THE URBAN SCENE: MYTHS AND REALITIES

THE URBAN SCENE: MYTHS AND REALITIES

SECOND EDITION

Edited by
JOE R. FEAGIN
University of Texas (Austin)

RANDOM HOUSE NEW YORK

To My Parents

Second Edition
987654321
Copyright ©1973, 1979 by Random House, Inc.

Library of Congress Cataloging in Publication Data

Feagin, Joe R.   comp.
   The urban scene.

   Includes bibliographical references.
   1. Cities and towns — United States — Addresses, essays, lectures. I. Title.
HT123.F4   1979   301.36′3′0973   78-11742
ISBN   0-394-32225-8

Manufactured in the United States of America. Composed, printed and bound by The Kingsport Press, Kingsport, Tenn.

Cover photo/design by Meryl Sussman Levavi
Text design by Judith Allan

Preface

TO THE SECOND EDITION

This revised edition of *The Urban Scene* reader is intentionally designed to provide those students interested in studying the American city with a shorter-than-average collection of articles and excerpts that present unconventional, critical, or particularly challenging analyses of urban life and urban structure. Selections have also been chosen with an eye toward their suggestions and implications for planning and policy-making. Of course, in designing a short reader of this type, *selectivity* is necessary. A number of important issues could not be considered here, and others could not be examined in great depth. However, my hope is that the relative brevity of this reader will allow it to be used in a broad variety of social science courses that would not otherwise be able to utilize a collection on urban issues and urban policy. This second edition of *The Urban Scene* is a substantially revised version of the first edition. Drawing on many useful suggestions from readers, I have added a number of new excerpts from recent books and articles on the urban scene. For example, an excerpt from the critical work of Manuel Castells now follows, and contrasts with, the updated excerpt from the work of Edward Banfield. Also, new excerpts have been added on Sunbelt cities, transportation and ecology, and remedies for urban fiscal crises, such as that of New York City. A few articles from the first edition have been deleted, and the entire volume has been reorganized into fewer, and more-focused, chapters.

For those students wishing to go beyond these readings, to probe more deeply into the issues raised here, the annotated bibliographies and the references in the footnotes to the general introduction and the chapter introductions provide excellent starting points.

In most undertakings of this character an author has received aid and support from more persons than he can possibly acknowledge. But I would particularly like to thank David Bartlett and Jane Cullen, my editors, for their wise guidance in the development and completion of this project; Charles Tilly, teacher and friend, who first seduced me into the study of the urban scene; and Clairece Booher Feagin, my wife, for extensive aid in typing and preparing this manuscript.

Contents

PREFACE   iii

GENERAL INTRODUCTION   1

1. THE URBAN CRISIS   11
Introduction   11
Edward C. Banfield, From *The Unheavenly City Revisited*:
     Introduction   16
     The Prospect   36
     Manuel Castells, The Wild City   42

2. WHITE MIDDLE AMERICANS   75
Introduction   75
Andrew M. Greeley, From *Why Can't They Be Like Us?*:
     The Future of Ethnic Groups   80
     Problem or Promise   85
Robert Coles and Jon Erikson, From *The Middle
Americans*   94
Bennett M. Berger, Suburbia and the American Dream   106

3. PERSPECTIVES ON POVERTY AND "SLUMS"   119
Introduction   119
Charles A. Valentine, From *Culture and Poverty*:
     Alternative Views of Poverty and the Poor — Present and
     Future   124
Postscript: A Proposal for Empowering the Poor to Reduce
     Inequality   134
David C. Perry and Alfred J. Watkins, People, Profit, and
     the Rise of the Sunbelt Cities   139
Marc Fried, From *The Urban Condition:* Grieving for a
Lost Home   167

4. BLACK AMERICANS IN URBAN GHETTOS   183
Introduction   183
Charles Tilly, From *The Metropolitan Enigma*: Race and
     Migration to the American City   188
Karl R. Taeuber, Racial Segregation: The Persisting
     Dilemma   208

William K. Tabb, From *The Political Economy of the
Black Ghetto*: Black Power — Green Power   219

5. **THE URBAN ENVIRONMENT: A FOCUS ON
TRANSPORTATION**   239
Introduction   239
Bradford C. Snell, American Ground Transport   241

6. **THE FUTURE OF URBAN SOCIETY: THE
STRUGGLE FOR POWER**   267
Introduction   267
Alvin Toffler, From *Future Shock*: The Strategy of Social
Futurism   270
David Mermelstein, Austerity, Planning and the Socialist
Alternative   297

THE URBAN SCENE: MYTHS AND REALITIES

General Introduction

To speak of American society is to speak of urban society, for three-quarters of this country's more than 210 million residents now live in urban places, with a large proportion of these urbanites residing in metropolitan areas. And even those Americans residing in rural sections are influenced in significant ways by life in nearby or distant urban places. Much of the talk about social problems, therefore, relates almost by definition to the past, present, and future character of American cities. The urban problems that have from time to time become the focus of popular and scholarly attention have varied a great deal in their scope and significance, running from rush-hour traffic jams to large-scale, collective violence. Many of the most widely discussed issues, as Edward C. Banfield suggests in the first selection in this reader, relate primarily to questions about the comfort and convenience of white or middle-class urbanites. While some of these comfort-and-convenience issues are important, they are *not* the most serious issues confronting contemporary urbanites.

A major purpose of this collection of articles and excerpts is to stress research and analysis which relate directly, or in a critical contextual way, to what are in my judgment some of the more serious urban issues, such as the unequal distribution of wealth and power, institutional racism, the impact of urban migration, and the pluralism of urban life styles. The intent here is to provide the student of urban affairs with selected materials offering unconventional or provocative insights into the complexities of the urban scene and the dilemmas of urban planning and policy. While some selections have been available for several years now, even a cursory glance at numerous textbooks touching on urban issues will make it clear that the perspectives developed by a number of the authors herein have not as yet penetrated many influential analyses of urban life.

Basic conceptions and images of urban life and urban structure are extraordinarily important, since they often shape the ends envisioned, and the means by which these ends are implemented, by those intent on reinforcing or remaking the existing urban scene. One prominent

1

urban sociologist, Scott Greer, has underlined the importance of images of the urban future in the lives of cities and their inhabitants:

> It is my assumption that images of the future determine present actions. They may or may not determine the nature of the future — that depends on a much more complex set of circumstances. But willy-nilly, much of our behavior is postulated upon images of a possible and/or desirable future.[1]

One might well extend Greer's observation about images of the future city to argue that dominant conceptions or images of the *present* city also shape behavior. The impact of conceptions of city life in shaping behavior appears particularly important in the case of urban policy-makers and planners, whose interpretations of phenomena such as poverty, slums, ghettos, suburbs, or migration have had a great impact on the formulation of urban policy and the channeling of urban development. Too often conventional wisdom about the city — the stuff out of which images are made or the means by which images are rationalized — is not carefully examined to see if it in fact does jibe with the best available evidence on urban life. Although it is never possible to be completely objective about urban issues, after careful analysis some conceptions about the city and its problems do appear more dated, restricted, or undocumented than others.

The selections included in this collection will not provide the reader with one "true" image of the city that can be used to replace other "faulty" ones. Rather, the selections will provide divergent and provocative interpretations which one may or may not be able to synthesize into a whole. The intention thus is to provoke the reader to formulate and integrate his or her own hypotheses and conclusions about the whys and wherefores of urban life.

Although the current diversity of perspectives on urban issues and urban policy is evident from the numerous analyses presented here, certain themes are reiterated — sometimes explicitly, sometimes implicitly — by various authors. For example, one important recurring theme that is viewed from several vantage points is the nature and extent of urban social structure or urban community. Conventional wisdom has often portrayed urbanites as somehow quite different from their counterparts in the country.

One widely quoted social scientist, Louis Wirth, argued some time ago that urban social life is characterized by the "substitution of secondary for primary contacts, the weakening of bonds of kinship, and the declining social significance of the family, the disappearance of the neighborhood, and the undermining of the traditional basis of social solidarity."[2] More recently, important authors such as Herbert Marcuse, Maurice R. Stein, and Robert A. Nisbet — to name just a few — have given emphasis to the disorganizing effects of the urbanization

process: eclipsed community, isolation, impersonality, and super-
ficiality.[3] Although criticism of this view of the decline of community
and family has appeared in recent urban sociology textbooks,
variations on the theme still appear in the literature on cities. Particularly common has been the application of Wirth-like arguments
about urbanization and urbanism in discussions of slum and ghetto
areas within central cities.[4] However, several studies in this collection
— including those by Marc Fried, Andrew M. Greeley, Charles Tilly,
and Bennett M. Berger — suggest the importance and persisting
structure of intimate and meaningful interpersonal relationships,
primary social networks, and other aspects of community in urban
areas, whether the specific focus is on poor or working-class
Americans, black Americans, suburbanites, or "white ethnics."
    Images of the city that utilize the language of disorganization and
pathology are not limited to those that focus on community. Scott
Greer has underlined the extent to which general conceptions of cities
have emphasized their negative dimensions: "A very common image
of cities in the United States is that of disorder, regression, decadence
— in short, disorganization."[5] Yet several authors in this collection
indicate the need for great caution in jumping to conclusions about
the disorganized nature of cities. At base there is the critical problem of
definition. What some would define as disorderly, decadent, or disorganized — for example, race riots, life in a slum, poverty subcultures
— others would see in terms of order, organization, and legitimacy.
Collective definitions of urban phenomena become particularly
problematical when they give legitimacy to the uprooting or manipulation of urban populations by planners and politicians — as has
happened all too frequently in urban redevelopment programs. Thus
a number of the analysts in this volume seem to be suggesting that
many commonly accepted definitions and images of urban phenomena must be carefully reexamined.[6] Worth examining, too, may be
the *political* character of the social-definition process itself.
    Yet another important motif in these discussions of urban life and
structure is that of heterogeneity. Some traditional images of
urbanization have envisioned a homogenizing process whereby
immigrants from rural areas (in the United States and elsewhere)
assimilate over time to a general urban type. In American history a
number of different images or models of assimilation have prevailed.
Perhaps the two most influential have been what Milton M. Gordon
has termed the "Anglo-conformity" and "melting pot" theories:
"Both the Anglo-conformity and the melting pot theories had
envisaged the disappearance of the immigrants' group as a communal
identity and the absorption of the later arrivals to America and their
children, as individuals, into the existing 'American' social
structure."[7] Utilizing these perspectives, both popular writers and
scholars have emphasized the insignificance or demise of ethnicity in

modern America.[8] However, a few authors in this reader raise serious questions about premature epitaphs for ethnicity. Important in this regard is Andrew M. Greeley's provocative argument for the survival of meaningful ethnic differences in *Why Can't They Be Like Us?* He views the persistence of the "old ties of blood, faith, land and consciousness of kind" as a fundamental aspect of urban social structure. Indeed, he sees the possibility that the particularistic modes of behavior of certain ethnic groups, and the general heterogeneity of ethnic life styles, provide the stuff that in fact makes — and will make — cities livable. And the data provided by Marc Fried on Italian-Americans residing in a low-income area of Boston lend further credibility to the argument that ethnic diversity persists. Thus, in a chapter of Robert Coles and Jon Erikson's *The Middle Americans* that is not reprinted here, a machinist movingly underscores this point:

> "I'm Polish. I mean, I'm American. My family has been here for four generations; that's a lot. My great-grandfather came over here, from near Cracow. . . . It's in your blood. It's in your background. But I live *here*. My wife is the same, Polish. We're just like other people in this country, but we have memories, Polish memories. . . . How *could* I forget? My wife won't let me. She says you have to stay with your own people. We don't have only Polish people living near us, but there are a lot. Mostly we see my family and my wife's family on weekends, so there's no time to spend doing anything else."[9]

Nor are ingroup ties salient only for white ethnic Americans. While institutionalized discrimination has been well documented as a major determinant in the living patterns of black Americans, the critical role of attachment to one's own kind among blacks is also substantiated in social science research.

The role of blue-collar or working-class life styles in adding pluralism and diversity to everyday life in the urban framework is also emphasized in the articles in this reader — life styles dominated not only by ethnic but also by class background. Until recently relatively few American social scientists had studied the sometimes distinctive way of life, the types of social choices, to be found among working-class Americans. Even in Levittown, Pennsylvania, which many had come to see as the personification of middle-class suburban conformity and homogeneity, Herbert J. Gans, in a pioneering study not excerpted here, found that life styles varied somewhat by class.[10] Furthermore, he noted that pluralism of life styles is a reality that urbanites have difficulty grasping: "People have not recognized the diversity of American society, and they are not able to accept other life styles." Of course, the variables of class and ethnicity are not the only determinants of pluralism or conflict between life styles within urban areas. Had we the space, we might examine other aspects of urban diversity — which are only briefly alluded to in this collection — such as counterculture developments among the younger generation or the communities of the encapsulated aged in numerous cities.[11]

Recognition of the importance of diversity leads in turn to the question of public policy. In his article reprinted in this volume, Bennett M. Berger has put the problems of planning for pluralism in relief by delineating three broad alternatives that planners can adopt: (1) they can ignore the consequences of their actions; (2) they can try in their work to bring the environments of groups with divergent life styles or values into line with planners' standards; or (3) they can foster the diversity of values and life styles that already exist. In his emphasis on the need for planners to recognize the importance of pluralism in cities, Berger develops a theme that is touched on in one way or another by a number of authors in this collection:

> In making their assumptions, planners might first of all assume (it is the most reasonable assumption) that most groups which are displaced by planning *will take their culture with them* if they can. Planners would do well to anticipate this, and to modify their plans accordingly, to facilitate the preservation of those parts of their culture that the groups want preserved.[12]

While there are a number of other reiterated motifs that could be singled out, perhaps the most important of these is the issue of unequal distribution of wealth and power in this urban society. The existence of poverty has traditionally been viewed as problematical by some Americans. Images of the poor, and of the nature and causes of economic inequality, may be among the most important images of urban life harbored by rank-and-file urbanites, as well as by urban planners and policy-makers. The writings of Charles A. Valentine, which deal with conflicting images and interpretations of poverty, are particularly thought-provoking in this regard. Even today, the dominant stereotype of poor persons emphasizes character flaws and individual failures. Poverty has long been blamed on the laziness or immorality of poor individuals rather than on the social and economic system.[13] Indeed, certain aspects of this popular image can be found in scholarly analyses that view the "culture of poverty" among the poor as the major determinant in perpetuating economic inequality. Valentine, however, suggests that there are serious problems in regard to prominent images of the urban poor and raises the question of stereotyping. He points up alternative portraits and explanations that give greater attention to the variability of lower-class values, to the diversity of life styles among the poor, and to the role of *external structural* factors in generating inequality, particularly exploitation by the better-off classes.

The problem of inequality encompasses the situation of black and other nonwhite urbanites. To a great extent the lack of wealth, resources, and power among black Americans is the result of overt and covert racial discrimination. Much recent discussion of black-white problems in American cities has focused on their sociopsychological aspects — on such things as prejudice and "white racism." Less attention, however, has been given to structural analysis, to the role of existing economic and political institutions in perpetuating racial inequality. In this volume William K. Tabb and Karl Taeuber touch on the issue of "institutional racism." Tabb, in his pioneering analysis, has underscored the importance of the point that "racism is perpetuated by elements of oppression within an economic and political system which must be understood *as a system*." Racial inequality in cities can be viewed as part of a larger system of race and class inequality.

Social stratification, the term social scientists often use for a social hierarchy in which certain groups differ sharply in income, wealth, or political power, takes a number of different forms in the United States. There is a racial hierarchy, with various white groups toward the top and several nonwhite groups — such as blacks, Chicanos, and Native Americans (Indians) — toward the bottom. There is sex stratification, with men in higher-level positions and women less well off. And there is an economic class system, with upper-class (elite) Americans (the capitalists) at the top, middle-class Americans in the middle, and working-class and lower-class Americans (the proletariat) toward the bottom. Whereas some, such as Edward Banfield, see social classes as differing mainly in terms of values (e.g., "culture of poverty" values), other urban analysts stress that it is much more important to look at differences in the way these economic classes tie into, or relate to, the capitalist economic system in the United States.

From this important perspective the members of the upper class, and the upper middle class, have maintained a high level in terms of such things as wealth or political power because of their more influential positions in the capitalist economic system. Included in the top ranks of these two classes are the owners of business and industrial enterprises, the managers of business and industrial enterprises, professional workers such as top doctors and lawyers, the larger ranchers and farmers, and major landowners. The size of the top ruling elites has been estimated at a few thousand, perhaps only 4,000—5,000 persons. Other Americans — including those in the affluent middle class, working-class Americans, and the poor — are tied into the capitalist economic system as *workers*, heavily dependent on the decisions of those at higher levels and usually relatively powerless to affect those decisions.

A number of the authors in this volume accent the critical political-economic theme that the drive for money profits by those in the controlling elites at the top of the class system has greatly shaped the structure and character of American cities. The quest for profits often leads to the neglect of human needs. Manuel Castells, for one, rejects the idea that the operation of the capitalist economic system is natural or accidental, asserting, rather, that those who control the economic system have by their economic decisions shaped the structure and life of the American city. Since the late 1800s the expansion of large American companies in the direction of monopoly control of markets, such as steel, food-processing, and banking, has been generated by this quest for forever-renewed private profit, significantly abetted by government involvement in the private sector, in such things, for example, as the protection of banks and loan associations through government subsidizing of the insurance of home mortgages. Together with the expansion of the automobile industry, the intentional killing off of much trolley, bus, and rail transportation by auto companies, and the proliferation of new highways — developments that Bradford Snell underscores in his article — recurring government intervention on behalf of certain large businesses and industries greatly shaped the growth, structure, and environment of cities. For example, suburbanization reflected and became dependent upon the government subsidization of an automobile-oriented, highway-oriented society. Suburbia could have grown only with government-subsidized roads and government-insured mortgages. The character of capitalist cities and their suburban areas also reflects the heavy influence of commodity advertising — especially in regard to the automobile and the single-family home. Castells and Snell both accent the importance of the capitalist economic system — one controlled by a relatively small business-industrial elite and its critical political allies — as a main force shaping American cities.

This profit-maximization theme reappears in some analyses of the increasing demographic shift in the last few decades away from Northern cities to those in the Sunbelt. Most cities in the South and Southwest have since 1950 seen an explosive growth in population, as businesses and industries — and workers as well — have left the North in very large numbers. In their paper reprinted in this volume Alfred Watkins and David Perry argue that this population shift signals a fundamental concern in business and industry for increased money profits. They note that poverty in U.S. cities is not the same everywhere, that the situation of poor workers in Sunbelt cities differs significantly from those in the Northeast. First, they provide evidence of the profit function of urban development by exploring the historical exploitation of white (e.g., Italian) and nonwhite (e.g., black) immigrants coming into the cities. Then, they proceed to show that the urban poor today were not barriers to capitalist economic growth; "in fact, they were in many ways just the opposite — as sources of cheap labor and as rental markets they were a source of 'locational advantage' for the capitalist city." By the 1960s the lack of economic vitality and opportunity in Northern cities played a role in triggering civil rights protest and ghetto revolts. Both poor and better-off workers were demanding and getting better wages and benefits. In the same period there was an incredible expansion of American industry in Sunbelt areas. The more affluent workers were following to the Sunbelt the drift of manufacturing, retail, and wholesale enter-prises seeking lower wages, lower taxes, and fewer urban social welfare problems. The less affluent workers were already there — in very large numbers. Watkins and Perry note that "it was not the poverty of the migrants, but rather the poverty of the region which helped stimulate the economic shift and the migration."

Given these fundamental American problems of race and class inequality, it is not surprising that observers such as Mermelstein and Toffler view solutions to the problems of wealth and power in terms of redistribution and community control. Indeed, many other urban problems — and solutions as well — are doubtless linked, directly or indirectly, to the basic problem of economic and political inequality. Given the diversity of disenfranchised and partially enfranchised groups in this urbanized society, one should not be baffled if the suggestions and proposals of the various authors presented in this book seem at times difficult to implement. Nonetheless, Toffler may indeed be quite correct in his argument that expansion of parti-cipatory democracy is required for the *survival* of this urban society, and not just for the satisfaction of those holding to egalitarian ideologies.

> Another way of stating this is that, as the number of social components grows and change makes the whole system less stable, it becomes less and less possible to ignore the demands of political minorities — hippies, blacks, lower-middle-class Wallacites, school teachers, or the proverbial little old ladies in tennis shoes. In a slower-moving, industrial context, America could turn its back on the needs of its black minority; in the new, fast-paced cybernetic society, this minority can, by sabotage, strike, or a thousand other means, disrupt the entire system. As interdependency grows, smaller and smaller groups within society achieve greater and greater power for critical disruption. Moreover, as the rate of change speeds up, the length of time in which they can be ignored shrinks to near nothingness.[14]

Reflecting the views of a growing number of more critical urban political-economic analysts, Mermelstein goes beyond Toffler's view to indicate the need for a *democratic* socialist alternative to current capitalist economic arrangements. Suggesting that the drive for profit maximization is at the root of the recurring crises of the capitalist city,

Mermelstein argues that only democratic socialism can overcome the fundamental problems faced by rank-and-file Americans. In this view, *profit-oriented* decisions must be replaced by *people-oriented* decisions. Decisions, economic as well as political, private as well as public, must also be democratized, and not left in the hands of small business and political elites. Privileges and resources must be redistributed in the direction of a more egalitarian class system. The alert reader will note that Mermelstein's well-articulated proposal for a socialist city, which would involve considerable government intervention, directly contradicts the proposals of more conservative analysts such as Edward Banfield, whose argument, as we shall see shortly, is that government should decline in size, or should at the very least now keep its hands off the "free" American economy. From Banfield's point of view government intervention will only make things worse, for the natural operation of the existing economic system will eventually make things better. For Mermelstein and other democratic socialists imaginative government intervention — this time on behalf of workers and controlled by workers — will be required to solve the urban crisis.[15]

NOTES

1. Scott Greer, *The Urbane View* (New York: Oxford University Press, 1972), p. 322.

2. Louis Wirth, "Urbanism as a Way of Life," *American Journal of Sociology*, 44 (July 1938), 20—21.

3. See Maurice R. Stein, *The Eclipse of Community* (New York: Harper Torchbooks, 1964); Herbert Marcuse, *One-Dimensional Man* (Boston: Beacon Press, 1964); and Robert A. Nisbet, *Community and Power* (New York: Oxford University Press, 1962).

4. See Genevieve Knupfer, "Portrait of an Underdog," in *Class, Status and Power*, R. Bendix and S. M. Lipset, eds. (Glencoe, Ill.: Free Press, 1953), pp. 257 ff; Gunnar Myrdal, *An American Dilemma* (New York: McGraw-Hill, 1964); Kenneth B. Clark, *Dark Ghetto* (New York: Harper and Row, 1965); Office of Policy Planning and Research, U.S. Department of Labor, *The Negro Family: The Case for National Action* (Washington, D.C.: U.S. Government Printing Office, 1965).

5. Greer, *The Urbane View*, p. 322.

6. For a critical assessment of the ghetto disorganization literature see David C. Perry and Joe R. Feagin, "Stereotyping in Black and White," in *People and Politics in Urban Society*, H. Hahn, ed. (Beverly Hills, Calif.: Sage Publications, 1972), pp. 433—463.

7. Milton M. Gordon, *Assimilation in American Life* (New York: Oxford University Press, 1964), p. 132.

8. See the discussion and authors cited in chaps. 2 and 3 of Will Herberg, *Protestant-Catholic-Jew* (Garden City, N.Y.: Anchor, 1960).

9. Robert Coles and Jon Erikson, *The Middle Americans* (Boston: Atlantic-Little, Brown, 1971), p. 43.

10. Herbert J. Gans, *The Levittowners* (New York: Random House, 1967), pp. 408—433.

11. On counterculture and cities see Theodore Roszak, *The Making of a Counter Culture* (Garden City, N.Y.: Anchor, 1969); on the aged see Rochelle Jones, *The Other Generation* (Englewood Cliffs, N.J.: Prentice-Hall, Inc., 1977).

12. Bennett M. Berger, "Suburbia and the American Dream," *The Public Interest*, no. 2 (Winter 1966), p. 90.

13. For a discussion of contemporary American views of the poor see Joe R. Feagin, "American Views of Poverty and Welfare," *Psychology Today*, 6 (November 1972), 101—110, 129; and Joe R. Feagin, *Subordinating the Poor* (Englewood Cliffs, N.J.: Prentice-Hall, Inc., 1977).

14. Alvin Toffler, *Future Shock* (New York: Random House, 1970), pp. 421—422.

15. For further analysis of this type, see the articles in Roger E. Alcaly and David Mermelstein (eds.), *The Fiscal Crisis of American Cities* (New York: Random House, 1976).

1

The
Urban Crisis

Americans have long been critical of their cities. This has been particularly true of writers and other intellectuals, who periodically have expressed a great amount of negative feeling for urban structure and urban life. From Thomas Jefferson and Ralph Waldo Emerson, to Frank Lloyd Wright and John Dewey, to contemporary commentators, influential Americans have expressed such antipathies:

> The American city has been thought by American intellectuals to be: too big, too noisy, too dusky, too dirty, too smelly, too commercial, too crowded, too full of immigrants, too full of Jews, too full of Irishmen, Italians, Poles, too industrial, too pushing, too mobile, too fast, too artificial, destructive of conversation, destructive of communication, too greedy, too capitalistic, too full of automobiles, too full of smog, too full of dust, too heartless, too intellectual, too scientific, insufficiently poetic, too lacking in manners, too mechanical, destructive of family, tribal and patriotic feeling.[1]

As this catalog of critiques clearly indicates, negative views of the city have been varied as well as inconsistent. Sometimes issues of comfort and convenience have been emphasized, while at other times critical questions about ethnic, racial, or economic trends have been raised. Sometimes the city has been viewed as too civilized; at other times it has been condemned as not civilized enough.

Focusing on the contemporary scene in his controversial analysis *The Unheavenly City Revisited*, Edward C. Banfield contends that current conventional wisdom about the American city views it as facing a crisis of great proportions, as being well on the road to a catastrophic disaster. Yet Banfield questions this interpretation. While admitting that many aspects of urban life need significant improvement, he argues that the majority of urbanites are better off than ever before, especially in terms of housing, schools, and even transportation. Urban Americans now live more comfortably than they or their counterparts in other countries did in the recent or distant past, at least in terms of material comforts. Moreover, in Banfield's view much of the "crisis" talk about the city has really been focused on problems involving the "comfort, convenience, and business advantage of the well-off white majority."

Consequently, Banfield distinguishes between *important* urban problems and really *serious* urban problems, the former involving situations that may be inconvenient or uncomfortable but could not possibly lead to a catastrophic disaster. Among these would be such things as the urban sprawl, long journeys to work, the decline of the central business district, taxes, and general architectural ugliness. One reason why Banfield questions whether many issues can really be viewed as crisis-level dilemmas is that in numerous cases solutions are already at hand but have not been implemented because of opposition either from the business community (as in the case of rush-hour traffic) or from the general public (as in the case of the revenue problems). The fact that urbanites have not alleviated many of these problems, even when the price is not great, suggests to Banfield that the problems are not critical.

Although these convenience and business-advantage problems touch the majority of urbanites, really serious urban problems — those conditions affecting the essential welfare of individuals or the society — in one sense directly involve only urban minorities. Poverty, racial injustice, and ignorance — these Banfield regards as crisis-level matters. "If there is an urban crisis in any ultimate sense, it must be constituted of these conditions."

In addition to raising provocative questions about the character of urban problems, Banfield points up other flaws in much of the talk about the urban crisis. For example, Banfield points to the issue of where urbanites actually reside. While it is true that three-quarters of the American people now live in urban areas, most do *not* live in the great metropolitan areas. In both 1960 and 1970 more than 70 percent of all Americans lived in cities with populations less than 250,000, in small towns, or in rural areas.[2] Thus the average American does not live in a great metropolis such as New York, Chicago, Los Angeles, or Detroit, although he may sometimes be affected by what happens there. Since much of the argument over the urban crisis relates to problems of these larger cities and derives from analysts residing there, reflection on these demographic statistics again leads to questions about conventional wisdom: In what sense, where, and for whom is there a real urban crisis?

Furthermore, in the course of his analysis Banfield lays out a series of controversial arguments about the nature of cities and the people dwelling therein. One of these arguments is that a distinctive feature of the lower-class life style, characteristic of many poor people, is that it is extremely "present-oriented," causing the lower-class person to live impulsively and irresponsibly, from one moment to another. In Banfield's stereotypical view, people in the upper class and middle class are much more future-oriented, planning and thinking ahead, even far ahead. From his perspective this feature of lower-class culture is defective, pathological, and leads to a significant number of urban problems, including individual violence, lack of mobility up the socio-economic ladder, crime, drug addiction, and the lack of social progress for many black Americans. Critics of Banfield consider this view a set of crude stereotypes.

We begin our readings with two selections from Banfield's book, the Introduction and a brief excerpt from the final chapter. In the latter, Banfield develops his thesis that current urban problems will eventually disappear and that these problems cannot, at any rate, be solved by large-scale government intervention. Here is the "benign neglect" perspective that has developed since the late 1960s, a perspective reflecting frustration at the (alleged) failures of such government-intervention programs as the War on Poverty and related Great Society programs of the 1960s. Numerous conservative critics have come to accept Banfield's forcefully argued thesis that "owing to the nature of man and society (more particularly, American culture and institutions) we cannot 'solve' our serious problems by rational management." Indeed, as he asserts periodically throughout his book, well-intended government intervention often makes things worse. In his view "powerful accidental forces," the natural operation of the capitalistic economic system together with demographic changes, are the most likely sources of real urban problem-solving.

The second author in this chapter, Manuel Castells, provides a quite different urban perspective, a well-supported argument that the urban crisis in the United States is at bottom *a crisis in American capitalism* and in the type of urban structure peculiar to this particular capitalist system. Castells first traces the impact and significance of those processes that shaped the social structure of U.S. cities. Metropolitanization, suburbanization, and political fragmentation into many local governments are viewed not only in their social effects but also in terms of their structural causes. The high concentration of Americans in a modest number of metropolises is linked to the concentration of capital in such areas in the monopolistic stage of American capitalism that has developed since the late 1800s. Beginning in earnest during the late 1800s, and continuing vigorously into the present, larger companies began buying up or coalescing with other companies, so that most major industries and business sectors came to be dominated economically by a few (often five or six) companies usually based in a few dozen urban areas.

The decentralization of Americans in the suburbanization process is not a "natural" social process but rather a reflection of the changes in transportation (automobiles and paved highways) and in housing (mass production and federal subsidy of mortgages). This much critics such as Banfield might acknowledge. But Castells goes beyond these facts to look at *why* such developments occurred. He argues that the continuing expansion of large companies (many with monopoly or near-monopoly control) reflected an even more aggressive quest for expanded profits. This quest led to large-scale government intervention in a way that expanded private profits — i.e., to a system of "welfare for the corporations." Government-insured mortgages meant "risk-free credit" could be given by banks and other lenders. Massive government subsidies for highways spurred the growth of the automobile industry and killed off most other types of public transportation. The persistent drive for money profits has led many companies to the suburbs, where land costs and taxes are lower; there, they can have the economic benefits of the urban scene without paying their share of the costs. These factors, together with advertising-spurred commodity consumption, have played a very significant role in U.S. suburbanization. State intervention since the 1930s has greatly benefited large corporations and the wealthy through what some have called "socialism for the rich." Castells is here emphasizing the overwhelming importance of the underlying economic structure manipulated by dominant business-industrial elites and their allies in government — something urban analysts such as Banfield ignore.

Suburbanization has increasingly meant a polarized urban scene, with the poor and the nonwhite in central cities and the more affluent whites in surrounding suburbs. To "save" central cities, where many corporations and elites still have significant economic interests, billions in government dollars have been poured into urban renewal and related development programs. Many urban social programs, such as the Great Society programs Banfield criticizes as failures, were designed by the ruling elites, in Castell's view, to preserve the peace disrupted by the growing number of people's revolts in the 1960s. Both of these types of government intervention — one for business, another for protestors — spurred further urban contradictions and conflicts.

For Castells the current urban crisis is real and consists of the breakdown of social order in the inner city, the crisis in housing and public transportation in central cities, the crisis in education, the crisis in public health and welfare services, and the fiscal troubles of central city governments. Much in his analysis here coincides with that of more establishment-oriented analysts. Castells traces recent shifts in government intervention, especially the shift to a revenue-sharing, locally-controlled program to replace reformist federal programs. Under revenue-sharing, more conservative local authorities have spent money for programs (e.g., buildings and other construction) they favored, which have encompassed interventionist reform programs for poor people much less often than the federal War-on-Poverty programs of the 1960s did.

In his concluding pages Castells seems optimistic about the growth of the urban protest movement since the early 1970s. Diversified and without a central focus, this movement consists of co-ops, health clinics, tenants' unions, utilities organizations, anti-renewal organizations, and other populist-oriented organizations.[3] What could result if these movements ultimately fail, Castells concludes, is "a new and sinister urban form: the Wild City."[3]

NOTES

1. Morton White, "Two Stages in the Critique of the American City," in *The Historian and the City*, Oscar Handlin and John Burchard, eds. (Cambridge, Mass.: M.I.T. Press and Harvard University Press, 1963), pp. 86—87.

2. U.S. Bureau of the Census, *Statistical Abstract of the United States: 1971* (Washington, D.C.: U.S. Government Printing Office, 1971), p. 17.

3. For an interesting discussion of people's organizations and why they succeed or fail, see Frances Fox Piven and Richard A. Cloward, *Poor People's Movements* (New York: Pantheon Books, 1977).

From
The Unheavenly City Revisited:

Introduction

Edward C. Banfield

. . . the clock is ticking, time is moving . . . . , we must ask ourselves every night when we go home, are we doing all that we should do in our nation's capital, in all the other big cities of the country.

— President Johnson, after the Watts Riot,
August 1965

A few years ago we constantly heard that urban America was on the brink of collapse. It was one minute to midnight, we were told. . . . Today, America is no longer coming apart. . . . The hour of crisis is passed.

— President Nixon, March 1973

The reason for juxtaposing the quotations above is not to suggest that whereas a few years ago the cities were in great peril now all is well with them. Rather it is to call attention both to the simplistic nature of all such sweeping judgments and to the fact that one's perception of urban America is a function of time and place and also, if one is a politician, of whatever winds are blowing. A few blocks' walk through the heart of any large city was enough in 1965 — and is enough in 1973 — to show much that was (and is) in crying need of improvement. That a society so technologically advanced and prosperous has many hundreds of blocks ranging from dreary to dismal is disturbing at least and when one takes into account that by the end of the century the urban population will be at least 20 percent larger than in 1970, with six out of every ten persons living in a metropolitan area of more than a million, the prospect may appear alarming.

There is, however, another side to the matter. The plain fact is that the overwhelming majority of city dwellers live more comfortably and conveniently than ever before. They have more and better housing, more and better schools, more and better transportation, and so on. By any conceivable measure of material welfare the present generation of urban Americans is, on the whole, better off than any other large group of people has ever been anywhere. What is more, there is every reason to expect that the general level of comfort and convenience will continue to rise at an even more rapid rate through the foreseeable future.

It is true that many people do not share, or do not share fully, this general prosperity, some because they are the victims of racial prejudice and others for other reasons that are equally beyond their control. If the chorus of complaint about the city arose mainly from these disadvantaged people or on behalf of them, it would be entirely understandable, especially if their numbers were increasing and their plight were getting worse. But the fact is that until very recently most of the talk about the urban crisis has had to do with the comfort, convenience, and business advantage of the well-off white majority and not with the more serious problems of the poor, the Negro, and others who stand outside the charmed circle. And the fact also is that the number of those standing outside the circle is decreasing, as is the relative disadvantage that they suffer. There is still much poverty and much racial discrimination. But there is less of both than ever before.

The question arises, therefore, not of whether we are faced with an urban crisis, but rather, *in what sense* we are faced with one. Whose interest and what interests are involved? How deeply? What should be done? Given the political and other realities of the situation, what *can* be done?

The first need is to clear away some semantic confusions. Consider the statement, so frequently used to alarm luncheon groups, that more than 70 percent of the population now lives in urban places and that this number may increase to nearly 90 percent in the next two decades if present trends continue. Such figures give the impression of standing room only in the city, but what exactly do they mean?

When we are told that the population of the United States is rapidly becoming overwhelmingly urban, we probably suppose this to mean that most people are coming to live in the big cities. This is true in one sense but false in another. It is true that most people live closer physically and psychologically to a big city than ever before; rural occupations and a rural style of life are no longer widespread. On the other hand, the percentage of the population living in cities of 250,000 or more (there are only fifty-six of them) is about the same now as it was in 1920. In Census terminology an "urban place" is any settlement having a population of 2,500 or more; obviously places of 2,500 are not what we have in mind when we use words like "urban" and "city."[1] It is somewhat misleading to say that the country is becoming more urban, when what is meant is that more people are living in places like White River Junction, Vermont (pop. 6,311), and fewer in places like Boston, Massachusetts (pop. 641,000). But it is not *altogether* misleading, for most of the small urban places are now close enough (in terms of time and other costs of travel) to large cities to be part of a metropolitan complex. White River Junction, for example, is now very much influenced by Boston. The average population density in all "urban areas," however, has been decreasing: from 5,408 per square mile in 1950 to 3,752 in 1960, to 3,376 in 1970.

A great many so-called urban problems are really conditions that we either cannot eliminate or do not want to incur the disadvantages of eliminating. Consider the "problem of congestion." The presence of a great many people in one place is a cause of inconvenience, to say the least. But the advantages of having so many people in one place far outweigh these inconveniences, and we cannot possibly have the advantages without the disadvantages. To "eliminate congestion" in the city must mean eliminating the city's reason for being. Congestion in the city is a "problem" only in the sense that congestion in Times Square on New Year's Eve is one; in fact, of course, people come to the city, just as they do to Times Square, precisely *because* it is congested. If it were not congested, it would not be worth coming to.

Strictly speaking, a problem exists only as we should want something different from what we do want or as by better management we could get a larger total of what we want. If we think it a good thing that many people have the satisfaction of driving their cars in and out of the city, and if we see no way of arranging the situation to get them in and out more conveniently that does not entail more than offsetting disadvantages for them or others, then we ought not to speak of a "traffic congestion problem." By the same token, urban sprawl is a "problem," as opposed to a "condition," only if (1) fewer people should have the satisfaction of living in the low-density fringe of the city, or (2) we might, by better planning, build homes in the fringe without destroying so much landscape and without incurring costs (for example, higher per-unit construction costs) or forgoing benefits (for example, a larger number of low-income families who can have the satisfaction of living in the low-density area) of greater value than the saving in landscape.

Few problems, in this strict sense, are anywhere near as big as they seem. The amount of urban sprawl that could be eliminated simply by better planning — that is, without the sacrifice of other ends that are also wanted, such as giving the satisfaction of owning a house and yard to many low-income people — is probably trivial as compared to the total urban sprawl (that is, to the "problem" defined simple-mindedly as "a condition that is unpleasant").

Many so-called urban problems (crime is a conspicuous exception) are more characteristic of rural and small-town places than of cities. Housing is generally worse in rural areas, for example, and so are schools. "Low verbal ability," Sloan R. Wayland of Columbia Teachers College has written, "is described as though it could only happen in an urban slum." Actually, he points out, all but a very small fraction of mankind has always been "culturally deprived," and the task of formal education has always been to attack such conditions.[2]

Most of the "problems" that are generally supposed to constitute "the urban crisis" could not conceivably lead to disaster. They are — some of them — important in the sense that a bad cold is important, but they are not critical in the sense that a cancer is critical. They have to do with comfort, convenience, amenity, and business advantage, all of which are important, but they do not affect either the essential welfare of individuals or what may be called the good health of the society.

Consider, for example, an item that often appears near the top of the list of complaints about the city — the journey to work. It takes the average commuter between 21 and 34 minutes to get to work (the difference in the average time depending upon the population of the metropolitan area).[3] It would, of course, be very nice if the journey to work were much shorter. No one can suppose, however, that the essential welfare of many people would be much affected even if it were fifteen minutes longer. Certainly its being longer or shorter would not make the difference between a good society and a bad.

Another matter causing widespread alarm is the decline of the central business district, by which is meant the loss of patronage to downtown department stores, theaters, restaurants, museums, and so on, which has resulted from the movement of many well-off people to suburbs. Clearly, the movement of good customers from one place to another involves inconvenience and business loss to many people, especially to the owners of real estate that is no longer in so great demand. These losses, however, are essentially no different from those that occur from other causes — say, a shift of consumers' tastes that suddenly renders a once-valuable patent valueless. Moreover, though some lose by the change, others gain by it: the overall gain of wealth by building in the suburbs may more than offset the loss of it caused by letting the downtown deteriorate.

There are those who claim that cultural and intellectual activity flourishes only in big cities and that therefore the decline of the downtown business districts and the replacement of cities by suburbs threatens the very survival of civilization. This claim is farfetched, to say the very least, if it means that we cannot have good music and good theater (not to mention philosophy, literature, and science) unless customers do their shopping in the downtown districts of Oakland, St. Louis, Nashville, Boston, and so on, rather than in the suburbs around them. Public efforts to preserve the downtown districts of these and other cities may perhaps be worth what they cost — although, so far as cultural and intellectual activities are concerned, there is no reason to assume that public efforts would not bring at least as much return if directed to metropolitan areas as wholes. The return, however, will be in the comfort, convenience, and business advantage of the relatively well-off and not in anyone's essential welfare.

The same can be said about efforts to "beautify" the cities. That for the most part the cities are dreary and depressing if not offensively ugly may be granted: the desirability of improving their appearance, even if only a little, cannot be questioned. It is very doubtful, however, that people are dehumanized (to use a favorite word of those who complain about the cities) by the ugliness of the city or that they would be in any sense humanized by its being made beautiful. (If they were humanized, they would doubtless build beautiful cities, but that is an entirely different matter. One has only to read Machiavelli's Florentine Histories to see that living in a beautiful city is not in itself enough to bring out the best in one. So far as their humanity is concerned, the people of, say, Jersey City compare very favorably to the Florentines of the era of that city's greatest glory.) At worst, the American city's ugliness — or, more, its lack of splendor or charm — occasions loss of visual pleasure. This loss is an important one (it is surely much larger than most people realize), but it cannot lead to any kind of disaster either for the individual or for the society.

Air pollution comes closer than any of these problems to threatening essential welfare, as opposed to comfort, convenience, amenity, and business advantage. Some people die early because of it and many more suffer various degrees of bad health; there is also some possibility (no one knows how much) that a meteorological coincidence (an "air inversion") over a large city might suddenly kill thousands or even tens of thousands. Important as it is, however, the air pollution problem is rather minor as compared to other threats to health and welfare not generally regarded as "crises."[4] Moreover, steps are being taken to clear the air. The Clean Air Act Amendment of 1970 is expected to reduce pollution from auto emissions (by far the most serious source) to half of what they were in 1967 (the base year) by 1980 and to a quarter by 1985.[5]

Many of the "problems" that are supposed to constitute the "crisis" could be quickly and easily solved, or much alleviated, by the application of well-known measures that lie right at hand. In some instances, the money cost of these measures would be very small. For example, the rush-hour traffic problem in the central cities (which, incidentally, is almost the whole of the traffic problem in these cities) could be much reduced and in some cases eliminated entirely just by staggering working hours in the largest offices and factories. Manhattan presents the hardest case of all, but even there, an elaborate study showed, rush-hour crowding could be reduced by 25 percent, enough to make the strap-hanger reasonably comfortable.[6] Another quick and easy way of improving urban transportation in most cities would be to eliminate a mass of archaic regulations on the granting of public transit and taxi franchises. At present, the cities are in effect going out of their way to place obstacles in the paths of those who might offer the public better transportation.[7] Metropolitan transportation could also easily be improved in those areas — there are a number of them — where extensive expressway networks link the downtown with outlying cities and towns. In these areas, according to the Harvard economist John F. Kain, "all that is currently needed to create extensive metropolitan rapid transit systems . . . is a limited outlay for instrumentation, some modification of ramp arrangement and design, and most importantly *a policy decision to keep congestion at very low levels during peak hours and to provide priority access for public transit vehicles.*"[8]

The "price" of solving, or alleviating, some much-talked-about city problems, it would appear from this, may be largely political. Keeping congestion at low levels at peak hours would necessitate placing high toll charges on roads at the very times when most people want to use them; some would regard this as grossly unfair (as indeed in a way it would be) and so the probabilities are that if any official had the authority to make the decision (none does, which is part of the problem), he would not raise tolls at rush hours for fear of being voted out of office.

If the transportation problem is basically political, so is the revenue problem. A great part of the wealth of our country is in the cities. When a mayor says that his city is on the verge of bankruptcy, he means that when the time comes to run for reelection he wants to be able to claim credit for straightening out a mess that was left him by his predecessor. What he means when he says that his city *must* have state or federal aid to finance some improvements is (1) the taxpayers of the city (or some important group of them) would rather go without the improvement than pay for it themselves; or (2) although they would pay for it themselves if they had to, they would much prefer to have some other taxpayers pay for it. Rarely if ever does a mayor who makes such a statement mean (1) that for the city to pay for the improvement would necessarily force some taxpayers into poverty; or (2) that the city could not raise the money even if it were willing to force some of its taxpayers into poverty. In short, the "revenue crisis" mainly reflects the fact that people hate to pay taxes and that they think that by crying poverty they can shift some of the bill to someone else.[9]

To some extent, also, the revenue problem of the cities arises from the way jurisdictional boundaries are drawn or, more precisely, from what are considered to be inequities resulting from the movement of taxable wealth from one side of a boundary line to another. When many large taxpayers move to the suburbs, the central city must tax those who remain at a higher rate if it is to maintain the same level of services. The "problem" in this case is not that the taxpayers who remain are absolutely unable to pay the increased taxes; rather, it is that they do not want to pay them and that they consider it unfair that they should have to pay more simply because other people have moved away. The simple and costless solution (in all but a political sense) would be to charge nonresidents for services that they receive from the city or, failing that, to redraw the boundary lines so that everyone in the metropolitan area would be taxed on the same basis. As the historian Kenneth T. Jackson points out, those central cities that are declining in numbers of residents and in wealth are doing so because their state legislatures will not permit them to enlarge their boundaries by annexations; even before the Civil War many large cities would have been surrounded by suburbs — and therefore suffering from the same revenue problem — if they had not been permitted to annex freely.[10]

That we have not yet been willing to pay the price of solving, or alleviating, such "problems" even when the price is a very small one suggests that they are not really critical. Indeed, one might say that, by definition, a critical problem is one that people *are* willing to pay a considerable price to have solved.

With regard to these problems for which solutions are at hand, we will know that a real crisis impends when we see the solutions actually being applied. The solution, that is, will be applied when — and only when — the inconvenience or other disadvantage of allowing the problem to continue unabated is judged to have become greater than that of taking the necessary measures to abate it. In other words, a bad-but-not-quite-critical problem is one that it would almost-but-not-quite pay us to do something about.

If some real disaster impends in the city, it is not because parking spaces are hard to find, because architecture is bad, because department store sales are declining, or even because taxes are rising. If there is a genuine crisis, it has to do with the essential welfare of individuals or with the good health of the society, not merely with comfort, convenience, amenity, and business advantage, important as these are. It is not necessary here to try to define "essential welfare" rigorously: it is enough to say that whatever may cause people to die before their time, to suffer serious impairment of their health or of their powers, to waste their lives, to be deeply unhappy or happy in a way that is less than human affects their essential welfare. It is harder to indicate in a sentence or two what is meant by the "good health" of the society. The ability of the society to maintain itself as a going concern is certainly a primary consideration; so is its free and democratic character. In the last analysis, however, the quality of a society must be judged by its tendency to produce desirable human types; the healthy society, then, is one that not only stays alive but also moves in the direction of giving greater scope and expression to what is distinctly human. In general, of course, what serves the essential welfare of individuals also promotes the good health of the society; there are occasions, however, when the two goals conflict. In such cases, the essential welfare of individuals must be sacrificed for the good health of the society. This happens on a very large scale when there is a war, but it may happen at other times as well. The conditions about which we should be most concerned, therefore, are those that affect, or may affect, the good health of the society. If there is an urban crisis in any ultimate sense, it must be constituted of these conditions.

It is a good deal easier to say what matters are not serious (that is, do not affect either the essential welfare of individuals or the good health of the society) than it is to say what ones are. It is clear, however, that crime, poverty, ignorance, and racial (and other) injustices are among the most important of the general conditions affecting the essential welfare of individuals. It is plausible, too, to suppose that these conditions have a very direct bearing upon the good health of the society, although in this connection other factors that are much harder to guess about — for example, the nature and strength of the consensual bonds that hold the society together — may be much more important. To begin with, anyway, it seems reasonable to look in these general directions for what may be called the serious problems of the cities.

It is clear at the outset that serious problems directly affect only a rather small minority of the whole urban population. In the relatively new residential suburbs and in the better residential neighborhoods in the outlying parts of the central cities and in the older, larger, suburbs, the overwhelming majority of people are safely above the poverty line, have at least a high school education, and do not suffer from racial discrimination. For something like two-thirds of all city dwellers, the urban problems that touch them directly have to do with comfort, convenience, amenity, and business advantage. In the terminology used here, such problems are "important" but not "serious." In many cases, they cannot even fairly be called important; a considerable part of the urban population — those who reside in the "nicer" suburbs — lives under material conditions that will be hard to improve upon.

The serious problems are to be found in all large cities and in most small ones. But they affect only parts of these cities — mainly the inner parts of the larger ones — and only a small proportion of the whole urban population. Crime is a partial exception, but in Chicago (so the Violence Commission was told) a person who lives in the inner city faces a yearly risk of 1 in 77 of being assaulted whereas for those who live in the better areas of the city the risk is only 1 in 2,000 and for those who live in the rich suburbs only 1 in 10,000.[11] Apart from those in the inner districts, which comprise about 10 to 20 percent of the city's total area, there are few serious urban problems. If what really matters is the essential welfare of individuals and the good health of the society, as opposed to comfort, convenience, amenity, and business advantage, then the problem is less an "urban" one than an "inner-(big)-city" one.

Although the poor and the black (and in some cities other minority groups also) are concentrated in the inner city and although the districts in which they live include many blocks of unrelieved squalor, it should not be supposed that the "poverty areas" of the inner cities are uniformly black, poor, or squalid. This can be seen from the findings of a special survey made in 1970 and 1971 by the Census of what it defined as the "low-income areas" of fifty-one of the largest cities.[12] A brief listing of some of these findings should dispel any notion that an inner-city "poverty area" is occupied only by the "disinherited."

Of the almost nine million persons aged sixteen or over who were counted, half were black and 35 percent non-Spanish white.

More than three-fourths reported incomes *above* the poverty level.

The median income of a male-headed family was $7,782 (the comparable figure for the United States population as a whole was $10,480).

Among such families, 25 percent of the white and 20 percent of the Negro reported incomes above $12,000.

Of the nearly two million persons below the poverty level, whites and blacks were distributed in about the same proportion as in the whole "poverty area" population. (Spanish families were considerably overrepresented among the poor in the nineteen cities where they were numerous enough to be surveyed separately.)

The median income of male-headed white families was $425 more than that of black and the median income of black $849 more than Spanish.

In twenty-one of the fifty-one cities, however, the blacks in poverty areas had higher median family incomes than whites and in twelve more cities the difference (in favor of the whites) was trivial -- less than 5 percent.

The median years of schooling for persons twenty-five years of age or older was almost identical — 10 and a small fraction — for whites and blacks, males and females; for persons twenty-five to thirty-four it was also almost identical and surprisingly high: twelve and a small fraction.

Although a large share of the income of many families went for housing, the reverse was also true: 40 percent of white and 25 percent of Negro (male-headed) families paid less than 10 percent of their income for housing. Ninety percent of the white and 80 percent of the black (male-headed) families had housing that was not overcrowded — that is, there was at least one room per person.

Of the nearly nine million persons aged sixteen or over, 478,000 (9.6 percent of those in the labor force) were unemployed. Less than half of these had been laid off; most had either quit or were just entering the labor force. Only 82,000 had been unemployed for as long as six months. Most were teenagers or unattached men and women in their early twenties, and many of these were students who wanted part-time or summer jobs.

The unemployment rate among male Negro family heads was 5.3 percent; among male white (non-Spanish) family heads it was 4.5 percent.

About 10 percent of those *not* in the labor force said that they intended looking for a job (most nonparticipants were housewives, of course). Asked why they did not look, "inability to find work" was given as a reason by 8,000 males and 24,000 females. Of these, 25 percent were aged 16-21. Asked what would be their minimum acceptable wage, the median figure given by black males in this age group was $83 weekly; whites expected one dollar more. Both black and white men who were heads of families expected $108.

Within or overlapping some "poverty areas" are huge enclaves — a few have populations of several hundred thousand — that are almost entirely Negro or, in some cities, Puerto Rican or Mexican-American.[13] These enclaves — they are often called ghettoes but . . . this usage is extremely ambiguous — constitute a problem that is both serious and unique to the large cities. The problem arises because the enclaves are psychologically — and in some degree physically — cut off from the rest of the city. Whatever may be the effect of this on the welfare of the individual — and it may possibly be trivial — it is clear that the existence of a large enclave of persons who perceive themselves, and are perceived by others, as having a separate identity, not sharing, or not sharing fully, the attachment that others feel to the "city," constitutes a potential hazard not only to present peace and order but — what is more important — to the well-being of the society over the long run. Problems of individual welfare may be no greater by virtue of the fact that people live together in huge enclaves rather than in relative isolation on farms and in small towns, although about this one cannot be sure (such problems *appear* greater when people live in enclaves, of course, but this is because they are too conspicuous to be ignored). The problem that they may present to the good health of the society, however, is very different in kind and vastly greater in importance solely by virtue of their living in huge enclaves. Unlike those who live on farms and in small towns, disaffected people who are massed together may develop a collective consciousness and sense of identity. From some standpoints it may be highly desirable that they do so: feeling the strength of their numbers may give them confidence and encourage them to act politically and in other ways that will help them. On the other hand, the effect of numbers may be to support attitudes and institutions that will hamper progress. There is no doubt, however, that such enclaves represent a threat to peace and order, one made greater by the high proportion of young people in them. As the Commission on Population Growth and the American Future recently remarked,

> The decade 1960 to 1970 saw a doubling of the number of young black men and women aged 15 to 24 in the metropolitan areas of every part of the nation except the south. This increase, twice that for comparable white youth, was the result of higher black fertility to begin with, participation in the post-World War II baby boom, and continued migration away from southern rural poverty. The result has been more and more young black people ill-equipped to cope with the demands of urban life, more likely to wind up unemployed or in dead-end, low-paying jobs, and caught in the vicious wheel of poverty, welfare degradation, and crime.
>
> The facts we have cited describe a crisis for our society. They add up to a demographic recipe for more turmoil in our cities, more bitterness among our "have-nots," and greater divisiveness among all of our peoples.[14]

The political danger in the presence of great concentrations of people who feel little attachment to the society has long been regarded by some as *the* serious problem of the cities — the one problem that might eventuate in disaster for the society. "The dark ghettoes," Dr. Clark has written, "now represent a nuclear stockpile which can annihilate the very foundations of America."[15] These words bring to mind the apprehensions that were expressed by some of the Founding Fathers and that Tocqueville set forth in a famous passage of *Democracy in America*:

> The United States has no metropolis, but it already contains several very large cities. Philadelphia reckoned 161,000 inhabitants, and New York 202,000, in the year 1830. The lower ranks which inhabit these cities constitute a rabble even more formidable than the populace of European towns. They consist of freed blacks, in the first place, who are condemned by the laws and by public opinion to a hereditary state of misery and degradation. They also contain a multitude of Europeans who have been driven to the shores of the New World by their misfortunes or their misconduct; and they bring to the United States all our greatest vices, without any of those interests which counteract their baneful influence.

As inhabitants of a country where they have no civil rights, they are ready to turn all the passions which agitate the community to their own advantage; thus, within the last few months, serious riots have broken out in Philadelphia and New York. Disturbances of this kind are unknown in the rest of the country, which is not alarmed by them, because the population of the cities has hitherto exercised neither power nor influence over the rural districts.

Nevertheless, I look upon the size of certain American cities, and especially on the nature of their population, as a real danger which threatens the future security of the democratic republics of the New World; and I venture to predict that they will perish from this circumstance, unless the government succeeds in creating an armed force which, while it remains under the control of the majority of the nation, will be independent of the town population and able to repress its excesses.[16]

Strange as it may seem, the mammoth government programs to aid the cities are directed mainly toward the problems of comfort, convenience, amenity, and business advantage. Insofar as they have an effect on the serious problems, it is, on the whole, to aggravate them.

Two programs account for a very large part of federal government expenditure for the improvement of the cities (as opposed to the maintenance of more or less routine functions). Neither is intended to deal with the serious problems. Both make them worse.

The improvement of urban transportation is one program. The federal contribution for urban highway construction and improvement, which as long ago as 1960 was more than $1 billion a year, has since doubled. The main effect of urban expressways, for which most of the money is spent, is to enable suburbanites to move about the metropolitan area more conveniently, to open up some areas for business and residential expansion, and to bring a few more customers from the suburbs downtown to shop. These are worthy objects when considered by themselves; in context, however, their justification is doubtful, for their principal effect is to encourage — in effect to subsidize — further movement of industry, commerce, and relatively well-off residents (mostly white) from the inner city. This, of course, makes matters worse for the poor by reducing the number of jobs for them and by making neighborhoods, schools, and other community facilities still more segregated. These injuries are only partially offset by enabling a certain number of the inner-city poor to commute to jobs in the suburbs.

The huge expenditure being made for improvement of mass transit — $1 billion in fiscal 1974 — may be justifiable for the contribution that it will make to comfort, convenience, and business advantage. It will not, however, make any contribution to the solution of the serious problems of the city. Even if every city had a subway as fancy as Moscow's, all these problems would remain.

The second great federal urban program concerns housing and renewal. Since the creation in 1934 of the Federal Housing Authority

(FHA), the government has subsidized home building on a vast scale by insuring mortgages that are written on easy terms and, in the case of the Veterans Administration (VA), by guaranteeing mortgages. Most of the mortgages have been for the purchase of *new* homes. (This was partly because FHA wanted gilt-edged collateral behind the mortgages that it insured, but it was also because it shared the American predilection for newness.) It was cheaper to build on vacant land, but there was little such land left in the central cities and in their larger, older suburbs; therefore, most of the new homes were built in new suburbs. These were almost always zoned so as to exclude the relatively few Negroes and other "undesirables" who could afford to build new houses and until late 1962 (when a presidential order barred discrimination in federally aided housing) FHA acted on its own to encourage all-white developments by instructing its appraisers to make low ratings of properties in neighborhoods occupied by what its Underwriting Manual termed "inharmonious racial or nationality groups" and by recommending a model racial restrictive covenant.[17] In effect, then, the FHA and VA programs have subsidized the movement of the white middle class out of the central cities and older suburbs while at the same time penalizing investment in the rehabilitation of the run-down neighborhoods of these older cities. The poor — especially the Negro poor — have not received any direct benefit from these programs. (They have, however, received a very substantial unintended and indirect benefit ... because the departure of the white middle class has made more housing available to them.) After the appointment of Robert C. Weaver as head of the Housing and Home Finance Agency, FHA changed its regulations to encourage the rehabilitation of existing houses and neighborhoods. Very few such loans have been made, however.

Urban renewal has also turned out to be mainly for the advantage of the well-off — indeed, of the rich — and to do the poor more harm than good. The purpose of the federal housing program was declared by Congress to be "the realization as soon as feasible of the goal of a decent home and a suitable living environment for every American family." In practice, however, the principal objectives of the renewal program have been to attract the middle class back into the central city (as well as to slow its exodus out of the city) and to stabilize and restore the central business districts.[18] Unfortunately, these objectives can be served only at the expense of the poor. Hundreds of thousands of low-income people, most of them Negroes or Puerto Ricans, have been forced out of low-cost housing, by no means all of it substandard, in order to make way for luxury apartments, office buildings, hotels, civic centers, industrial parks, and the like. Insofar as renewal has involved the "conservation" or "rehabilitation" of residential areas, its effect has been to keep the poorest of the poor out of these neighborhoods — that is, to keep them in the highest-density slums.

"At a cost of more than three billion dollars," sociologist Scott Greer wrote in 1965, "the Urban Renewal Agency (URA) has succeeded in materially reducing the supply of low-cost housing in American cities."[19]

The injury to the poor inflicted by renewal has not been offset by benefits to them in the form of public housing (that is, housing owned by public bodies and rented by them to families deemed eligible on income and other grounds). With the important exception of New York and the less important ones of some Southern cities, such housing is not a significant part of the total supply. Moreover, the poorest of the poor are usually, for one reason or another, ineligible for public housing.

Another housing program that has subsidized the relatively well-off and hastened their movement out of the central city is seldom thought of as a housing program at all. It consists of benefits to homeowners under the federal income tax laws. *The President's Fourth Annual Report on National Housing Goals*, issued in 1972, estimated that by allowing homeowners to deduct mortgage interest and property taxes from their gross incomes federal revenues had been reduced by $4.7 billion the previous year.[20] The subsidies, the report said, "are worth relatively more to higher income homeowners." Renters were not benefited at all except as owners might pass some of their tax savings on to them. To dramatize the inequity of these arrangements, a tax authority testifying before a Senate subcommittee imagined what it would sound like if a housing program having the same effects were to be proposed to Congress:

> We have a program to assist people who own homes. . . . If there is a married couple with more than $200,000 of income, why for each $100 of mortgage that they have, HUD will pay that couple $70. On the other hand, if there is a married couple with an income of $10,000, then under this HUD program we will pay that married couple only $19 on their $100 mortgage interest bill. And, of course, if they are too poor to pay an income tax then we are not going to pay them anything.[21]

Obviously these various government programs work at cross-purposes, one undoing (or *trying* to undo) what another does (or *tries* to do). The expressway and (with minor exceptions) the housing programs in effect pay the middle-class person to leave the central city for the suburbs. At the same time, the urban renewal and mass transit programs pay him to stay in the central city or to move back to it. ". . . [F]ederal housing programs over the years," the presidential report cited above acknowledges, "have contributed to rapid suburbanization and unplanned urban sprawl, to growing residential separation of the races, and to the concentration of the poor and minorities in decaying central cities."[22] In the opinion of the economist Richard Muth, expressways ("the major contributor to urban decentralization in the postwar period") and federal aids to home ownership may have caused the land area of cities to be as much as 17 percent larger than it would otherwise be and the central city's share of the urbanized area population to be 3 to 7 percent smaller.[23]

In at least one respect, however, these government programs are consistent: they aim at problems of comfort, convenience, amenity, and business advantage, not at ones involving the essential welfare of individuals or the good health of the society. Indeed, on the contrary, they all sacrifice these latter, more important interests for the sake of the former, less important ones. In this the urban programs are no different from a great many other government programs. Price production programs in agriculture, Theodore Schultz has remarked, take up almost all the time of the Department of Agriculture, the agricultural committees of Congress, and the farm organizations, and exhaust the influence of farm people. But these programs, he says, "do not improve the schooling of farm children, they do not reduce the inequalities in personal distribution of wealth and income, they do not remove the causes of poverty in agriculture, nor do they alleviate it. On the contrary, they worsen the personal distribution of income within agriculture."[24]

It is widely supposed that the serious problems of the cities are unprecedented both in kind and in magnitude. Between 1950 and 1960 there occurred the greatest population increase in the nation's history. At the same time, a considerable part of the white middle class moved to the newer suburbs, and its place in the central cities and older suburbs was taken by Negroes (and in New York by Puerto Ricans as well). These and other events — especially the civil rights revolution — are widely supposed to have changed completely the character of "the urban problem."

If the present situation is indeed radically different from previous ones, then we have nothing to go on in judging what is likely to happen next. At the very least, we face a crisis of uncertainty.

In a real sense, of course, *every* situation is unique. Even in making statistical probability judgments, one must decide on more or less subjective grounds whether it is reasonable to treat certain events as if they were the "same." The National Safety Council, for example, must decide whether cars, highways, and drivers this year are enough like those of past years to justify predicting future experience from past. From a logical standpoint, it is no more possible to decide this question in a purely objective way than it is to decide, for example, whether the composition of the urban population is now so different from what it was that nothing can be inferred from the past about the future. Karl and Alma Taeuber are both right and wrong when they write that we do not know enough about immigrant and Negro assimilation patterns to be able to compare the two and that "such evidence as we could compile indicates that it is more likely to be misleading than instructive to make such comparisons."[25] They are certainly right in saying that one can only guess whether the pattern of Negro assimilation will resemble that of the immigrant. But they are wrong to imply that we can avoid making guesses and still compare things that are not known to be alike in all respects except one. (What, after all, would be the point of comparing immigrant and Negro assimilation patterns if we knew that the only difference between the two was, say, skin color?) They are also wrong in suggesting that the evidence indicates anything about what is likely to be instructive. If there were enough evidence to indicate that, there would be enough to indicate what is likely to happen; indeed, a judgment as to what is likely to be instructive is inseparable from one as to what is likely to happen. Strictly speaking, the Taeubers' statement expresses *their* guess as to what the evidence indicates.

The facts by no means compel one to take the view that the serious problems of the cities are unprecedented either in kind or in magnitude. That the population of metropolitan areas increased during the 1960's by nearly 17 percent to a record high of 139,374,000 persons need not hold much significance from the present standpoint: American cities have frequently grown at fantastic rates (consider the growth of Chicago from a prairie village of 4,470 in 1840 to a metropolis of more than a million in fifty years). In any case, the present population increase is leaving most cities less rather than more crowded. In the 1960's, 130 of the 292 central cities lost population, and the aggregate of their loss was 2.25 million persons; this was a greater decline than in the previous decade. Density of population in the central cities fell from 7,786 per square mile in 1950 to 4,463 in 1970; the comparable figures for suburban areas are 3,167 and 2,627.[26] Looking to the future, there is every reason to expect the trend toward "decongestion" to continue. But even if it were to reverse itself, there would be no obvious cause for concern. As Irving Hoch, a researcher for Resources for the Future, has remarked, there has been much sound and fury about the presumed ill effects of city size and density on health and welfare but there is little hard evidence on the subject; moreover, such evidence as points in one direction can be countered by other evidence pointing in the opposite direction.[27]

The movement of farm and rural people (mostly Negroes and Puerto Ricans) to the large Northern cities was much smaller in the 1960's than in the previous decade and the outlook is for a continued decline both because natural increase was less during the 1960's and because rural areas appear to be retaining a higher proportion of their growth.[28] But even at its height the migration of Negroes and Puerto Ricans to the big cities was not more than about equal to immigration from Italy in its peak decade. (In New York, Chicago, and many other cities in 1910, two out of every three schoolchildren were the sons and daughters of immigrants.) When one takes into account the vastly greater size and wealth of the cities now as compared to half a century or more ago, it is obvious that by the only relevant measure — namely, the number of immigrants relative to the capacity of the cities to provide for them and to absorb them — the movement from the South and from Puerto Rico has been not large but small.

In many important respects the material conditions of life in the cities have long been improving. Incomes have increased steadily. In the 1960's, for example, white income rose by 69 percent and black income by 100 percent. Despite this relative gain, the income of black families was still somewhat less than two-thirds that of whites. Housing is also better and consumption of it more than doubled in real per capita terms between 1950 and 1970. As Dean Dick Netzer has written,

> Not only has the housing improved, but also there have been huge investments in supporting public and institutional facilities — schools, roads, transit, hospitals, water supply and sewerage, airports, etc. In the twenty-year period, about $200 billion has been invested by state and local governments in new public facilities in metropolitan areas, almost as much as the total investment in new housing in these areas during the period. This hardly supports the charge that ours is a society of "public squalor amidst private opulence."[29]

At the turn of the century only one child in fifteen went beyond elementary school; now well over half finish high school. In this period blacks have increased the amount of their schooling faster than whites; in 1900 they averaged three years less than whites, but the present generation of pupils is expected to get almost as much, or — if comparison is made among pupils with about the same test scores — slightly more.[30] (In 1972, for the first time, the percentage of black and other minority-race high school graduates enrolling in college was the same as for whites.) As these figures imply, racial discrimination has declined dramatically since the Second World War. Studies made over a period of almost thirty years by the National Opinion Research Center reveal a trend "distinctly toward increasing approval of integration" with the highest pro-integration scores among the young and among residents of the largest metropolitan areas.[31]

The very movements that in some cities or parts of cities signalize, or constitute, an improvement in the situation tend, of course, to make matters worse in other places. For example, in Philadelphia the population of the districts designated "low income" by the Census dropped from more than 900,000 to nearly 800,000 in the 1960's. This happened partly because many families, black as well as white, became able to afford to move to better neighborhoods. The consequence of their moving out of the "low-income" areas, however, was to widen the income gap between those areas and the rest of the city. In other words, the poverty of the "low-income" areas has been intensified relative to other areas even though — conceivably — it may be that no one in any of them is poorer than before. (As a practical matter, there can be little doubt that the departure of the better-off families *does* entail disadvantages for those who remain.)

Surprising as it may seem, most Americans are reasonably well satisfied with their neighborhoods. A recent poll found that those who live in rural areas and in small towns are more likely to say that they are satisfied than those who live in cities, and, as one would expect, the well-off are more likely to be satisfied than the poor. But even among blacks (seven out of ten of whom are city dwellers) only 17 percent say that they are dissatisfied with their neighborhoods.[32]

If the situation is improving, why, it may be asked, is there so much talk of an urban crisis? The answer is that the improvements in performance, great as they have been, have not kept pace with rising expectations. In other words, although things have been getting better absolutely, they have been getting worse *relative to what we think they should be.* And this is because, as a people, we seem to act on the advice of the old jingle:

> Good, better, best,
> Never let it rest
> Until your good is better
> And your better best.

Consider the poverty problem, for example. Irving Kristol has pointed out that for nearly a century all studies, in all countries, have concluded that a third, a fourth, or a fifth of the nation in question is below the poverty line.[33] "Obviously," he remarks, "if one defines the poverty line as that which places one-fifth of the nation below it, then one-fifth of the nation will always be below the poverty line." The point is that even if everyone is better off there will be as much poverty as ever, provided that the line is redefined upward. Kristol notes that whereas in the depths of the Depression, F.D.R. found only one-third of the nation "ill-housed, ill-clad, ill-nourished," Leon Keyserling, a former head of the Council of Economic Advisers, in 1962 published a book called *Poverty and Deprivation in the U.S. — the Plight of Two-Fifths of a Nation.*

Much the same thing has happened with respect to most urban problems. Police brutality, for example, would be a rather minor problem if we judged it by a fixed standard; it is a growing problem because we judge it by an ever more exacting standard. A generation ago the term meant hitting someone on the head with a nightstick. Now it often means something quite different:

> What the Negro community is presently complaining about when it cries "police brutality" is the more subtle attack on personal dignity that manifests itself in unexplainable questionings and searches, in hostile and insolent attitudes towards groups of young Negroes on the street, or in cars, and in the use of disrespectful and sometimes racist language. . . .[34]

Following Kristol, one can say that if the "police brutality line" is defined as that which places one-fifth of all police behavior below it, then one-fifth of all police behavior will always be brutal.

The school dropout problem is an even more striking example. At the turn of the century, when almost everyone was a dropout, the term and the "problem" did not exist. It was not until the 1960's, when for the first time a majority of boys and girls were graduating from high school and practically all had at least some high school training, that the "dropout problem" became acute. Then, although the dropout rate was still declining, various cities developed at least fifty-five separate programs to deal with the problem. Hundreds of articles on it were published in professional journals, the National Education Association established a special action project to deal with it, and the Commissioner of Education, the Secretary of Labor, and the President all made public statements on it.[35] Obviously, if one defines the "inadequate amount of schooling line" as that which places one-fifth of all boys and girls below it, then one-fifth of all boys and girls will always be receiving an inadequate amount of schooling.

Whatever our educational standards are today, Wayland writes, they will be higher tomorrow. He summarizes the received doctrine in these words:

> Start the child in school earlier; keep him in school more and more months of the year; retain all who start to school for twelve to fourteen years; expect him to learn more and more during this period, in wider and wider areas of human experience, under the guidance of a teacher, who has had more and more training, and who is assisted by more and more specialists, who provide an ever-expanding range of services, with access to more and more detailed personal records, based on more and more carefully validated tests.[36]

To a large extent, then, our urban problems are like the mechanical rabbit at the racetrack, which is set to keep just ahead of the dogs no matter how fast they may run. Our performance is better and better, but because we set our standards and expectations to keep ahead of performance, the problems are never any nearer to solution. Indeed, if standards and expectations rise *faster* than performance, the problems may get (relatively) worse as they get (absolutely) better.

Some may say that since almost everything about the city can stand improvement (to put it mildly), this mechanical rabbit effect is a good thing in that it spurs us on to make constant progress. No doubt this is true to some extent. On the other hand, there is danger that we may mistake failure to progress as fast as we would like for failure to progress at all and, in panic, rush into ill-considered measures that will only make matters worse. After all, an "urban crisis" that results largely from rising standards and expectations is not the sort of crisis that, unless something drastic is done, is bound to lead to disaster. To treat it as if it were might be a very serious mistake.

This danger is greatest in matters where our standards are unreasonably high. The effect of too-high standards cannot be to spur us on to reach the prescribed level of performance sooner than we otherwise would, when that level is impossible of attainment. At the same time, these standards may cause us to adopt measures that are wasteful and injurious and, in the long run, to conclude from the inevitable failure of these measures that there is something fundamentally wrong with our society.

To extend the range of present Department of Health, Education and Welfare services equitably — to all those similarly situated in need — would require an *additional* cost roughly equivalent to the *entire federal budget*, Elliot L. Richardson reported as he left the secretaryship of that department.[37] His point was that expectations, indeed claims authorized by Congress, far exceeded the capacity of the government to provide. "One can imagine," he said somberly, "a point of reckoning at which the magnitude of the ill-treated problems is fully perceived — along with a profound sense of failure. And one can only hope that the troubled reaction toward the institutions held accountable would be reasoned and responsible."

The Prospect

It is probable that at this time we are about to make great changes in our social system. The world is ripe for such changes and if they are not made in the direction of greater social liberality, the direction forward, they will almost of necessity be made in the direction backward, of a terrible social niggardliness. We all know which of those directions we want. But it is not enough to want it, not even enough to work for it — we must want it and work for it with intelligence. Which means that we must be aware of the dangers which lie in our most generous wishes.

—Lionel Trilling

It is impossible to avoid the conclusion that the serious problems of the cities will continue to exist in something like their present form for another twenty years at least. Even on the most favorable assumptions we shall have large concentrations of the poor and the unskilled, and — what, to repeat, is by no means the same thing — the lower class in the central cities and the larger, older suburbs. The outward movement of industry and commerce is bound to continue, leaving ever-larger parts of the inner city blighted or semi-abandoned. Even if we could afford to throw the existing cities away and build new ones from scratch, matters would not be essentially different, for the people who move into the new cities would take the same old problems with them. Eventually, the present problems of the cities will disappear or dwindle into relative unimportance; they will not, however, be "solved" by programs of the sort undertaken in the past decade. On the contrary, the tendency of such programs would be to prolong the problems and perhaps even make them worse.

For the most part, the problems in question have arisen from and are inseparably connected with developments that almost everyone welcomes: the growth and spread of affluence has enabled millions of people to move from congested cities to new and more spacious homes in the suburbs; the availability of a large stock of relatively good housing in the central cities and older suburbs has enabled the Negro to escape the semi-slavery of the rural South and, a century late, to move into industrial society; better public health measures and facilities have cut the deathrate of the lower class; the war and postwar baby boom have left the city with more adolescents and youths than ever before; and a widespread and general movement upward on the class-cultural scale has made poverty, squalor, ignorance, and brutality — conditions that have always and every-where been regarded as inevitable in the nature of things — appear as anomalies that should be removed entirely and at once.

What stands in the way of dealing effectively with these problems (insofar as their nature admits of their being dealt with by government) is mainly the virtues of the American political system and of the American character. It is because governmental power is widely distributed that organized interests are so often able to veto measures that would benefit large numbers of people. It is the generous and public-regarding impulses of voters and taxpayers that impel them to support measures — for example, the minimum wage and compulsory high school attendance — the ultimate effect of which is to make the poor poorer and more demoralized. Our devotion to the doctrine that all men are created equal discourages any explicit recognition of class-cultural differences and leads to "democratic" — and often misleading — formulations of problems: for example, poverty as lack of income and material resources (something external to the individual) rather than as inability or unwillingness to take account of the future or to control impulses (something internal). Sympathy for the oppressed, indignation at the oppressor, and a wish to make amends for wrongs done by one's ancestors lead to a mis-representation of the Negro as the near-helpless victim of "white racism." Faith in the perfectibility of man and confidence that good intentions together with strenuous exertions will hasten his progress onward and upward lead to bold programs that promise to do what no one knows how to do and what perhaps cannot be done, and therefore end in frustration, loss of mutual respect and trust, anger, and even coercion.

Even granting that in general the effect of government programs is to exacerbate the problems of the cities, it might perhaps be argued that they have a symbolic value that is more than redeeming. What economist Kenneth Boulding has said of national parks — that we seem to need them "as we seem to need a useless dome on the capitol, as a symbol of national identity and of that mutuality of concern and interest without which government would be naked coercion"[1] — may possibly apply as well to Freedom Budgets, domestic Marshall Plans, and other such concoctions. That government programs do not succeed in reducing welfare dependency, preventing crime, and so on, is not a weighty objection to them if, for want of them, the feeling would spread that the society is "not worth saving." There is an imminent danger, however, that the growing multitude of programs that are intended essentially as gestures of goodwill may constitute a bureaucratic juggernaut which cannot be stopped and which will symbolize not national identity and mutual concern but rather divisiveness, confusion, and inequity. If a symbol is wanted, a useless dome is in every way preferable.

That government cannot solve the problems of the cities and is likely to make them worse by trying does not necessarily mean that calamity impends. Powerful accidental (by which is meant, nongovernmental and, more generally, nonorganizational) forces are at work that tend to alleviate and even to eliminate the problems. Hard as it may be for a nation of inveterate problem-solvers to believe, social problems sometimes disappear in the normal course of events.

. . .

NOTES

Introduction

1. The 1970 Census defined as "urban" places, unincorporated as well as incorporated, with 2,500 inhabitants or more (excluding persons living in rural portions of extended cities) as well as other territory within Urbanized Areas. An "Urbanized Area" comprises at least one city of 50,000 inhabitants (the "central city") plus contiguous, closely settled areas ("urban fringe"). A "Standard Metropolitan Statistical Area (SMSA)" is a county or group of contiguous counties (except in New England) containing a city (or "twin" cities) of at least 50,000 population; contiguous counties are included in an SMSA if they are essentially metropolitan in character and are socially and economically integrated with the central city. That part of the United States lying outside of any SMSA is "non-metropolitan." All of these definitions were somewhat different in 1960 and also in 1950.

    See Daniel J. Elazar, "Are We a Nation of Cities?" *The Public Interest*, 4 (Summer 1966), pp. 42—44.

2. Sloan R. Wayland, "Old Problems, New Faces, and New Standards," in A. Harry Passow, ed., *Education in Depressed Areas* (New York: Columbia University Teachers College, 1963), p. 66.

3. Irving Hoch, "Urban Scale and Environmental Quality," in *Population, Resources, and the Environment*, vol. III of task force reports of Commission on Population Growth and the American Future, Ronald G. Ridker, ed. (Washington, D.C.: Government Printing Office, 1972), p. 243. The figures are for 1966.

4. According to the U.S. Public Health Service, the most polluted air is nowhere near as dangerous as inhaled cigarette smoke. It is of interest also that the mortality rate from emphysema is higher in rural parts of New York than in metropolitan ones (*New York Times*, October 30, 1970) and that the state with the highest death rate from respiratory disease is Vermont (*New York Times*, December 20, 1972).

5. For data see U.S. Environmental Protection Agency, *Air Quality Data*, an annual, *Air Pollution Measurements of the National Air Sampling Network, 1957—1961*, and *The Fourth Annual Report of the Council on Environmental Quality*, U.S. Government Printing Office, September 1973, pp. 265—275.

6. This was the finding of a six-year study directed by Lawrence B. Cohen of the Department of Industrial Engineering of Columbia University and reported in the *New York Times*, December 16, 1965.

7. J. R. Meyer, J. F. Kain, and M. Wohl, *The Urban Transportation Problem* (Cambridge, Mass.: Harvard University Press, 1965), p. 359.

8. John Kain, "How to Improve Urban Transportation at Practically No Cost," *Public Policy*, 20 (Summer 1972): 352. Italics are in the original.

9. Arnold J. Meltsner titles his contribution to a collection of essays "Local Revenue: A Political Problem." He explains: "Officials are sometimes reluctant to raise taxes because they believe that taxes have reached a political limit. How do you know, Mr. Mayor, that the property tax has reached a political limit? Answer: I do not know; I just feel it. A political limit is a fuzzy constraint, perhaps fictitious, that local officials worry about, but have difficulty predicting. Even social scientists cannot tell when a political limit is about to be reached." In John P. Crecine, ed., *Financing the Metropolis*, Urban Affairs Annual Reviews, vol. 4 (Beverly Hills, Calif.: Sage Publications, 1970), p. 108.

    In 1973 a survey of thirty cities with "serious financial problems" "failed to locate any cities in which conditions were such that timely action by local, or in a few cases, State officials could not avert or promptly relieve a financial emergency." Advisory Commission on Intergovernmental Relations, *City Financial Emergencies: The Intergovernmental Dimension* (Washington, D.C.: U.S. Government Printing Office, July 1973), p. 4.

10. Kenneth T. Jackson, "Metropolitan Government versus Suburban Autonomy," in Kenneth T. Jackson and Stanley K. Schultz, eds., *Cities in American History* (New York: Alfred A. Knopf, 1972), pp. 446 and 456.

11. *Final Report of the National Commission on the Causes and Prevention of Violence* (Washington, D.C.: U.S. Government Printing Office, 1969), footnote p. 29.

12. U.S. Bureau of the Census, *Census of Population: 1970, Employment Profiles of Selected Low-Income Areas*, Final Report PHC(3)-1, United States Summary — Urban Areas (January 1972). The low-income areas were defined by the Census Bureau in the middle 1960's for the use of OEO and Model Cities agencies. The following (equally weighted) criteria were used: family income below $3,000, children in broken homes, persons with low educational attainments, males in unskilled jobs, and substandard housing. Census tracts in the lowest quartile were defined as "low income." In 1970 the boundaries so established were re-examined by the Census in consultation with local planning and other officials; in most instances areas were enlarged somewhat.

    A Census report (distributed after the text of this book was in type) provides data for the low-income areas of the fifty largest cities using figures from the decennial census (a 15 percent sample) and defining a low-income area to consist of all census tracts in which 20 percent or more of all persons were below the poverty line in 1969. On this basis, there were 10,555,918 persons in the poverty areas, 60 percent of whom were Negro. The median family income was $6,099; 27 percent of the families were below the poverty line and 22 percent had incomes at least three times greater than the poverty standard. About one-third of the families in the low-income areas paid rents of less than 20 percent of their income; however, of the renters whose incomes were below the poverty line, more than half paid more than half of their incomes in rent. Census tracts with a poverty rate of 40 percent or more had 2,017,513 persons nearly three-fourths of whom were Negro. U.S. Bureau of the Census, Census of Population: 1970 Subject Reports, Final Report PC(2)-9B, Low-Income Areas in Large Cities.

13.   In *Dark Ghetto*, Kenneth B. Clark presents 1960 Census data showing that eight cities—New York, Los Angeles, Baltimore, Washington, Cleveland, St. Louis, New Orleans, and Chicago—contain a total of sixteen areas, all of at least 15,000 population and five of more than 100,000, that are exclusively (more than 94 percent) Negro (New York: Harper & Row, 1965), table, p. 25.

14.   Commission on Population Growth and the American Future, *Population and the American Future* (Washington, D.C.: U.S. Government Printing Office, 1972), p. 74.

15.   Kenneth B. Clark, "The Wonder Is There Have Been So Few Riots," *New York Times Magazine*, September 5, 1965, p. 10.

16.   Alexis de Tocqueville, *Democracy in America*, trans. by Henry Reeve (New York: Alfred A. Knopf, 1945), 1: 289—290.

17.   George Grier, "Washington," *City Magazine* (February 1971), p. 47, quoted by Bennett Harrison, *Education, Training and the Urban Ghetto* (Baltimore: The Johns Hopkins University Press, 1972), p. 167.

18.   Cf. Robert C. Weaver, "Class, Race and Urban Renewal," *Land Economics*, 36 (August 1960): 235—251. On urban renewal in general, see James Q. Wilson, ed., *Urban Renewal: The Record and the Controversy* (Cambridge, Mass.: M.I.T. Press, 1966).

19.   Scott Greer, *Urban Renewal and American Cities* (Indianapolis: Bobbs-Merrill, 1965), p. 3.

As William G. Grigsby has pointed out, the "flight to the suburbs," which most renewal projects in central cities have been intended to stop or reverse, may be a good thing from the standpoint of the society as a whole even if undesirable from that of the central city. "It is not understood that . . . exodus from the city has produced a much higher standard of housing than could otherwise have been attained, and that the market forces that produced this shift should, therefore, be stimulated." *Housing Markets and Public Policy* (Philadelphia: University of Pennsylvania Press, 1963), p. 333.

20.   *The President's Fourth Annual Report on National Housing Goals*, 92d Congress, 2d Session, House Document No. 92—319, June 29, 1972. The report includes a table (p. 48) showing the revenue cost for 1971 by gross income class.

This and another form of concealed subsidy (the noninclusion of imputed net rent in gross income reported for tax purposes) are discussed by Henry J. Aaron, *Shelter and Subsidies: Who Benefits from Federal Housing Policies?* (Washington, D.C.: The Brookings Institution, 1972), ch. 4.

21.   Stanley S. Surrey, Professor of Law, Harvard University, in U.S. Congress, Senate, Subcommittee on Priorities and Economy in Government of the Joint Economic Committee, *Hearings, The Economics of Federal Subsidy Programs*, 92d Congress, 1st Session, January 13, 14, and 17, 1972, p. 45.

22.   *The President's Fourth Annual Report*, p. 32. The report goes on to add: "While housing programs have contributed to these problems and in many cases intensified them, it is important to emphasize that they did not *cause* them. The causes stem from the complex interaction of population migration, community

attitudes and prejudices, consumer preferences, local government fragmentation, and the impact of other federal programs such as urban renewal and the highway programs."

23. Richard Muth, "The Urban Economy and Public Problems," in John P. Crecine, ed., *Financing the Metropolis*, p. 454. See also Muth's book, *Cities and Housing: The Spatial Pattern of Urban Residential Land Use* (Chicago: University of Chicago Press, 1969), pp. 319—322.

24. Theodore W. Schultz, *Economic Crises in World Agriculture* (Ann Arbor: University of Michigan Press, 1965), p. 94.

25. Karl E. and Alma F. Taeuber, "The Negro as an Immigrant Group: Recent Trends in Racial and Ethnic Segregation in Chicago," *American Journal of Sociology*, 69 (January 1964): 382.

26. Executive Office of the President, Domestic Council, *Report on National Growth, 1972* (Washington, D.C.: U.S. Government Printing Office, 1972).

27. Irving Hoch, "Income and City Size," *Urban Studies*, 9 (1972): 320.

28. Peter A. Morrison, *The Impact and Significance of Rural-Urban Migration in the United States* (Santa Monica, Calif.: The Rand Corporation,#P-4752, March 1972), p. 2.

29. Dick Netzer, *Economics and Urban Problems: Diagnosis and Prescriptions* (New York: Basic Books, 1970), p. 21.

30. Christopher Jencks et al., *Inequality: A Reassessment of the Effect of Family and Schooling in America* (New York: Basic Books, 1972), pp. 141—142.

31. Andrew M. Greeley and Paul B. Sheatsley, "Attitudes Toward Racial Integration," *Scientific American*, 225 (December 1971): 13 and 15.

   Thomas F. Pettigrew has found that "white attitudes toward open housing have become increasingly more favorable over the past generation." See his paper on "Attitudes on Race and Housing: A Social-Psychological View," in Amos H. Hawley and Vincent P. Rock, eds., *Segregation in Residential Areas* (Washington, D.C.: National Academy of Sciences, 1973), pp. 21—84. See also Joel D. Aberbach and Jack L. Walker, *Race in the City* (Boston: Little, Brown and Company, 1973), which presents data on attitudes of blacks and whites in Detroit in surveys made in 1967 and 1971.

32. William Watts and Lloyd A. Free, eds., *State of the Nation* (New York: Universal Books, 1973), p. 80.

33. Irving Kristol, "The Lower Fifth," *The New Leader*, February 17, 1964, pp. 9—10.

34. Robert Blauner, "Whitewash Over Watts," *Trans-action 3* (March—April 1966): 6.

35. Burton A. Weisbrod, "Preventing High-School Drop-outs," in Robert Dorfman, ed., *Measuring Benefits of Government Investments* (Washington, D.C.: The Brookings Institution, 1965), p. 118.

36. Wayland, "Old Problems," p. 67.

37. Elliot L. Richardson, *Responsibility and Responsiveness (II): A Report on the HEW Potential for the Seventies* (Washington, D.C.: U.S. Department of Health, Education, and Welfare, January 18, 1973).

The Prospect

1. Kenneth Boulding, book review in the *Journal of Business* (January 1963): 121.

The Wild City

Manuel Castells

INTRODUCTION:
BEYOND THE MYTHS OF THE URBAN CRISIS

"There was an urban crisis at one time," said William Dilley 3d, Deputy Assistant Secretary of Policy Development at the Department of Housing and Urban Development. But now, according to President Ford's aides, "the urban crisis of the 60's is over."[1]

What the officials wanted to express was that the black ghettoes were under control in spite of the recession. As right-wing ideologist Daniel Moynihan declared in the Congress, there is not an urban problem but a Negro problem.[2]

Is that really true? Is the urban crisis just the ideological expression used by the ruling class to "naturalize" (through an implicit ecological causation) the current social contradictions?[3]

This is the most current understanding of the political elite. So, Senator Ribicoff, opening the famous Congressionial "Ribicoff hearings" on urban problems in 1966 put it in unambiguous terms:

> To say that the city is the central problem of American life is simply to know that increasingly the cities are American life; just as urban living is becoming the condition of man across the world. ... The city is not just housing and stores. It is not just education and employment, parks and theaters, banks and shops. It is a place where men should be able to live in dignity and security and harmony, where the great achievements of modern civilization and the ageless pleasures afforded by natural beauty should be available to all.[4]

The popular mood is similar. A survey conducted by Wilson and Banfield on a sample of homeowners in Boston in 1967 in order to

Manuel Castells, "The Wild City," *Kapital state*, Nos. 4—5 (Summer 1976), pp. 2—30.

identify what the "urban problems" were for the people concluded that

> the conventional urban problems — housing, transportation, pollution, urban renewal and the like — were a major concern of only eighteen per cent of those questioned and these were expressed disproportionately by the wealthier, better educated respondents.... The issue which concerned more respondents than any other was variously stated — crime, violence, rebellious youth, racial tension, public immorality, delinquency. However stated, the common theme seemed to be a concern for improper behavior in public places.[5]

Nevertheless, while the urban crisis of the sixties remained largely associated with poverty and racial discrimination and with the social programs designed to control blacks and unemployed, the urban crisis of the 1970's has progressively developed rather different connotations:

- The urban crisis has been used to speak of *the crisis of some key urban services*, like housing, transportation, welfare, health, education, etc., characterized by an advanced degree of socialized management and a decisive role of the state intervention.[6]
- The urban crisis is also *the fiscal crisis of the cities*, the inability of the local governments to provide enough resources to cover the required public facilities because of the increasing gap between the fiscal resources and the public needs and demands.[7]
- The urban crisis is, at another level, the development of *urban movements and conflicts* rising up from the grass-roots community organizations and directed towards urban stakes, that is towards the delivery and management of particular means of socialized consumption.[8]
- And, currently, the urban crisis is also the impact of the *structural and economic crisis* on the organization of the cities and on the evolution of social services.[9]

Is the multiplicity of meanings of the urban crisis an ideological effect? It is, if by this we would mean that the roots of the different levels of crisis that we have cited are produced by a particular form of spatial organization. But if the crude use of the term "urban crisis" is an ideological artifact, the association between the different connotative levels is not an arbitrary one. It is a biased reading of actual connections experienced in social practice.

In fact, *our hypothesis is that the U.S. urban crisis is the crisis of a particular form of urban structure that plays a major role in the U.S. process of capitalist accumulation, in the organization of socialized consumption and in the reproduction of the social order.* Since the urban role is performed at multiple levels, so is the crisis, its connections and its effects. This is the unifying perspective that will underlie our exploration of the multidimensionality of the urban crisis.

1. The U.S. model of capitalist accumulation and the U.S. pattern of urban structure: economic dualism, class domination, and spatial segregation.

The specificity of the U.S. urban structure since World War II — underlying the crisis of American cities — results from the historical articulation of the processes of *metropolitanization, suburbanization,* and *social-political fragmentation.*[10]

(A) *Metropolitanization:* concentration of the population and activities in some major areas at an accelerated rate. Such population concentration follows from the process of uneven development and from the concentration of capital (means of production and labor) in the monopolistic stage of capitalism. At the periphery, regional economies and agriculture are devastated/restructured by the penetration of their markets and the transformations in productivity under the hegemony of financial capital. Mass migration follows. In the dominant urban centers, the combined effect of externalities, transportation networks, urban markets, and concentration of the management units and of the institutions of circulation of capital concentrate workers, means of production, means of consumption, and organizations. These major cities are soon called metropolitan areas as an expression of their dominance over the "hinterland," that is, over the entire society.[11,12]

(B) *Suburbanization:*[13] the process of selective decentralization and spatial sprawl of population and activities within the metropolitan areas, starting at a large scale after World War II, accelerating during the fifties and maintaining its trend in the sixties. This is a selective process in that the new suburban population has a higher social status. There is a double differentiation of economic activity. On the one hand, business activities and major administrative services remain in the urban core while manufacturing and retail trade tend to decentralize their location. On the other hand, within the industrial and commercial sectors large-scale monopolistic plants and shopping centers go to the suburbs, leaving in the central cities two very different types of firms: a small number of technologically advanced activities and luxury shops; the mainstream of industrial and service activities of the so-called "competitive sector" (backward) as well as the marginal activities known as the components of the "irregular economy."

In the U.S. urban structure,[14] this process is a self-reinforcing one. The immigration of poor blacks expelled from the agricultural South has been concentrated in the inner cities.[15] The exodus of the upper and middle income groups attracts trade and service activities to the suburbs. "Competitive sector" jobs locate in geographical proximity to the low-income workers residing in central cities. Service and industrial employment locate in terms of the transportation system for suburban workers. The ecological patterns of residence will be increasingly differentiated:[16] yard-surrounded suburban single-family houses versus increasingly obsolete inner-city apartment dwellings. The cultural style, rooted mostly in the social class and family practices, will be symbolically reinforced by the social-spatial distance and by the environmental imagery. The two worlds will increasingly ignore each other until they will develop reciprocal fears, myths, and prejudices, often articulated to racial and class barriers.[17] The segregated school will become a major instrument of self-definition and perpetuation of the two separate and hierarchically organized universes.[18]

The suburbanization process has been facilitated by major technological changes in transportation, in the mass production of housing, and in the increasing spatial freedom of the plants and services in terms of the functional requirements for their location. Suburbanization is not a consequence of the automobile. On the contrary, the massive auto-highway transportation system and the new locational patterns of residence and employment express the new stage of capitalist accumulation and have been made possible primarily by the policies of the state designed to serve this purpose.[19] Let us summarize briefly the specific connections between capital accumulation, state policies, and suburbanization.

The recovery of U.S. capitalism after the Great Depression of the thirties was made possible by the war and three major postwar economic trends:[20] (a) the internalization of capital and the increase of the rate of exploitation on a world scale under U.S. hegemony, as a direct consequence of the economic and political situation of each country after World War II; (b) the rapid expansion of new profitable outlets through the development of mass consumption; (c) the decisive structural intervention of the state in the process of accumulation, in the creation of general conditions for capitalist production, and in the socialization of costs of social investment and the reproduction of labor power. As a simultaneous cause and consequence of this accelerated capitalist growth, the stability of the social relationships of exploitation was achieved through the combined use of economic integration and political repression of the mainstream of the working class.

How do these trends relate themselves to the process of suburbanization? On the one hand, the increasing profits of monopoly capital allowed the expansion of material production and of the investment in new technology and transportation facilities that led to the decentralization of larger plants. On the other hand, the

economic growth allowed a less than proportional raise of the
workers' wages and gave some of them a prospective job stability,
increasing their purchasing power and their financial reliability. The
requirement for immediate and massive new outlets was met just in
time by the sudden expansion of mass production of new housing,
highway-auto transportation, and all complementary public
facilities. In twenty years, America practically built up a new set of
cities, contiguous to the preexisting metropolises. The reason that
improved housing conditions were realized through new suburban
settlements was that land was much cheaper in the urban fringe, that
mass production of housing with light building materials required
new construction, and that the whole impact on the economy was considerably higher, particularly if we consider the implied necessity of a
decentralized individual transportation system.[21] Under these conditions of production and relying on a system of easy installment
credit, the construction and auto industry could draw into their
market a substantial proportion of the middle-class American
families, later including in this new world a sector of the working
class.

Nevertheless, the decisive element in the feasibility of this
economic, social, and spatial strategy was the role of the state,
particularly of the federal government, introducing key mechanisms
for the production of housing and highways, in a form subordinated
to the interests of monopoly capital. In the case of housing, as the most
recent U.S. government's report on housing writes:

> In the 1930's Congress made two fundamental policy decisions which remain
> basically intact to this day. The first was the complete restructuring of the
> private home financing system through the creation of the Federal Housing
> Administration (mortgage insurance); the Federal Home Loan Bank Board and
> Bank System (savings and loan industry); institutions like the Federal Deposit
> Insurance Corporation and the Federal Savings and Loan Insurance
> Corporation (insurance on deposits of commercial banks, mutual savings
> banks, and savings and loan associations); and finally, the Federal National
> Mortgage Association (secondary mortgage market). Creation of these
> institutions, resulting in the acceptability of long-term, low down payment,
> fully amortizing mortgage and a system to provide a large flow of capital into
> the mortgage market, are probably the most significant achievements of the
> Federal Government in the housing area.[22]

With the provision of a mortgage system that provided risk-free
credit for financial capital, the state overcame the major obstacle to the
profitable mass production of housing within capitalism: the absence
of a reliable home-ownership market. Once the government
undertook the risk of mortgage foreclosures, the middle-class families
could afford to enter the market, starting the process that allowed the
relative modernization of the building industry and the lowering of

costs which further enlarged the suburban market. In addition, the government issued (during the past forty years) a number of fiscal measures to protect real estate investors and to favor home ownership.[23]

Concerning the development of the *highway-auto transportation system*, three elements have to be considered:[24] (a) the deliberate destruction by the auto corporations (under the tolerance of the state and federal authorities) of alternative means of transportation, namely by acquiring the streetcar and railway companies and dismantling them;[25] (b) . . . the federal government paid 90 percent of the highway construction and it has spent, in 1973, sixty times more in this category than in the urban collective transportation for the whole country;[26] (c) the residential and industrial sprawl was necessarily connected to the highway-auto transportation, and in that sense the capitalist interests and the state policies created a set of mutually reinforcing trends. The auto, and therefore the highway, *became a need.*

The role of the suburbs in the process of capitalist accumulation was not limited only to providing outlets for the capital directly invested in their production. The whole suburban social form became an extremely effective *apparatus of individualized commodity consumption.*

Shopping centers and supermarkets were made possible by suburban sprawl. A new set of leisure activities (from the drive-in to the private swimming pool) was linked to suburbanization. But even more important was the role of the suburban single-family house as the perfect design for maximizing capitalist consumption. Every household had to be self-sufficient, from the refrigerator to the TV, including the garden machinery, the do-it-yourself instruments, the electro-domestic equipment, etc.

At the same time, the suburban model of consumption had a very clear impact on the *reproduction of the dominant social relationships.* Because the (legally owned) domestic world was in fact borrowed, it could be kept only on the assumption of a permanent preprogrammed job situation. Any major deviation or failure could be sanctioned by the threats to (job-dependent) financial reliability. The mass consumption was also mass dependency upon the economic *and cultural* rules of the financial institutions.

The social relationships in the suburban neighborhood also expressed the values of individualism, conformism, and social integration, reducing the world to the nuclear family and the social desires to the maximization of individual consumption.

Without discussing here the alternative hypotheses about the suburbs being produced by the combination of technological possibilities and of subjective values towards suburbanism, three remarks must suffice: (a) Peoples' consciousness and values are produced by their practice, a practice determined by their place in the

social relationships of production and consumption.[27] (b) It is true
that there is a "return to nature" dream linked to the myth of
recovering, at least in the evening, the autonomy of the petty
commodity and peasant production from which salaried labor power
was historically drawn. (c) This myth is as strong in Europe as in the
U.S. and nevertheless the suburban pattern *has not been the same*. In
this sense the U.S. is *unique* in the world. Obviously the suburbs have
grown everywhere with the expansion of the metropolitan areas, but
the pattern of social segregation is not the same (with the non-U.S.
central cities having frequently a higher social status on the average).
Suburban owner-occupied housing is much less diffused outside the
U.S. and the automobile is not the major mode of urban
transportation. Indeed, this is not a matter of "inferior level of
development": the "suburban-like-U.S. pattern" [began to reverse] in
Paris in the last ten years after having increased in some extent in the
early sixties.[28] This is not to claim the irreducible specificity of each
society but to show how the process of U.S. suburbanization was
determined and shaped by a particular pattern of capitalist
development at a particular critical stage characterized by the decisive
intervention of the state.[29]

*The other face of the process of suburbanization was the new role
played by the central cities* in the process of accumulation and in the
reproduction of the labor power. There is a major differentiation
between the Central Business District (CBD) and the central cities at
large.[30] The CBD kept the major directional and organizational
economic functions, as well as a number of luxurious commercial
activities and several major cultural and symbolic institutions, while
losing a large proportion of the retail trade and many residents. The
central cities lost jobs especially in large-size manufacturing plants
and a significant residential proportion of the middle-class as well as
monopoly workers. On the other hand, central cities received increasing numbers of black and poor white immigrants, mostly from
the Southern depressed areas, as a consequence of the mechanization
of agriculture and of the destruction of the backward regional
economies.[31] The central cities became the location, at the same time,
of the "competitive sector" activities, of the corresponding low-skilled
and low-paid segment of the labor market, of the surplus population
(unemployed and underemployed), and of the discriminated ethnic
minorities. Therefore, the central cities organized consumption on an
entirely different basis than the suburbs. The housing market, in
particular, was supposed to work according to a "filtering down"
theory. Namely, the upper strata of central-city residents (exluding
from our analysis the top elite, mostly concentrated in self-defended
high-society ghettoes) left their urban dwellings for their new
suburban homes. This allowed the middle strata to occupy the vacated
houses, freeing their standard housing for the bottom level that could

leave their slums to the newcomers. In fact, such a theory never corresponded to reality, since its basic assumption was the extension of upward income mobility to the whole population.[32] Given a process of uneven development, the low and middle strata of the inner city were not able to afford the level of rents or interest payments necessary to jump to the following housing level. In addition, the racial discrimination operated against any actual access of the minorities to an equivalent standard of living, imposing a "race overprice."[33] The result for inner-city housing was that to maintain profit levels, the landlords combined lower rents with overcrowding and lack of maintenance. Some neighborhoods were *nevertheless* well-maintained on the base of ownership through savings and loan associations linked to nonmonopolistic financial markets, mostly ethnically (white)-based.[34]

The fixed assets of the inner-city residents were reduced in value:[35] what was occasion of profit for capital in the suburbs was cause of impoverishment for the inner-city white working class, of indebtedness for the suburban middle class, and of deterioration of living conditions for the slum dwellers. The reduction of the economic base of the central-city revenues also reduced the public services needed by the social groups that could not afford commodified consumption. Thus, the process of suburban expansion was, at the same time, the process of the central-city decay. Both were produced by the dominant capitalist interests which differentially affected the different social class segments.[36]

(C) The specific model of the postwar U.S. urban structure is completed by the functioning of a third major trend: *the political fragmentation of autonomous local governments*, and their role in the maintenance of the social residential segregation and the corresponding organization of consumption.[37]

"Separate and unequal," the communities of the metropolitan areas have transformed the Jeffersonian ideal of grass-roots local democracy into a barbed-wire wall of municipal regulation which prevents redistribution of income through the public delivery of goods and services.[38] An interesting analysis by Richard Child Hill on a large number of metropolitan areas shows a close relationship between the level of metropolitan income inequality and social status, and local government resource inequality.[39] This reflects both the major cleavage between central cities and their suburbs, and intra-suburban stratification. So, the more low-income residents are dependent on socialized consumption, the less the local government, major agency of provision of public facilities, has the resources to meet those needs and demands. Thus, not only are exploited people trapped in the labor market, but, in addition, public institutions are *structurally regressive* concerning the mechanisms of redistribution. Furthermore, fragmentation becomes a social and racial barrier that connects cultural prejudices to real estate interests. The school system plays a major role in channeling expectations of generational social mobility within each particular stratum and reproducing the whole system, economically and ideologically.[40] The wage-earning population is split so that each social position is crystallized in physical and social space, in consumption of services, in organizational networks, and in local government institutions. Future conflicts are channeled towards intracity competition among equally exploited residents for a structurally limited pie. The suburban local governments enforce this situation through all kinds of discriminatory land-use regulations: large-lot zoning, minimum-house-size requirements, exclusion of multiple dwellings, obstacles to nonreliable building permits, etc.

Thus, class-based metropolitan inequality is derived from uneven capitalist development. Expressed in the unequal social composition of the urban structure, it is ultimately preserved and reinforced by the state through the institutional arrangement of local governments and the class-determined fragmentation of the metropolitan areas.

The U.S. urban development pattern individualizes and commodifies profitable consumption, while simultaneously deteriorating nonprofitable socialized consumption. At the same time the institutional mechanisms for the preservation of the social order are structurally provided.

The coherence and the elegance of this model appeared as neat, well ordered, and impeccable as the uniforms of the guards who stand behind the smiling facade of the advertising society.

The new metropolitan world seemed able to go on and on. . . .

2. The social contradictions of the model of urban development and the attempts at regulation through urban policies.[41]

The new dynamic stability attained by the capitalist model of suburban growth did not last very long. Several structurally implicit contradictions within the model have expanded at an accelerated rate.

Urban crises have been generated by the contradictions inherent in (a) *the corporate-business and political-elite response to the decay of central cities;* and (b) *the loss of social control over the minorities and the lower working class of the inner city.*[42]

(a) The first process had three major consequences that were highly dysfunctional for dominant interests: (i) deterioration of municipal services and the social environment threatened the existence of the Central Business District, yet the preservation of the CBD was essential because of the ecological requirements for concentration of some directional functions, and because of the need to maintain the value-fixed capital investments and real estate interests held by large corporations; (ii) threat to functions of centrality, at the level of the symbolic dominance, [and to the] cultural institutions and "higher circles" residence and leisure that had to be preserved; (iii) potential erosion of political influence over the oldest white ethnic working class which had to be maintained as a base of institutional power, yet which required a city fiscally able to provide a minimum level of services and jobs.

To counter these consequences, it was crucial to restore the city's fiscal viability. The central city moved inexorably towards a gap between shrinking local property tax revenues on the one hand and expanding expenditures on the other. Corporate strategy involved giving up most of the central city, to concentrate on a program of *downtown redevelopment*, combining urban renewal, real estate initiatives, and easy access to the wealthy outer suburban ring through new highways reaching into the urban core over ghetto roofs. This strategy required the mobilization of the dominant forces of the largest cities around a program which articulated specific capitalist interests, local political elites, and the federal government. As Mollenkopf has shown in a critical paper, during the 1950's "pro-growth coalitions" formed to elect several strong mayors to implement and to legitimize this downtown redevelopment program (Daley in Chicago, Alioto in San Francisco, Lindsay in New York, White in Boston, etc.).[43]

The strategy's success was contingent on its articulation with urban renewal programs. Using the provisions of the 1949 Housing Act, this program accelerated in the sixties, federally financed.[44] This downtown program, carried out in cities like Boston, Newark, Baltimore, and Los Angeles, was predominantly aimed at attracting commercial and corporate interests in order to increase the tax base, to preserve the centrality functions, and to protect the CBD against the surrounding ghettoes. The program, with current costs of $8.2 billion in direct outlays and $22.5 billion in local government bonded debt, together with the highway program displaced over 250,000 *families* per year. These families were generally not relocated and received compensatory payments averaging $80, or less than one percent of the direct federal outlays. The results are twofold. On the one hand, the downtown districts have been partially "saved," the deterioration of the municipal budgets was slowed, and some central functions (for instance, some urban universities) were preserved. On the other hand, a number of communities were disrupted, a mass of sound housing stock was destroyed without equivalent replacement, the displaced families suffered serious difficulties and the central-city housing and public services situation worsened.[45]

No wonder that urban renewal was under grass-roots attack and that a number of urban struggles started as a reaction to the program.[46] In that sense, the partial economic benefits that corporate and elite interests received from progrowth policies were counteracted by the ensuing problem of maintaining the social order. These problems were exacerbated by another parallel set of expanding contradictions.

(b) The inner-city residents were submitted not only to the urban bulldozer but increasing unemployment and inflation. "Poverty" suddenly became a reality that nobody could ignore. The very serious depression of 1957—58, which developed once the economic stimuli of the Korean War had been spent, particularly struck the "competitive sector" workers and the newcomers to the large cities. Without collective political challenge to their situation, many inner-city dwellers, particularly the youth, reacted individually. So-called "crime in the streets" rose dramatically. Neighborhood gangs spread in the ghetto. The city's social order was seriously threatened.[47]

At the same time the civil rights movements, launched by black people in the South with white liberal support in the Northeastern cities, had started to transform the consciousness of the uprooted black immigrants. The ghetto organizations became more militant.

Those tendencies contributed to a new strategy of the federal political elite on the behalf of the ruling class. The late fifties (particuarly the 1957—58 depression and the Soviet Sputnik) directed the attention of the American dominant interests to the need to introduce some regulatory mechanisms at the social level. Labor unions reacted to the crisis by threatening to revise their support for labor-saving technological improvements. While a fraction of American capital, and most of the political personnel, wanted to pursue the trend that had been so successful during the fifties, adding more repression if necessary, the most class-conscious faction of the establishment supported a new reformist strategy in order to preserve the most precious advantage of U.S. capital: the stability of the exploitative social order. To them this "new frontier" appeared useful and without political danger. Internally, the McCarthy period had eliminated any possible alternative from the Left. The socialist forces had been isolated, discredited, and dismantled. The unions had either been coopted or repressed. The ideological order had been secured by the combined effect of the cold war, the hot (Korean) war, and the economic boom. Externally, the nuclear equilibrium limited the possibility of defeating the Soviet Union: the "peaceful coexistence" that followed permitted greater maneuverability and rendered the continuous mobilization of conservative myths superfluous. In sum, in the late fifties the most enlightened sector of the ruling class realized that the model of development required social reform for which they had the requisite political strength. The purpose: to enlarge their social base, to increase their political and ideological legitimization, and to modernize the economy by rectifying mechanisms of over-exploitation that were only required by backward sectors of capital. One of the major objectives of this reformist strategy was to provide mechanisms of black integration, or at least to give symbolic channels to prevent a mass-based social revolt. Furthermore, the specific political instruments that had to be used by the reformist wing required a mobilization of the black vote (particularly in the Northern cities) in order to compensate for the loss of the right-wing democrat vote in the South.[48] In fact, Kennedy won the key vote of Chicago in 1960 by relying on the black vote. If it is true that the ghettoes traditionally voted democrat, what was new in 1960 was the exceptional turnout of blacks voting for Kennedy. Yet, the rationality of this strategy did not convince a significant proportion of the American rulers. Its implementation was not a "structural necessity" but the result of a political struggle (the 1960 Nixon-Kennedy election) that gave a narrow victory to the man that was at the same time the candidate of the Establishment and the hope of the over-exploited against short-sighted "middle America."

The "New Frontier policies" and the "Great Society" programs were aimed at two major targets:[49] (a) the implementation of "civil rights," particularly against legal discrimination in the South; (b) the reduction of the consequences of uneven development by establishing special services and benefits for "the poor," trying at the same time to maintain social order. On both sides, the central cities became the natural battleground for the new reformers. A pioneer program, New York City's East Side Mobilization for Youth, "discovered" that the best way to prevent juvenile delinquency was to organize the young people in order to obtain their collective demands on jobs, services, and revenues. . . . The only "trouble" being that the program became increasingly contradictory with the social order that had generated it. Also, War on Poverty programs undertaken through the Office of Economic Opportunity had to be complemented, at the grass-roots level, with the Community Action Program which tried to organize and to mobilize neighborhood residents to put pressure on the bureaucracies in order to obtain the required services.[50] How is it possible that some bureaucracies were pushing other bureaucracies? Because they were different bureaucracies: it was clear, at the *federal level*, that all efforts of even modest social reform would be absorbed by the interests vested in the *local government bureaucracies* unless some controlled grass-roots pressure could be organized. Such control was eventually lost, not because of the naive idealism of the reformers (as some conservative bureaucrats think[51]) but because of a set of contradictions internal and external to the reformist programs. Internally, how to mobilize people without convincing them? And how to convince and be trusted without engaging in some actual economic or institutional reform? And how to do this without hurting the particularistic interests of the locally established cliques? Externally, the expansion of the Great Society programs was histori-cally connected to five major disruptive trends in the crucial period of the sixties: (1) the uprising of black people and the development of a black movement; (2) the Viet Nam War that absorbed more and more public resources, preventing the federal government from matching the expectations provoked by the social programs; (3) student revolt and the major breakdowns in the capitalist ideology with the emergence of the counterculture as a symptom of the legitimacy crisis; (4) the development of neighborhood struggles that opposed the "progrowth coalition."; (5) the inflationary process that undermined standards of living and faith in the market mechanisms, turning people towards the issue of service delivery.

The interaction of the "urban programs," designed to improve social peace, with these various trends initially transformed the programs into disruptive mechanisms. In a second phase, this led to their dismantlement (started by Johnson in 1967—68 and accelerated by Nixon) and the use of massive repression in the inner city, under the newly reinforced control of local bureaucracies.

Thus, both urban renewal and urban social programs, policies designed to improve the economic situation and the social stability of the decaying inner city accelerated the social conflicts as expressed by community mobilizations in the neighborhoods and by mass disruptions in the ghettoes. Combined with the problems arising within the services themselves, these led to a new, more dangerous form of urban crisis that exploded in the 1970's

3. Dimensions and processes of the current U.S. urban crisis.

The failure of the urban policies to handle the problems generated by uneven urban-suburban development and the maturation of the contradictions underlying the production and delivery of services precipitated during the sixties a multidimensional crisis that violently shook the urban structure and endangered its crucial function in the process of accumulation and segregated consumption. This crisis developed along several different lines that, although interrelated, will be better understood considered separately.

3.1 The breakdown of social order in the inner city. The most direct and most disruptive expression of the urban crisis was a series of different phenomena that broke suddenly and radically the reproduction of the social order. The breakdown rooted in central-city social order was in the social structure of exploitation and the political and ideological experiences of oppression. Nevertheless, since the central city was, on the one hand, a material apparatus for the directional functions of the economy and of the society, and on the other hand, a form of organization of the labor power in the stagnant economic sector, the revolt of the overexploited against the symbols and practices of the rulers was expressed through the material base and organizational supports of the inner city's everyday life.

This major disruption of the dominant social order took several forms that, *without being equivalents*, all expressed the rejection of a given situation and produced a similar impact on the functioning and structure of the central city. The most important forms of breakdowns of social control were the following:

(A) *The rapid increase of so-called "crime"* and particularly of "crime in the streets" that was clearly linked to an individual reaction against structural oppression coupled with the absence of a stable mass-based political alternative.[52] "Crime" is not only explained by "deprivation." For example, in the 1930's depression crime rates actually *went down* and only went up again in the late fifties and early sixties. In the current depression crime rates are higher still (+20 percent in 1974/1975). This implies that the collective movement that during the thirties forced the government to launch the New Deal was viewed by most urban dwellers as an adequate response and a hopeful trend. Today the inner city concentrates the structurally unemployed and lacks an effective channel for mass action. But we also observe that the most rapid crime-rate increase was during the sixties, when in fact, until 1966 the economic situation was improving on the average. So it seems that the major factor has been the collapse of the system of social control by the family, the school, or the Southern communities from where many inner-city dwellers came. Not only was urban crime a challenge to the social order but it became a way of living, economically and culturally, for a large sector of inner-ghetto youth that had no chance outside the irregular economy to which some forms of crime are structurally connected.

(B) On a totally different dimension, another source of challenge to the established social-spatial division of labor and consumption was *the development of community organizations and urban protest movements* that defied the logic of functioning and delivery of specific services as well as the legitimacy of traditional local authorities.[53] The most widespread urban movements were mobilizations against urban renewal in order to protect the neighborhood from demolition or to obtain adequate relocation and compensation. Given urban renewal's direct threat, the mobilizations were at the same time relatively easy to develop but defensive and limited in their scope. Nevertheless, after several years of experience, the movements progressively shifted towards demands for comprehensive neighborhood planning forcing a new approach to urban redevelopment.

The *rent strikes*, as analyzed by Michael Lipsky,[54] particularly in New York, in St. Louis, in Philadelphia, in Chicago, etc., marked a new period where the "filtering down" process was blocked by requirements of adequate repairs and by demands for controlled rents according to some public standards instead of at the landlord's will.[55] All social services (health and education in particular) as well as social welfare were subject to assault by central-city residents. Frances Piven and Richard Cloward have shown how, in fact, the spectacular increase in the welfare rolls during the sixties was not due to the increasing *needs* (that already existed) but to the increasing *demands*.[56] Thus, urban protest was not the effect of an urbanization process but the grass-roots attempt to overcome the segregated model of collective consumption, an expression of the loss of social control from the combined impact of the internal contradictions of urban services and of generalized unrest in the American society.

The poor and black mobilizations were paralleled by Alinsky-type *community organizations* trying to develop middle-class citizens' participation and control over the local governments and social services. Bailey[57] has shown how this very moderate populist approach developed mostly where middle-class groups found "poor people types of problems," that is where the inner-city crisis struck the remaining middle-class dwellers. Thus, in spite of their ideological conservatism and pragmatic approach, the Alinsky experiences were a real threat (as opposed to the opinion expressed by Bailey) to the social order, since they were channeling groups towards protests that were generally supportive of local institutions. Certainly, their localism and economicism kept them within the mainstream of the consumer movement but their growing influence was a factor pushing in the direction of a multiclass movement that could have been developed on a more conflictual base in a different political context. In summary, while limited, localistic, and strictly economic, the urban movements during the sixties clearly limited the overexploitation implicit in the until-then predominant pattern of urban development.

(C) Nevertheless, the most significant factor in the breakdown of the social order in the cities during the sixties was the *riots*, mostly in the black ghettoes. After the explosions of Harlem (1964) and Watts (1965) they were generalized in the famous hot summer of 1967, in 1968 as a mass response to the murder of Martin Luther King, and followed in 1969, 1970, and 1971 in a very important number of less publicized riots.[58] Certainly, the riots are not "urban movements" in the sense that they were not exclusively linked to a protest related to the living conditions in the inner city. They were a form of general protest and struggle of the black people against the general conditions of their oppression. After many debates and empirical research on the courses of riots, the best statistical systematic analysis, carried out by Spilerman,[59] shows that the only variables significantly correlated with the occurrence and intensity of riots were the size of the black population in the city (the larger the black population, the more riots) and the region (the Northern cities have higher probabilities). Statistically speaking, the riots were strongly linked to the large inner-city ghettoes of the largest metropolitan areas. This can be interpreted either in organizational terms (the largest possible base for sustained mass organization) or in terms of the specific effects of the segregated organization of work, services, and everyday life, as expressed in the largest ghettoes. The hypotheses are complementary. The riots were mass protests against the racist society, including one of its dimensions, the specific pattern of racial segregation in the ghetto and its effects on the delivery of services and jobs.[60]

If the black movement, in its different expressions, could not overcome its isolation and if its vast radical component was destroyed by repression, the struggles of the sixties forced the state, at the federal and at the local level, to a major reexamination of the use of central cities as a reservation for ethnic minorities. Access of blacks to local governments and to the state agencies was given in increasing proportion, more and better services were distributed (at least for a period), and more public jobs were available for inner-city residents. Very often this was part of a process of cooptation of the community leaders to disorganize the grassroots but nevertheless the overall effects produced a decisive breach in the social logic dominating the urban services and local governments. So, the mobilization and protest from the grassroots, at the same time, obtained tangible social benefits, challenged the structural logic, and eventually precipitated the crisis of the urban services.

3.2. The crisis in the system of production and distribution of the means of collective consumption.[61]   The crisis of the postwar pattern of urban development also reflects an increasing inability to keep the segregated delivery of urban services functioning smoothly. The most significant examples include housing, transportation, and education.

(A) The crisis of the *housing market*, particularly acute *in the central cities* of large metropolitan areas, is revealed in a total failure of the "filtering down" theory, the relative deterioration of the resources of the poor, the rising level of property taxes and maintenance costs, depreciation of the housing stock by the overall decay of the city, overcrowding and lack of maintenance.

Many landlords faced declining purchasing power and profitability.[62] The incomes of a large proportion of central-city families were insufficient to provide landlords with acceptable profit margins and meet maintenance costs. Thus many families: (1) overcrowded small dwellings, accelerating the rate of deterioration, (2) *abandoned housing units* in the quest for cheaper housing, (3) launched rent strikes and either were evicted or the landlord abandoned the house to deterioration and subsequent renewal and compensation.

On the other hand, many central-city landlords faced increasing costs and property taxes, could not obtain higher rents because of the low income of tenants, and could not sell because of tenant resistance and lack of buyers. So, they stopped repair and maintenance. Later on, they stopped paying property taxes, obtaining superprofit during the two or more years before the city could legally take over the house.[63] Since the cost of demolition was high and without profitable purpose, the empty houses were quickly occupied by squatters, and very often by drug-addict communities and inner-city gangs. Violence, prejudice, actual assaults, and widespread fear contributed to the abandonment of the entire sector by the neighbors, creating a process of contagion that literally produced no-man's-land zones in large parts of the cities. This trend is developing very fast in the U.S. Some official figures for 1973[64] estimated ("conservatively") 100,000 units abandoned in New York City, 30,000 in Philadelphia, 12,000 in Baltimore, 10,000 in St. Louis, etc. The process of abandonment has been going on in New York for the last eight years at a rate of 50,000 housing units each year, which (with corrections for demolition and adding previously abandoned stock) gives an estimate of between 400,000 and 450,000 abandoned apartments.

(B) The crisis in central-city housing stock is paralleled by a crisis *in the mechanisms of production and distribution of suburban housing*, reflected in creeping inflation and the instability of financial markets.[65] Financial intermediaries are decisive in the families' ability to purchase a home. The major contradiction is manifested in increasing individual, corporate, and state debt in general, and residential debt in particular. Residential debt as a proportion of total debt rose from 9.5 percent in 1947 to 23.7 percent in 1972. More and more resources have to be devoted to pay the past debt. With the sky-rocketing of interest rates and stagnation of real income the cost of new suburban housing threatens a financial collapse that could start an explosive chain of reactions.

Housing investments are becoming more and more risky and therefore the leading financial institutions are retreating from the mortgage-holding market. In the process the federal government has assumed an increasing share of the debt, avoiding a mass of fore-closures in the suburbs and in the central cities. Increasing government debt and thus inflation were crucial for maintaining the demand for housing between 1968 and 1972.[66]

But there are major unresolved contradictions linked to this process. Either interest rates grow faster than inflation, and families will be increasingly unable to pay them, or inflation speeds up and financial institutions will refuse to make unprofitable investments. The federal government intervenes, but is increasingly unable to stop inflationary expenditures and simultaneously meet other priorities.

(C) *The pattern of transportation* in the dual model of urban-suburban structure produced several contradictions during the sixties.[67] The most important was the differential speed of residential sprawl and decentralization of activities in the CBD. The under-supported public transportation network became increasingly over-crowded and deteriorated and the new urban highways were not enough to support the amount of peak-hour traffic. An increasing proportion of central land was devoted to parking lots and the downtown streets were more and more submerged by the traffic. Federally backed use of the automobile created a permanent financial crisis in public transit and reinforced the downgrading of the service, thus expanding a vicious circle.[68]

Urban crises have been generated by the contradictions inherent in (a) downtown-redevelopment interests that required renewed public support for mass transit in order to make the facilities they were building more accessible; (b) the inner-city residents who had problems driving in the city and were disadvantaged in their travels to suburban work places. As a response, the federal government started a new program funding 80 percent of city projects proposing mass-transit development.[69] The most important initiative under this new provision was the BART system in the San Francisco Bay Area. But as several analysts have shown, this experience, as well as the general trend in other ongoing mass-transit programs, has favored middle-class suburban residents commuting to work in the central business district rather than the increasingly isolated city residents or the mass of workers commuting from the working-class suburbs.

But the model came under attack from the suburbs as well. Car maintenance costs increase and a significant proportion of the suburban population cannot drive. A study conducted by the Berkeley Institute of Urban Research estimated the proportion of those deprived of daily access to the car in the San Francisco area as 30 percent of the population *over sixteen*. Also, the measures to protect the environment against pollution have emphasized the critique of the automobile, mobilizing one dimension of the suburban model (living "within Nature") against another (traveling by car).

Ultimately, the oil crisis is producing a major breakdown in the perspectives of unlimited car-based transportation. With the 55 mph speed limit on the highways, commuting time increases substantially and the absurdity of extra-large superpowerful cars running slowly in twelve-lane express highways is starting to strike many North American minds.

(D) Another key mechanism in the class model of urban structure that is currently crumbling is the *school system*. We will not refer here to the whole complex set of contradictions concerning education, but exclusively to its role in the reproduction of the system of urban segregation through the "separate and unequal" rule. The autonomy of the school districts over the functioning of their schools has come under attack from the grass roots and from the institutions at the same time. The neighborhood movements, particularly in the minority sectors of the city, have developed a campaign asking for *community control* over the school, namely for the mobilization of the parents in order to improve the quality of the service and to break down the differential class logic of the educational bureaucracies in the inner-city schools. Without challenging segregation, this movement opposes the effects of segregation on services calling into question the structural inequality in the distribution of public resources.[70]

On the other hand, the impact of mass protest and liberal pressures on the institutional system led to a potentially explosive trend: the *busing* of schoolchildren among different school districts in order to keep a racial balance and to avoid segregation.[71] This measure is one way to by-pass the vicious circle between the social status determined by the quality of education and the quality of education determined, through residential segregation, by social status. Some cities have court-ordered two-way busing in order to improve integration in the schools. While the upper and middle class do not care too much, being "protected" in the suburbs or having the possibility of sending their children to private schools, the white working-class neighborhoods have reacted strongly (rioting and demonstrating in Boston, Louisville, etc.) against what they consider a threat against the social chances of their children or even their physical security.

The system of "educational vouchers" to families who can use them in the school of their choice, each school receiving funding proportionately to the demand, is an attempt to make the schools work through the market mechanisms. Experiences in California do not seem very convincing either in terms of efficiency or equality since the mechanisms of reciprocal selection by schools and parents work to keep in general the same social recruitment.

What is clear through this process of contradiction and conflict over school segregation is that the U.S. urban model is being shaken not only in its daily functioning but also in its mechanisms of self-reproduction.

(E) Similar problems appear in other basic public services, such as health, garbage collection, welfare, etc. Analysis of these service areas would provide additional evidence about the general breakdown of the organization of the means of collective consumption settled during the expanding period that followed World War II.

The most striking effects of these trends are undoubtedly *the growing abandonment and physical destruction of large sectors of the central cities, particularly in the ghettoes.* Baltimore's Pennsylvania Avenue, Boston's West Point, St. Louis' Pruitt and Igoe, etc., are symbols of the potential massive destruction that could happen if the current pattern is not reversed. The most famous example is the South Bronx district in New York, where 600,000 people live. The process of abandonment, the deterioration of real estate values, and the loss of control by the system have induced the landlords to stimulate fires in order to obtain some payment from the insurance companies. In other cases it is just to obtain plumbing and some building materials. They pay children to start the fires: $3 to $10 each. There were 12,300 fires in

South Bronx in 1974, with more than one-third proved intentional, ten every night! And that is not a unique district: Brownsville-Brooklyn, Bushwick, etc., are also burning. Zones of New York appeared as if they had been bombed. And among the ruins, the structurally unemployed, and kids without schools, sit and chat waiting to see what is coming next.

The crisis of urban services and the breakdown of the social order at the individual and at the collective level had a major impact on the management of the urban system itself, striking deeply the state apparatus and its internal operations: this is what emerged openly as the urban crisis of the seventies.[72]

3.3 The crisis of the local level of the state apparatus in the large central cities.[73] The most visible effect of the impact of the urban contradictions and conflict on the state apparatus is the *fiscal crisis of the central cities*. This is the direct expression of the articulation of the different processes that I have described. The fiscal crisis of the central cities is a particularly acute expression of the fiscal crisis of the state: the increasing gap between expenditures and revenues through the process of socialization of costs and privatization of profits. The crisis is even more acute in the local governments of large central cities because they express the contradictory expansion of the "service sector."[74]

On the one hand, corporate capital must build directional centers which require concentration of service workers and public facilities. On the other hand, in order to maintain the social order, the state must absorb the surplus population and provide welfare and public services to the large fraction of structurally exploited population, mostly concentrated in the inner cities. During the fifties, the accumulation requirements had the top priority and local finance started to recover. During the sixties the mass protest in the inner cities forced some redistribution through social expenses as well as the provision of jobs.

The increasing number of *municipal workers* triggered a process of escalating demands and economic struggles that was favored by the absence of established bargaining patterns in the public sector. Teachers, municipal service workers, public health workers, sanitation workers, firemen, and policemen have been among the most militant strikers and union-organizing sectors of American labor. They have improved their position substantially even if they are yet behind the level of wages in the private monopoly sector. *The entire set of labor relationships has been disrupted in the local public sector*, creating inflationary trends in the cost of labor-intensive services. The city [reacted not] by raising new taxes on the corporations, who were the most expensive municipal-service consumers, but by raising taxes on central-city residents and trying to oppose between them taxpayers, the welfare-consuming poor, and municipal workers. In spite of renewed fiscal effort and higher public service fares, the city had to increase public debt, issue municipal bonds, and count on the expected future revenues in order to equilibrate the budget. This is what happened to New York City in 1974—76, provoking a world-famous fiscal crisis that will become a test of the U.S. policies to handle the economic crisis in general.[75]

During the 1950's the New York City budget expanded at an annual rate of approximately 6 percent. Since 1965, after pressures from communities and workers started, the budget increased at an annual rate of 15 percent. One-eighth of New Yorkers are on welfare. New York maintains the largest system of public hospitals, of subsidized mass transit, of welfare payments, of free-tuition universities, of cultural facilities, etc. Nevertheless, the "bankruptcy" of New York City is not a consequence of the "excessive" services and jobs distributed as the elite circles have tried to argue. It is the combined result of corporate rejection of increased taxes that could pay for the social services and, even more important, the decision of the financial community to discipline the New York City social welfare policy.

If the case of New York City is perhaps the most extreme example of the tendency implicit in the whole evolution of the urban contradictions, most central cities face similar problems. In Cleveland, the ratio of the city's debt service to its current budget expenditures is 17.9 percent, even higher than New York. In Milwaukee, this ratio (indicator of potential imbalance) is 15.2 percent in spite of the very high local taxes. Detroit also has a structural deficit and laid off 15 percent of its municipal workers in 1975. Buffalo has a debt-service-to-operating-budget ratio of $17 million to $229 million. Boston reduced its municipal work force by 10 percent in 1975, particularly in the health sector. San Francisco faced in September 1975 a strike of firemen and police that forced the mayor to keep their jobs and to raise their salaries, provoking the indignation of the financial community and submitting the mayor to embittered attacks . . . .

The potential consequences of the urban fiscal crisis are very serious because they could *threaten* the already unstable *political legitimacy of the local governments*. Let us explain this important point.

The municipal reformers of the thirties replaced the pork-barrel and patronage policies of the political machines [with] the urban-development schemes of the city managers. They risked the loss of the person-to-person ties that had founded machine control of inner-city neighborhoods. The pressures from the grass roots during the sixties forced open local bureaucracies to the poor and to the ethnic minorities. If "all out business" policies predominate, the local governments of the largest cities are going to be increasingly isolated from the different conflicting social interests and are going to lose all the past sources of legitimacy, either in terms of clientele, in terms of management, or in terms of specific interests being served. First line of the revision of the social policies of the sixties, the cities are actually under the cross fire of the business interests claiming restraint and the workers and consumers refusing to carry the burden of a crisis which is not theirs. Thus the state apparatus in the central cities, besides supporting increasing contradictions at the level of fiscal policies and being shaken by demands for services, jobs, and wages, is also losing political control over the social conflicts growing up from the urban issues.

3.4. The crisis of the model of urban development.   The postwar pattern of urban development itself is now at stake. The converging trends of the social conflicts, the crisis of services, and the economic and political crackdown of social governments have put into question the urban-suburban structure that emerged as a powerful factor in the process of capitalist accumulation and segregated commodity consumption. Actually, even the trend of metropolitanization is now being reversed. For the first time in U.S. urban history, between 1970 and 1973 five of the eight major metropolitan areas have *decreased* instead of increasing in size. The New York metropolitan area had a net decrease of 305,000 inhabitants. The decrease in Chicago was 124,000; for Philadelphia 75,000; for Detroit 114,000; Los Angeles in 1972—73 showed a net out-migration of 119,000. Boston (+0.4 percent) and San Francisco (+0.5 percent) remained stable after their growth during the sixties. Only Washington grew, by 1 percent, largely because of federal government employment.

A new and major contradiction arises. If the flight of activities and residence continues towards the nonmetropolitan areas (which gained 4.2 percent population in 1970—73), the depression of the large cities will accelerate. But the large metropolitan areas remain organizational forms of major economic and political interests of the ruling class, as well as the dwelling of a large proportion of American people. The new urban form arising from the current crisis will be largely a function of urban social movements and political conflicts.

4. Policies for the Urban Crisis, Grass-Roots Movements, and the Political Process.

There is no alternative model to the crumbling pattern of urban-suburban development within the parameters of the unrestrained dominance of corporate capitalist interests. The almost perfect functionality of this urban form, at the same time, for the accumulation of capital, the organization of centralized management, the stimulation of commodity consumption, the differential reproduction of labor power, and the maintenance of social order, explains why the dominant capitalist interests will tend, in all circumstances, to respond to the multilevel crisis by mechanisms that, ultimately, will reestablish the already proven model with slight modifications. There has been some speculation about the lack of interest of corporate capital in maintaining the central cities, but this is pure science fiction. As Roger Friedland says:

> Such a scenario is highly unlikely, given the importance of the big city vote for national elections, the continued concentration of corporate and financial head-quarters in the major central cities, and the economic imperative of maintaining the value of public infrastructure and private construction in the central cities. ... The value of central city properties is the bedrock upon which the residential, commercial, and municipal loans are based. Thus the viability of the financial institutions of this country and ultimately the nation's capital market itself are dependent on maintaining the value of central city properties.[76]

But then, how are corporate interests to handle the growing contradictions shown by our analysis? The virtue and shortcoming of U.S. capitalism is its pragmatism. Instead of launching big national projects — "à la française" — urban policy makers tried specific successive solutions to the specific problems following the moment and intensity of their appearance. The "trouble" with this piecemeal approach is that eventually it triggers new contradictions and conflicts less and less susceptible to control.

Thus, the opposition to urban renewal did not stop the program which actually expanded during the seventies under new forces and accelerated in some cities, like Los Angeles. The failure of the Great Society programs in controlling the social order led to a total revision of the strategy and progressive dismantlement of the programs since 1968, at the same time that new laws were approved and massive funds were devoted to the reinforcement of repressive policies. The Model Cities program, for instance, was a transitional measure with emphasis given to the problems of coordination and to demonstration effects, rejecting explicitly the idea of autonomous community mobilization, the whole under the supervision of local authorities whose power was restored. With Nixon's revenue-sharing policy in 1972, the change of direction in social and political terms was completed. By cutting off the funding of the programs and by replacing them [with] a distribution of federal tax-raised funds to states and local governments, the dominant interests succeeded, with a single movement, in by-passing the excessively reformist federal agencies, reducing considerably the social welfare expenditures and the re-distribution of services, and elevating the burden of political responsibility over the shoulders of the local authorities.

In the U.S., local authorities are more socially conservative than the federal government, since they are embedded in the network of socially dominant interests in each city, rarely representative of grass-roots needs and demands. The analysis of the first two years of the revenue-sharing program shows that in half of the cases the money was not spent but used to reduce local taxes. Concerning the funds actually used, the two more important areas were law enforcement (police) and education, which are the usual responsibility of local authorities. Less than 3 percent was spent on welfare or some kind of special social program. In most larger cities there was no expenditure at all in activities that could replace the cancelled federal programs.[77]

Using repression more than integration in handling the central-city problem, the next step was to reorganize the productivity of services in the public sector and to coordinate more effectively at the technical and economic level the socially and politically fragmented metropolis. But in order to improve productivity and to mobilize resources to increase the functionality of the metropolis without affecting either the major privileges of corporations or the established political network, it necessitated cutting off social services, reducing wages, and increasing fares. This was to deny the sixties, to reorganize the model of metropolitan accumulation with tougher policies and tightened controls.

The implementation of this hard line in urban policies is not going to be easy since the heritage of the sixties is not only more services and higher public wages but also more experience of struggle and organization at the grass-roots level. In fact, the evolution of urban structure and of urban services in the U.S. will depend upon the contradictory interaction between the capitalist-oriented hard-line urban policies and the mass response that could emerge from city dwellers.

In that sense, more recent information seems to point towards a surpassing of the shortcomings of community movements during the sixties.[78] These were stalled by two major problems, almost inevitable in the early period of their development: (a) their localism, defining themselves more in terms of their neighborhood and/or ethnicity than in regard to some specific issues; (b) partly as a consequence of the latter trend, their *social* and *political isolation*, at the same time with respect to other groups and in relation to the political system.

Making alliances (and then winning allies) and penetrating the political system (and then winning positions in the network of power) seem to be the major requirements for the shift from grass-roots pressure to grass-roots power in the shaping of the urban policies. Contrary to Cloward and Piven's insightful analysis, the problem with the 1960's protest movements was not their integration by the system and the loss of their spontaneity but, on the contrary, their insufficient level of organization and their role as political outsiders. Thus, the results were the absence of any cumulative mass movement, the inability to ensure the advantages obtained in urban services, and their political isolation, opening the way to their repression and dismantlement.[79]

The lessons were well learned to a large extent. The 1970's urban movement grew up mostly around particular issues, organizing a large sector of people not on the grounds of their spatial togetherness but on the base of their common interests and in a long-run perspective: tenants' unions, mass-transit riders' committees, schools' parents and teachers, public-utilities users, etc., spread all over the country in the process of creation, step by step, of a huge decentralized network of protest-oriented mass organizations and activities.[80]

This movement is extremely diversified. On the one hand, there is a proliferation of self-help activities at the level of the community: co-ops, health centers, independent schools, community radio stations, local construction, local agricultural and industrial production (obviously on a very small scale), and, even black cooperative capitalism in some ghettoes.

At a second level, defensive movements of resistance against the consequences of the urban policy for people (i.e., to stop urban renewal) or to fight back the attack on the quality or level of services (i.e., protests against the reduction of hospital facilities in San Francisco, unrest in the New York subway to oppose the rise of subway fares, etc.) are general to all large metropolitan areas.

At a third level, some of these movements are trying to recover the initiative along two major lines of development:

(1) The transformation of a reaction into a specific demand capable of being translated into a progressive measure potentially implying a new social content for urban policy. Perhaps the best example is the evolution of the tenants movement facing the process of residential abandonment in New York. After having realized that most attempts to launch a rent strike led to abandonment by the landlord, many tenants' committees stopped their action. But after verifying that some abandoned houses were rehabilitated by the city and sold at a low price to another landlord, groups implemented a new tactic. They triggered a process of rent strikes forcing abandonment and then applied to the city for a rehabilitation grant that transformed them into cooperative owners, eventually using the rents saved through the strike for paying for the repairs. The logic of urban decay was reversed, not by urban planners but by urban movements.

(2) The other developing line is the emergence of real "public facilities consumers unions" that try to respond to the deterioration of social services and to their growing weight in the family budgets by sustained economic action concerning the production, distribution, and management of collective goods and services. An example is the nation-wide campaign launched in 1975 against the rise in electricity rates by a movement of several thousand members significantly called "Just Economics."

Finally, these alternative perspectives in urban policies seem also to appear, for the first time in the last thirty years, at the level of local and state governments — not only as "social welfare programs" within the general context of corporate-interest-dominated policies but as actual priorities given to the immediate interests of the grass roots combined with the search for an increase in the rationality of urban management. Propositions to municipalize urban land or electricity companies, to expand a public system of urban transportation, to develop community control over schools and hospitals, etc., are widespread now in cities like Madison, Wisconsin, or Austin, Texas, which are run by progressive coalitions elected with huge support and which are developing a clear social-democratic trend in urban policies. Certainly, these cities are atypical (because they are the settings of major universities) but the first conference on "Alternative State and Local Public Policies" sponsored by the Institute of Policy Studies, gathered in Madison, in June 1975, nearly 200 elected public officials from all over the country, in order to define a "populist" tendency within the public sector and to establish a permanent system of exchange of experience and resources. Even if this trend is not yet so visible in the large cities' local institutions, it represents the mobilization of a growing organized force that could eventually connect with the relatively progressive black mayors of some big cities.

In the development of this trend of populist-oriented new urban policies, there is obviously the need of some connections with the national political process. And this is precisely one of the most significant effects of U.S. urban movements on the general system of class relationships. As Roger Friedland writes, "By transforming urban daily life into national partisan issues, the large number of poor and working class people who have no meaningful connection or place in the national electoral system could be given choices that make a difference."[81]

Now, if we consider the developing trends towards urban policies from both sides (that is, on the one hand, from the point of view of monopoly capital and big-city bureaucracies; on the other hand, from the point of view of a multiclass populist form) a major social clash over urban policies appears clearly possible in the near future.

The exploitative and increasingly contradictory model of urban-suburban expansion that dominated metropolitan America in the last thirty years will be transformed only if the people's forces win decisive gains in upcoming battles. But such a result would be an almost intolerable setback to the corporate interests. This explains why the Establishment has been so violent in repressing New York City and also why the dominant emphasis in current local policies is given to the development of the repressive apparatus. The aftermath of the sixties has provided an incredible mass of sophisticated weaponry for repressing mass protests in the large cities. Since it has become clear now that the costly desperate riots have been replaced by long-run—oriented, permanent mass movements, the FBI has reconverted hundreds of special agents and sent them to infiltrate the grass-roots organizations. Emergency procedures and day-to-day repression have now been articulated to pave the way for a new edition of the monopoly-capital pattern of urban development. The stake is important, so "they" are ready to pay a high price, even in terms of political legitimacy.

So, unless the progressive forces of the U.S. are able to develop a major movement, with enough social and political support, to rectify the dominant trend in forthcoming urban policies, what could emerge from the current urban crisis is a simplified and sharpened version of the exploitative metropolitan model with the addition of mass police repression and control and in a largely deteriorated economic setting. The suburbs will remain fragmented and isolated, the single-family homes closed over themselves, the shopping centers a bit more expensive and a lot more surveyed, the highways less maintained and more crowded, the central districts still crowded during office hours and more deserted and curfewed after 5 p.m., city services increasingly crumbling, public facilities less and less public, the surplus population more and more visible, the drug culture and individual violence necessarily expanding, gang society and high society ruling the bottom and the top in order to keep a "top and bottom" social order, the urban movements repressed and discouraged, and the urban planners eventually attending more international conferences in the outer, safer world. What could emerge of a failure of urban movements to undertake their present tasks is a new and sinister urban form: the Wild City.

NOTES

1. Quoted by Ernest Holsendolph, "Urban Crisis of the 1960's is Over, Ford Aides Say," *The New York Times*, March 23, 1975.

2. Quoted in Charles O. Jones and Layne D. Hoppe, *The Urban Crisis in America*, Washington National Press, Washington, 1969.

3. See, for example, M. Castells, "Urban Sociology and Urban Politics," *Comparative Urban Research*, 6, 1975.

4. *The Ribicoff Hearings*, U.S. Congress, 1966, p. 25.

5. See James Q. Wilson, "The Urban Unease," *The Public Interest*, Summer 1968, pp. 26—27.

6. See Alan Gartner and Frank Riessman, *The Service Society and the Consumer Vanguard*, Harper and Row, New York, 1974. And also Paul Jacobs, *Prelude to Riot. A View of Urban America from the Bottom*, Vintage Books, New York, 1966.

7. See Daniel R. Fusfeld, "The Basic Economics of the Urban and Racial Crisis," Conference Papers of the Union for Radical Political Economics, December

1968. And also Barbara Bergeman, "The Urban Crisis," *American Economic Review*, Sept. 1969.

8. See John Mollenkopf, *Growth Defied: Community Organization and the Struggle Over Urban Development in America*, forthcoming book on the base of a 1973 Harvard Ph.D. dissertation, the best research that we know on urban movements in the U.S. Also, the useful reader, Robert H. Connery (ed.), *Urban Riots: Violence and Social Change*, Vintage Books, New York, 1969. And the now classic article by Michael Lipsky, "Protest as a Political Resource," *American Political Science Review*, LXII, no. 4, December 1968.

9. City Bureau of the San Francisco Socialist Coalition, "Cities in Crisis," Package on the Economic Crisis of the Union of Radical Political Economists, 1975.

10. For some data concerning the basic information on the characteristic functions and transformation of the process of metropolitan growth and urban structure in the United States, see Leo Schnore, *The Urban Scene*, The Free Press, Glencoe, Ill., 1965; Beverly Duncan and Stanley Lieberson, *Metropolis and Region in Transition*, Sage Publications, Beverly Hills, Ca., 1970; Sylvia F. Fava and Noel P. Gist, *Urban Society*, Thomas Y. Crowell, New York, 1975; Leonard E. Goodall, *The American Metropolis*, Charles E. Merrill, Columbus, Ohio, 1968; Amos H. Hawley and Basil G. Zimmer, *The Metropolitan Community*, Sage Publications, Beverly Hills, Ca., 1970; Jeffrey K. Hadden and Edgar F. Borgatta, *American Cities: Their Social Characteristics*, Rand McNally Co., Chicago, 1965, etc. For a well-informed presentation of the historical evolution on American cities, see Charles N. Glaab, *The American City: A Documentary History*, The Dorsey Press, Homewood, Ill., 1963.

11. For this crucial point on the urban analysis in the U.S., see the forthcoming paper by David Gordon, "Toward a Critique of Capitalopolis: Capitalism and Urban Development in the U.S.," 1975, which we had the chance to discuss personally.

12. The specificity of Los Angeles can be better understood by consulting the insightful monograph by Robert M. Fogelson, *The Fragmented Metropolis, Los Angeles, 1850—1930*, Harvard University Press, Cambridge, Mass., 1967.

13. The best source of data, bibliography, and interpretations on the suburbanization process is the reader edited by Louis H. Masotti and Jeffrey K. Hadden, *The Urbanization of the Suburbs, Urban Affairs Annual Reviews*, Sage, Beverly Hills, Ca., 1973. Elliott Sclar (Brandeis Univ.) is finishing an important book on the subject: we have benefitted from one discussion on the topic as well as of a chapter ("Levels on Entrapment"). For additional references on the topic, until 1971, we suggest consulting Timothy Schiltz and William Moffitt, "Inner City—Outer City Relationships in Metropolitan Areas: A Bibliographic Essay," *Urban Affairs Quarterly*, Vol. 7, 1, Sept. 1971.

14. See Bennett Harrison, *Urban Economic Development: Suburbanization, Minority Opportunity and the Condition of Central City*, The Urban Institute, Washington, D.C., 1974.

15. See Ira Katznelson, *Black Men, White Cities, Race, Politics and Migration in the United States, 1900—30 and Britain 1948—68*, Oxford University Press, London, 1973, for an explanation of the mechanisms, although the period studied is not exactly the same.

16. See Leo Schnore, *Class and Race in Cities and Suburbs*, Markham, Chicago, 1972.

17. Reminder: Herbert J. Gans, *The Urban Villagers: Group and Class in the Life of Italian Americans*, Free Press of Glencoe, New York, 1962; *The Levittowners, Ways of Life and Politics in a New Suburban Community*, Pantheon Books, New York, 1967; "Urbanism and Suburbanism as Ways of Life," in Arnold M. Rose (ed.), *Human Behavior and Social Processes*, Houghton Mifflin, Boston, 1962.

18. See Reynolds Farley and Alma F. Taeuber, *Racial Segregation in the Public Schools*, Institute for Research on Poverty, University of Wisconsin, Madison, May 1972, mimeo.

19. See the different analyses contained in Robert H. Haveman and Robert D. Hamrin (eds.), *The Political Economy of Federal Policy*, Harper and Row, New York, 1973. And for the specific and crucial point on transportation, George M. Smerk, *Urban Transportation: The Federal Role*, Indiana University Press, Bloomington, 1965.

20. I will be here necessarily schematic on this major topic. My analyses and references on the postwar development of U.S. capitalism are contained in my draft paper *The Graying of America: The World Economic Crisis and the U.S. Society*, University of Wisconsin, Madison, August 1975.

21. For an outline of the interaction between these three levels (the process of capital accumulation, the process of urbanization, and the state) see the fundamental paper by David Harvey, "The Political Economy of Urbanization in Advanced Capitalist Societies: The Case of the United States," *Urban Affairs Annual Review*, Sage Publications, 1975.

22. The most important source of data on housing for the U.S.: *Housing in the Seventies*, Hearings on Housing and Community Development Legislation, 1973, Part 3, House of Representatives Subcommittee on Banking and Currency, 93rd Congress, First Session, Government Printing Office, Washington, D.C., 1973.

23. A clear description of the financial mechanisms of the housing market is Rogert Starr, *Housing and the Money Market*, Basic Books, New York, 1975.

24. We are looking forward to the development of research by Glenn Yago (Sociology Department, University of Wisconsin, Madison) on "State policy, corporate planning and transportation needs: the development of the U.S. Urban Ground Transportation System." We have learned many things about U.S. transportation through our discussions.

25. Glenn Yago, "How Did We Get to the Way We Are Going?, General Motors and Public Transportation," University of Wisconsin, Sociology Department, Madison, 1974, mimeo.

26. See George M. Smerk, *op. cit.*, 1965; and especially the readings included in the chapter on "The Politics of Transportation" in Stephen M. David and Paul E. Peterson (eds.), *Urban Politics and Public Policy: The City in Crisis*, Praeger Publishers, New York, 1973.

27. See Francis Godard, "De la notion de besoin au concept de pratique de classe," *La Pensée* (Paris), n. 166, December 1972: and also, Edmond Preteceille, "Besoins sociaux et socialisation de la consommation," *La Pensée*, n. 180, March—April, 1975.

28. See M. Freyssinet and T. Regazzola, *Segregation urbaine et deplacement sociaux*, Centre de Sociologies Urbaine, Paris, 1970; and Christian Topalov, "Politique Monopoliste et propriété du logement," *Economie-et-Politique*, March, 1974.

29. Leo Schnore has insisted several times on the dependency of the social patterns of the cities upon the specificity of the historical processes and stages. For a reassessment of this perspective, see Leo F. Schnore (ed.), *The New Urban History*, John Wiley, New York, 1975.

30. The best available source of data and references on the problem of the central city in the U.S. and its social and economic interactions is the study prepared by the Congressional Research Service for the Subcommittee on Housing and Urban Affairs, United States Senate, *The Central City Problem and Urban Renewal Policy*, 93rd Congress, Government Printing Office, Washington, D.C., 1973. See also for a detailed analysis of the functioning of the irregular economy, William Tabb, *The Economy of the Black Ghetto*, W. W. Norton, New York, 1971.

31. See Karl E. Taeuber and Alma F. Taeuber, *Negroes in Cities: Residential Segregation and Neighborhood Change*, Aldine Publishing Co., Chicago, 1965.

32. See *The Central City Problem, op. cit.*, 1973, p. 103.

33. See Stanley H. Masters, "The Effect of Housing Segregation on Black-White Income Differentials," Institute for Research on Poverty, Univ. of Wisconsin, Madison, 1972, mimeo.

34. See David Harvey, *op. cit.*, 1975.

35. Elliott Sclar, *op. cit.*, 1975.

36. See "Exploitative Transfers in the Metropolis," Part I, of the interesting reader edited by Kenneth E. Boulding, Martin Pfaff, and Anita Pfaff, *Transfers in an Urbanized Economy: The Grants Economics of Income Distribution*, Wadsworth Publishing Co., Belmont, Ca., 1973.

37. I have borrowed several interesting ideas from a paper by Ann Markusenn (Economics Department, University of Colorado). Since she does not want to be quoted, I do not quote the paper.

38. See the now classic analysis on the subject by Norton E. Long, "Political Science and the City," in Leo F. Schnore and Henry Fagin (eds.), *Urban Research and Policy Planning*, Urban Affairs Annual Review, Vol. 1, Sage, Beverly Hills, Ca., 1967.

39. Richard Child Hill, "Separate and Unequal: Governmental Inequality in the Metropolis," *American Political Science Review*, Dec. 1974.

40. See Alan K. Campbell and Philip Meranto, "The Metropolitan Education Dilemma: Matching Resources to Needs," in Marilyn Gittell (ed.), *Educating an Urban Population*, Sage Publications, Beverly Hills, Ca., 1967; and also, James S. Coleman *et al.*, *Equality and Educational Opportunity*, U.S. Government Printing Office, Washington, D.C., 1966.

41. For a useful reader on the evolution and social meaning of the urban policies see Stephen M. David and Paul E. Peterson (eds.), *Urban Politics and Public Policy: The City in Crisis*, Praeger Publishers, New York, 1973. Also, for a more traditional view, J. Wilson (ed.), *City Politics and Public Policy*, John Wiley, New York, 1968.

42. [Footnote missing in original.]

43. We have largely relied on the excellent analysis of the relationships between urban structure, urban politics, and urban policies by John Mollenkopf, "The Post-War Politics of Urban Development," to be published (1975) by *Politics and Society* and by *Espaces et Sociétés*.

44. The most comprehensive research that we know on American urban renewal has now been almost completed by Roger Friedland (Sociology Department, University of Wisconsin, Madison, Ph.D. dissertation, 1975). I have used Friedland's comments and information to update my own research on American urban renewal, written in 1969 ("La rénovation urbaine aux U.S.A.," *Espaces et Sociétés*, n. 1, 1970).

45. In my quoted article (1970) there are many bibliographical and data references to support this statement. Friedland's thesis will expand both theoretically and empirically the basic assumptions of the radical critique on U.S. urban renewal.

46. See, for instance, Chester Hartman's *Yerba Buena*, 1974, on the popular resistance against urban renewal in San Francisco. Mollenkopf studies also several struggles on urban renewal (book quoted, 1976).

47. See Report by the President's Commission on Law Enforcement and Administration of Justice, *The Challenge of Crime in a Free Society*, Avon Books, New York, 1968.

48. Frances Fox Piven, "The Great Society as Political Strategy," in Richard A. Cloward and Frances F. Piven, *The Politics of Turmoil*, Pantheon Books, New York, 1974.

49. For a more detailed interpretation, see our forthcoming paper, Michael Aiken and Manuel Castells, "From the Great Society Dreams to the Inner-City Nightmares," 1975.

50. Basic references on the subject are Peter Marris and Martin Rein, *Dilemmas of Social Reform*, Routledge and Kegan Paul, London, 1970 (it is better to consult this second edition); Daniel P. Moynihan, *Maximum Feasible Misunderstanding*, Free Press, New York, 1969; Frances F. Piven and Richard A. Cloward, *Regulating the Poor*, Vintage Books, 1971; same authors, *op. cit.*, 1974; Roland L. Warren, Stephen M. Rose, Ann F. Bergunder, *The Structure of Urban Reform*, Lexington Books, Lexington, Mass., 1974.

51. Moynihan, *op. cit.*, 1969.

52. We have extensively used the summary of research on the subject written by Howard S. Erlanger, *Interpersonal Violence*, University of Wisconsin, Madison, 1974, typed paper.

53. See Norman Fainstein and Susan Fainstein, *Urban Political Movements*, Prentice Hall, Englewood Cliffs, N.J., 1974; and also, John Mollenkopf, "On the Causes and Consequences of Neighborhood Political Mobilization," paper delivered at the meeting of American Political Science Association, New Orleans, September 1973.

54. Michael Lipsky, *Protest in City Politics: Rent Strikes, Housing and the Power of the Poor*, Rand McNally, Chicago, 1970.

55. See John Mollenkopf and Jon Pynoos, "Property, Politics and Local Housing Policy," *Politics and Society*, Vol. 2, n. 4, 1972.

56. *Op. cit.*, 1971.

57. Robert Bailey, Jr., *Radicals in Urban Politics: The Alinsky Approach*, The University of Chicago Press, Chicago, 1972.

58. The best *summary* and discussion of the research available on the 1960's riots is Joe R. Feagin and Harlan Hahn, *Ghetto Revolts: The Politics of Violence in American Cities*, Macmillan Co., New York, 1973. For an excellent case study of the development of the black movement in Detroit see Marvin Surkin, *I Do Mind*

Dying. A Study on Urban Revolution, St. Martin's Press, New York, 1975.

59. See Seymour Spilerman, "The Causes of Racial Disturbances: A Comparison of Alternative Explanations," *American Sociological Review*, 35, August 1970; "The Causes of Racial Disturbances: Tests of an Explanation," *American Sociological Review*, June 1971.

60. The connection between the black movement as a social protest movement and the open-housing movement as a service-reform movement has been shown in detail by a case study on Milwaukee carried on by a working group of my University of Wisconsin seminar on urban politics: Ron Blascoe, Kim Burns, David Gillespie, Greg Martin, and Linda Wills, *Milwaukee Open Housing and the Grass Roots*, Sociology Department, University of Wisconsin, Madison, August 1975.

61. For a general documentation see David Gordon (ed.), *Problems in Political Economy: An Urban Perspective*, Heath, Lexington, Mass., 1971. And also, J. Pynoos, R. Schafer, and C. Hartman (eds.), *Housing Urban America*, Aldine Publishing Co., Chicago, 1973.

62. See *The Central City Problem, op. cit.*, 1973, Part I, Section 6.

63. See the insightful study of George Sternlieb and Robert W. Burchell, *Residential Abandonment: The Tenement Landlord Revisited*, Center for Urban Policy Research, Rutgers University, New Brunswick, N.J., 1973. The study is centered on Newark but the analysis has a more general scope.

64. *The Central City Problem, op. cit.*, 1973, p. 107.

65. See David Harvey, *op. cit.*, 1975.

66. [Footnote missing in original.]

67. See Wilfred Owen, *The Metropolitan Transportation Problem*, Doubleday Anchor Books, New York, 1966.

68. See Michael N. Danielson, *Federal-Metropolitan Politics and the Commuter Crisis*, Columbia Univ. Press, New York, 1965.

69. James F. Veatch, "Federal and Local Urban Transportation Policy," *Urban Affairs Quarterly*, Vol. 10, n. 4, June 1975.

70. See Norman I. Fainstein and Susan S. Fainstein, *The Future of Community Control*, Bureau of Social Applied Research, Columbia University, New York, Sept. 1974, mimeo.

71. I have relied on the very detailed summary research paper done by a working group of my University of Wisconsin seminar on urban politics: Mary A. Evans, Alfonzo Thurman, Anthony Edoh, and Augusto Figueroa, "Busing and Urban Segregation: The Continuing Struggle," Sociology Department, University of Wisconsin, Madison, August 1975.

72. See J. David Greenstone and Paul E. Peterson, *Race and Authority in Urban Politics: Community Participation and the War on Poverty*, Russell Sage Foundation, New York, 1973.

73. In addition to my own observations and data-gathering, I have used two excellent papers on the urban crisis within a largely shared perspective of concrete Marxist analysis of urban contradictions: Richard Child Hill, "Black Struggle and the Urban Fiscal Crisis," Conference on Urban Political Economy, New York, Feb. 1975, mimeo; and Roger Friedland, "Big Apple and the Urban Orchard," Berkeley, August 1975, typed paper.

74. See William J. Baumol, "Macroeconomics of Unbalanced Growth: The

Anatomy of the Urban Crisis," *The American Economic Review*, June 1967. Also, George Sternlieb, "The City as Sandbox," *The Public Interest*, Fall 1971. And Alexander Ganz, "The City-Sandbox, Reservation or Dynamo?" *Public Policy*, 21, Winter 1973. Also, the recent careful statistical analysis of the *determinants* of central-city decay by Franklin D. Wilson, *The Organizational Components of Expanding Metropolitan Systems*, Center for Demography and Ecology, University of Wisconsin, Madison, July 1975.

75. I have used, besides reading the *New York Times* and speaking with some friends in New York (particularly Marvin Surkin, Allan Wolfe, Robert Cohen, Bill Tabb, Ron Lawson, etc.), the well-documented paper done by one of my students at the University of Wisconsin: Joel Devine, "Working Paper on the Urban Fiscal Crisis — A Case Study: New York City," Madison, Wisconsin, August 1975.

76. Roger Friedland, *op. cit.*, 1975.

77. See M. Aiken and M. Castells, *op. cit.*, 1975.

78. See Ira Katznelson, "Community Conflict and Capitalist Development," paper delivered at the Annual Meeting of the American Political Science Association, San Francisco, Sept. 1975.

79. I have trusted (and perhaps misunderstood) information provided personally by John Mollenkopf, Roger Friedland, Janice Perlman, Ira Katznelson, Marvin Surkin, and Ron Lawson. Also, I have done in some cases, a bit of "tourist participant observation."

80. [Footnote missing in original.]

81. Roger Friedland, *op. cit.*, 1975.

[Ed. note: Asterisked note and prefatory credits paragraph have been omitted.]

CHAPTER 1   SUGGESTIONS FOR FURTHER READING

Banfield, Edward C. *The Unheavenly City Revisited* (Boston: Little, Brown, 1974). This volume, from which the first excerpt in this chapter is drawn, offers a thorough introduction to the urban crisis as seen through the eyes of one of America's most prominent political scientists. This is a revised version of his earlier book, *The Unheavenly City*, one which provoked a great deal of controversy and many review articles. See, for example, the set of articles, with Banfield's reply, in a symposium on Banfield's book in the *Social Science Quarterly*, 51, 4 (March 1971), 816—859.

Pickvance, C. G. (ed.). *Urban Sociology: Critical Essays* (London: Tavistock, 1976). This volume consists of eight articles on urban sociology and urban problems, both in the United States and in Europe. All of the articles, including two by Manuel Castells, are critical of the conventional wisdom on cities espoused by critics such as Edward Banfield.

Warner, Sam Bass. *The Urban Wilderness* (New York: Harper and Row, 1972). In a critical but sympathetic fashion this provocative analysis digs deeply into the historical origins and contemporary problems of landowning and land use in the capitalist city in the United States.

2

White
Middle Americans

At least for the last half-century many Americans have adopted a "melting-pot" perspective in describing or prescribing the social and cultural adaptations made by the millions who migrated to the United States from other countries. The melting-pot theme is found not only in the speeches of presidents but also in the conversations of ordinary Americans, and it was given an influential formulation by Zangwill in an early-twentieth-century play about the struggle of a Russian immigrant, who at one point argues that

> America is God's Crucible, the great Melting-Pot where all the races of Europe are melting and re-forming! Here you stand, good folk, think I, when I see them at Ellis Island, here you stand in your fifty groups, with your fifty languages and histories, and your fifty blood hatreds and rivalries. But you won't be long like that, brothers, for these are the fires of God. ... A fig for your feuds and vendettas! Germans and Frenchmen, Irishmen and Englishmen, Jews and Russians — into the Crucible with you all! God is making the American.[1]

Although America-the-Crucible ideas have taken a variety of forms and have been countered with alternative interpretations, they still maintain a powerful grip on American thinking about the assimilation process — past, present, and future.

For example, many would argue that the current trend is — and ought to be — toward a precipitous decline in the significance of ethnicity in American society. Although there has been debate over the character and operation of this adaptive process, until quite recently few seemed to question the view that ethnic differences were no longer of any real consequence.

In *Why Can't They Be Like Us?* sociologist Andrew Greeley argues convincingly for the survival of meaningful ethnic differences in contemporary American society. In addition to the data cited in the excerpts from Greeley's book reprinted here, extensive research evidence for the persistence of ethnic differentials is provided throughout that book. To illustrate, examination of survey research (opinion poll) materials on Catholic immigrant groups (including the Irish, Germans, Italians, and Poles) has revealed very important variations among white ethnics not only in socioeconomic status but also in racial attitudes and general outlook on life. Particularly important, too, is the reported tendency for these white Americans to socialize and marry within their own ethnic groups. Thus, Greeley argues that the ethnic neighborhood is still a part of urban society:

> Considerable numbers of human beings continue to live in neighborhoods and continue to be deeply attached to their social turf, to view the geography and the interaction network of their local communities as an extension of themselves and to take any threat to the neighborhood as a threat to the very core of their being.[2]

Rejecting the view that there is really a "blue-collar ethnic problem," Greeley further proposes that existing ethnic diversity, as well as the apparent resurgence of ethnic self-consciousness among whites, can be viewed positively. Thus, the intimate primary ties of these predominantly urban groups provide a social location and a context for the development of strong personal identity. From this perspective ethnic groups do, and in the future can, provide cultural richness and liveliness in an urban environment, perhaps preventing the emergence of the much-feared specters of "mass society" and the "lonely crowd."

In the second selection in this chapter we are introduced in a rather intimate way to a few of those Americans often maligned in discussions of "blue-collar ethnic" or "hard-hat" Americans. Similarly rejecting the notion that these middle Americans should be viewed as a "problem," Robert Coles provides vivid verbal portraits, the result of long hours spent interviewing a number of Americans who described themselves simply as "plain people" or "average people." Relatively little analysis accompanies Coles' ethnographic sketches, but the surprising diversity and complexity of the views represented are particularly underscored. In the excerpt reprinted here the variety and inconsistency of working class perspectives are conspicuously evident. At times Joe — a man who works at several blue-collar jobs — certainly seems to fit the image of a hard-hat bigot, espousing negative, prejudiced views of college students and black Americans. However, a few minutes later Joe confounds those who would neatly classify him with unexpected comments like the following: "If I was a Negro, I'd be madder than hell. I'd stand up to anyone who tried to keep me away from my share."[3] Nor is his view of students as monolithic or inflexible as some might make it out to be. "And soon Joe switches, says maybe, says yes, says it is true that some of the students are good, mean well, are on the workingman's side against the big corporations."[4]

While Coles' interviews reflect views that many have come to associate with popular images of blue-collar Americans, including firm commitment to the work ethic, entrenched patriotism, devotion to home and family, and criticism of students and racist attitudes toward black Americans, they also accentuate the confusion, the complexity, the honesty, and even the *radicalism* of middle Americans. Perhaps most striking is the strain of economic radicalism, which is often mixed with more conservative points of view; the comments of a young Vietnam veteran, a welder, are instructive:

> We argue during coffee break. One guy will say that Nixon is cracking down on nigger-bums, and the welfare-bleeders. . . . But pretty soon the next guy will open up with a reminder that the Negro is only trying to get *his*, just like we tried to get *ours*, the workingman did. And who won't give anyone an extra dime, unless he's pushed? I'll tell you. It's the banker and the big businessman. . . . I've never been asked what I think in a poll, and no one I know has ever been asked. If they did come around and talk with us at work and ask us their questions, I'll bet we'd confuse them. One minute we'd sound like George Wallace, and the next we'd probably be called radicals or something.[5]

Misconceptions about middle Americans extend as well to blue-collar and white-collar Americans in suburbia. Conventional wisdom about suburbs suggests that much there can be described in terms of sickness and social pathology. In his now classic study, *Working-Class Suburb*,[6] Bennett M. Berger was one of the first to argue that serious misconceptions about the social and cultural life of suburbanites had recently arisen, a set of misconceptions he termed "the myth of suburbia." Herbert J. Gans provides a concise statement about some key elements of this myth:

> . . . the suburbs were breeding a new set of Americans, as mass produced as the houses they lived in, driven into a never ending

round of group activity ruled by the strictest conformity. Suburbanities were incapable of real friendships; they were bored and lonely, alienated, atomized, and depersonalized. As the myth grew, it added yet more disturbing elements: the emergence of a matriarchal family of domineering wives, absent husbands, and spoiled children, and with it, rising marital friction, adultery, divorce, drunkenness, and mental illness.[7]

Working-Class Suburb not only criticized this suburban myth but also presented detailed data on the way of life common to a group of blue-collar families who had moved from the industrial city of Richmond, California, to a new suburb just outside San Jose. Berger carefully documented in that work his contention that the blue-collar families who had moved to the suburban fringe "had not been profoundly affected in any statistically identifiable or sociologically interesting way."[8] Thus, he found no evidence of status-striving or status anxiety but did find a general feeling of well-being. While couple-visiting and activity in formal associations were relatively rare (in contrast to patterns in some white-collar suburbs), there was a considerable amount of visiting with relatives and family activity. These important findings are reported and further underscored in a subsequent article, which is reprinted in this chapter, a paper in which Berger reviews the earlier arguments in the light of recent research and examines the sources and implications of misconceptions about suburban life. The role of a curious group of bedfellows — realtors, businessmen, city planners, intellectuals, the mass media — in the development of suburban stereotypes is suggested; and the serious implications of these stereotypes for present and future urban planning are carefully weighed. Moreover, in his policy-oriented concluding comments Berger seems to be developing arguments compatible with Greeley's discussion of pluralism in life styles. Social and cultural variety is a reality in the suburban fringe, as well as elsewhere in American cities, and in his view this pluralism should be recognized and taken seriously by those planners intent on shaping and reshaping the social and physical environments of American urbanites.

NOTES

1. Israel Zangwill, *The Melting Pot* (New York: Macmillan, 1925), p. 33.
2. Andrew M. Greeley, *Why Can't They Be Like Us?: America's White Ethnic Groups* (New York: Dutton, 1971), p. 100.
3. Robert Coles and Jon Erikson, *The Middle Americans* (Boston: Atlantic-Little, Brown, 1971), p. 9.

4. Ibid., p. 6.

5. Ibid., pp. 138—139.

6. Bennett M. Berger, *Working-Class Suburb* (Berkeley: University of California Press, 1969).

7. Herbert J. Gans, *The Levittowners* (New York: Pantheon, 1967), pp. xv—xvi.

8. Bennett M. Berger, "Suburbia and the American Dream," *The Public Interest*, no. 2 (Winter 1966), p. 81.

From
Why Can't They Be Like Us?:

The Future of Ethnic Groups

Andrew M. Greeley

It is now time to address ourselves to three general questions: (1) Are ethnic groups likely to survive in American society? (2) Can anything be done to mitigate ethnic conflicts? and (3) What kind of research would help shed some of the light we need on this subject?

As to the first question — whether ethnic groups have a future in American society — the previous chapters have, I hope, provided sufficient answer. There is no reason to think they will not continue to play an important role, at least for the rest of this century, despite the fact that the compositions of the groups are changing, as well as the kind of identification they provide for their members. (Joshua Fishman, in his large and impressive study of language loyalty,[1] indicates that there is apparently an inevitable decline across generation lines in the use of a foreign tongue, although he and many of his coauthors entertain some hope that the decline can be arrested and even reversed.)

Although immigration has by no means come to an end, and hundreds of thousands of immigrants enter the United States each year, the ratio of immigrants to the total population is obviously much smaller than it was at the turn of the century. And while the new immigrants do provide clients for the hard core of purely ethnic services (especially the press and radio programs identified with the mother tongue), they no longer represent the major focus of concern for most American ethnics.

Poles, Norwegians and Italians, for example, are far more concerned with shaping their future within the American environment than preserving their cultural links with the past. The cultural links are preserved, however, in two fashions — first, by the unconscious transmission of role expectations, some rooted in the past and others in the early experience in this country; and second, through a scholarly or artistic interest in the customs of the past. Thus, though the ethnic groups in this country have taken on a life of their own, more or less independent of the national cultures and societies where their roots lie, many of the old links survive, indirectly and undeliberately, or in a highly self-conscious academic fashion.

Again we can see how blurred the picture is and how difficult it is to be confident in the absence of more careful research. The American Irish are different, let us say, from the American Poles in part because they come from different cultural backgrounds, in part because they came to the United States at different times, in part because the two groups have had vastly different experiences in the American society, and in part because there are conscious efforts — at first from an intense determination to survive, and later out of leisurely academic and artistic interests — to keep a lot of the traditions and customs of the past.

The American Irish, I suspect, are only slightly moved by the current Londonderry riots in which Catholics in the north of Ireland have adopted some of the tactics of American blacks in their own civil rights movement. Not long ago, during a visit to a Catholic girls' college in the heartland of America, I noticed a sign on the bulletin board announcing that the Irish Club of the college would shortly hold its monthly meeting. I asked the young lady who was showing me through the college if she belonged to the Irish Club; it turned out that she not only belonged, she was its president. "Peggy," I asked her, "do you know what the six counties are?" She admitted that she did not. "Have you ever heard of the Sinn Fein?" She had not. "Have you ever heard of the Easter rising, or the I.R.A.?" She conceded her ignorance. Finally, I said "Peggy, do you know who Eamon de Valera is?" She brightened. "Isn't he the Jewish man that is the Lord Mayor of Dublin?" she asked.

And yet Peggy is Irish, and proudly so, though she is part of the fourth generation. She might be hard put to say specifically how she differs from her Polish classmates, but the political style of her family, the shape of its commitment to Roman Catholicism, perhaps even its interpretation of the meaning of the good life, are rooted in the Irish past; and even though Peggy later married a boy with a German name (it was all right, her relatives assured me, because his mother was Irish), she continues to be Irish, and I suspect her children will too, no matter what their name happens to be.

For Jews, the issue of ethnic identity is, it seems to me, even more subtle and complex. The horrifying disaster of the Second World War made most Jews much more explicitly conscious of their background and cultural traditions, and the existence of Israel as a modern nation state embodying these traditions reinforces this consciousness. Thus, while Jews are one of the most thoroughly acculturated groups in American society, they are also extremely conscious of their origins and history, and even in the third and fourth generation they make greater efforts to preserve their own culture than any other major immigrant group.

INTERMARRIAGE AND IDENTITY

Those who doubt that ethnic groups have much of a future usually point to intermarriage as proof that ethnicity is vanishing on the American scene. The truth is, however, that there is almost nothing in the way of detailed literature on ethnic intermarriage except the studies on intermarriage between Jews and gentiles.[2]

Harold Abramson's study, referred to in Chapter 7 [not reprinted here], finds that ethnic intermarriage does, indeed, increase with generation, education and occupational success. But ethnic intermarriage hardly seems to be a random event. A typical ethnic in Abramson's population was some two and one-half times more likely to choose a mate from his own ethnic group than he would if ethnicity were irrelevant in a choice of spouse. Furthermore, even intermarriage seems to take place along certain ethnically predictable lines — that is to say, if someone does marry outside his ethnic group, he is more likely to choose someone from a group considered relatively close to his own. Thus an Irishman, for example, is much more likely to marry a German than a Pole or an Italian.

Abramson's data, which were collected for another purpose, do not supply the answers to two critical questions. First, what sort of ethnic identification, if any, does the new family choose for itself? While there is not much in the way of precise data, impressionistic evidence (reported by Moynihan and Glazer) seems to indicate that a choice of ethnic identity is made either by the spouses themselves or by their children.

The second and more complicated question is: Which traits are passed on to which children in an ethnic intermarriage? Let us consider, for example, the apparent political liberalism of the Irish in comparison with the other Catholic groups described in the previous chapter. In a marriage between an Irish male college graduate and a Polish female college graduate, holding all the other variables constant, whose social attitudes are likely to affect the children? Will the father, rather than the mother, prevail because the father is political leader of the family? Will the father influence his sons and the mother her daughters, or will the flow of influence be vice versa? Or will it all cancel out, with the Polish-Irish children assuming positions on social issues somewhere between those of the two ethnic groups?

Of course we also have no way of knowing whether the social attitudes reported in the previous chapter will survive into the next generation, even in ethnically endogamous marriages. These complicated questions simply underscore how precious little we know about the later stages of acculturation and assimilation. What we do know, however, scarcely justifies the popular assumption that the ethnic groups are disappearing.

But if they are likely to persist, how is society to cope with the problems that ethnicity generates? For it seems to me we must, above all, recognize that ethnic problems are also likely to persist, and that it does little good to lament them or moralize about them. We must also be carefully aware of our own ethnic biases and not permit ourselves the luxury of superior attitudes towards behavior which, if the truth be told, we dislike mostly because it's not the sort of thing "our kind of people" might do. And thirdly, we must be wary of turning correlations into causes. In Chapter 6 [not reprinted here], for example, we described correlations between "Polishness" and certain ethnocentric attitudes. It would be quite easy to make a leap and say that being Polish "causes" the ethnocentric attitudes — and some Polish critics of the data I've discussed have assumed I was making such a leap, even though there were no grounds for such an assumption. There may be something in the Polish cultural background to explain anti-Semitism, but there is nothing I can think of that would explain racism. Thus, I would be much more inclined to see the conflict between the Poles and the blacks in terms of the particular stage in the ethnic assimilation process that the Poles happen to have reached at the time when the black group has become militant. In other words, I am inclined to think we can explain the conflict between the Poles and the blacks almost entirely in economic, social and psychological terms, without having to fall back on cultural traditions at all.

The problem is not much easier with respect to the somewhat less intense controversies separating white ethnic groups, one from another. I have no clear notions of how to cope with an apparent increase in Jewish animosity toward Catholics in recent years ... or with the antagonism between Irish Catholics and other Catholic groups. I suspect we need intergroup dialogue, cultural exchanges and serious interest in the cultural institutions of those groups with which we are most likely to compete. I am also inclined to think we need leaders who are less demagogic since ethnic groups seem to have a genius for flocking to demagogic leadership. And we must show great self-restraint in attacking the leadership of other groups, even though that leadership is likely to leave itself wide open to such attacks. But having repeated suggestions which must be considered as little more than truisms of intergroup work, I am at a loss as to how to proceed further. We simply do not know enough; not enough data are available, not enough experiments have been done, and all too few theories have been advanced to enable us either to understand what is going on or to prescribe remedies for the pathology we may observe.

It does seem to me, however, that it is essential for political leaders, social planners and influential figures in the ethnic communities to abandon the rather foolish controversy of whether ethnicity is a good thing or a bad thing — particularly since it clearly has both good and bad effects — and settle down to a better understanding of what it means and how we may live with it, not merely tolerably, but fruitfully.

A number of people have made some concrete suggestions for helping to "cool" the tensions among America's ethnic groups. Some try to deal with the problems "where they're at," that is, at the actual point of collision. The American Arbitration Association, for example, has organized a new Center for Dispute Settlement which will offer free mediation and arbitration services to help resolve differences between racial and ethnic groups, students and school administrators, landlords and tenants, businessmen and consumers, and other groups involved in clashes that might otherwise escalate into dangerous confrontations.

Others address themselves to efforts to get at the underlying causes. If competition for scarce, or presumably scarce, opportunities and services is at the root of much of the conflict among ethnic groups, they reason, one way to reduce such conflict is to "enlarge the pie" through economic and social programs aimed at improving the overall quality of life for all Americans. Such proposals have come from a variety of sources, including the carefully detailed Freedom Budget, outlined a few years ago by economists Leon Keyserling and Vivian Henderson and others, and the broad *Agenda for the Nation* published by the prestigious consultants of the Brookings Institution. All of these proposals envision a shift in national priorities to channel some of our enormous productive capacities into programs to provide jobs, schools, housing, recreation, health services and other essentials, not only for the hard-core poor who, in our less affluent past, have been consistently squeezed out in the competition for these needs, but also for the many millions of hard-working lower middle-class ethnics embittered by poor schooling, dead-end jobs and an unrelenting, unfair tax burden.

· · ·

Problem or Promise

As someone who has insisted for a decade and more that American social science ought to be concerned about the continuation of ethnicity in American society I have mixed feelings about the current fascination with the subject in academic, governmental, foundation and mass media offices. Obviously, I am delighted that people don't look at me as though I were crazy when I say that ethnic groups have survived in American society, but I am considerably less than pleased to discover that from a state of nonexistence white ethnic groups have become a social problem without anybody bothering to do any careful study in between. My feeling is that most members of American ethnic groups are going to be unpleasantly surprised to discover that they are a problem or that they are a "blue-collar problem" and, much worse, a "hard hat problem." As much of a shock as it may be to elite groups in American society, there are considerable numbers of white ethnics who are not blue-collar workers, and even substantial numbers who are college graduates and professionals; but they still have some recollection of what it was like to be a social problem, to be an object of the ministrations of welfare workers and settlement house do-gooders and they are, unless I am mistaken, quite disinclined to become that once again. Nor are they to be bought off by an increase in real income or by "community services." Indeed, the American white ethnics realize almost as much as do their black brothers that when the elite groups define you as a problem you are in for trouble. There was a time when the white ethnics had no choice but to be a "problem," but they have a choice now and I think they want no part of it.

Nonetheless, the elites persist in talking about the "blue-collar ethnic problem" and find themselves now joined by some of those alienated ethnics who only recently were seeking their own self-validation by crusading for rights for blacks. When the blacks made clear to them that they no longer could play their paternalistic roles, some of these leaders — most notably Catholic clergymen — rediscovered their own ethnic heritage and, with barely a change in vocabulary, they are now crusading for white ethnic rights. Indeed, one of them went so far recently as to observe that in a couple of years white ethnics would catch up to the blacks in matters of ethnic self-consciousness — a statement well calculated to offend, if possible, everyone.

In the final analysis, I suspect more harm will be done by this "social problem" approach than was done by simply ignoring the existence of white ethnic groups. It should be obvious by now that the perspective of this book assumes that ethnic diversity is an opportunity rather than a problem. Why the social problem approach is being emphasized and the "positive contribution" approach largely ignored is in itself a subject for further investigation.

The great theme of classical sociology is that in the last centuries Western society has moved from *gemeinschaft* to *gesellschaft*, from community to association, from primary group to secondary group, from mechanical solidarity to organic solidarity, from traditional authority to bureaucratic authority, from primordial drives to contractual drives. Weber, Durkheim, Tonnies, Toreltsch and Talcott Parsons have merely arranged different orchestrations on this architectonic theme. Under the impact of rationalization, bureaucratization, industrialization and urbanization, it is argued, the old ties of blood, faith, land and consciousness of kind have yielded to the rational structural demands of the technological society. In the conceptual framework of Professor Parsons's famous pattern variables, the immense social changes of the last two centuries have moved the race or at least the North Atlantic component of it from the particularistic to the universal, from ascription to achievement, from the diffuse to the specific. And other observers see a shift from the mythological to the religionless, from the sacred to the profane to the secular, from the folk to the urban. In other words, in organized society at the present time, the rational demands of the organization itself — or the organizations themselves — provide the structure that holds society together. Nonrational and primordial elements, if they survive at all, survive in the "private sphere" or in the "interstices." The old primordial forces may still be somewhat relevant in choosing a wife or a poker or bridge partner, but they have no meaning in the large corporate structures — business, labor, government, education, or even, for that matter, church. In the private sphere and in the interstices, the nonrational and primordial ties are seen as everywhere in retreat. Ethnic groups are vanishing, religion is losing its hold, men and women are becoming so mobile that they need no geographic roots. Professor Bennis[1] argues that there is emerging a "temporary society" made up of those members of the social elite for whom geographic, institutional and interpersonal stability are no longer necessary. These men, according to Bennis, move from place to place, occupation to occupation, and relationship to relationship without feeling any sense of personal or physical dislocation. Wherever they go, they are immediately able to relate intensely to their fellows, and sitting but lying back, "in the perfect position for television." He watches television when he can, and if he were home more he would watch more television. He likes to view sports — football, basketball, hockey. He will watch golf, but not very enthusiastically. He has never played golf. The game is too slow for him, and there is, too, a touch of the fancy in those clubs and the carts and the caps a lot of golfers wear. So he thinks, anyway; and he knows why. His father used to tell him that golf was a rich man's game. He now knows better; even his father knows better. But knowing is not being convinced. In his words: "You can know something, but you can't change the way you feel." (So much for whole textbooks of psychology and psychiatry.)

As a matter of fact, the game of golf can prompt him to reflect. He has a friend who plays golf. The city golf course is crowded, though. In order really to enjoy the game one must belong to a club, have access to a first-rate, uncrowded course. The friend has a friend — his lawyer, in fact — who takes him to a fine country club. Every Saturday morning the two men play golf, then go home and meet again the next Saturday. They don't have lunch afterwards, or breakfast beforehand. They don't talk much to each other. What they have in common is golf, period. And there is a lesson in that. It's hard to "move away from your own kind of people."

Joe and Doris see no reason to make lists of "criteria" that characterize the people they feel comfortable with, or on the contrary don't; but upon occasion they will spell things out rather clearly. Joe will talk about "brainy people." One of his friends has a son who is just studying and studying, not in order to become a doctor or a lawyer (which is fine) but to stay out of the draft (Joe thinks) and "because he's so shy he can't talk to people, so he lives in the library." The subject of libraries and the universities that own them leads to other matters. Joe and Doris want those libraries and universities for their children, and indeed, their oldest son is in his first year of college. But no one can be snobbier, more arrogant and condescending than "a certain kind of professor" or a lot of those "professional students," which mean students who are not content to study and to learn, but make nuisances of themselves, flaunt themselves before the public, disrupt things, behave like fools. He gets angry as he gets further into the discussion, but his wife slows him down, and even manages to cause a partial reversal of his views. After all, she insists, he is always complaining about certain things that are wrong with the country. He is always saying that the rich are getting richer, and the ordinary man, he can barely keep up with himself. Someone has to do more than complain; someone has to say unpopular things. Doris herself does so, says unpopular things, at least at certain times — though only to her husband, when they are having a talk. And soon Joe switches, says maybe, says yes, says it is true that some of the students are good, mean well, are on the workingman's side against the big corporations.

ethnics] are simply a barrier to social progress, though I suppose they have their own problems, too." And at the same conference a panel discussion about white ethnics labels them as "social conservatives." Serious discussions are held under the sponsorship of government agencies or private foundations in which the white ethnic "problem" is discussed as something about which "something must be done." One cannot speak to an academic group on the subject of ethnicity without some timid soul rising in the question period to inquire whether it might not be immoral to discuss the question of ethnic groups since ethnicity stresses the things which separate men and we ought to be concerned about those things which unite them. The bias in these reactions is apparent: the survival of the primordial is a social problem. The evolution from the nonrational to the rational, the sacred to the profane, the primordial to the contractual, the folk to the urban is seen not merely as a useful analytic model, but as profoundly righteous moral imperative. As some people have not completed their pilgrimage through this simple evolutionary model, obviously they are a social problem and "something must be done about them," such as, for example, seeing that their real income goes up at the rate of 5 percent a year or providing day care centers for their neighborhoods. If one does enough of such things for them, maybe then they or at least their children will someday become more enlightened and be just like us.

It is certainly not my intention to deny the great utility of the official model of classical sociology. Obviously, a great transformation has come over the North Atlantic world since 1750. I need only to visit Ballendrehid, County Mayo, Ireland, to know that it is different from Chicago, Cook County, Illinois. The insight of the great sociologists is extraordinarily valuable but the trouble with their model as a tool for analysis is that the temptation is strong either to ignore or to treat as residual phenomena whatever can't be made to fit the model. I would contend that it is the very elegance of the official model of classical sociology that has blinded us to an incredibly vast range of social phenomena which must be understood if we are to cope with the problems of contemporary America.

I would suggest, then, that another model must be used either in conjunction with the official one or as the component of a more elaborate model which will integrate the two. According to this model, the basic ties of friendship, primary relationship, land, faith, common origin and consciousness of kind persist much as they did in the Ice Age. They are the very stuff out of which society is made and in their absence the corporate structures would collapse. These primordial, prerational bonds which hold men and women together have of course been transmuted by the changing context. The ethnic group, for example, did not even exist before the last of the nineteenth century. It came into existence precisely so that the primordial ties of the peasant commune could somehow or other be salvaged from the immigration experience. But because the primordial ties have been transmuted does not mean that they have been eliminated. They simply operate in a different context and perhaps in a different way. They are, according to this second model, every bit as decisive for human relationships as they were in the past. In fact, a strong case could be made that one primordial relationship — that of marriage — has in one respect become far stronger than it ever was in the past, because prospective marriage partners now require more rather than fewer ties of interpersonal affection; and while such ties of affection may appear structurally tenuous, they can be far more demanding on the total personality than were the structural ties of the past.

To the extent that this model has validity, a simple, uni-dimensional and unidirectional evolution from *gemeinschaft* to *gesellschaft* has not taken place. What has happened, rather, has been a tremendous increase in the complexity of society, with vast pyramids of corporate structures being erected on a substratum of primordial relationships. Since the primoridal ties tend to be the infrastructure, or at least to look like the infrastructure to those who are interested primarily in corporate bureaucracies, it is possible to ignore them or at least to give them minimal importance. One does not, after all, think about the foundation of the Empire State Building when one sees it soaring into the air above Manhattan Island — not at least unless one happens to be an engineer.

From this second model, if it has any validity, one would conclude that the persistence of primordial bonds is not merely a social problem, but also a social asset. Communities based on consciousness of kind or common faith or common geography would be seen in this model not merely as residues of the past, but rather as a basic sub-component of the social structure. Membership in such communities would be seeen as providing personal identity and social location for members as well as making available a pool of preferred role opposites whose availability would ease stress situations at critical junctures in modern living. In other words, collectivities grouped around such primordial bonds would be seen not merely as offering desirable cultural richness and variety, but also as basic pillars of support for the urban social structure. A city government would view itself as fortunate in having large and diverse ethnic groups within its boundaries because such collectivities would prevent the cities from becoming a habitat for a "lonely crowd" or a "mass society." Psychologists and psychiatrists would be delighted with the possi-bilities of ethnic group membership providing social support and self-definition as an antidote to the "anomie" of the mass society. Another way of putting the same matter would be to say that to the extent the second model is a valid one, the lonely crowd and the mass society do not really exist.

But to what extent does the second model have any validity? My inclination would be to say that, if anything, much more research data can be fitted into the second model than into the first one. This is not the appropriate place to review in detail all the available evidence about the survival of the primordial, but one can at least list the principal research efforts. The now classic Hawthorne experiments of Elton Mayo and his colleagues demonstrated how decisive in the supposedly rationalized and formalized factory was the influence of informal friendship groups. Ruby Jo Reeves Kennedy proved in the early 1940's that there had been no change in patterns of religious inter-marriage for a half century and thirty years later the research done at the National Opinion Research Center on young college graduates indicates that denominational (which includes Baptists, Lutherans, Methodists, etc., as separate denominations) intermarriage is still not increasing in the United States. The *American Soldier*[4] showed how decisive personal loyalty was in holding together the combat squad. The work of Morris Janowitz and Edward Shils proved that the Wehrmacht began to fall apart only when the rank and file soldier began to lose faith in the paternalistic noncom who held his unit together. The voting studies of Paul Lazarsfeld and his colleagues proved that voting decisions were not made by isolated individuals but rather by members of intimate primary groups; and the similar studies of Elihu Katz and others on marketing decisions and the use of innovative drugs showed how such decisions were strongly influenced by informal personal relationships. Will Herberg's classic, *Protestant, Catholic, Jew*, suggested a model explaining that religion is so important in the United States precisely because it provides self-definition and social location. James Q. Wilson's study of police discovered that sergeants of different ethnic groups have different administrative styles and the work of Edward Levine and others on the Irish as politicians has made clear — to those who are yet unaware of it — that the Irish have a highly instinctive political style (a political style, be it noted, that assumes the persistence and importance of primordial groups).

Manpower research done at NORC indicates that ethnicity is a moderately strong predictor of career choice. (Germans go into science and engineering, Jews into medicine and law, Irish into law, political science and history and the foreign service.) Studies of hospital behavior show that different ethnic groups respond differently to pain in hospital situations. (The Irish deny it and the Italians exaggerate it.) The Banfield and Wilson school of political science[5] emphasizes urban politics as an art of power brokerage among various ethnic and religio-ethnic groups. More recent research at NORC has shown that there is moderately strong correlation between ethnicity and a number of behavioral and attitudinal measures — *even when social classes have held constant*. Other research studies suggest that in large cities professional practices — medical, dental, real estate, construction — tend to be organized along religious or ethnic lines, and yet other work would indicate that some groups choose to create a form of self-segregation, even in the suburbs. Louis Wirth was right; there would indeed be a return to the ghetto but the ghetto would not be in Douglas Park (Chicago), it would be in Skokie and Highland Park (the suburbs).

I could go on, but it hardly seems necessary. Weep not for *gemein-schaft*; it is still very much with us. On the contrary, the burden of evidence ought to be on those who claim to see it vanishing. When it is argued that at least among the social elites secular, technological, religionless man seems to dominate, we need only point out that precisely the offspring of these elites seem presently most interested in recreating the tribal in the world of the psychedelic, neo-sacral communes. The model of classical sociology obviously is not to be abandoned, but it must be freed from a simple-minded, evolutionary interpretation. Furthermore, it is even more necessary to divest the model from the moralistic overtones which it has acquired in popular sociology and, unless I am very much mistaken, in professional sociology as well. To assume that religious or ethnic or geographic ties are unenlightened, reactionary, benighted or obscurantist is to make a moral judgment for which there are no grounds in serious social analysis.

The issue of the two models is not by any means just a theoretical one for, if one uses only the first model, then the angry white ethnic groups are seen basically as a social problem. But if one uses also the second model, one might conclude that ethnic loyalty could be a strong, positive force which might make available vitality and vigor for the preservation and enrichment of urban life for all members of the city. Thus, I would hypothesize that taking the propensity to desert the city as a dependent variable, one would find a strongly ethnic neighborhood scoring much lower on that variable than a cosmopolitan neighborhood. I would even go further and suggest that in an ethnic neighborhood under "threat" there would be less inclination to desert the city than in a less threatened cosmopolitan neighborhood. In one study of the 1969 mayoral election in Gary, Indiana, it was discovered that Poles who are more strongly integrated into the Polish community were more likely to vote for Mayor Hatcher than Poles who were less integrated into the ethnic community (though, obviously, in absolute numbers not many were likely to vote for him). There has been so little positive research done on the subject of white ethnic groups that one hesitates to state conclusively that ethnic identification and loyalty might be a positive asset for promoting social change in the city. Unfortunately, the rigid theoretical limitations of the official model have made it difficult to persuade funding agencies that such research might be appropriate. We are now faced with the rather bizarre situation in which many funding agencies are almost pathetically eager to do something about "the white ethnic problem," without ever having established that it is in fact a problem. It might be a distinct advantage.

If the second model has any utility at all, one could also call into question much of the romantic criticism and equally romantic utopianism of contemporary American society. It may turn out that there is, after all, rather little anomie. It may be that the mass society does not exist beyond Los Angeles and the university campuses around the country. It may be that the young who are seeking to create new clans, new tribes or new communes could achieve the same goals by moving back into their grandparents' neighborhood — an experiment which would also have the happy advantage of revealing to them that intimate communities can be narrow, rigid, doctrinaire and, in many instances, quite intolerant of privacy, creativity and diversity. If such romantic utopians would at least spend some time in their grandparents' neighborhood, they would be a bit more realistic about the problems that they will encounter in the Big Sur or along the banks of the Colorado River.[6]

American social scientists have to put aside their underlying assumptions if they are intelligently to investigate and understand ethnic pluralism in the large cities of our Republic. Social policy makers must likewise put aside most of *their* underlying assumptions. A considerable number of both the social scientists and social policy makers are currently announcing that black is beautiful (whether they really believe it or not is another matter) but if black is beautiful (and it is) then so is Irish, Polish, Italian, Slovenian, Greek, Armenian, Lebanese and Luxembourger.[7] All these represent valid and valuable cultural heritages. They all represent sources of identification and meaning in a vast and diverse society. They all have a positive contribution to a richer and more exciting human community.

Let me conclude with a story whose point I think I need not elaborate. I was standing in front of a church in the west of Ireland, camera in hand, attempting to record the church which I thought just possibly was the place of my grandfather's baptism. The parish priest, who was out cutting his hedge despite the rain, approached me, noted that I was a new man around here, and introduced himself. I must say I was a bit surprised when, on hearing my name, he remarked, "Ah, yes, you'd be the sociologist fellow from Chicago." Then he added, "Would you be wantin' your grandfather's baptismal record now?"

I admitted that the idea hadn't occurred to me. He shook his head in discouragement. "Ah," he said, "fine sociologist you are."

"Do a lot of people come seeking such records?" I asked.

He nodded gravely. "Indeed they do," he said, "indeed they do. Those poor people, you know, they've been in the States now for three generations and they come seeking roots; they want to know who they are; they want to know all about their past and their ancestors. The poor people, I feel so sorry for them. That's why I had all their baptismal records put on microfilm. It makes it a lot easier for people to find their roots."

NOTES

The Future of Ethnic Groups

1. Joshua Fishman *et al.*, *Language Loyalty in the United States* (London and The Hague: Mouton, 1966).
2. Marshall Sklare, "Intermarriage and the Jewish Future," *Commentary*, April 1964, and Erich Rosenthal, "Studies of Jewish Intermarriage in the United States," *American Jewish Year Book*, Vol. 64 (1963), two of the best research reports on this subject.

Problem or Promise

1. Warren G. Bennis and Philip E. Slater, *The Temporary Society* (New York: Harper & Row, 1968).
2. To make my own biases in the matter perfectly clear, if I had to choose between the temporary society and a commune, I wouldn't have much difficulty choosing the latter.
3. John Schaar, "Reflections on Authority," *New American Review*, vol. 8, 1970, p. 671.
4. Samuel A. Stouffer *et al.*, *The American Soldier: Adjustment During Army Life* (Princeton, N.J.: Princeton University Press, 1949).
5. See E. C. Banfield and J. Q. Wilson, *City Politics* (Cambridge: Harvard University Press, 1963).
6. I here rely heavily on a paper of mine, "The Positive Contributions of Ethnic Groups in American Society," which was done for the American Jewish Committee, 1968.
7. In Chicago we have a colony of Luxembourgers.

From
The Middle Americans

Robert Coles and Jon Erikson

"We are proud of ourselves, that's what I'd like to say. We're not sure of things, though; we're uncertain, I'm afraid, and when you're like that — worried, it is — then you're going to lose a little respect for yourself. You're not so proud anymore." There he goes, like a roller coaster; he is up one minute, full of self-confidence and glad that he is himself and no one else, and the next minute he is down, enough so to wish he somehow could have another chance at his life, start in again and avoid the mistakes and seize the opportunities and by God, "get up there."

Now, where is "there" for him? In the observer's mind the question is naturally asked, but the man who speaks like that about his destination would not understand why anyone would feel the need to do so, require a person to say the most obvious things in the world. In fact, if the question were actually asked, the man would have one of his own in return, which out of courtesy he might keep to himself: you mean you don't know? And that would be as far as the man would want to take the discussion. He has no interest in talking about life's "meanings," about his "goals" and his "values." At least, he has no interest in a direct and explicitly acknowledged discussion of that kind. He feels more comfortable when he slides into such matters, when he is talking about something quite concrete and of immediate concern and then for a few minutes finds himself "going off." It is not that he minds becoming introspective or philosophical or whatever; he likes to catch himself "getting carried away" with ideas and observations. What he dislikes is the self-consciousness and self-congratulation and self-display that go with "discussions." Perhaps he is "defensive" about his lack of a college education. Perhaps he feels "inferior," suffers from a poor "self-image." Sometimes a visitor slides into that way of looking at a person, even as sometimes the person being branded and pinioned comes up with considerably more than the self-justifications he at first seems intent upon offering: "Maybe we should ask ourselves more questions, Doris and me, like you do. I don't have time for questions; and neither does my wife. Mind you, I'm not objecting to yours. They're not bad questions. I'll have to admit, there'll be a few seconds here and there when I'll put them to myself. I'll say, Joe, what's it all about, and why in hell kill yourself at two jobs? I'll ask myself what I want out of life. My dad, he'd do the same, I can remember."

He can indeed remember. At forty-three he can remember the thirties, remember his father's vain efforts to find work. He can remember those three letters, WPA; he can remember being punished, shouted at, and grabbed and shouted at some more, because he dropped an ice-cream cone. Did he know what a nickel meant, or a dime? Did he know how few of them there are, how hard they are to come by? Now, his youngest son has a toolbox, and once in a while tries to pound a nail through a nickel or a dime, or even a quarter. The father gets a little nervous about such activities, but soon his apprehension gives way to those memories — to an amused, relaxed moment of recall. Indeed, it is just such ironies, both personal and historic, that get him going. And that is how he often does get going, with an ironic disclaimer: "I don't want to go on and on about the depression. My dad will do that at the drop of a hat. We've never had another one so bad since the Second World War started, so I don't believe we're in danger. But you can't forget, even if you were only a kid then. When my kids start complaining, I tell them they should know what their grandfather went through. I start telling them what it was like in America then; but they don't take in what you say. They listen, don't get me wrong. No child of mine is going to walk away from me when I'm talking. I have them looking right at me. But they think I'm exaggerating. I know they do. My wife says it's because they were born in good times, and that's all they've ever known. Maybe she's right. But even now for the workingman, the average guy, it's no picnic. That's what I really want my kids to know: it's no picnic. Life, it's tough. You have to work and work and work."

Then he adds that he likes work. No, he *loves* work. What would he do without it? He'd be sitting around. He'd go crazy. He'd last maybe a few weeks, then go back and be glad to be back. True, he'd like to get rid of his second job. That's not work, what he does in the evenings — after supper, or on weekends and some holidays. He needs the extra money. The bills have mounted and mounted. Prices are not merely "up"; they are "so high it's a joke, the kind of joke that makes you want to cry." So, he finds "odd jobs," one after the other, but when he talks about them he doesn't talk about his *work*; he refers to the *jobs*, and often enough, the damned jobs.

He can even be heard talking about the "slave time" he spends, and his mind is as quick as anyone else's to pursue that particular image: "You've got to keep ahead of the game, or you drown. The more money you make, the more you spend it, even if you're careful with money; and we are. We've so far kept up, but it's hard. I get odd jobs. I'll work around the clock sometimes, with just a few hours off to nap. I wire a building. I can do plastering and painting. I'm a steam fitter, but I'm handy at anything. A man wants some work on his house and he gets me to do it. He doesn't want to pay high union wages and doesn't want to register every change he makes in his house with the city officials, who'll make him lose his shirt doing unnecessary things — or paying them off. If he could do the work himself, like I can, he wouldn't hire anyone — because he's in the same tight squeeze I'm in, we're all in. But he's a schoolteacher, you see, or he works in an office, and he can't do anything with his hands, so I get the work. I feel bad taking the money from them, I mean it. But I do the job good, real good, and I've got to have the extra money. I get a good salary every week. We live in a real good house. We live as comfortably as anyone could ever want. I work for one of the biggest real estate companies in the city. They keep me going. I'll be in one building, then I move on to the next one. I put in heating systems, fix boilers. I do everything. In the winter there's emergencies, a pipe has frozen, you know. In the summer we get ready for the winter. Even so, with good wages, we can barely keep our heads up over the water. Doris and I, we go wild with those bills. I tell her we've got to stop buying everything. Once I said we're going into the woods and live in a tent and hunt our food and grow it. She said that was fine with her, and I had no argument. So, I laughed; and she did, too.

"No, I guess we're where we are and we have to stay here, and so long as I've got my health, my strength, we'll do all right; we'll get by. The niggers are moving toward us, you know. They're getting big ideas for themselves. I hear they're making more money than ever before. They're pushing on us in the unions. They want to be taken in fast, regardless of what they know. A man in the trades, he's got to prove himself. You can't learn to be a good steam fitter or electrician over-night. But they're pushing for quickie jobs, that's what. I say to hell with them. Let them take their turn, like everyone else. That's another reason to make more money on the side. If we ever had to leave here, because they started coming in, then we could. There are times when I feel like a nigger myself; I'll admit it. I've been going all day, and I'm back at work after supper, and I'll be sweating it with a pipe or a radiator, and I'll say to myself: Joe, you're a goddamn slave, that's what you are; you might as well be picking cotton or something like that. And my face is black, too, from the dirt in the cellar!"

He smiles and moves toward a cup of coffee nearby. He stretches himself on a leather chair, the kind that unfolds in response to the body's willful selective pressure and has the occupant no longer sitting but lying back, "in the perfect position for television." He watches television when he can, and if he were home more he would watch more television. He likes to view sports — football, basketball, hockey. He will watch golf, but not very enthusiastically. He has never played golf. The game is too slow for him, and there is, too, a touch of the fancy in those clubs and the carts and the caps a lot of golfers wear. So he thinks, anyway; and he knows why. His father used to tell him that golf was a rich man's game. He now knows better; even his father knows better. But knowing is not being convinced. In his words: "You can know something, but you can't change the way you feel." (So much for whole textbooks of psychology and psychiatry.)

As a matter of fact, the game of golf can prompt him to reflect. He has a friend who plays golf. The city golf course is crowded, though. In order really to enjoy the game one must belong to a club, have access to a first-rate, uncrowded course. The friend has a friend — his lawyer, in fact — who takes him to a fine country club. Every Saturday morning the two men play golf, then go home and meet again the next Saturday. They don't have lunch afterwards, or breakfast beforehand. They don't talk much to each other. What they have in common is golf, period. And there is a lesson in that. It's hard to "move away from your own kind of people."

Joe and Doris see no reason to make lists of "criteria" that characterize the people they feel comfortable with, or on the contrary don't; but upon occasion they will spell things out rather clearly. Joe will talk about "brainy people." One of his friends has a son who is just studying and studying, not in order to become a doctor or a lawyer (which is fine) but to stay out of the draft (Joe thinks) and "because he's so shy he can't talk to people, so he lives in the library." The subject of libraries and the universities that own them leads to other matters. Joe and Doris want those libraries and universities for their children, and indeed, their oldest son is in his first year of college. But no one can be snobbier, more arrogant and condescending than "a certain kind of professor" or a lot of those "professional students," which mean students who are not content to study and to learn, but make nuisances of themselves, flaunt themselves before the public, disrupt things, behave like fools. He gets angry as he gets further into the discussion, but his wife slows him down, and even manages to cause a partial reversal of his views. After all, she insists, he is always complaining about certain things that are wrong with the country. He is always saying that the rich are getting richer, and the ordinary man, he can barely keep up with himself. Someone has to do more than complain; someone has to say unpopular things. Doris herself does so, says unpopular things, at least at certain times — though only to her husband, when they are having a talk. And soon Joe switches, says maybe, says yes, says it is true that some of the students are good, mean well, are on the workingman's side against the big corporations.

They don't like those big corporations; Joe and Doris don't, and their neighbors don't. If the students are at different times called vulgar, wild, crazy, insulting, and obscene, the corporations are declared clever, wily, treacherous, dishonest, and powerful beyond belief. Doris believes in "balancing things," and she believes in keeping her cool. She wants her husband, also, to have a certain distance on events. When he takes after college students, she reminds him that they have one in the family, hope to have more in the family as the years go by. And she brings up the corporations, and the way they "behave." They are decorous and restrained, but in Doris's mind they are no less outrageous than "the bad element" among the students, the ones who "look so awful" and make her and everyone she knows feel uncomfortable and puzzled and really, at a loss.

After a while one can see that Doris and Joe are just that: at a loss to figure certain things out, at a loss to know how their own various opinions can ever become reconciled into some consistent, believable and coherent viewpoint. To some extent, they well know, the task is hopeless, because like the proudest, most knowing social critic, they are thoroughly aware of the ambiguities and ironies they, we, everyone must face: "I try to slow Joe down. He'll be watching the news, and he shouts at the demonstrators, you know. He doesn't like the colored very much. He says they're pushing too hard on the rest of us. I agree, but I think we ought to be careful, because the children will hear, and they'll repeat what they listen to us saying in Sunday School, and that's no good. Our son wants to be an engineer. He is in college. He is a sensible boy. He'll never be a radical or a militant. But he tells his father to go easy, and I agree. Where I go wild is on prices. They go up and up and no one seems to want to stop them. I voted Republican for the first time last year, because I thought they'd do something. But they're like the Democrats. They're all the same. They're all a bunch of politicians, every one of them. Joe says I'm as nutty when I talk about politicians and the prices in the supermarket as he is when he talks about the colored and the college students.

"There are times when I wonder who really runs this country. It's not people like us, that I know. We vote, we do what we're supposed to do and we go fight in the wars — I lost a brother in the Second World War and a cousin in the Korean War, and I hope to God my son doesn't end up in Vietnam, like my nephew, his cousin — but we don't get any place for being good citizens. There are some big people, in Washington I guess, and they make all the decisions; and then it's left for us to go and send our boys to fight, and try to pay the high prices that the politicians have caused us to have. Don't ask me more. I don't know who the big people are. But it's a clique. They own the stocks in the banks and the corporations. It's up to them, what the country does. We get these letters from our congressmen, that he sends around, and it's just a lot of talk. Why, even my thirteen-year-old daughter knows better. She read the newsletter and she said he was just talking out of both sides of his mouth. Well, I went up and hugged and kissed her. I put my name on a list at the supermarket, protesting high prices. I guess that's how he got my name in the first place, that congressman. To tell the truth, I don't remember his name, and I don't want to."

Not that she or her husband spend much time talking about such frustrating, mystifying and upsetting issues. By and large they shun what Doris calls "current events." There is more than enough to do from day to day. Joe works almost all the time. Doris does, too. She has four children to look after. She has a house to keep clean, very clean. She has her aged mother to visit, who lives nearby with Doris's older sister. And then of late Doris has also had to find work. She doesn't "always" work, but she "helps out" at a luncheonette for two hours, eleven to one, five days a week. Her husband did not want her to do so, but she insisted, and she got her way. She rather likes the work, serving the crowded tables. She gets a view of the outside world. She meets people. She hears people talk, and she learns what is on their minds. She makes a few dollars. She feels more independent. She feels that time goes by more quickly. And much as she dislikes talking about all the world's problems, she finds herself listening rather intently to what others have to say about those problems: "I can't help it. I'll be coming over to a table with food, and serving it, and I'll hear them, the men on their lunch hour, and the women, too. They all talk the same way, when you come right down to it. They're worried about where the country is going. Yesterday I waited on a man who lost his son in Vietnam. You know how I know? I heard him telling his friend that the boy died so we could be safe over here. I'm sure he's right. I couldn't help wondering what I'd say if it happened to me, if I lost my son. I guess I'd say what he did, that man. My husband says there's nothing else you *can* say. You have to believe your own government. I mean, if you start turning on your own country, then what have you got left? The answer is nothing, I guess.

"I don't think the country is being run the way it should be. Don't ask me how I'd do better, but everyone I know agrees we're in trouble: boys dying every day over there in the jungle, and here the criminals taking over. There's the big gangsters, the Mafia, and there's the demonstrators, and downtown there's the colored — little boys, no more than ten or twelve a lot of them, looking for things to steal. I've seen them steal in the department stores. They knock down women and run away with their pocketbooks. I don't even carry one any more when I go shopping in town. And I only go there to do holiday shopping, because most of the stores have branches out in our plaza. Why don't the students and the college people demonstrate against the criminals? My sister-in-law was knocked down by three colored boys.

They had a knife! They said they'd kill her. They took her pocketbook and ran. And you hear the Negro people asking for more, more, more!"

She would go so far and no further. She would never use the word "nigger." Her husband does, all the time he does; but when he goes further, starts cussing and swearing, starts sending people to hell, starts making sweeping, utterly unqualified judgments, she tries to stop him, and usually manages to succeed. She even gets him to reverse himself somewhat — which means, she gets him to say a number of *other* things he believes. For example, he believes that at birth "we're all just about the same," and he believes "it's the education a child gets that makes the difference," and he believes that "if a child is born poor and he doesn't get good food, then he's going to pay for it later."

As a matter of fact when he is feeling reflective and not pushed into a liberal corner by anyone, Joe will come up with some rather strong-minded rebuttals of his own assertions: "I can see how the niggers feel cheated out of things. If I was a Negro, I'd be madder than hell. I'd stand up to anyone who tried to keep me away from my share. We have a couple of them, carpenters, working with us on the job now. They're the best guys you could want. They work hard, and they're smart. They speak good, as good as anyone I know. If all the Negro people were like those two, then I can't believe we'd be having the trouble we are. A man is a man, that's what I believe; I don't care what his skin color is, or where he goes to church. This country has every kind of people in it; and it's all to the good, because that way no one group runs the show. The thing that bothers me about the Negro people is this: they're not like the rest of us, and I don't mean because their skin is a different color. I drive through their neighborhood. I've worked in the buildings where they live. I'd be working on the pipes and I'd hear them from another apartment or down in the cellar. (The sound carries!) If you ask me, they're slow, that's what I think. They're out for a good time. They want things made easy for them — maybe not all of them, but plenty of them. They actually want relief. They think they're entitled to it!"

He stops. He lifts his head up, ever so slightly but noticeably nevertheless, and significantly. He is about to reminisce. After several years of visiting his home and getting to know him and his family, one can anticipate at least that much, the several directions his mind will pursue, if not the particular message he will deliver on a given day. So, he takes a slightly longer swallow of beer, and waits a few seconds, as if to pull them all together, all his memories. And then he is on his way: "I remember my father, how it killed him to take money from the government, the WPA, you know. I remember him crying. He said he wished he was never born, because it's not right that a man shouldn't be able to earn a living for his family. He could have stayed on relief longer, but he got off as fast as he could. He hated every day he didn't work. I guess they made some work for people, the WPA did; but no one was fooled, because it was phony work. When a man really wants to do something, and instead he's raking leaves and like that, he's even worse off than sitting on his porch all day — except that without the money, I guess we all would have starved to death.

"Now with the niggers it's different. They want all they can get — for free. They don't really like to work. They do work, a lot of them, I know. But it's against their wish, I believe. They seem to have the idea that they're entitled to something from the rest of us. That's the big thing with them: they've suffered, and we should cry our heads off and give them the country, lock, stock and barrel, because we've been bad to them, white people were. I have friends, a lot of them; and let me tell you, not one of them goes along with that way of thinking. You know why? It's an insult, it's an insult to you and me and everyone, including the niggers themselves. If I was a Negro, and someone came up to me and told me how sorry he was — sorry for what he'd done, his people had, and sorry for the Negro people — I'd tell him to get away fast, real fast, if he wanted to keep his good health. Pity is for the weak; my grandfather used to tell us kids that. But your niggers, a lot of them want pity; and they get it. You know who gives it to them? The rich ones out in the fancy suburbs, they're the ones — the bleeding hearts, always ready to pat people on the head and say you're wonderful, and we love you, and just sit back, we'll take care of you, with welfare and the rest, just like we do with our pet dogs."

There is more, much more. He fires himself up as he gets deeper and deeper into the subject, the issue, the argument he is setting forth. He reaches for more beer, and his wife gets slightly worried, then obviously nervous, then somewhat alarmed. She wants him to stop. She wants us to change the subject. She doesn't necessarily disagree with the thrust of his remarks; but the more he speaks, the longer the exposition, the more explicit the references and criticisms and illustrative examples, the more uncomfortable she feels. Why? What bothers her about her husband's ideas? He asks her that. She has told him that he is getting "carried away." He says yes, he is getting carried away with the truth, and if that is wrong, it is also rare "in this country, today." He invokes the "credibility gap." He reminds us that politicians and businessmen tell lies all the time. He insists that "a lot of very proper types" delude themselves and fool others. It is hard to be honest, and for that reason most of us shirk saying what we know "in our hearts" is true. People are afraid to speak out, say certain things, because they know they'll be called "prejudiced," and in fact they are not at all that; rather they are "letting the chips fall where they do."

But yes, he goes on to acknowledge, she is right, his wife; she always is, as a matter of fact. What is the point of working oneself up into a virtual frenzy over people who themselves never let anything really trouble them? In his own words and manner he says that he actually rather accepts his wife's disapproval — and anticipates exactly why she "really" was made anxious: "She doesn't want the kids to hear that kind of talk. They admire this minister, and he's always worrying out loud over someone, or some problem." Joe dislikes all those sermons; they make him feel uncomfortable, accused, a criminal of sorts. The minister can talk as he wishes, and if need be, move on to another church; whereas people like Joe and Doris have to stay — or so Joe feels. And anyway, ministers have a way of making things much too simple and stark and apocalyptic: "To hear him talk on Sunday, you'd think we were on the verge of ruin, America, unless we solve every problem we have and especially the race problem. He's got the Negro people on his brain, our minister. He must dream about them every night. He says we're to blame, the white people, for all that's happened. I went up once after the sermon and asked him what I've done that's to blame. He said he didn't mean any one person, just the whole white world. I didn't know how I could answer him. I said I'd never want to hurt a Negro, all I wanted was for them to leave me alone and I'd leave them alone. But that got him going again, and I pretended that I had to leave, because we had to be somewhere. On the way home I told Doris I'm ready to start shopping for a new church, but she and the children like him, the minister. They say he's 'dynamic.' He either makes me mad or puts me to sleep. So you see, we don't agree on *everything* in this house."

Joe is at times envious. His sister is married to a schoolteacher who is a Catholic. In the Catholic Church, he believes, one is spared those sermons. In the Catholic Church one goes for mass, for communion, not to be lectured at over and over again. But his sister and brother-in-law disagree. They have also had to sit through sermons, and they have their misgivings about the direction the church is taking. Here is what his sister says: "It's not any one church, it's them all. I listen to my neighbors talk. A lot of church people are always scolding the ordinary man. If you ask me, the rich people and the college professors have too much influence with the cardinal. Even the Catholic Church can be pushed around. All of a sudden, these last few years, we've been hearing these letters from him, the cardinal. He tells us this is wrong and that is wrong, and it seems all he has on his mind is the colored people. I'm sick and tired of them and their complaining. And they've stirred up everyone; my husband tells me the children in junior high school are 'organizing.' That's what they call it. They have 'grievances,' and they want to talk about them with the teachers and the principal. I'd give them the back of my hand. I'd read them the riot act. But no, the principal is afraid that if they get 'too strict,' the teachers, then the kids will get even more aroused, and there will be more trouble. Can you imagine that? And he's talking with them — hour after hour, I hear.

"There's something wrong, that's what I say; and it all started with this civil rights business, the demonstrations, and then the college radicals and on and on. It used to be that you could go to church and pray for your family and country. Now they're worried about colored people and you even get the feeling they care more about the enemy, the people killing our boys in Vietnam, than our own soldiers. And the schools, the radicals and the colored are both trying to destroy the schools — I mean, take them over, that's what. They don't like what's being taught, and they don't like the teachers, and a day doesn't go by that they don't have something bad to say, or a new threat for us to hear. My husband says he'd quit tomorrow if he didn't have so much seniority, and if he could get another job. It's pretty bad for you these days if you're just a law-abiding, loyal American and you believe in your country, and in people being happy with their own kind, and doing their best to keep us the first in the world. And, God forbid, if you say we need to keep the streets safe, and stop those riots and marches, then the priest will pull you aside and tell you that you don't 'understand.' But I do, that's the point. I understand what's happening. We're losing our freedom. We can't be ourselves anymore. There are those that want to change the country completely. They are dictators. A lot of priests are with us; but some have been fooled, and two of them are in our parish, I'll tell you."

There are differences, of course, in the two families. A teacher is not a steam fitter. Once the teacher felt himself "higher," a man of education, a man who wears a suit to work. Now the teacher feels hard pressed and bitter. His salary has for a decade been inadequate, and for half a decade he has had to work in the evenings and on weekends, even as his brother-in-law does. The high school children seem harder to control. The educational critics are constantly saying bad things about people like him, or so he feels. And everyone's sympathy seems to go elsewhere: "The priests, a lot of them feel sorry for the Negroes and the North Vietnamese. The college students love Asians and Africans, love to go work in the ghetto. Their professors keep on saying how bad our schools are. College professors make three and four times what we do, and they have the nerve to say we're not 'motivated' enough, and we don't teach the way we should. They can cry with sympathy for some insolent, fresh-talking Negro demonstrator, who wants the world delivered into his hands within twenty-four hours, but if we even try to explain our problems, they start telling us how wrong we are, and how we need to learn how to be 'open' with the children, and 'accepting,' and how we are 'rigid' and 'prejudiced,' and everthing bad. I've heard them on television.

"No one asks people like me to be on television. I'm a teacher, but no educational television people come and ask me my opinion. They get these writers and 'experts' and let them say one bad thing after the other, and we're supposed to say: that's right, that's absolutely right. Not one of them impresses me as anything but a sensationalist. They love tearing things down. And you know who eats it all up, don't you: the intellectuals, the rich people out in the suburbs, the people who send their children to private schools, and then say it's awful, how we're treating the Negroes, and not keeping up with all those 'progressive' ideas, which (mind you) change every other year."

One can, of course, go on and on with tape-recorded conversations such as these, toned down here, edited there, abbreviated necessarily. One can call upon a bank teller or a barber or a repairman for the telephone company or a truck driver or a man who works in a large factory or a man who works in a small warehouse. One can call upon the electricians and carpenters who work with Joe, or other teachers who work with his brother-in-law in a high school. And then, there are clerks, accountants, salesmen, bus drivers, firemen, and policemen. If an observer wants to lump them all together, millions and millions of men, women and children, he can resort to labels and phrases, some of them more traditional than others. For a long time there have been "blue-collar workers" and "white-collar workers"; and there has been the "lower middle class." More than any other expression, though, the people themselves (as we have mentioned) like to use "ordinary man" or "average American" or "plain person." Again and again one hears those words, all the time spoken with pride and conviction and a touch of sadness, a touch of worry — as if the country has not learned to appreciate such people, and maybe even makes them pay for the sins of others, pay with their lives, their savings, their energies. And they have indeed paid. They have seen their savings mean less, or disappear, as inflation gets worse and worse. They have had to take second jobs to keep up with prices. They have sent their sons abroad, and thousands of them have died — all of which an observer knows and reads and repeats to himself from time to time and then is likely to forget.

Is it, then, a certain vulnerability that they share, those "ordinary people"? Are they best thought of as socially insecure, economically marginal, politically unorganized, hence weak? Ought we be talking about millions and millions of people in such a way; that is, do they all lend themselves to the generalizations that social scientists, journalists and politicians persist in using? Needless to say, statistics and indices of one kind or another certainly do tell a lot; they quite precisely tell us how much money comes into homes, much is spent and by whom — that is, people employed where and of what educational "level" or background. But again, one must ask whether expressions like "social class" quite explain what it is that so many Americans have in common when they call themselves "ordinary." Money is part of the answer; they have some, enough to get by, *just* get by, *barely* get by, *fairly* comfortably get by. (Qualifications like "just" or "barely" or "fairly" are always there and say a good deal.) But there are other things that matter to people. How much schooling did I get? How much do I wish I'd had? How much do I want for my children? What kind of work do I do, apart from the money I make, and what kind would I like to do? Where do I live? Where would I prefer to live, if I could have my choice? Which church do I attend? How do I like to dress? And finally, do I feel at ease about my life and my future, even though I live in a good, strong house, well supplied with gadgets and appliances on the inside and surrounded by a nicely tended lawn on the outside?

Suburbia and the American Dream

Bennett M. Berger

Americans have never been other than ambivalent in their commitment to cultural variety, as against their longing for cultural uniformity. Today, this ambivalence is becoming a central concern of public policy. For, as urban planning becomes an increasingly visible and legitimate part of the activity of the public sector, its power will grow to support or to undermine cultural diversity in the traditional seat of that diversity — the cities. Like the myth of a homogeneous "suburbia," which for a long time obscured, and to some extent still obscures, the actual variety of suburban life, complacence about the cultural diversity of cities may blind us to the conditions which sustain it. My aim in this essay is to take what I and others have learned about the variety of suburban styles of life, and to relate this knowledge, first to some of the more pervasive pluralisms of American culture, and then to a few of the problems of planning for urban diversity.

THE PERSISTENCE OF THE MYTH OF SUBURBIA

Some years back, I undertook a study (reported in *Working-Class Suburb*, Univ. of Calif. Press, 1960) in order to observe the transformation of a group of automobile assembly line workers into the "suburbanities" who had become stock figures in American popular culture in the 1950's through the satirical and other efforts of a variety of popular magazines. It seemed to me that, having found a working

From **Bennett M. Berger**, "Suburbia and the American Dream," in *The Public Interest*, No. 2 (Winter 1966). Copyright © National Affairs, Inc., 1966. Reprinted by permission, pp. 80—91.

class population more than two years settled in a new suburb, I was provided with an almost natural experimental setting in which to document the processes through which "suburbia" exercised its profound and diffuse influence in transforming a group of poorly educated factory workers into those model middle-class Americans obsessed with the problems of crab-grass and "conformity."

Well, it is now a matter of public record that my basic assumption was wrong. As the interview evidence piled up, it became clearer and clearer that the lives of the suburbanites I was studying had not been profoundly affected in any statistically identifiable or sociologically interesting way. They were still overwhelmingly Democrats; they attended church as infrequently as they ever did; like most working class people, their informal contacts were limited largely to kin; they neither gave nor went to parties; on the whole they had no great hopes of getting ahead in their jobs; and instead of a transient psychology, most of them harbored a view of their new suburban homes as paradise permanently gained.

But (appropriately enough for a Ph.D. candidate) I was cautious in the general inferences I drew from that study. It was, after all, based only on a small sample, of one suburb, of one metropolitan area, in one region, and it suffered from all of the methodological limitations inherent in small case studies. None of my findings gave me any reason to doubt the truth of what William H. Whyte, for example, had said of his organization men; but it also seemed to me that there was little reason *not* to believe that my findings in San Jose would be repeatedly confirmed in many of the less expensive suburbs around the country whose houses were priced well within the means of unionized workers in heavy industry, and of lower white collar employees as well. I did, in short, question the right of others to generalize freely about suburbia on the basis of very few studies of selected suburbs which happened to be homogeneously middle or upper class in character — especially when it seemed apparent that suburban housing was increasingly available to all but the lowest income levels and status groups.

The considerable bulk of research that has been done on suburbs in the years since I did my work has given me no reason to alter the conclusions I drew then. Indeed, none of this research can be expected to give much comfort to those who find it convenient to believe that a suburb exercises some mysterious power over its residents, transforming them into replicas of Whyte's practitioners of "The Outgoing Life." There seems to be increasing consensus among students of suburbia that suburban development is simply the latest phase of a process of urban growth that has been going on for a long time, that the cultural character of suburbs varies widely in terms of the social make-up of its residents, and of the personal and group dispositions that led them to move to suburbs in the first place; that the variety of physical and demographic differences between cities and suburbs (and there *are* some) bears little significance for the way of life of their inhabitants, and that some of these differences, although statistically accurate, are sociologically spurious, since the appropriate comparisons are not between residential suburbs and cities as wholes, but between suburbs and urban residential neighborhoods. In general, the reported changes in the lives of suburbanities were not *caused* by the move to suburbia, but were reasons for moving there in the first place. In suburbs, as in city apartments, social class, the age-composition of residents, the age of the neighborhood, etc., are much more profound predictors of the style of life than is residential location with respect to the city limits. Analysis of national samples has provided confirmation neither of a trend to Republicanism in politics nor a return to religion. Suburbs, in short, seem — as Reissman and Ktsanes have characterized them — to be "new homes for old values."

It appears, then, that there are no grounds for believing that suburbia has created a distinctive style of life or a new social character for Americans. Yet the myth of suburbia persists, as is evident from the fact that it is still eminently discussable over the whole range of our cultural media, from comic books to learned journals. One should not be surprised at this, for myths are seldom dispelled by research; they have going for them something considerably more powerful than mere evidence. And though nothing I say here can change this fact, it may give us some comfort to understand the sources of the myth, the functions it performs for the groups by whom it is sustained, and the nature of its appeal to America's image of itself.

In my book, and then, again, later in an article, I undertook a functional explanation of the myth of suburbia. I pointed first to the fact that suburbs were rich with ready made visible symbols: patios and barbecues, lawnmowers and tricycles, shopping centers, station wagons, and so on, and that such symbols were readily organizable into an image of a way of life that could be marketed to the non-suburban public. I also pointed out that this marketing was facilitated by the odd fact that the myth of suburbia conveniently suited the ideo-logical purposes of several influential groups who market social and political opinion — odd because these groups could usually be found disagreeing with each other, not only about matters of opinion, but about matters of fact as well. Realtor-chamber-of-commerce interests and the range of opinion represented by the Luce magazines could use the myth of suburbia to affirm the American Way of Life; city planners, architects, urban design people and so on could use the myth of suburbia to warn that those agglomerations of standardized, vulgarized, mass-produced cheerfulness which masqueraded as homes would be the slums of tomorrow. Liberal and left-wing culture-critics could (and did) use the myth of suburbia to launch an attack on complacency, conformity, and mass culture, and found in this myth an up-to-date polemical vocabulary with which to rebuke the whole slick tenor of American life: what used to be disdained as "bourgeois" was now simply designated as "suburban." In short, the *descriptive* accuracy of the myth of suburbia went largely unchallenged because it suited the *prescriptive* desires of such a wide variety of opinion, from the yea-sayers of the right to the agonizers of the center to the nay-sayers of the left.

But though I still think this analysis of the myth makes good sense, I think too that there is something more — something, if I may be permitted to say so, deeper, profounder, and which I was only dimly aware of then. I think now that the myth can be understood also as our society's most recent attempt to come to terms with the melting pot problem, a problem that goes straight to the heart of American ambivalence about cultural pluralism.

CULTURAL PLURALISM AND THE MELTING POT

America has never really come to terms with the legend of the melting pot. That legend, if I may quote the windy text of its original source, saw America as the place where "Celt and Latin, Slav and Teuton, Greek and Syrian, Black and Yellow, Jew and Gentile, the palm and the pine, the pole and the equator, the crescent and the cross" would together build "the Republic of Man and the Kingdom of God." Despite the hope that a unified American culture might emerge from the seething cauldron, it didn't happen; instead, the formation of ethnically homogeneous communities — ghettoes — helped the immigrants preserve large segments of their cultures, and the tendency to endogamy helped them preserve it beyond the first generation. But in spite of the evident facts of our cultural pluralism (by which I mean the persisting correlation of significant differences in values and behavior with ethnic, regional, and social class differences), attempts are continually made to create an image of *the* typical or representative or genuine American and his community. These attempts have usually succeeded only in creating stereotypes — most familiarly, perhaps, a caricature of one or another variety of Our Town: white, anglo-saxon, Protestant, and middle class. *Saturday Evening Post* covers, white picket fences, colonial houses, maple hutches and the like have historically played an important role in such attempts. *The myth of suburbia is the latest attempt to render America in this homogeneous manner*, to see in the highly visible and proliferating suburban developments a new melting pot which would receive the diverse elements of a new generation from a society fragmented by class, region, religion, and ethnicity, and from them create *the* American style of life. Suburbia as America is no more false a picture, probably, than Babbitt or Our Town as America; but it fails as a melting pot for the same reason that the original melting pot idea failed: like many other urban neighborhoods, specific suburbs developed a tendency to homogeneity, almost always in terms of social class and very often in terms of ethnicity.

The myth of American cultural homogeneity and the stubborn fact of heterogeneity reflect a persistent ambivalence in American society regarding cultural unity and diversity, between the melting pot idea and the pluralist idea. During and after the period of rapid immigration into the "teeming cities," for example, free public education expressed the need for some minimum "Americanization," whereas the ghetto expressed the impulse to cultural self-preservation (both by the natives who excluded and the immigrants who segregated themselves). In the rest of the country, 4th of July style patriotic rhetoric expressed the gropings toward an elementary national identity, whereas provincial arrogance — and hostility to "the government" and to centers of cosmopolitan influence — expressed the affirmation of narrow local autonomies. The ambivalence was really a double ambivalence; each polar position was itself unstable: to be truly tenable, a pluralist ideology must accord intrinsic honor and value to a diversity of life styles, and this it has never completely done. The salient features of minority subcultural styles have more often than not been regarded as stigmata by dominant groups, tolerable so long as they were temporary, that is, *transitional* to something approaching the dominant cultural style. On the other hand, the attempts of provincial, nativist ("WASP") groups to secure their own style as *the* American style stopped short of supporting the emergence of broadly inclusive *national* institutions which would have facilitated that transition. The most enthusiastic celebrators of "Americanism" were precisely the groups who were most wary of integrating the varieties of the national life into a unified culture.

Indeed, a unified national culture has until quite recently been a most improbable prospect, since the United States has traditionally been a society without very powerful national institutions with which to promote that unity and pass it on down the generations. Without an established church or a powerful federal government, without national political parties or a standardized educational system, enormous distances and poor communications enabled local economies to breed a highly differentiated system of *native* subcultures — in addition to those created by the immigrants. Even today, there are probably dozens of distinctive American types, to some extent stereotypes, perhaps, but which nevertheless call attention to the wide variety of *native* styles: Vermont farmers and Boston Brahmins, Southern Bourbons and Tennessee hillbillies, Beatniks and organization men, Plainvillers, Middletowners, and cosmopolitan intellectuals, to say nothing of teenagers, the jet set, and many, many more, all American, all different, and none probably very eager to be integrated into an idea of "*the* American" at a level of complexity suitable for a *Time* cover story or a patriotic war movie.

It is not surprising, then, that when one tries to abstract from American life a system of values which can be called distinctively or representatively American, the task is immensely difficult. The most systematic attempt by a sociologist, that of Robin Williams in his book *American Society*, is foiled by the fact that important groups in American society do not share the 15 or 16 values which he offers as basically American. There is no question that values such as "achievement," "work," "efficiency," "equality," and the rest have played a significant role in creating the quality of American life, but important parts of the lower and working classes (important because of their numbers) do not share them, and important parts of the upper class (important because of their influence) do not share them — although they may affirm them when a journalist is nearby.

MYTHS AND STYLES OF LIFE

The persistent attempts to find some transcendent principles or values which define the unity of American culture have been defeated by the persistence of important class and ethnic differences. Even under natural or "organic" conditions, then, "American" patterns of culture are enormously difficult to describe with any accuracy. This difficulty is exacerbated when a society becomes sophisticated enough to be self conscious about its culture and rich enough to do something about it. The maturity and the luxury of our civilization constrain its elites to define an "American" style, and the miracle of our technology arms us to manufacture it. Our society is wealthy enough to support a substantial class of intellectuals devoted to staying on top of contemporary events to "spot the trend," "see the pattern," "find the meaning," "discover the style." And our media are such that these spottings and seeings are more or less instantaneously communicated to audiences of millions, whose demand upon the marketers of opinions and interpretations for sensible and coherent syntheses is greater than the available supply. Under such conditions, we do not get serious historical interpretation of contemporary events; we do not even get responsible journalism; we get myths, which themselves become part of the forces shaping what is happening, and which hence function ideologically. The myth of suburbia fosters an image of a homogeneous and classless America without a trace of ethnicity but fully equipped for happiness by the marvelous productivity of American industry: the ranch house with the occupied two-car garage, the refrigerator and freezer, the washer and dryer, the garbage disposal and the built-in range and dishwasher, the color TV and the hi-fi stereo. Suburbia: its lawns trim, its driveways clean, its children happy on its curving streets and in its pastel schools. Suburbia, California style, is America.

Most American intellectuals have sustained this myth in order to hate it; but the bases of their antipathy have never really been made clear. Somehow associated with these physical symbols of suburbia in the minds of most intellectuals are complacency, smugness, conformity, status anxiety, and all the rest of the by now familiar and dreary catalogue of suburban culture. But the causal connection between the physical character and the alleged cultural style of suburbia has never been clearly established. It is almost as if American intellectuals felt, like some severe old Calvinist prophet, that physical comfort necessarily meant intellectual sloth. Perhaps it is because we have been too well trained to believe that there is somehow a direct relationship between the physical structure or the esthetic shape of a residential environment and the sort of values and culture it can possibly engender — so that the esthetic monotony of suburbia could house nothing but a generation of dull, monotonous people, and its cheerful poverty of architectural design could breed nothing but a race of happy robots. The only trouble with this view is that there is little evidence and less logic to support it. Most of the adult suburbanites were *urban* bred, and hence presumably already shaped by the time they became surburbanites. And although it is still a little too early to tell what kind of culture will be produced by the generation bred in the manufactured environment of suburbia, we might remember that the generation bred in the endless and prison-like New York tenements did not do badly.

But becoming aware of the myth of suburbia, and pointing to the disparities between it and what we actually know of suburbs we have closely studied, should not be confused with a *defense* of suburbia. Nor should anything I have said about the critics of suburbia be interpreted as an expression of my personal bias in favor of suburbia. As I suggested earlier, myths are potent enough to survive evidence; they are not disarmed by understanding. Quite the contrary. Once myths gain currency, once they go, as we say, "into the cultural air," they *become real*, and function frequently as self-fulfilling prophecies. Life copies literature; fact is affected by fiction; history is constrained by myth. "If a situation is defined as real," said William I. Thomas, "it is real in its consequences," and I have no doubt (though I have no data) that family decisions regarding whether to move to the suburbs have been affected (both pro and con) by the myth of suburbia. And despite everything reasonable I have said about suburbs, I *know* that the fact that I unreasonably dislike them has been conditioned, *beyond the possibility of redemption by mere research*, by the very myth of suburbia I have helped explode.

In the sense in which I have been speaking of them, myths are more or less noble fictions; fictions in that they are *made*, and noble depending on the art with which they are made, the extent to which one is in favor of the consequences they foster, and, most particularly, the forms of solidarity they promote. In the context of the debate over "suburbia," what is usually at stake is whose version of America shall become "American."

PLURALISM AND PLANNING

Whose shall? I want to suggest that the question is relevant to the way in which the future quality of urban life is planned. Like Emile Durkheim, who suggested that the punishment of crime was significant less as a deterrent or as simple revenge than as a collective re-affirmation of cultural values, I want to suggest that we look more closely at the images of solidarity which inform the proposals for dealing with social problems in general, and with urban problems in particular. For social problems, of course, have no objective existence — although the facts to which they refer may. It is objectively true that some people have always lived in dilapidated, unsafe, unheated, vermin-infested residences, but "slums" have not always been a social problem. Slums become a social problem when a large enough group of important people decide that poor people ought not to live in such places.

Americans have a propensity to find social problems. By defining them as real and hence setting ameliorative forces into action, we affirm our liberal heritage. To find problems, to mobilize opinion about them, to shake our social structure by its metaphorical shoulders and force it to *pay attention* to these matters, nourishes our beliefs in progress and perfectibility. America is a country dedicated to the propositions that no evils are ineradicable, no problems insoluble, no recalcitrance beyond conciliation, no ending need be unhappy; we are a most un-Greek democracy. Finding and dealing with problems, then, are necessary conditions for the verification of these propositions; the very existence of social problems to ameliorate, reaffirms our principles more than any imaginable utopia could. But not just any problems at any time. Because at any given moment there is an indefinitely large number of social problems which are theoretically identifiable, public concern with some (to the exclusion of others) can be understood not only in terms of the salience of the difficulties of those who *have* the problems but also in terms of the relevance of proposed solutions to the dominant forms and rhetoric of solidarity.

When we set out to improve the quality of urban life, what we are most likely to be doing is altering the conditions under which weak and vulnerable sections of the population live. The wealthy, who also have problems, are protected from the welfare impulses of others. The strong and the autonomous grant no one the right to alter the conditions of their lives — that is what strength and autonomy are about. Public concern over, and desire to plan for, "the problem of" the increasing proportions of aged persons in our society, for example, do not extend to Dwight Eisenhower, Harry Truman, or H. L. Hunt, all of whom qualify for the statistical category "aged," but not for our image of those who need help — although, if consulted, I might have several suggestions as to how they might spend their declining years more wholesomely. The people who have the problems which are defined as "real" are those who are vulnerable to public action, and thus to the implicit images of solidarity which underlie that action. I think it is essential that we be very clear about these images, for to plan for the *quality* of urban life is to be concerned with the *culture* of urban life, and hence with the forms of human solidarity which planning is likely both to foster and discourage.

I see three broad alternatives for those who are confronted with the problem of planning the quality of urban life. First of all, planners can simply abdicate from any concern for the cultural consequences of what they do, and instead interpret their mandate narrowly — for example, the improvement of the physical environment for the poorly housed. To the extent that they have been planned at all, most new, inexpensive suburbs have been developed in this way — with occasional exceptions, as in the gestures by the Levittowns toward the provision of some institutional facilities. More centrally located urban residential development for the poor and the less-than-affluent has also been dominated by considerations such as square footage, hygiene, and domestic technology. Now to provide room, cleanliness, comfort, and convenience to people who have previously been without them is an important achievement; but it is not planning for the quality of urban life. Quite the contrary; the *quality* of urban life is precisely what is usually left out of consideration — perhaps as a luxury rendered expendable by the need to bring large numbers of people up to some minimum physical standard. Under these conditions of planning, images of human solidarity seem limited exclusively to *households* within which *family* solidarity may be symbolized by culinary and recreational technology (refrigerators, freezers, barbecues, TVs, etc.), whereas solidarities beyond that of the family and household seem irrelevant, alien, or distant. There is a sense in which this alternative is evasive because such planning *does* engender a quality in urban life, but it is the quality that most cultivated foreign observers complain about in most American cities.

Planning's second alternative, it seems to me, is to make a conscious effort to alter the environments of certain groups, with the overt intention of bringing their culture closer to some monolithic or homogeneous ideal. Presumably, this would be some more advanced version of the melting pot idea, in which either a bureaucratic or entre-preneurial version of a middle class life-style would be given as an ideal toward which the poor should be encouraged to reach. Here the aim would be to make the society more monolithically what it already dominantly is. This alternative founders on its utopianism, on its assumption that a cultural consensus can be engineered or induced in a society in which conflict is endemic and which will remain so as long as the interests of groups and classes remain opposed. In the absence of any ability by planners to wipe out class differences, we must expect, in any multi-class community, controversy not only over the appropriate means to reach agreed-upon goals but over the goals themselves and the priorities to be assigned to them. This is the stuff of politics and culture, and where interests and norms are rooted in a class-based style of life, the attempt by one group to elicit the commit-ment of the entire community to a specific goal will very likely threaten another group and elicit its opposition. Moreover, these political and cultural diversities have a right to exist and persist. We can be reasonably sure that the vulnerable and dependent groups most readily affected by planning would gladly be rid of their slums, their poverty, and the discrimination against them. Beyond this it is difficult to assume anything with great assurance except, perhaps, that groups develop an attachment to those aspects of their culture which have not been imposed by necessity, an attachment made evident by their tendency to take the culture with them when they move from one environment to another, and to preserve whatever of it that circumstances permit. On the other hand, utopian planning dominated by visions of profound cultural changes is always interest-ing, and such planners might well devote more energy to making these visionary ideals manifest and rhetorically vivid, if only in order to help others to know whether to be for or against the form of solidarity they envision.

THE PLURALIST ALTERNATIVE

Finally, there is the pluralist alternative, an alternative perhaps best expressed in the recent work of Herbert Gans, and, to a lesser extent, of Jane Jacobs. Whatever reservations one may have about the work of either, each of them projects an unambiguous image of the kind of human solidarity they would like to see fostered by urban planning. This solidarity is loose and heterogeneous, composed of more or less autonomous groups and neighborhoods formed on the basis of ethnicity and social class; communities attached, perhaps, to the notion that good fences make good neighbors, but necessarily related to one another through those political and economic accommodations long characteristic of urban life. If they are open to criticism as "romanticists" (although it is not clear to me why a preference for dense street life, or an insistence that an ethnic working-class neighborhood is not necessarily a slum, renders one vulnerable to such criticism), it should at least be said in their defense that they obviously care enough about the *quality* of urban life to evoke a strong and clear image of it (something their critics do not always do) — strong enough in Mrs. Jacobs' case and clear enough in Professor Gans' case to make it easy for a reader to be for or against them.

I am mostly for them, since planning for pluralism seems to me not only the most sensible way of responding to the fact of persisting cultural diversities but the most honorable way as well. In making their assumptions, planners might first of all assume (it is the most reasonable assumption) that most groups which are displaced by planning *will take their culture with them* if they can. Planners would do well to anticipate this, and to modify their plans accordingly, to facilitate the preservation of those parts of their culture that the groups want preserved. This means that planning would have to be done *for specific types of people with distinctive cultural styles*, that is, for a variety of specific, known tastes rather than for faceless densities with a given amount of disposable income for housing. A working class group with a durable pattern of sexual segregation (husbands and wives living largely separate extra-familial lives) requires for its sustenance residential and community facilities different from those required by a middle class group with a culture pattern emphasizing companionable family togetherness.

If the strain put upon the middle class biases of professional planners by such considerations seems excessive, I ask only that you think of the problem of the Negro ghetto and the potential controversy about whether *its* subculture ought to be preserved. People as different as a sociologist like Lee Rainwater and a Negro leader like James Baldwin have remarked (without clearly deploring it) upon the Dyonisianism prevalent in the Negro ghetto. Now, this is a culture pattern which clearly is both at once an adaptation to the trapped character of ghetto life, and a means of providing compensatory satisfactions for that blocked access to middle class life. If the satisfactions are not only compensatory but real, planners might think about providing facilities for the nourishment of this psycho-cultural pattern — even as they think about eliminating the enforced segregation and demoralization which make it more attractive.

Even after discrimination on the basis of race disappears, however, we have no evidence to suggest that segregation will ever disappear. If the experience of other ethnic groups is any guide (and I know of no better guide), many Negroes will choose to live among their own "kind" even after they have formally free choice of housing. However "kind" may be defined in the future, there is no reason *not* to expect social class and ethnicity to continue to play an important role — although it is quite conceivable that color may eventually not have much to do with ethnicity. We know little enough about the nature of ethnicity — and even less, perhaps, about which members of an ethnic group *prefer* to live in ghettoes, or why, even after they can live almost wherever they please. But the *fact* that many of them do is beyond question. We have no reason *not* to expect this to be true of Negroes also, particularly of those whose views are represented by the most militant Negro leaders, insistent upon the acceptance of Negroes into American society *as Negroes* — with all that this historically implies.

I hope it is clear that these remarks are not the elaborate rationalizations of a conservative searching for an acceptable rhetoric to defend the *status quo*. Quite the contrary; they are the remarks of a sociologist who, being for the extension of the widest possible range of choice to all segments of the population, nevertheless knows that choices are hardly ever random, and that no man is so free that he is not constrained by the norms of the groups to which he belongs or would like to belong. This is as it should be; but the sense of choice rests on the existence of real alternatives. Cultural diversity has somehow been maintained in the suburbs without much help from planners. We may not be so lucky in the cities unless planners begin to understand the conditions of cultural distinctiveness and to design for it.

CHAPTER 2   SUGGESTIONS FOR FURTHER READING

Howe, Louise Kapp (ed.). *The White Majority* (New York: Vintage Books, 1970). This is a collection of essays by a number of scholars on the conditions faced by, and the politics and prejudices of, rank-and-file white workers. Here authors such as Robert E. Lane, Andrew Hacker, and Seymour M. Lipset examine the lives of the so-called "silent white majority."

Levy, Mark R., and **Michael S. Kramer**, *The Ethnic Factor* (New York: Simon and Schuster, 1972). A considerable portion of this volume is focused on the politics and political impact of the prominent "white ethnic" segment of Middle America. Groups examined include the Irish, the Jews, and the Italians.

Novak, Michael. *The Rise of the Unmeltable Ethnics* (New York: Macmillan, 1972). This hard-hitting, controversial book makes a strong case that non-WASP (White-Anglo-Saxon-Protestant) Americans, including Poles, Slavs, Italians, and Greeks, have suffered greatly at the hands of WASP Americans, yet have prospered and maintained a great degree of ethnic consciousness and identity.

3

Perspectives on Poverty and "Slums"

One of the most serious problems in U.S. cities is persisting poverty. In 1970 more than 24 million Americans were counted as poor using the government poverty line of $4,000 for an urban family of four. The majority of these persons resided in urban places. Over the years a variety of interpretations of poverty have been developed in both popular and scholarly writings. Popular perspectives have usually blamed poverty *on the poor themselves*. Doubtless the most famous scholarly conceptualization has been that of Oscar Lewis, an anthropologist whose ethnographies of the Mexican and Puerto Rican poor are widely read. Developing the concept of a "culture of poverty" in the book *Five Families*, Lewis argued that this culture is "a way of life which is passed down from generation to generation along family lines." In class-stratified, capitalistic societies—including the United States—the poor adapt in distinctive ways to their oppressive conditions, and these adaptations are transmitted from one generation to the next through the socialization process.[1] The culture of poverty transcends national differences; it consists of at least seventy distinctive traits, such as chronic unemployment, the lack of saving, a short childhood and early initiation into sex, a high rate of illegitimacy and family troubles, authoritarianism, and a pervasive sense of marginality and fatalism. As for policy implications, Lewis has noted that "by the time slum children are age six or seven they have usually absorbed the basic values and attitudes of their subculture and are not psychologically geared to take full advantage of changing conditions or increased opportunities which may occur in their lifetime."[2]

One of a growing number of critics of this culture-of-poverty approach is Hyman Rodman, whose book *Lower-Class Families* argues that although this approach can provide a useful way of cataloging poverty characteristics, it often leads to a *stereotyped view* of the poor that emphasizes negative aspects. Problematical, too, for culture-of-poverty theorists is the heterogeneity of life styles among the poor. Indeed, Rodman contends that there are at least four major responses made by lower-class persons in adapting to deprivations. Many poor individuals share dominant middle-class aspirations while at the same time adhering to alternative lower-class values; thus, the repertoire of values is usually greater for lower-class individuals.[3] If this "biculture" of poverty is actually characteristic of more of the poor than is the culture of poverty, then Rodman's policy-oriented argument in *Lower-Class Families* seems particularly relevant to government programs: "Opening up opportunities, rather than changing the values of the poor, may therefore be the crucial practical problem in attacking poverty."[4]

The first selection in this chapter, an excerpt from Charles A. Valentine's *Culture and Poverty*, delineates three important models or conceptualizations of poverty. One perspective depicts the lower class as a "self-perpetuating subsociety with a defective, unhealthy subculture." A second model describes the lower class as an "externally oppressed subsociety with an imposed, exploited subculture." Yet a third approach synthesizes certain points made in the other two perspectives: the lower class is seen as a "heterogeneous subsociety with variable, adaptive subcultures." The first model, basically similar to Lewis' culture of poverty, seems to be the prevailing orientation toward the poor among many academic analysts and social planners and has shaped numerous governmental attempts to grapple with the problem of poverty. Yet much of the evidence relevant to this first model is contradictory, and Valentine asserts that "in this form it is little more than a middle-class intellectual rationale for blaming poverty on the poor and thus avoiding recognition of the need for radical change in our society."

Valentine's preference here is for the synthesis model, which like Rodman's concept of the "lower-class value stretch," depicts the poor as having some distinctive subcultural values, positive and negative, but also as sharing middle-class patterns. Very important is the emphasis on the role of external social factors in determining poverty. Further, arguing that the subculture of poverty is not the main determinant behind the perpetuation of poverty, Valentine is sharply critical of various antipoverty programs directed either at maintaining dependency or altering the values of the poor. As an alternative policy, he suggests that positive remedies on behalf of low-income workers in the job market would be a way of providing the poor with expanded resources and thereby reducing poverty in America—basically a proposal for major *structural* change.

More recently, Valentine has responded to some of the critics of *Culture and Poverty* by admitting that problems exist in his conceptualization of culture, particularly in his acceptance of the assumption that the continuity of cultural patterns can be explained solely in terms of the socialization process; thus he has subsequently admitted that "many replicated patterns are the result of the response of successive generations to similar conditions of social life."[5] In addition, he has expressed the view that more attention should have been given in his analysis to the critical economic factors that determine the situation of poor Americans — those given some stress in Model 2 — and to the fact that many Americans actually profit from the perpetuation of an unequal distribution of resources.[6] Apparently for this reason, Valentine has become less hopeful in regard to the prospects for his job proposal for eradicating poverty. Perceiving this proposal as a last appeal for change within the existing system, he asserts that "my answer today is that a fundamental and revolutionary restructuring of society is the only solution, that to support anything short of this is effectively to defend a grossly inhumane status quo, and that there are some grounds for cautious hope that national and world conditions may be moving toward a point at which this necessary solution will come about."[7]

The second selection in this chapter, by David Perry and Alfred Watkins, takes a perspective on the urban poor that is close to Valentine's Model 2. In "People, Profit, and the Rise of the Sunbelt Cities" Perry and Watkins underscore the point that people are poor primarily because of the behavior of better-off Americans, particularly those who are leaders in the business and industry sectors of this capitalist society. Urban growth is here seen in terms of the money profit that it gives to members of the dominant economic elite. The urban poor in the older cities of the North and in the emerging cities of the Sunbelt (a new term for the South and the Southwest) are exploited, underpaid, unemployed — whatever the system requires to sustain the profits, and thus the life styles and wealth, of owners and managers. The experiences of several waves of the urban poor moving to cities of the North are examined, including those of the Irish, the Italians, and the blacks. Then the focus shifts to the poor in the cities of the Sunbelt. In the Sunbelt the recent in-migration is of business and industry, with (white) managers and (white) skilled workers from the North pouring in. Yet the poor workers, those needed to do the "dirty work" for growing industries, have long been there in Sunbelt cities. Indeed, an attraction for Northern industries has been the poverty of Southern and Southwestern cities. Simply put, lower wages and lower taxes mean higher profits than can now be secured in the North, with its strong unions (meaning higher wages) and better urban social services (meaning higher taxes). As workers in the North have gained a more reasonable standard of living, capitalists have seen their profits slipping. So the capitalists move or open new plants in the Sunbelt.

Subemployment is a central focus in the last part of the essay by Perry and Watkins. Subemployment is much broader than the more commonly and publicly discussed problem of *unemployment*. The subemployed poor include the discouraged jobless, involuntary part-time workers, workers with substandard wages, and those officially considered unemployed (the active jobless). The statistics (Tables 1 and 2) on wage earners in eighteen Northern and Sunbelt cities clearly show that over half of the workers in these areas fall into the category of the subemployed poor, with the proportions a bit higher in Sunbelt cities. Yet the components of subemployment are substantially different in the two regions. In the Sunbelt a much higher proportion of poor workers — who are often black and Chicano workers — are in jobs paying substandard wages than in the North: "What emerges from this analysis is the conclusion that people living below the poverty line in the urban South and Southwest represent a profitable resource to be exploited by employers of low skilled labor." Conversely, the workers in the North, poor and otherwise, are seen, by those capitalists in the aggressive quest for higher profits, as forcing government and unions too fast in the direction of increased social benefits and health and welfare services. In their conclusions Perry and Watkins explore the implications of two proposed profit-oriented solutions for the troubled cities of the North: (1) letting the inner cities die, or (2) drastically reducing redistributive social health-welfare programs. Both they regard as unacceptable. Here then is an in-depth probing of the implications of a Model-2 analysis, a critical political-economic assessment of cities North and South.

The third selection in this chapter, a report on poor Bostonites by Marc Fried, seems to reflect the thrust of Valentine's Model 3: that most of the poor in "slum" and "ghetto" areas share with middle-income groups normal patterns of social and psychological life. The focal point here is the West End of Boston, an area that in the 1950's came to be viewed by powerful local figures in business and politics as a "slum," a "dangerous" area that should be leveled by the urban renewal process so as, the leaders argued, to rejuvenate the downtown area of Boston and improve the tax base. Relatively little attention was given to the poor and working-class persons who lived in the renewal area. One sociologist, Herbert Gans, conducted an in-depth research study of the Italian-American segment, that made up about half the West End population. Carefully researching the social structure and living patterns of this community, Gans concluded that the area was not a "slum." Rather, the Italian section of the West End could best be described as a low-rent area of solidary kinship networks and stable working-class families; his suggestion is that the district could not be (and had not been proved to be) harmful to most of the local residents or to the larger community.[8]

Fried's article examines the grief reactions of rank-and-file urbanites who were *forced* by the urban renewal process to leave the West End area of Boston, the same area that Gans had studied just prior to the bulldozing process. The urban renewal plan had been approved in 1956; by 1960 only debris existed where thousands had once lived; by 1962 new residents had begun to move into the luxury housing that replaced the homes of the West Enders. The despair, the grieving for a lost home, that Marc Fried found among those relocated is not surprising in light of Herbert Gans' data on the vital social ties that existed there prior to urban renewal. Fried's data clearly indicate the importance of urban social structure, including peer-group societies, in integrating individuals and providing a sense of belonging — both spatial and social — within the urban context. Given the findings of Gans and Fried, critical policy questions about the traditional process of remaking American cities arise; Fried's answers to these questions seem sensible and challenging.

NOTES

1. Oscar Lewis, *La Vida* (New York: Random House, 1965), p. xliii.
2. Ibid., p. xlv.
3. Hyman Rodman, *Lower-Class Families* (New York: Oxford University Press, 1971), pp. 4—5, 192—193.
4. Ibid., p. 6. For discussion of social life in a "slum," see note 8 below.
5. Charles A. Valentine, "Models and Muddles Concerning Culture and Inequality: A Reply to Critics," *Harvard Educational Review*, 42, 1 (February 1972), 98. He continues: "The programming received may even be different from the actual patterns; in other words people may be enculturated to behave in one way but be obliged by situational or functional factors beyond their control to behave in another way."
6. See Charles A. Valentine, "Black Studies and Anthropology: Scholarly and Political Interests in Afro-American Culture," in *Addison-Wesley Modular Publications*, no. 15 (1972), pp. 39—40.
7. Valentine, "Models and Muddles," pp. 101—102.
8. Herbert J. Gans, *The Urban Villagers* (New York: Free Press, 1962).

From
Culture and Poverty:

Alternative Views of Poverty and the Poor—Present and Future

Charles A. Valentine

CONCEPTIONS FOR THE PRESENT

A number of ideas have been reviewed here, a variety of problems explored, and some suggestions offered for future research. From this discussion there emerge three broad formulations or intellectual models representing varying views of the lower class as a subsociety, its lifeways as a subculture, the sources of subcultural patterns, and associated questions of public policy looking to the future.

These three models emerge from the foregoing discussion in the sense that they are logical alternatives growing out of available knowledge about poverty, society, and culture. While these models can be said to have their roots in different schools of thought, they are not meant to represent positions taken by particular writers.

Model 1: Self-perpetuating Subsociety with a Defective, Unhealthy Subculture

a. The lower-class poor possess a distinct subculture, and in the areas covered by this subculture they do not share the dominant larger culture typified by the middle class.
b. The main distinctiveness of the poverty subculture is that it constitutes a disorganized, pathological, or incomplete version of major aspects of middle-class culture.

*[Editor's note: This is one of the last chapters in *Culture and Poverty* and thus represents Valentine's conclusions based on an extensive review of the literature on poverty. The earlier literature discussion mentioned has not been reprinted here.]

c. The poverty subculture is self-generating in the double sense that socialization perpetuates both the cultural patterns of the group and consequent individual psychosocial inadequacies blocking escape from poverty.

d. The poverty subculture must therefore be eliminated, and the poor assimilated to middle-class culture or working-class patterns, before poverty itself can be done away with.

e. These changes may occur through revolution in underdeveloped societies where the poor are the majority; in the West they will be brought about by directed culture change through social work, psychiatry, and education.

Model 2: Externally Oppressed Subsociety with an Imposed, Exploited Subculture

a. The lower-class poor are a structurally distinct subsociety, and their life is therefore situationally distinct from that of all other social strata.

b. Elements of pathology, distortion, and incompleteness in the life of the lower class have their source in the structure and processes of the total system, mediated by denial of cultural resources to the poor.

c. The disadvantaged position of the poor is maintained primarily by the behavior of the higher strata, acting in their own interest as they see it, to preserve their advantages by preventing a redistribution of resources.

d. The structure of the whole society must therefore be radically altered, and the necessary redistribution of resources accomplished, before poverty can be eliminated.

e. Short of a presently unforeseeable willingness of the other subsocieties to share their advantages, these changes can come about only through revolutionary accession to power by representatives of the poor.

Model 3: Heterogeneous Subsociety with Variable, Adaptive Subcultures

a. The lower-class poor possess some distinct subcultural patterns, even though they also subscribe to norms of the middle class or the total system in some of the same areas of life and are quite nondistinctive in other areas; there is variation in each of these dimensions from one ethnic group to another.

b. The distinctive patterns of the poverty subcultures, like those of the other subsocieties, include not only pathogenic traits but also healthy and positive aspects, elements of creative adaptation to conditions of deprivation.

c. The structural position and subcultural patterns of the poor stem from historical and contemporary sources that vary from one ethnic or regional group to another but generally involve a multicausal combination of factors, often including some of those cited above in both 1c and 2c.

d. Innovation serving the interests of the lower class to an optimal degree will therefore require more or less simultaneous, mutually reinforcing changes in three areas: increases in the resources actually available to the poor; alterations of the total social structure; and changes in some subcultural patterns.

e. The most likely source for these changes is one or more social movements for cultural revitalization, drawing original strength necessarily from the poor, but succeeding only if the whole society is affected directly or indirectly.

   (1) Such a movement would reinvigorate the poor as it developed, sweeping away subcultural patterns that are merely static adjustments to deprivation.

   (2) Particularly where the poor are a numerical minority, such a movement would have to rely significantly on suasion other than physical force to achieve its wider objectives, so that revolution on the classical model would probably not be sufficient.

   (3) Social work and education, perhaps psychiatry, might serve important secondary and supportive functions if they were re-oriented in terms of the movement.

   (4) The American civil rights movement is perhaps a prototype in some respects, but a successful revitalization movement serving the interests of the poor would have to be much more radical in its aims and command far greater strength.

Among the authors whose works we have reviewed here there are several whose views overlap the boundaries between these formulations.* The three conceptualizations are not by any means altogether mutually exclusive. While there are many important inconsistencies between the first two, one of the intentions behind Model 3 obviously is to reconcile some of these differences by providing a framework to accommodate certain items from both of the other formulations. Thus the third model is, in part, an eclectic synthesis involving the contention that major propositions from the first two may be simultaneously valid.

At the same time, these three outlines do contain the principal theoretical themes touched upon earlier. Model 1 will be recognized as

*[Editor's note: The authors mentioned here were discussed in earlier chapters of *Culture and Poverty*, which are not reprinted here.]

representing the dominant view in most respects. This is the case despite the fact that some of its proponents, notably Oscar Lewis, also subscribe with varying vigor to certain propositions in the other formulations. Model 1 seems to be the prevailing orientation not only among academic poverty experts but also among liberal intellectuals in general, as well as in relevant national policy-making circles. My own view of this model is that the main weight and prevailing direction of available evidence are inconsistent with it, even though most of those reporting the evidence seem to be more or less committed to this interpretation. When it is presented as a total picture of the culture of the lower class, in my considered judgment this portrayal is absurd. In this form it is little more than a middle-class intellectual rationale for blaming poverty on the poor and thus avoiding recognition of the need for radical change in our society.

It seems obvious that Model 1 constitutes the chief conceptual underpinning for dominant public policy initiatives, preeminently the "war on poverty." In this respect the influence of this conception is profoundly pernicious, unless one adopts the position that the worse relations become between the poor and the rest of society, the more likely it is that constructive change will come about. The basic message of this approach to the poor is that only after they have become conventionally respectable can they hope for a chance to leave poverty behind them. As virtually every good-sized city in the country becomes a battlefield from time to time through the 1960's, it should be apparent that this approach does not work because its intellectual foundation is a woeful distortion. The social-work solution has been given a new rationale in terms of "culture," but the policies have clearly failed and their intellectual justifications could hardly have been more thoroughly discredited.

On the other hand, none of this means that the logic of Propositions 1*a*, 1*b*, and 1*c* is inherently unreasonable or universally invalid. From a theoretical standpoint, there must be few if any cultures or subcultures with *no* dysfunctional or pathogenic elements. More concretely, there is certainly empirical evidence of pathology, incompetence, and other kinds of inadequacy among the people of the ghettos and slums, as there is in the rest of society. There can be no doubt that living in poverty has its own destructive effect on human capacities and that these impairments become part of the whole process perpetuating deprivation. The vital questions are, how important are the internal disabilities of the lower class, and how are they related to significant external factors? An incomplete but important answer seems plain already: subcultural disabilities are definitely not the whole problem and almost certainly not the principal problem. More adequate answers await research not yet done, including the kind of field work suggested earlier.

Model 2 has its roots in scholarship animated by philosophical positions of the radical left. Phrased rather broadly as it is, it is perhaps reasonably consistent with a fairly wide range on this ideological quarter, from the pessimistic orthodox Marxian view of the "lumpen-proletariat" to Fanon's more optimistic vision of "the wretched of the earth." These views find no systematic or wholehearted proponents among the authors we have considered in detail. Nevertheless, the general shape of the evidence not infrequently suggests that the propositions of this model must be taken seriously. Moreover, some interpretations in our sources raise intriguing questions in this connection, such as Lewis' suggestion that poverty cultures may have been eliminated in socialist states.

In my opinion, Model 2 is another inadequate formulation, by virtue of incompleteness. That is, it covers part of the available evidence but not all of it. Nevertheless, it seems that, in a general way at least, this theory is consistent with a considerably larger part of the evidence than the first model considered. The broad structural features of Model 2 are difficult to argue against, as are its propositions on the general processes of relationship between subsocieties. The associated strategies for change are more open to question. It seems clear that stratified inequalities in both wealth and power continue to exist in societies that have undergone socialist revolutions, including some where such upheavals occurred decades ago. On the other hand, this does not necessarily mean that either poverty or lower-class subcultures persist in these societies. Again, obviously, more information is needed. On one point, however, general knowledge does seem a sufficient basis for a reasonably secure conclusion. In the United States, and perhaps in other advanced systems of mixed capitalism where the poor are distinctly in the minority, a socialist revolution by violent seizure of power in the interests of the lower class does not appear practicable.

The final model is clearly superior to the others, if it succeeds in its design. It is intended to resolve some of the major difficulties found in the present literature on poverty subcultures, as well as to synthesize the strong points of Models 1 and 2. Most of it is self-explanatory, and supporting arguments for it will be found widely scattered through this entire essay. The predictive propositions dealing with movements for culture change follow logically from the descriptive phases of the model. Nevertheless, one could hardly consider these suggestions anything more than speculative. This remains true partly because existing empirical information is nowhere nearly adequate either to validate convincingly or to discredit fully any of these abstract conceptions. What is most needed is fresh research leading to real ethnographies of the poor.

SCENARIOS FOR THE FUTURE

The suggested research will best achieve its aims if it is oriented and animated by a universalistic concept of culture. Within this conception of panhuman adaptation, each particular culture need not be viewed as an alien mode inimical to one's own lifeways. Each way of life can be seen as a uniquely creative and continually developing synthesis in which human universals and group particularities are inseparable. Similarly, this view will grant a basic human worth and dignity to all subsocieties and to each subculture. This requires a consistent refusal to derogate any subsystem simply because it seems to violate one's own sectional values or to threaten one's own subgroup interests. These are requirements not easily fulfilled, as we have seen.

Anthropologists have succeeded well in living up to these difficult requirements while working with exotic peoples in every faraway part of the world. They also succeeded notably with the American Indians, though it should be remembered that this was achieved mainly after the Indians had ceased to pose any threat to white Americans or their interests. Can we now accomplish the same achievement with our more familiar exotics, the savage underclasses here at home — the potentially predatory nomads who wander with the seasonal cycles of our crops, the pockets of primitive mountain folk still living by a coal-age culture, or the marauding hostile tribes on the frontiers of our inner cities? We have not succeeded as yet in meeting this contemporary challenge to anthropology, though some of us have made valiant attempts. These attempts by the new anthropologists like Oscar Lewis should certainly not be scorned, even if we cannot yet praise them very highly by the older standards. The present challenge of ethnography at home is a far more difficult one than yesterday's fieldwork problems. It is much more difficult here and now to preserve the necessary social distance and creative tension between ourselves and the governors, the missionaries, the purveyors of trade goods, or the labor recruiters. We are much more directly involved in the larger system, which makes it harder to achieve the necessary quality of involvement in certain of the smaller subsystems. More pointedly, we have personal and professional interests that are firmly embedded in the dominant subsociety of this system.

Yet perhaps even this need not disqualify us entirely or make our task impossible. In the old anthropology we had to loosen our intellectual and emotional ties with Western culture considerably, engaging in a sort of professsional semialienation to achieve a kind of transcendent viewpoint. The problem of the new anthropology is to achieve sufficient intellectual and emotional independence from the middle class, and from its dominant subculture, so that we can spend substantial time actually living our whole existence with the indigenes on the other side of the tracks, within the black ghetto, or in a public housing project. As in the old pattern, some us might even go native, slightly and temporarily, though this is certainly a relative matter and an individual problem for each ethnographer. In short, the new problems may not differ so much in kind from the old ones, even though they certainly differ in degree.

If we can really regain the art of living with the natives, it seems reasonable to hope that the rest will flow rather naturally. We should be able to learn to see the world as it is from within the alien subsociety. We should find it possible, by following out the inner logic of the exotic subculture, to discover through direct experience the similarities of the subsystem to others as well as its differences, its order as well as its disorganized facets, its strengths and virtues along with its dysfunctions and pathologies. Gradually we should become less dependent on images of our people communicated to us by outsiders such as policemen or social workers, for we shall know the people ourselves at firsthand. Eventually we will come to regard those outsiders, not as authoritative sources of information, but as objects of study, to be examined in light of our growing experience of and through the subculture. Thus we shall then be investigating relationships between our temporarily chosen subsociety and others. Ultimately we should be able to view the total system with new eyes.

If this point is ever reached, there will be further consequences. The changed vision of the new ethnographer must sooner or later include within its focus the programs of agencies dealing with the subculture, and the policies of governments that rule over the subsociety. We are so far from this point at present that it seems hardly plausible to predict in detail what this reexamination might yield in new understanding or initiative for change. Yet some broad possibilities do appear highly likely. It seems probable that the future ethnographer of the poor will have clear knowledge of what lower-class people want; he will have considerable understanding of what they are willing and able to do, to get what they want. From this viewpoint it will seem obvious that policies and programs to "eliminate poverty" have failed partly because they were designed and launched without any such knowledge or understanding. It will be clear that this lack of success is analogous to the earlier failure of colonial regimes whose knowledge of their subjects was both superficial and distorted. Another obvious conclusion will be that uniform "antipoverty" policies lacking either understanding or respect for ethnic subcultural diversity within the subsociety, based on the shallow simplification of a homogeneous "culture of poverty," could not succeed. Again the historical parallel will be clear: imperial confusion and failure stemming from stereotyped thinking about primitives and savages.

The old arguments about whether the material condition of poverty or its "culture" must be changed first will seem as futile and irrelevant as the still older debates over the question whether subject peoples could be freed before they were "civilized," "modernized," or "prepared." It will be recognized that the many discussions about whether there was anything "worth preserving" in the poverty subcultures, essentially like those other arguments about the viability of non-Western lifeways in the modern world, suffered an irrelevance born of arrogance: they failed to recognize that the answers to these questions would ultimately depend, in significant part, on the people most directly concerned; not on the rulers but on those whom they ruled. From this perspective, the whole strategy of imposing conformity to middle-class manners and codes with the proffered reward of future affluence will have the quality of another historical echo. It will seem no less bankrupt and no less corrupt than the colonial strategy of offering the material comforts of the West to the rest of the world's peoples if only they would accept Western dictates in religion, politics, and economics.

Similarly, the "social-work solution" for the dilemmas of poverty at home will stand revealed as the latter-day equivalent of Christian education and uplift for the faraway heathen, and all the other baggage of the white man's burden. What has been called "maximum feasible participation of the poor" or "working with indigenous leadership" was earlier labeled indirect rule in a different but analogous context. The earlier version, like the later one, was also presented as a civilizing force, but the older policymakers were somewhat more candid about using their appointed chiefs and designated satraps to further the interests of the governors' home constituencies. Perhaps we shall come to see how, even as segregation and discrimination were being officially "prohibited," the newer forms of apartheid and the latter-day bantustans were being established here at home: "compensatory education" as a substitute for integration, whether of races or classes; training those without jobs to do the dirty work still left over after automation; painting and patching the ghetto instead of allowing people to live decently where they choose; "self-examination" and "self-help" by the poor rather than the sharing of wealth and power by the privileged; helping the poor to build "positive identities" and lots of pride — but no prosperity or power — in their slums. Further parallels will abound. Decreeing "equal rights" and "equal opportunities" for people who do not have and are not allowed equality in anything else (e.g., achievement, power) is as empty and hypocritical as the older shibboleths of "dual development" and "separate but equal." "Voting rights" for the poor, when the candidates are chosen and the parties controlled by the rich, are no more meaningful than being a British subject or holding French citizenship is for a South Sea Islander whose homeland is economically, politically, and militarily ruled by a regime of Europeans, by Europeans, for Europeans.

It may be that thinkers of another day will look back with special interest on the spirited and sophisticated debate of the 1960's between the proponents of the "services strategy" and those who favored "income strategies" in the "war against poverty." Like most activities to which the middle class attached real importance and value (seeing them as affecting their own interests), the poor did not play much part in this, even under the doctrine of maximum feasible participation. Nevertheless, it involved a lively division between those who favored winning the war with a lot of social services for the poverty-stricken few, and others who preferred victory by the weapon of a little money for everyone. The income strategists accused their opponents of advocating outmoded approaches that would merely perpetuate the problem by reinforcing the "dependency" universally considered a prime feature of poverty culture. A few even suggested that perhaps some social-service warriors enjoyed fighting poverty (and being depended on), with the implication that subtle motives might therefore prolong the war. The pro-income forces laid great stress on the importance of independence, healthy masculine economic roles, and the therapeutic effect their strategy would have on the sordid sexuality and brutish home life known by all to characterize the depraved lower class.

Moreover, they showed that these benefits would be a bargain for the whole society at only a few billion dollars per year. According to one widely publicized plan, healthy male identities and stable families would flower from Harlem to the Delta if every child in the nation were supported in the style to which public assistance recipients have become accustomed in Mississippi. A handful of reactionaries argued that such income strategies would have bad effects on the incentive to work. This carried little weight, however, for liberals and sophisticates knew that the poor had no motivation anyway, and they had other programs to take care of that problem. So the doctrine of income supports, or "transfer payments," gained supporters from the right as well as the left. Indeed, within a few years even what had previously been generally regarded as a crackpot scheme, the "guaranteed annual income," came to be discussed by congressmen. Perhaps this was partly accountable by the fact that the level of support proposed amounted to guaranteed poverty. Presumably, to some, good morals and healthy home life among the poor began to seem cheap at this price.

Although our future scholars might thus find it easy to discern absurdities by hindsight, it seems possible that they may discern something more important in these income plans and in the general disposition of the 1960's to seek some scheme for minimal relief to the poor. It is possible that these accumulating crumbs may add up to something that those dispensing them are not bargaining for at all. Again there may be a valid analogy with the cumulative effect of minor concessions granted by the colonialists to their subjects in the mistaken belief that token acquiescences would keep the empire secure. It has been widely true that the most severely oppressed peoples and subsocieties have seldom rebelled or risen up effectively. Yet even slight improvements in the level of life and hope have often liberated quite unsuspected strengths, and rising hopes have led, not just to frustration, but to creative forms of action for change. These are commonalities in the history of many revitalization movements, some of which have succeeded in overthrowing old orders and creating new ways of life.

Possibly something like this may be what the confused struggles of the 1960's portend for the poor in America and elsewhere. We must hope that a new anthropology will soon be able to tell us whether this is the case and if so, something about what form it may be expected to take. We must hope also that the beginning of a coming confrontation between the poor and the rest of society has not already so angered and embittered crucial groups that no ethnographer can study them. There is a tragic possibility that the issue is already joined, on battlefields ranging from exploding ghettos to bullet-scarred land claims in the mountains and deserts of the Southwest or to the violently disputed fishing grounds of Pacific Northwest rivers. Our nation, and through its dominion the Western world as a whole, seems little prepared to meet the foreseeable revitalization of the poor with anything other than the reflexes of the cop on the beat in the ghetto, the posse in National Guard uniforms, and the world policeman. Perhaps there will be no new anthropology, no creative resynthesis by the oppressed, but only another long night of blood and pain.

Postscript:
A Proposal for Empowering
the Poor to Reduce Inequality

BACKGROUND

The proposal outlined in the following pages springs from the same concerns and is shaped by the same framework of thought as the rest of this book. Yet the plan suggested here goes well beyond the central purpose of the book. Those purposes were to evaluate existing interpretations of poverty; to probe the implications for social policies; and to propose measures for improving our knowledge and understanding of the poor. This may lead to more effective policies in the future. It is all too obvious, however, that our society needs new ways of dealing with the problems of poverty now — not merely at some future point to be determined by progress in research. This postscript proposes a way of meeting this immediate need.

This proposal reflects the urgency of dealing with the national crisis of poverty and related forms of social disadvantage. Such plans must not proceed from any illusion that present knowledge provides a clear guide to foolproof measures. On the contrary, social planners must originate fresh initiatives for change even as they recognize that existing knowledge is extremely imperfect. This will certainly deprive us of any confidence that total answers or certain solutions are at hand. At the same time, however, this recognition should also free us from the limitations of using presently accepted theories of poverty as the only bases for action. One reasonable response to the inadequacy of widely accepted interpretations of poverty is to propose action programs based on alternative interpretations.

A major source of the need for new solutions is the demonstrated failure of existing antipoverty programs and the predictable failure of additional approaches now on the horizon. It is widely agreed that the traditional programs of the welfare establishment have proved inadequate. A principal reason for this is that these programs have not enabled the poor to act in behalf of their own interests, either individually or collectively. Indeed, conventional welfare approaches have often had the opposite effect of perpetuating and reinforcing the dependency and powerlessness of the poor.

The "war on poverty" of the last few years was supposedly designed to overcome these very deficiencies in older approaches. It has neither accomplished this aim nor shown much promise that it will do so. The recent federal antipoverty effort has contributed substantial new resources to old-line social service and welfare agencies. Federal help has typically not required any basic change in agency policies, and thus in effect it has reinforced their traditional orientation. Moreover, it is generally true across the country at the local level, where antipoverty programs are actually carried out, that control over policy lines and action decisions has changed little. By and large this control is firmly held by the traditional power centers of municipalities, counties, and states. This remains true despite the myths of federal intervention and the ornaments of token "participation by the poor."

This means that there has been no significant increase in the power of poor people to act in behalf of their own interests. Under these conditions, there is little or no reason to expect that results from the newer combinations of services, training programs, and "community action" projects will be much different from the older ones. It is equally discouraging that the "war on poverty" is mainly aimed at changing the "culture of poverty" rather than altering the condition of being poor. Not only are the culture patterns of the poor very imperfectly understood, but it is highly doubtful that any "culture of poverty" is the main force perpetuating socioeconomic inequality. As long as the "war on poverty" is focused mainly on changing the supposed customs and values of the poor — rather than on altering the economic and political structure of the nation — it will have little effect on poverty.

The main ideas presently being widely discussed, tried out experimentally here and there, and possibly scheduled for national implementation within the foreseeable future are various forms of direct income support for the poor: guaranteed annual income, negative income tax, family allowances. The main contribution of these programs would be to establish an absolute minimum below which no family's or unattached individual's disposable income could fall. Such an approach can be expected to fail because it is based on a misunderstanding of the poverty problem in an affluent society with an ideology of equality. The segments of the poor and their partisans or supporters who are in motion today, creating a national crisis by their outbursts of protest, are not demanding some absolute minimal level of economic security. On the contrary, they are demanding equality — if not total equalization then radically greater equality. This demand applies not merely to economic welfare but to all the material and psychic benefits of membership in our society. This is not to say that a minimum livelihood should not be vouchsafed to all; nor is it implied that this security would not be welcomed by many among the poor. The point is that no measures of minimal income support, whether presented as welfare payments or as guaranteed subsistence, can solve the basic problem of inequality.

With all this in mind, the proposal put forward here is consistent with Model 3, outlined in Chapter 6 above, portraying the poor as a heterogeneous subsociety with variable subcultures. The key to this proposal is to place substantial new economic, social, and political resources under the control of the poor so that they will have the power to act in such a way as to reduce their inequality significantly. Reducing inequality does not mean what has come to be called "equal opportunity." It means equitability of results in the sense of achievement, fulfillment, and enjoyment of the rewards and satisfactions already generally available to citizens outside disadvantaged groups.

THE NEED

It has long been a cherished belief in this country that the poor should overcome poverty themselves. We now know that under modern conditions this has proved impossible for about one quarter of our citizens. Because of historically developed inequalities, equal rights today do not bring about genuinely equal opportunity for these people. Laws that guarantee equal rights cannot create actual equality for those who control only the most inadequate economic, educational, and political resources. We are all paying for this failure of our society. The cruel loss of lives and property in our burning cities makes it imperative that we find new responses to unemployment and powerlessness among the poor. In order to deal with these problems effectively, we must transcend the principle of guaranteed equality even though this principle itself is only barely established in national life. It is necessary to move on immediately to special rights and positive discrimination in favor of the human groups heretofore most disadvantaged.

The program suggested here does not deal with all aspects of poverty. No doubt comprehensive programs will be proposed by others in fields of current interest such as family structure and community organization. The present proposal is focused on the immediate and long-range economic problems of the unemployed, the underemployed, and the unskilled poor. To deal effectively with these problems it is necessary that the program cover the fields of employment and economically valuable training, as well as the related phenomenon of the powerlessness of the poor.

There are three principal reasons for choosing this focus. One is the belief that solutions in the economic realm are both urgent in the sense of great immediate need, and fundamental in the sense that little else seems possible without substantial progress in this area. Second is the hope that a concrete and radical plan in the field of employment may have an immediate appeal to people who suffer economic deprivation every day and who can readily perceive connections between employment difficulties and some of their other problems.

In the third place, germs of a radically new approach already exist in certain employment proposals that have come in the past from civil rights organizations and related sources. One of these germs is the principle of compensatory hiring articulated by Whitney Young of the Urban League. Another is the demand sometimes made by the movement for Negro advancement, that employers who claim qualified workers cannot be found, should hire people whom they consider unqualified and give them the necessary qualifications through on-the-job training.

These ideas clearly go beyond the formulas of equal rights and equal opportunities. The common principle underlying them is that after centuries of severe denial of opportunity the victims of this deprivation cannot possibly catch up through merely equal opportunity. Carried to their logical conclusion, these ideas lead to the demand for a comprehensive national program of positive discrimination in favor of the presently underprivileged. Bayard Rustin has recently pointed out that to win World War II we effectively employed huge numbers of workers without standard qualifications. We must do the same on a larger scale, and with more imagination, to avoid losing today's war of the cities.

THE PROGRAM

Employment. The heart of this proposal is a national commitment to positive discrimination in employment. Present patterns and past trends of employment and job advancement, as reflected in group unemployment rates and median family income, must be reversed to the positive advantage of the unemployed and the poor. The program should cover as many employers as possible, certainly including government agencies at all levels, extending to public utilities under government regulation and private businesses holding government contracts, and ideally encompassing educational institutions receiving government aid and all other employers engaged in interstate commerce.

The ruling consideration should be that all individuals who are unemployed or earn less than an adequate yearly income must be given realistic good-faith opportunities for employment or advancement as soon as possible. This will mean that job opportunities must frequently be opened up regardless of applicants' existing qualifications as traditionally defined. The emphasis should be on full-time work, and all employment under the program should carry reasonable hope of both permanence and advancement. The jobs to be produced should pay no less than an adequate family income for workers who are household heads, and no less than the national minimum wage or union rates, whichever is higher, for other employees.

Hiring under such a program would have to be in accordance with group priorities. The highest priority would be assigned to heads of households who are members of the nonwhite ethnic group which has the highest rate of unemployment in each local area. In practice this would mean that adult Negro males would receive first preference in most but not all areas. The remainder of the priority system could be defined in terms of the measurable relative deprivation of each significant ethnic group in each local area, including of course poor unemployed whites.

An important key to administration of the priority system would be that whenever employers claimed they could not find qualified high-priority applicants for entering positions, they should be required and enabled to establish on-the-job training for such positions. While it should be the responsibility of each employer to find and recruit high-priority applicants for all job openings, a file of such applicants could be maintained by the administering agency for the use of employers in each local area.

. . .

People, Profit, and the Rise of the Sunbelt Cities

David C. Perry and Alfred J. Watkins

The dominant characterizations of the present state of uneven urban development mask a telling contradictory view of urban America. For the urban poor, the "rise of the Sunbelt" and the "decline of the Northeast" are meaningless descriptions. Their poverty is not a regional issue. But the vast outpourings of many journalists, academics, and politicians seem to indicate otherwise: low income in the Northeast represents "poverty" while low income in the Sunbelt represents the advantage of cheap labor and is part of a "good business climate."

At the heart of this disagreement are competing definitions over the role the city should play in a society. For the established analysts, the primary function of the American city is its productivity function — the generation of profit. The prime measures of urban health or dynamism are economic and these analysts discuss the growth of cities in terms of their success or failures as centers of profit; sorting them out along continuums of central city and suburb and Northern and Sunbelt. For the poor, the function of the city is only secondarily associated with its productivity function. The city, whether it is economically profitable or not, should be first and foremost a center of social well-being, providing a community which is at once materially and socially renewing.

These divergent conceptions of the fundamental role of the city in America form the basis of this essay. In the two sections which

Source: "People, Profit and the Rise of the Sunbelt Cities" by **David C. Perry** and **Alfred J. Watkins** is reprinted from *Urban Affairs Annual Review*, Vol. 14, David C. Perry and Alfred J. Watkins, Editors © 1978, pp. 277—305 by permission of the publisher, Sage Publications, Inc. (Beverly Hills London) and by permission of the authors.

immediately follow we briefly discuss the emergence of the city as first and foremost a center of profit in America. In the third section we review three waves of migration to American cities testing the notion that the conditions of urban poverty are not irrevocably altered by the economic rise or decline of a city. What is altered during such periods of change in urban productivity is the ability of the capitalist society to economically utilize and otherwise socially control the poor. In the last two sections of this essay we argue that continued adherence to the dominant role prescribed for the American city will have no significant impact on the existence of a permanent urban underclass. Unless we begin the socially necessary task of recasting the role of the city in our society so that it is primarily a center of people and not profit, we will never fully understand much less witness an end to the domestic tensions fostered by the contradictions emanating from competing definitions of the purpose of our urban society.

THE URBAN FUNCTION IN AMERICA

Before proceeding to the empirical tasks set forth in the introduction, a short discussion of our concept of the prevailing role assigned to the American city is in order. It is axiomatic to say that every society, in order to survive, must be productive — that is, it must generate material surplus. What differentiates societies are the purposes to which this surplus is directed. At the most basic level, societal productivity can be either accumulative or redistributive. If it is accumulative, it allows for an uneven distribution of surplus to its citizens, each individual rightfully accruing his share of the surplus because of his owned share of the means of production. On the other hand, surplus used redistributively accrues to citizens evenly, based on their political right to share equally in the productive fruits of society. Both these pure political-economic states can and do use surplus *replacively* to guard against disaster or refurbish the productive infrastructure, and *wastefully*, misspending surplus on luxuries which have no redeeming productive value. Finally, we would argue both political economies can *misallocate* surplus. That is, capitalist economies can err and use surplus in a nonreplacive and overly redistributive way and socialist economies have the untoward potential to use capital in a nonreplacive and overly accumulative manner.

Obviously this simple political-economic conceptualization of societies is an "ideal type." There are no pure politically individualistic, economically accumulative, nation states and no pure politically collective, economically redistributive states. The real world is characterized by the thin line that nations dance between preserving their predominant political economic nature and committing irreversible errors in the misallocation of their productivity. The government is the institution called upon to "choreograph" such a "dance" and such a role is usually called the social control function. Ira Katznelson captures the essence of the social control function of the American state when he declares: "The state's function of social control consists in managing the consequences of making capitalism work and can best be understood as an attempt to manage but not overcome the contradictions of the capitalist system" (1976 : 220). Interpreting this description for our purposes, we can say that if the state fails in such management or choreography of the tension between the redistributive demands of the "nonowners," or the poor, and the predominant political economic order, then misallocation of surplus (in the name of rising public services) or the implementation of a police state follows. In either case, the predominant order, the legitimacy of the society, has been threatened by the presence of militant or at least economically "unmeltable" citizens. The presence of a socially uncontrollable and economically unprofitable class of people represents a crisis in the legitimacy of the capitalist society itself.

In this context, it can thus be argued that studying the migration of various groups of poor people to the American city gives us a clear opportunity to place in larger perspective what is meant in the prevailing discourse by the "decline" of the urban Northeast and the "rise" of the Sunbelt cities. Indeed it is our thesis that urban poverty has become a symptom of decline in the Northeast because it is no longer viewed as either economically or politically manageable. Northeastern cities are constantly "misallocating" larger and larger shares of public surplus to meet the increased demands of economically "illegitimate" people. A contemporary way of describing this misallocation is to talk of an urban "fiscal crisis." Conversely, the "rise" of the Sunbelt cities represents a "good business climate" because poverty implies that people are willing to work for low wages and because public service burdens have not yet reached the stage where they could be defined as a misallocation of our productive surplus.

However, the veracity of this version of regional uneven development is not found in the simple model presented here; it is found in the experience of successive waves of urban migrants as they come to our nation's cities. We now turn or rather, in this paper, "dash" through history in an attempt to provide a first approximation of our thesis on the evolving role of the city in America.

THE CITY, THE PROFIT FUNCTION, AND THE EARLY IMMIGRANTS

Few nations have grown to urban status in quite the way of the United States. The American city did not evolve so much as it exploded. In less than 160 years we have changed from a time when less than 10% of our population lived in urban places to a time when three-quarters of us are urbanites. Relative to other advanced nations, our cities are not the result of centuries of cultural growth; they are the inventions of decades — manufactured as if overnight, out of whole cloth (Bookchin, 1973 : 90—93). As a result even the oldest of our cities have no long-standing cultural history derived from a singular people; rather they have served as sorting-out and resocialization centers for successive waves of racially and culturally diverse outsiders. From the beginning, our cities fueled the dreams of materially oppressed immigrants; they were centers of individual gain, with "streets paved with gold." The fulfillment of such a dream was more than enough to force the immigrants into a Faustian contract with the New World; to exchange the "soul" of their home-land for the "gold" of the open land and later the cities of America. In short, the history of the American city — Yankee and Sunbelt — is the history of the rise of the *capitalist city* (the center of material profit) on the initially expansive urbanless *tabula rasa* of the New World.

This conception of the economic function in the New World was not central to the immediate dream or assumptions the early settlers had about their lot in life. For the first 200 years it appears that the New World settlers were basically hopeful of being "less poor," but poor just the same. Their heritage of Old World poverty was far from an entrepreneurial one. Robert Bremner (1956 : 3) points out that "during the first two centuries of the country's development most Americans took it for granted that the majority of men would always be poor. Poverty was the state from which thousands of emigrants fled when they embarked in hope or despair on the difficult journey to the New World, in the form of hardship, privation and suffering it was the lot, not of the first settlers on the alien coast, but of generations of pioneers on successive inland frontiers."

However, the growth of our first cities into mercantile centers and later on the transformation of others into industrial centers of profit brought about unprecedented wealth for some. This overall process is depicted by historian Sam Bass Warner as the process of "privatism." He describes the requirements of life in the American city as follows:

> Under the American tradition, the first purpose of the citizen is the private search for wealth; the goal of a city is to be a community of private money-makers. Once the scope of many city dwellers' search for wealth exceeded the bounds of their municipality, the American city ceased to be an effective community. Ever afterwards it lacked the desire, the power, the wealth, and the talent necessary to create a humane environment for all citizens. From that first moment of bigness, from the mid-nineteenth century onward the successes and failures of American cities have depended upon the unplanned outcomes of the private market's demand for workers, its capacity for dividing the land, building houses, stores and factories, and its needs for public services have deter-

mined the shape and quality of America's big cities. What the private market could do well American cities have done well, what the private market did badly, or neglected, our cities have been unable to overcome [1968 : x].

Thus, the city in America emerged as a market place for competitive material productivity: a profit place not a social place. The social well-being of its immigrating citizens could be accomplished through their economic renewal (James, 1972 : 22—30). While it became rationalized economically, the city remained a socially disintegrated community, sorting out successive waves of immigrants within the criteria of profitable productivity. Beyond this, immigrants were left relatively alone with the cultural heritage of their immediate past to salvage their own social community (or, as we have come to call it, ghetto).

PROFIT, POVERTY, AND THREE WAVES OF URBAN MIGRATION

Our thesis in this section, quite boldly, is that for most of our history the place of the urban poor has been comfortably "hidden" under the "rock" of urban profit. America becomes concerned with its urban poor when their conditions can no longer be hidden; when they pose a barrier to economic growth and a threat to the social order, thus exacerbating a developing crisis in the legitimacy of the city as a center of profit. More precisely, we will argue that the poor emerge as burdens when they can no longer be used productively (as a supply of cheap labor or rental income) or controlled (as they come to represent a threat to the social order through health hazards, riots, racial tensions, increased wage demands, anarchistic acts of violence, or organized political movements).

The European immigrant and the new city of profit

Early in the 19th century, as Americans began to experience the first dramatic blush of urban-based affluence, they also began to observe new levels of urban poverty (Greeley, 1972). The close proximity of rich and poor in the city set out in dramatic relief growing social disparities arising from rapid immigration, industrialization, and urbanism. Such a [disparate] condition did not scare people away; in fact it had the opposite result. It removed the vision that the state of man was inherently one of poverty; replacing this notion was the dream that America was the place of opportunity, of the *economic* "Horatio Alger," of the *political* "Lincoln Ideal" (Ginger, 1973). The emigrant from the Old World or the farm could go to the city and literally walk along streets "paved with gold." The American city was the place for living the liberal-capitalist dream, where ostensibly one was at last free to contract one's labor, and where one was free to accumulate wealth, through ownership and even profit making.

Evidence of such dreams lies in the demographics of 19th century America which exhibited one of the most dramatic immigration and urbanization rates in the history of the Western world. The national population sorted out in two different ways: first, through an explosion and expansion across the breadth of the continent spurred by an entrepreneurial process of frontier development (Wade, 1959; Chudacoff, 1975); and, second, through a veritable population implosion in our industrializing cities. This second demographic pattern was a boon to the capitalist city in two major ways. It provided an apparently limitless supply of cheap labor, thus ensuring low wages and high profits in the emerging manufacturing structure. Second, the very presence of literally millions of new people in our cities made for an almost inexhaustible source of residential demand. "Proper" land development in the city — filling every available foot of a slum lot with cheap housing and filling every available foot of a house with humans — represented a highly profitable practice of land development. Perhaps tenement slum development did not offer quite the dramatic level of profit to be found in frontier land speculation, but the returns to investment were more immediate and the speculative risks were negligible.

By the 1840s tens of thousands of immigrants, many from Ireland, were streaming into Northeastern American cities. Numerous authors have given us chilling descriptions of the housing conditions found there. In New York tenements Charles Dickens saw attics filled with startled wretched creatures who would crawl from infested nests and corners "as if the judgment hour were at hand and every obscene grave was giving up the dead" (1972 : 137—138). Jane Addams (1910) witnessed the impact of similar conditions on tenement dwellers in Chicago, and William Ellery Channing reported that many tenements in Boston consisted of "cellars and rooms which could not be ventilated, which want for benefits of light, free air and pure water, and the means of removing filth" (Bremner, 1956:5).

However appalling the conditions of slum dwellers during the middle of the 19th century, these were rarely viewed as evidence of an "urban crisis." On the contrary these people and the very oppression of their existence represented a true economic resource in the American process of urban dynamism. Their very numbers worked against them, providing the city with a limitless pool of labor and reducing the bargaining power of the unskilled workman with industrial owners to near zero. Because the male worker was further forced to compete not only with other incoming immigrant males but with women and children (Bremner, 1956 : 4), his wages often never exceeded $5.00 a week (Gambino, 1975 : 92).

Italians, largely farmers before their emigration, moved to the cities of the United States in great numbers after 1880. Upon their arrival, they were employed in the "hard, dirty, usually menial labor . . . left behind by the North and West Europeans who had moved up the socio-economic scale" (Feagin, forthcoming). Their work conditions, like those before them, were also abominable:

> The Italian immigrant may be maimed and killed in his industrial occupation without a cry and without indemnity. He may die from the "bends" working in the caisons under the river, without protest; he can be slowly asphyxiated in crowded tenements, smothered in dangerous trades or occupations (which only the ignorant immigrant pursues, not the native American); he can contract tuberculosis in unsanitary factories and sweatshops* [Feagin, forthcoming, Chapter 6].

In fact, tuberculosis, a rarity in Italy, was a major source of death in the urban tenements of our cities' "little Italies" (Feagin, forthcoming).

Moreover, by the late 1880s, the history of the Italian in-migration shows that labor conditions for immigrants and tenement dwellers had not been substantially altered, even with a growing union movement (Grob, 1969). In 1895, the day scale of work for manu-facturing laborers, in the "gold paved" streets of New York, was listed in a newspaper advertisement as follows (Gambino, 1975 : 77):

- Common labor, white, $1.30 to $1.50;
- Common labor, colored, $1.25 to $1.40;
- Common labor, Italian, $1.15 to $1.25.

In short, as the 1910 Industrial Commission on Immigration put it: "Where an Irishman or a German demands meat, an Italian will work upon stale bread and beer, and, although his physical efficiency is not as great, he works for so much less that it is *profitable* to employ him" (Gambino, 1975 : 87, emphasis added).

At about the same time, the front sections of the newspapers of New York heralded the emergence of the city as the rightful new center of American life, growth, and prosperity (McCabe, 1882). Historian Roy LuBove describes the end of the 19th century as the time when cities "shattered the Jeffersonian-Jacksonian vision of the yeoman, agrarian republic. The economic vitality of the new era centered in the factory, not the farm. The city, rather than the small town, became the *undisputed symbol of America's productive energies*, cultural and intellectual attainments, economic and social opportunities" (1962 : 40). The measures of the city's success as a center of profit hid its failures as a center of social well-being.

---

*Editors' note: This quote is originally from Antonia Stella, *Some Aspects of Italian Immigration to the United States* (San Francisco: R and E Associates, 1970), p. 94.

There were those who argued for social reform, and against the impact of the excesses of profit making on poor city dwellers. But such critics were few and far between and their propositions for reform, as well as their critiques, rarely made them advocates for redistributively reshaping the city's character in the name of the people. In fact, one group of advocates for slum renewal put the blame for depressed wages and slum conditions at the feet of the immigrant. This early form of the social control strategy of "blaming the victim" for urban poverty argued that our cities could be returned to a wholesome state when we stopped admitting overwhelming numbers of inferior aliens to our cities (Morse, 1835; Greeley, 1864).

A more sympathetic version of such ethnocentric reform argued that even though the immigrants were marginal earthlings, to be treated by all normal souls with understandable repugnance, their very presence and life-styles could not be ignored (Bremner, 1956:6; Hartley, 1842 : 18; Dickens, 1972). The slum, along with the disease it spawned, was a potential threat to *all* city dwellers. And the most *successful* early reformers quickly couched arguments for changing the outrageous living conditions of slum dwellers from Boston to Chicago to St. Louis in terms, not of helping the poor, but of controlling their presence in order to protect the social order. A three-part platform of 19th century urban reform emerged looking something like this: (1) establish standards for sanitation in the slums to guard the *public* health; (2) rectify living conditions in the slum as a guard against the *spread of the "dangerous classes";* and (3) remove slum conditions in areas *unprofitably close* to the business districts of the city (Brace, 1872; Hartley, 1842; Griscom, 1845). The reform for both public and private sectors now took the form of regulating the victim rather than simply blaming him (Piven and Cloward, 1971; Trattner, 1974).

LuBove (1962:48) points out that the first major public hygiene reforms occurred in New York City with the creation of the Metropolitan Board of Health. The board was created not out of a concern for the living conditions of the poor, but after a cholera epidemic threatened the health of the entire city. The first public standards affecting the structure and design of tenements were not directed at the inhuman nature of poor housing conditions; rather they were offered as a way of mollifying the "dangerous" residents who had rioted over military draft conscription policies in 1863. Indeed, it appears that "terror had succeeded where reason, enlightened self-interest and pleas of humanitarians had failed" (LuBove, 1962 : 23).

The reforms for greater welfare were further modified by the opportunities of profit realized in the tenement districts. Besides the bounty of cheap labor, the urban slums of the 19th century also represented a growing place for rental profit. Thus a successful reform soon became one that balanced the rights of people to decent housing against the rights of the urban entrepreneur.

On the surface, local legislation dictating the construction of tenements with light shafts, air vents, fire escapes, larger water closets, privies, and other amenities appeared to be quite sensible when compared with the conditions described by Dickens, Hartley, and others.

However, even these basic changes were not often provided. Attempts were made to include these amenities in the construction of "model tenements," which were designed to reduce overcrowding and profit gouging. To accomplish the latter, it was argued that the profits generated by these structures should be limited to 4% or 5% rather than the usual 15% to 18%. Few such structures were ever built (LuBove, 1962 : 25—33, 86—115). Another reform-based architectural structure was very popular — the "dumb-bell"-shaped tenement. It was the winning entrant in a nationwide contest designed to develop the most "health and morally" spacious tenement that could be constructed on a city lot measuring 25 by 100 feet. The purpose of the structure was to reconcile the tenant's welfare and the investor's profit. Overnight it became a characteristic type of tenement in working-class New York and other cities. It usually stood around six stories high, with 14 rooms to a floor, and it housed two dozen families.

Such forms of social reform obviously did little to benefit the slum but they do not appear to have hurt the tenement landlords. Indeed, the "dumb-bell" and other such reforms appear to have been good business. By 1890, 35,000 of New York's 81,000 dwellings were tenements ("reformed" or otherwise). Of the 1.5 million people living in New York, 1 million of them lived in these slum dwellings. By 1916, the number of New York tenements had increased by 5,000, yet the number of tenement dwellers had increased to an incredible 2,082,000 (LuBove, 1962). While the absolute magnitude of this trend was not as great in other industrial cities, they did exhibit similarly dramatic practices of urban profit at the expense of an exploited underclass (Chudacoff, 1975).

Again it is important to point out that these cities were viewed as the vital new social and economic centers of America (LuBove, 1962). Their poor were not barriers to growth; in fact, they were in many ways just the opposite. As sources of cheap labor and as rental markets, they were a source of "locational advantage" for the capitalist city.

Urban poverty was certainly not defined as an "urban crisis." From this time forward the depressed conditions of urban life would only come to be viewed as an urban crisis when they posed a threat to the economic dynamism (profitability) of the city. Public and private sector reforms would be instigated primarily to control such threats, thus protecting the economic vitality of the "private city."

The preceding historical discussion can now be used to frame two more recent patterns of migration to American cities: the emigration of rural Southern blacks to the cities of the North and West; and the most recent movement of Northern urbanites to the cities of the Sunbelt.

The black migrant and the changing nature of urban profit

There are significant differences as well as significant parallels between the black American's arrival in industrial cities and the earlier entry of European migrants. Like many of its ethnic predecessors, the black population which pushed north after 1940 was a basically *rural* and *unskilled* group. Blacks were also a marginal group; they brought with them a heritage, race, and presence that were highly unacceptable to white America. But their racial marginality represented a form of social identity which had not accompanied the European immigrants. Blacks were not aliens emigrating from a foreign country. On the contrary, they were American residents of long-standing second-class status: a status which had evolved historically as predominantly Southern, rural, and poor.

Between 1940 and 1966, the migration of 4.7 million of these people to the industrial North and the West precipitated a profound change in their residential and geographical character. They were reduced by technological changes in agriculture to a position of uselessness and, driven by "imminent starvation and eviction" (Cloward and Piven, 1974 : x), they made their way to the cities. Thus, where 80% of our black population lived in the South in 1940, today only 53% reside there. And where, in 1940, 32% of all employed blacks worked on farms, today only 2% are farm workers. The result of these shifts is that a higher proportion of blacks than whites now live in metropolitan areas (Farley, 1977:189). In less than four decades black Americans suffered a dramatic dislocation that had a profound effect on their previous social and economic status.

While blacks did not move directly from farms to the major cities, once in urban areas, they were forced by discrimination to gather in ghetto communities. In many cases these ghettos were the slum-worn neighborhoods that had acted as staging areas for the advancement of past marginal groups. But while these areas would serve as places of cheap housing, communal centers of social reinforcement and friendship, and supply centers of public services as they had for past groups, they would not be the economic launching pads they had been previously. On the contrary, these neighborhoods have become final repositories for vast numbers who were pushed by poverty from the farm to the city, only to be "pushed around" again.

It is too simple to conclude that if blacks had come 50 years earlier such slums would have been launching pads for their socioeconomic integration. Their present-day economic position is tied to a variety of features which differentiate their arrival in the industrial city from that of other immigrants. First, their position in American society as a racially marginal group is one of long-standing historical duration. The vestiges of racism remain fundamentally intact to this day. As the agricultural economy of the United States diversified and its productivity increased with technological change, blacks lost rather than gained ground. On the other hand, the urban economies to which they moved no longer needed the large numbers of unskilled labor that had originally primed and fueled their early growth. The Northeastern industrial economies were just not growing very rapidly anymore and where there was growth, blacks had to compete with *white* unskilled labor for jobs (Grob, 1969).

As in their days in the rural South, changes in the urban economy have meant growing sectors of black unemployment and poverty. In short, a racial group, which outlived the economic value society had assigned to it after the Civil War, found the same history of socio-economic uselessness assigned to it in the city.

However, one component had changed; the economic vitality of the cities themselves was now, in some cases, becoming somewhat suspect. As the power of the accumulation function waned, not only as an avenue of profit, but also as a manipulator of the cheap labor and slum conditions of the poor, the legitimacy of the role of the cities as centers of this accumulation was weakened. In the Northeastern urban areas, characterized by increasing wages, job benefits, and union organizing, rising material expectations among consumers and growing civil rights legislation, the black urbanite was justifiably incensed by the failures of the declining city. The riots of the 1960s are ample evidence not only of black rage but also of the growing failure of the city's accumulative capacity to utilize and thus manage poverty profitably. Blacks were not needed as cheap labor and without jobs they represented limited consumption power. Without such consumption ability, they did not represent a new profit market of immigrant renters. *The Northeastern city was as useless to them as they were to it.*

As such, by the 1960s the presence of black immigrants represented more than an economic liability; they also represented social control burdens in urban centers already feeling the first major ripples of economic stagnation and decline. The explosion of these cities into riot-torn war zones displayed in dramatic relief the failing legitimacy of these cities in the eyes of urban black America. It is important to note that the major riots of this era did not break out in Sunbelt cities like Houston, Dallas, Austin, Miami, or Phoenix. For the most part, the major race riots occurred in economically declining urban centers of the North where, as our analysis suggests, the poor could no longer be profitably absorbed or efficiently managed by the economic and political sectors of the city.

Finally, the national political climate of the nation between the end of World War II and the beginning of the 1970s was substantially different than it was during previous eras of urban in-migration. The most dramatic difference was the centralization of many urban social services at the federal level. Again, race had much to do with this. While urban blacks had come to represent a significant electoral force in our nation's cities, few had become integrated into the political machinery of city politics. They did not receive, in the form of social services, public jobs, and political power, the patronage due them for their vote. Frances Piven argues that this time-honored form of integration of the urban underclass into city society did not occur because, although national democratic presidents such as Kennedy and Johnson owed much of their strength to the Northern urban black vote, local city politicians derived their structural power from old, predominantly white, political ties (Cloward and Piven, 1974 : 274—275). In part, in an attempt to break the blockage of black integration through patronage, the Kennedy-Johnson administrations launched a full phalanx of "categoric" urban aid programs, many of which were specially targeted toward the politically vote-rich, yet slum-infested, wastelands of our Northeastern industrial cities.

With the advent of the riots in cities losing both economic vitality and social control over the poor, the federal government, like social reformers of bygone eras, responded not simply out of political patronage, but also out of fear. The "war on poverty" escalated in cities of declining profit to the point that by 1969, it appeared that the most profit to be made in some of these cities was in the "inefficiency-laden" public service delivery systems themselves. If one reads the legacy of these programs, setting aside for the moment that they were born primarily out of political pragmatism rather than a redistributive spirit of social well-being, it is apparent that their failure has been measured more by how costly they were than by how little they changed the lives of the urban poor. In short, the "war on poverty" has been reduced to a "war against welfare cheaters." A rather sophisticated new welfare-labor-housing political rhetoric of blaming the "able-bodied" victim has emerged as the urban "fiscal crisis" of the 1970s, replacing the urban social crisis of the late 1960s. The political strategy of spending the economically declining Northeastern cities out of their 1960s malaise failed because the private sector was deserting the Northeast at a time when the social welfare dollars of federal and state governments were not enough to trigger social renewal in a milieu of both declining profit and declining urban legitimacy. Within the frame of this essay, then, continuation or expansion of the social reforms of the 1960s in this climate represented for the dominant order a serious *mis*allocation of declining surplus; indeed it came to be deemed one cause of our Northeastern "fiscal crisis."

Hence, 130 years after Charles Dickens walked the tenement streets of Manhattan, another journalist, Jimmy Breslin, walked the Brownsville section of Brooklyn and wrote not of teeming tenements but of a semi-deserted, physically decimated, and rat-infested community of economically vanquished people:

> At night, the streets of Brownsville are like a well bombed target. On each block there are half-demolished buildings. Their corroded insides of staircases and broken walls and sagging floors are outlined by the car headlights. ... The people in these lone apartments must keep somebody awake all night, because the kids from the neighborhood come into these buildings and set fires in the empty apartments.... Here and there in the ruins of Brownsville there are neatly painted wooden signs proclaiming that a housing project will be erected on the spot. Under the proclamation is the name of the politician, and of the various urban experts, in charge of the housing program. These signs have been standing in Brownsville for many, many months. Just as the same signs have been standing for the same months and months on Roosevelt Avenue in Chicago and Twelfth Avenue in Detroit and Joseph Avenue in Rochester. The story of a city in this nation in the 1960s is a sign with a politican's name on it, and only the name on the sign changes [Breslin, 1971:233].

Brownsville represents more than poverty; its declining condition represents a society pulling back on the reins of social reform. Apparently there is no redeeming productive value (Baer, 1976; Starr, 1976) to be found in the ghettos anymore and the shift in the social control strategy of the state is as clear as the fading paint on the state program signs.

The contradiction represented by Brownsville and scores of other Northeastern inner cities is that millions of their residents are useless to the city — their needs represent a strain on the accumulation function with no returns to urban profit. Conversely, the historic racial and economic illegitimacy of blacks is only matched by the political and economic illegitimacy of the city to urban blacks. In 1976 it is estimated there were 30,000 burned residences in the South Bronx section of New York City alone. Nationally, thousands of assaults reportedly occurred against inner-city school teachers and welfare workers, and the welfare system is in shambles. Daily, guerilla warfare is waged with city policy. In such a standoff, the Northeastern cities are indeed "declining" because they have lost the ability to control what were once neighborhoods of profit and social order.

The rise of the Sunbelt cities and the "Yankee Immigrant"

Since 1950, while the majority of the older Northeastern cities was suffering a relentless loss in its white, skilled, and upwardly mobile population, the cities of the Sunbelt were experiencing, almost without exception, significant increases in population. In the space of three decades, the population of the region doubled, from 40 to 80 million. The impact of this shift was felt in both regions: dramatic increases in urban population growth in the Sunbelt were matched by significant declines in the Northeast. This shift did not occur in an economic vacuum. People are attracted by jobs and moved by the job market. Thus, by 1972, the major cities of the Northeast had lost anywhere from 14% to 18% of their 1958 employment in manufacturing, retailing, and wholesaling. The major cities of the Sunbelt had average employment gains of between 60% and 100% in these same three sectors (Perry and Watkins, 1977). Further, fully 60% of the South's industrial growth can be traced to the capture of rapidly growing high wage industries.

The migrants attracted to the jobs generated by this competitive edge registered in the Sunbelt economy represented a substantially different group from black migrants. They were, often as not, skilled rather than unskilled, urban rather than rural, and white rather than racially marginal. In the main, therefore, they were not pushed by abject poverty to the Sunbelt. They did not move to slums; they moved very quickly to suburban-type housing. They did not represent useless labor power to the emerging Sunbelt centers of accumulation; they represented profitable, integratable, workers. They did not represent a gross infusion of high cost, socially disruptive, citizens; they represented consumer affluence and a burgeoning housing market. And, quite often, they were Northeasterners who were tired of high taxes, high welfare burdens, and a society shattered by the disorganized impact of large numbers of an "unreasonably" militant racial underclass.

Therefore, this last wave of urban migrants does not, for the most part, represent a massive infusion of a new low-income urban underclass. The urban poverty of Southern and Southwestern cities preceded the new migrants by a century and a half (Perry and Watkins, 1977). In fact one of the attractive features for many labor-intensive Northeastern industries was this large regional pool of docile, low-skilled labor (Harris, 1952; Fuchs, 1963). Thus, it was not the poverty of the migrants but rather the poverty of the region which helped stimulate the economic shift and the migration.

In as much as the growth of Sunbelt cities has been, in part, predicated on these differences, such cities have come to represent a new legitimation of the city as a center of profit rather than a center of wasteful social service delivery. As such, the "rise" of the Sunbelt cities does not represent the practice of a new urban function in America: it represents a regional reaffirmation of the prevailing urban function. Returning to the dilemma posed at the beginning of this essay, the apparent contradiction in the distinction between the "poverty-stricken Northeast" and the "low income Sunbelt" can now be resolved.

SUBEMPLOYMENT: THE NORTHEAST VERSUS THE SUNBELT

We posited in the introduction that the economic "rise" or "decline" of a city does not irrevocably alter the depressed life-style conditions of poverty. What is altered during such periods of change in productivity is the ability of the urban center to economically utilize low-income, unskilled residents. Using a subemployment index as a measure of poverty in the economically productive Sunbelt and the declining Northeast, we will now test this assertion, especially in light of the previously discussed waves of urban immigration.

We use the subemployment index to indicate the economic condition of the urban poor in both the "affluent" Sunbelt and the "depressed" Northeast. Further, this index represents an attempt to overcome the limitations inherent in using the incomplete measure of unemployment. Unemployment, at best, tells us only the amount of people affected by cyclical movements in the job market. Thus, in addition to those officially designated as unemployed by the Bureau of Labor Statistics, the subemployment index includes the following components:

The discouraged jobless.   This includes workers who say that they want a job, but for a number of reasons are not looking. The reasons include such economic ones as lack of transportation or that jobs are not available and that looking would be a waste of time; also such personal ones as family responsibility, an absence of adequate day-care facilities, or ill health which could be alleviated by adequate medical attention. Since they are not actively looking for work, the discouraged workers are reported neither as unemployed nor as members of the labor force. Yet since these people indicate a desire for work, an adequate indication of the impact of a city upon the social well-being of its poor cannot be constructed by simply relegating these residents to the status of nonpersons.

Involuntary part-time workers.   This category separates persons who work part time because they are unable to find full-time work from persons working full time by choice. It also represents a departure from currently accepted Bureau of Labor Statistics practices which count any individual as fully employed irrespective of how many hours per week they work. But again, following the traditional guidelines would only hide an important aspect of a city's performance with respect to its employment capacity.

Workers earning substandard wages.   Qualitatively and quantitatively this is the most significant component of subemployment and represents the one element which has traditionally served as the watershed in measuring the potential utility of human beings in the city. The local economy can be said to be providing adequate avenues out of a poverty life-style if there is significant movement from substandard jobs to "good" jobs. While the subemployment index cannot measure the movement of individuals between these groups of jobs since time series data are not available, it can determine the percentage of workers who, at one specific moment, fall on one side or the other of the cutoff point used to separate a good job from a bad job. Two possible standards will be used to enumerate workers who are fully employed by earning substandard wages. The Bureau of Labor Statistics has defined a lower level family budget, which distinguishes a living wage and a substandard wage. The national urban average "lower level" family budget in 1970 was $6,960 per year, or about $3.50 per hour for a family of four; and for 1973 it was $8,181 per year or about $4.00 per hour. The Social Security Administration has, on the other hand, defined for 1970 $4,200 or $2.00 per hour as an adequate income for a family of four, and this is the basis of the official poverty line.

The data for this index is derived from the 1970 Census Employment Survey conducted by the Bureau of Labor Statistics in the low-income neighborhoods of 51 major central cities. Extensive questionnaires were administered in each inner-city area to determine the respondent's recent work experience as well as past labor-market history. In this fashion, unemployed workers were identified and separated from the discouraged jobless and those correctly listed as not in the labor force. Similarly, involuntary part-time workers were accurately distinguished from those working full time but earning less than $2.00 per hour, between $2.00 and $4.00 per hour, or greater than $4.00 per hour. Overall, we have constructed separate indices for two categories of low-income residents: (1) primary wage earners of each family unit and (2) individuals 16 years or older and not in school.

In Tables 1 and 2 both variants of the subemployment index are computed for 18 of the largest central cities in the industrial Northeast and the Sunbelt. These cities can be properly regarded as prime centers of Northeastern and Sunbelt productivity. Hence, with this sample, both the quantitative and qualitative dimensions of the job-related sources of low income patterns found in the Northeast and the Sunbelt should be apparent.

As the overall subemployment totals suggest, the rising levels of Sunbelt affluence have done little for the poor. The total magnitude of poverty as captured by the two indices is almost identical, with the Sunbelt showing a slightly greater incidence of subemployment than the Northeast.

At the qualitative level, regional variations in subemployment patterns suggest that poverty represents very different urban conditions in the two regions. If we take the first two components — i.e., the

TABLE 1

Comparison of Inner-city Subemployment Rates for Individual Wage Earners in 18 Selected Northeastern and Sunbelt Cities (in percentages)

| | (1) | UNEMPLOYED | | UNDEREMPLOYED | | | | TOTAL |
| | | (2) | (3) | (4) | (5) Full-Time Workers | (6) | (7) | |
Cities:	Unemployed	Discouraged workers	Subtotal (1 + 2)	Involuntary Part-Time Workers	$0.00–$2.00	$2.00–$3.50	Subtotal (4 + 5 + 6)	(3 + 7)
			a. NORTHEASTERN INNER-CITY SUBEMPLOYMENT					
New York	5.6	30.7	36.3	1.6	6.1	26.9	33.6	69.9
Chicago	7.6	28.2	35.8	2.2	7.8	26.0	36.0	71.8
Philadelphia	7.6	12.4	20.0	4.0	10.1	25.3	39.4	59.4
Detroit	10.1	27.4	37.5	3.4	8.9	17.4	29.7	67.2
Boston	5.7	32.7	38.4	1.8	6.3	20.7	28.8	67.2
Pittsburgh	7.8	20.8	28.6	2.5	0.8	24.8	38.1	66.7
Cleveland	6.4	27.1	33.5	3.0	9.1	22.7	34.8	68.3

TABLE 1 (continued)

Newark	7.4	31.3	2.2	8.6	24.3	35.1	73.8
Buffalo	6.9	29.6	2.6	9.0	19.8	31.4	67.9
Average	7.2	26.6	2.5	8.5	23.1	34.1	67.9
Summary	10.6	39.2	3.7	12.5	34.0	50.2	100.0
b. SUNBELT INNER-CITY SUBEMPLOYMENT							
Memphis	8.8	22.3	3.8	21.5	19.9	45.2	76.3
Birmingham	7.5	25.2	3.3	19.5	17.9	40.7	73.4
Oklahoma City	6.3	22.5	3.2	19.6	18.1	40.9	69.7
Miami	8.3	19.0	4.2	19.6	22.5	46.3	73.6
Fort Worth	8.6	18.6	4.0	10.6	21.0	45.6	72.8
Houston	4.7	19.8	3.9	17.2	22.8	43.9	68.4
Dallas	7.3	18.9	4.5	19.3	24.4	48.2	74.4
Phoenix	7.2	25.1	4.2	12.9	21.1	38.2	70.5
Atlanta	6.3	23.4	4.1	18.2	23.1	45.4	75.1
Average	7.2	21.7	3.9	18.7	21.2	43.8	72.7
Summary	9.9	29.8	5.4	25.7	29.2	60.2	100.0

SOURCE: U.S. Bureau of the Census, 1970 Census of Population and Housing (1972). Census Employment Survey for Selected Low Income Neighborhoods. Washington, D.C.: U.S. Government Printing Office.

TABLE 2

Comparison of Inner-city Subemployment Rates for the Primary Wage Earner in Each Family in 18 Selected Northeastern Sunbelt Cities (in percentages)

	UNEMPLOYED			UNDEREMPLOYED				TOTAL
	(1)	(2)	(3)	(4)	(5)	(6)	(7)	
					Full-Time Workers			
	Unem- ployed	Discour- aged workers	Sub- total (1 + 2)	Involun- tary Part- Time Workers	$0.00— $2.00	$2.00— $3.50	Sub- total (4 + 5 + 6)	(3 + 7)
Cities:								
a. NORTHEASTERN INNER-CITY SUBEMPLOYMENT								
New York	4.8	22.5	27.3	1.6	5.0	33.2	39.8	67.1
Chicago	4.8	16.9	21.7	1.7	4.8	14.8	21.3	43.0
Philadelphia	5.2	6.2	11.4	3.9	6.6	28.3	38.8	50.2
Detroit	7.6	19.6	27.2	3.4	7.2	20.9	31.5	58.7
Boston	5.0	21.8	26.8	1.6	4.6	22.7	28.9	55.7
Pittsburgh	6.6	14.4	21.0	2.6	6.8	28.5	37.9	58.9
Cleveland	4.8	12.0	16.8	2.5	5.9	23.2	31.6	48.4

TABLE 2 (continued)

Newark	6.7	23.7	30.4	1.6	5.4	29.2	36.2	66.6
Buffalo	5.5	20.9	26.4	2.2	7.0	24.8	34.0	60.4
Average	5.6	17.6	23.2	2.3	5.9	25.1	33.3	56.5
Summary	9.9	31.2	41.1	4.1	10.4	44.4	58.9	100.0
b. SUNBELT INNER-CITY SUBEMPLOYMENT								
Memphis	4.6	11.3	15.9	3.3	17.2	31.7	52.2	68.1
Birmingham	3.7	12.8	16.5	2.9	16.9	27.2	47.0	63.5
Oklahoma City	5.0	14.1	19.1	3.4	14.5	30.5	48.4	67.5
Miami	6.7	9.7	16.4	4.2	13.0	29.9	47.1	63.5
Fort Worth	5.2	8.5	13.7	4.0	12.1	28.5	44.6	58.3
Houston	2.5	8.0	10.5	3.7	13.0	32.3	49.0	59.5
Dallas	5.3	10.7	16.0	3.9	14.8	30.1	48.8	64.8
Phoenix	5.2	15.0	20.2	3.8	9.4	25.5	38.7	58.9
Atlanta	4.4	14.9	19.3	3.9	9.0	21.8	34.7	54.0
Average	4.7	11.6	16.3	3.7	13.3	28.6	45.6	62.0
Summary	7.6	18.7	26.3	6.0	21.4	46.1	73.5	100.0

SOURCE: U.S. Bureau of the Census, 1970 Census of Population and Housing (1972). Census Employment Survey for Selected Low Income Neighborhoods. Washington, D.C.: U.S. Government Printing Office.

unemployed and the discouraged jobless — we can derive a first major qualitative dimension of subemployment: the lack of opportunity for work of any quality. Measured along these two components, the Northeastern central cities clearly emerge as less successful than their Sunbelt counterparts. A person residing in the ghetto area of a major Northeastern central city will be much more likely to be without a job — either because he is unable to locate one or more likely because he perceives that none are available and therefore searching would be futile. In fact, among the old cities, the discouraged jobless component is responsible for 49.8% of the total subemployed population. Limiting the definition of the relevant labor supply to encompass only the primary wage earner in each family widens the disparity between Northeast and Sunbelt cities although in all instances the magnitude of unemployment and discouraged jobless is less for family heads than for all individuals. Joblessness makes up 41.1% of the subemployed in Northeastern cities and 26.3% of the subemployed in Sunbelt cities.

The remaining three components of the subemployment index comprise a second major dimension of the urban labor market: substandard wages and the inability to find full-time work. On this basis, the Northeastern cities have clearly outperformed the Sunbelt irrespective of which subemployment index is used. The evidence is particularly striking for the category enumerating full-time workers earning less than $2.00 per hour. A worker, either individual or head of household, in a Sunbelt city is more than twice as likely to be working full time and receiving wages which are insufficient to provide a level of income above the poverty level. Ghetto residents in new cities, while much more likely to be working, are also more likely to be earning substandard wages. In the Northeast, however, the incidence of joblessness is greater but for those individuals or family heads who are working, the labor market has provided them with a larger share of good jobs.

Thus poverty in the Sunbelt is in large part the result of low paying jobs, with 73.5% of subemployed inner-city heads of households employed at jobs which do not bring them a living wage. The pattern is less dramatic (58.9%) but similarly the case when Sunbelt subemployment is traced for individuals. In both cases, these characteristics of Sunbelt poverty far exceed the percentage of poor working at substandard jobs in the Northeast. Relative to the Sunbelt, substantially larger shares of the Northeastern urban poor are unemployed or refuse to look for jobs in a market that does not provide an avenue out of material deprivation. They see little difference between taking a job which guarantees them poverty and remaining unemployed.

What emerges from this analysis is the conclusion that people living below the poverty line in the urban South and Southwest represent a profitable resource to be exploited by employers of low-skilled labor; while people living in poverty in the North are more likely to be unemployed because there is no job, or because they cannot find a job which meets their qualitative needs. As such, poverty levels in the North represent people who are economically unmanageable or unuseable; these people represent a barrier to profit and can emerge as a threat to the predominant social order.

DOMINANT VISIONS FOR THE URBAN FUTURE

To state this most recent pattern of growth another way, Sunbelt poverty is maintained and managed by the private sector, while Northeastern poverty, now economically unmaintainable, is becoming increasingly the management problem of the state. What is a "cheap labor" supply in the South is a source of rising "fiscal crisis" in the Northeast, demanding, from the dominant perspective, a damaging *misallocation* of public funds away from surplus-stimulating investment ventures and into redistributive social programs designed to control social unrest and somehow restrain or reshape the poor into some accumulatively useful group. From this perspective, therefore, urban poverty comes to be confronted, not because it represents human misery and a center of declining social well-being, but because it represents a failure in the city as a center of profit.

As such, the *primary* issue of social reform in the late 1970s has become reform of the social welfare and urban renewal structures and not of the declining conditions of human social well-being. Norton Long characterizes the shift of industries and people out of the Northeastern cities, leaving large numbers of economically useless and socially costly residents behind, as residential and industrial "disinvestment" of our historically dynamic centers of profit. For Long, rising conditions of urban blight are not viewed as failures in social well-being but as economic failures: this disinvestment manifests itself in "empty, blighted, gutted, and abandoned factories, office buildings, warehouses, lofts, houses and apartments. The reasons for this disinvestment have to be faced if the process is to be halted and reversed. The single most important explanation is profitability" (Long, 1977 : 51). City expenditures are being sadly "misallocated" in his eyes; they "are treated as pure 'merit consumption' and not as investments of scarce resources that, to some important degree, must generate a return if they are to be sustained" (Long, 1977 : 50).

As if heeding the siren call of Long, two new highly similar directions are emerging in urban policy which place primary emphasis upon the reform of what they view as *misallocative* urban programs that generate no return on their "investment." One perspective catalogues cities in terms of healthy and dying sections. It argues that urban policy should be directed toward the economically and residentially renewable areas, leaving blighted areas to die. The second approach suggests that both private and public policies must adhere to the realities of the societal crisis emerging in the Northeast and cut back on social spending, rising wage floors, costly labor benefits, inflated tax programs, and other redistributive expenditures which divert scarce funds from region-renewing investment strategies. If the regional pattern of urban disinvestment is to be halted, then, from this perspective, Eastern cities cannot afford to continue strategies which are not devoutly attractive to accumulative interests. Thus, while one approach would have us discard sections of cities, or whole cities themselves, which have outlived their primary accumulative utility, the other approach would have us discard public and private activities which divert too much surplus from accumulatively attractive reinvestment schemes.

The urban-death theorists supply a new analytic vocabulary for the increasing human misery and communal blight found in the cities of the Northeast. They relegate sections of our older cities, and some entire cities, to the level of economically useless backyard "sandboxes" (Sternlieb, 1971) and to the socially illegitimate status of barren Indian "reservations" (Long, 1971). William Baer (1976) takes the analysis one step further: these cities, and the poor who reside in them, are really representative of urban "cemeteries." They are actually "dying." They have outlived their profit function and [as with] any organism whose function has waned and which can no longer adapt to change in its environment, natural decline and death are inevitable. Like latter day Social Darwinists, they assume the accumulative function to be the "natural" urban state, and progressively insurmountable failures in the accumulative power of this state must eventually come to be viewed as a sign of death. Baer infers that ineffective social renewal programs, after a certain time, are no more useful to the urban areas than embalming fluid is to a corpse — they preserve the corpse but do not generate its economic rebirth. Those who would continue to pour money and programmatic support into the most blighted of our cities are, in Baer's eyes, no more than urban morticians. Hence, our policy agenda for the urban future should include a contemplation of "the various aspects of urban death and . . . suggest what can be done to ameliorate its consequences. Contemplation is meant as just that: a considered exposition that treats urban death as very much in the *natural order* of things, to be taken in stride — not an apocalyptic pronouncement in the currently fashionable vein" (Baer, 1976 : 4).

Such policies have already begun to emerge. In a recent article, Roger Starr (1967) argues that in order to rejuvenate New York, we must make it smaller. To do this he suggests a form of selective neighborhood *triage* whereby certain sections of the city (including, in particular, the Brownsville section described earlier by Jimmy Breslin) would be systematically allowed to self-destruct with the help and encouragement of the city and the nation. According to Starr, we must begin to think in terms of shrinkage because this is the fate which has been prescribed for New York City by the ultimate arbiter of all economic decisions — the Invisible Hand.

While this first group of policy advocates argues that the best way to manage the crisis of poverty is to "pull the plug" on the terminally ill patient, the other approach suggests a drastic alteration in the mode of treatment. Their new prescription of social control suggests drastic reductions in the amounts and forms of redistributive medicines. The approach in essence punishes cities for their misallocative excesses and accumulative shortcomings. It calls for a substantial change in the amount and character of public- and private-sector activities in order to attract new industrial activity and cut down on the drain of disinvestment. In calling upon Northeastern governors to create an economy renewing Regional Energy Development Corporation, Felix Rohatyn captures the essence of this approach well. He argues that the billions of dollars such an investment could generate will only be forthcoming when and if the Northeastern states and cities are willing to cut back on public service spending. In order to attract such new investment and renewed industrial activity he has argued: "we need to make changes in the (business) tax structure, or changes are needed in union work rules. . . . Because of the possibility of economic activity, the governors will accept political change. What we are creating is a way to give politicians the excuse to do what they know ought to be done anyway. That's the way we got reforms in New York City's government. Every few weeks another bond issue had to be sold. Each required concessions" (McManus and Weil, 1976 : 375).

The concessions Rohatyn and his Big MAC fiscal oversight body exacted from the workers and poor of New York flow directly from the assertion that "political change" in our Northern cities must constitute a reduction in the "wasteful" excess of "misallocated," overly redistributive, policies in an urban community whose role is primarily accumulative.

Recently, Daniel Moynihan has argued that the fiscal plight of the major cities of New York is in large part the result of federal programs which forced the cities to become bloated centers of welfare for unrealistic numbers of people. In a report to President Carter, he states:

> one person in six in New York City is on welfare, and . . . [the] . . . other cities in the State have great welfare rolls. If a personal note may be allowed, as far back as 1965 I persuaded the third President before the present one that this was going

to happen. To use an economist's term, the welfare system is exogenous. This is [to] say the influence comes from outside the system. New York State did not create the present welfare system — the Federal government did. If the system were changed, a great many of its symptoms might disappear, which would prove they had nothing to do with New York as such [Moynihan, 1977: S10829].

Moynihan finds it unrealistic to expect the cities of his region to supply the amount of social services they now deliver. In his mind, a reduction in such redistributive activity is essential if cities are to survive the chaotic "excesses" that contine to materialize as citizens demand more and more services from the state.

Indeed, the demands of the poor for high-paying jobs and the concomitant leisure-oriented luxuries of a consumer society are, in Norton Long's view, also unrealistic goals for the urban poor in America (Long, 1977 : 55). Citing data which suggest that the primary way a poor family can expect to receive an adequate income is by having multiple earners in the family working at low wages, Long argues we must cut back on "union and liberal policy" (1977 : 55) which drives up the wage costs and the expectations of jobholders in low-skill industries to the point where the jobs disappear all together or the economic activity is removed to the low-wage Sunbelt.

These forms of policy redirection have their roots in the overall condition of uneven urban development between the Northeast and the Sunbelt. The impact of the policies offered by Rohatyn, Long, Starr, and others would cheapen Northeastern labor, reduce corporate taxes, decrease the public service burdens, and otherwise ameliorate the rising social well-being costs which dulled the competitive edge of the Northeastern urban centers. Thus, just as the present-day profit emanating from the Sunbelt economy now looks very much like the latter-day profit levels of the Northeast, social welfare policies are now being abandoned in the Northeast in an attempt to bring industrial rim redistributive activities down to the low level of the Sunbelt (Harris, 1952).

THE DECLINE OF THE SUNBELT AND THE RISE OF URBAN SOCIAL WELL-BEING

Against all this, the "rise of the Sunbelt cities" represents a geographical shift in the "successful" practice of the city as the dominant unit of profit. The migrants to the Sunbelt, while substantially different from the other waves, have been profitably integrated into the accumulation process and are highly manageable. Therefore, at present, social reform in the South is in no danger of "erring" through a misallocation of surplus. The poor in the South are also highly employable and a substantial share of their poverty results from the low wages they receive. From this perspective, the new cities of the Sunbelt represent nothing new for the poor — their social well-being is no more ensured in Sunbelt cities than it is in cities of the Northeast.

For us, therefore, the "rise" of the Sunbelt means a new legitimation of the capitalist city and the "decline" of the Northeast is evidence of a crisis in the legitimacy of America's political economy. The new proposals of established policy analysts reflect a concern with this regionally based legitimation crisis.

If the rise of the Sunbelt and the present prescriptions for urban change reflect no alteration in the historical tradition of a permanent urban underclass, and if history repeats itself, then the time will come when Sunbelt cities begin to experience an eclipse in their social legitimacy. The advantageous "low-income pool" of Southern workers will be transformed into "poverty-stricken" urbanites. Indeed the cities of the Sunbelt will have achieved a state of "crisis" parity with the Northeast. As the rising social and economic tensions of the Northeastern cities have demonstrated, the poor do not go away. They do not lose their desire for human renewal; they do not lose their frustration, discouragement, and anger. While the capitalist system can temporarily escape such social dislocation by moving to the suburbs and to the Sunbelt — trading in old urban centers, like used cars, for new models — it cannot proceed in this manner forever. Unlike used cars, declining centers of profit cannot be removed to a junk yard, slipped into a coffin, or pushed to a controlled reservation. They remain filled with humans who are more than simply units of labor, more than "good business climates."

The social unrest of a declining Northeast is a sign of a rising crisis in the legitimacy of the city as first and foremost a center of profit and it cannot be hidden by the "rise" of the Sunbelt. More than ever, it is time to recast the definition of the city in America. It is time to measure urban success in terms of the climate of social well-being the cities represent for people. We must become aware of economic measures of urban health that have at their source the economic exploitation of human lives and temper our definitions of urban growth accordingly. We should test social welfare programs against criteria of social well-being rather than social control. Unless we begin this task of political economic renewal, and consider the American city first and foremost as a center for people rather than profit, then the traditional definitions of the "rise" and "decline" of American cities will become meaningless measures of American development for more than simply the urban poor.

REFERENCES

Addams, J. (1910). Twenty years at Hull House. New York: Macmillan.

Baer, W. C. (1976). "On the death of cities." Public Interest, 45(fall) : 3—19.

Bookchin, M. (1973). The limits of the city. New York: Harper and Row.

Brace, C. L. (1872). The dangerous classes of New York and twenty years work among them. New York: Wynkoop and Hallenbeck.

Bremner, R. H. (1956). From the depths: The discovery of poverty in the United States. New York: New York University Press.

Breslin, J. (1971). "Moonwalk on Sutter Avenue." Pp. 231—234 in D. M. Gordon (ed.), Problems in political economy: An urban perspective. Lexington, Mass.: D.C. Heath.

Chudacoff, H. P. (1975). The evaluation of American urban society. Englewood Cliffs, N.J.: Prentice-Hall.

Cloward, R. A., and Piven, F. F. (1974). The politics of turmoil: Essays on poverty, race and the urban crisis. New York: Random House.

Dickens, C. (1972). American notes for general circulation. J. S. Whitley and A. Goldman (eds.). Baltimore, Md.: Penguin.

Farley, R. (1977). "Trends in racial inequalities: Have the gains of the 1960s disappeared in the 1970s? American Sociological Review, 42 (2) : 189—208.

Feagin, J. R. (forthcoming). Race and ethnic relations. Englewood Cliffs, N.J.: Prentice-Hall.

Fuchs, V. R. (1963). Changes in the location of manufacturing in the United States since 1929. New Haven, Conn.: Yale University Press.

Gambino, R. (1975). Blood of my blood: The dilemma of the Italian-American. Garden City, N.Y.: Doubleday.

Ginger, R. (1973). Altgeld's America: The Lincoln ideal versus changing realities. New York: New Viewpoints.

Greeley, A. M. (1972). That most distressful nation: The taming of the American Irish. Chicago: Quadrangle.

Greeley, H. (1864). "Tenement houses — their wrongs." New York Daily Tribune, November 23 : 4.

Griscom, J. H. (1845). The sanitary condition of the laboring population of New York and suggestions for its improvement. New York: Harper and Row.

Grob, G. N. (1969). Workers and utopia: A study of ideological conflict in the American labor movement, 1865—1900. Chicago: Quadrangle.

Harris, S. E. (1952). The economics of New England: Case study of an older area. Cambridge: Harvard University Press.

Hartley, R. (1842). "An historical, scientific and practical essay on milk, as an article of human sustenance; with a consideration of the effects consequent upon the present unnatural methods of producing it for the supply of large cities." Eighth annual report of the New York Association for Improving the Condition of the Poor. New York: Jonathan Leavitt.

James, D. B. (1972). Poverty, politics and change. Englewood Cliffs, N.J.: Prentice-Hall.

Katznelson, R. (1976). "The crisis of the capitalist city: Urban politics and social control." Pp. 214—229 in W. D. Hawley et al. (eds.), Theoretical perspectives on urban politics. Englewood Cliffs, N.J.: Prentice-Hall.

Long, N. E. (1971). "The city as reservation." Public Interest, 25 (fall):22—38.

——— (1977). "A Marshall plan for cities?" Public Interest, 46 (winter):49—60.

LuBove, R. (1962). The progressives and the slums: Tenement house reform in New York City, 1890—1917. Pittsburgh: University of Pittsburgh Press.

McCabe, J. D. (1882). New York City by sunlight and gaslight, a work descriptive of the great metropolis. Philadelphia: National Publishing Company.

McManus, M. J., and Weil, F. A. (1976). "No one is in charge." Empire State Report, (October—November):364—375.

Morse, S. F. B. (1835). Foreign conspiracy against the liberties of the United States. New York: Leavitt and Lord.

Moynihan, D. P. (1977). The federal government and the economy of New York State. Congressional Record Senate. June 27, pp. S10829—S10833.

Perry, D. C., and Watkins, A. J. (1977). "To kill a city: A critical reevaluation of the status of yankee and cowboy cities." Studies in Politics: Series I: Studies in Urban Political Economy, Paper no. 6. Austin: University of Texas.

Piven, F. F. (1974). "The great society as political strategy." Pp. 271—283 in R. A. Cloward and F. F. Piven, The politics of turmoil: Essays on poverty, race and the urban crisis. New York: Random House.

Piven, F. F., and Cloward, R. A. (1971). Regulating the poor: The functions of public welfare. New York: Random House.

Report of the National Advisory Commission on Civil Disorder (1968). New York: Random House.

Starr, R. (1967). "Making New York smaller." New York Times Magazine, November 1:32—33, 99—106.

Sternlieb, G. (1971). "The city as sandbox." Public Interest, 25 (fall): 14—21.

Trattner, W. I. (1974). From poor law to welfare state: A history of social welfare in the United States. New York: Free Press.

U.S. Bureau of the Census (1972). 1970 Census of Population and Housing, Census employment survey for selected low income neighborhoods. Washington, D.C.: U.S. Government Printing Office.

Wade, R. C. (1959). The urban frontier: The rise of western cities, 1790—1830. Cambridge: Harvard University Press.

Warner, S. B., Jr. (1968). The private city: Philadelphia in three periods of its growth. Philadelphia: University of Philadelphia Press.

Watkins, A. J., and Perry, D. C. (1978). "Regional change and uneven urban development." In D. C. Perry and A. J. Watkins (eds.), The rise of the sunbelt cities. Beverly Hills, Calif.: Sage.

From
The Urban Condition:
Grieving for a Lost Home
Marc Fried

INTRODUCTION

For some time we have known that the forced dislocation from an urban slum is a highly disruptive and disturbing experience. This is implicit in the strong, positive attachments to the former slum residential area — in the case of this study the West End of Boston — and in the continued attachment to the area among those who left before any imminent danger of eviction. Since we were observing people in the midst of a crisis, we were all too ready to modify our impressions and to conclude that these were likely to be transitory reactions. But the post-relocation experiences of a great many people have borne out their most pessimistic pre-relocation expectations. There are wide variations in the success of post-relocation adjustment and considerable variability in the depth and quality of the loss experience. But for the majority it seems quite precise to speak of their reactions as expressions of *grief*. These are manifest in the feelings of painful loss, the continued longing, the general depressive tone, frequent symptoms of psychological or social or somatic distress, the active work required in adapting to the altered situation, the sense of helplessness, the occasional expressions of both direct and displaced anger, and tendencies to idealize the lost place.[1]

At their most extreme, these reactions of grief are intense, deeply felt, and, at times, overwhelming. In response to a series of questions concerning the feelings of sadness and depression which people experienced *after* moving, many replies were unambiguous: "I felt as though

Excerpted from Chapter 12, "Grieving for a Lost Home," by **Marc Fried**, in *The Urban Condition: People and Policy in the Metropolis*, edited by Leonard J. Duhl, © 1963 by Basic Books, Inc., Publishers, New York, pp. 151—164, 167—170.

I had lost everything," "I felt like my heart was taken out of me," "I felt like taking the gaspipe," "I lost all the friends I knew," "I always felt I had to go home to the West End and even now I feel like crying when I pass by," "Something of me went with the West End," "I felt cheated," "What's the use of thinking about it," "I threw up a lot," "I had a nervous breakdown." Certainly, some people were overjoyed with the change and many felt no sense of loss. Among 250 women, however, 26 per cent report that they still feel sad or depressed two years later, and another 20 per cent report a long period (six months to two years) of sadness or depression. Altogether, therefore, at least 46 per cent give evidence of a fairly severe grief reaction or worse. And among 316 men, the data show only a slightly smaller percentage (38 per cent) with long-term grief reactions. The true proportion of depressive reactions is undoubtedly higher since many women and men who report no feelings of sadness or depression indicate clearly depressive responses to other questions.

In answer to another question, "How did you feel when you saw or heard that the building you had lived in was torn down?" a similar finding emerges. As in the previous instance, the responses are often quite extreme and most frequently quite pathetic. They range from those who replied: "I was glad because the building had rats," to moderate responses such as "the building was bad but I felt sorry," and "I didn't want to see it go," to the most frequent group comprising such reactions as "it was like a piece being taken from me," "I felt terrible," "I used to stare at the spot where the building stood," "I was sick to my stomach." This question in particular, by its evocative quality, seemed to stir up sad memories even among many people who denied any feelings of sadness or depression. The difference from the previous result is indicated by the fact that 54 per cent of the women and 46 per cent of the men report severely depressed or disturbed reactions; 19 per cent of the women and about 31 per cent of the men report satisfaction or indifference; and 27 per cent of the women and 23 per cent of the men report moderately depressed or ambivalent feelings. Thus it is clear that, for the majority of those who were displaced from the West End, leaving their residential area involved a moderate or extreme sense of loss and an accompanying affective reaction of grief.

While these figures go beyond any expectation which we had or which is clearly implied in other studies, the realization that relocation was a crisis with potential danger to mental health for many people was one of the motivating factors for this investigation* In studying the impact of relocation on the lives of a working-class population through a comparison of pre-relocation and post-relocation interview data, a number of issues arise concerning the

---

*This is implicit in the prior work on "crisis" and situational predicaments by Dr. Erich Lindemann under whose initiative the current work was undertaken and carried out.

psychology of urban living which have received little systematic attention. Yet, if we are to understand the effects of relocation and the significance of the loss of a residential environment, it is essential that we have a deeper appreciation of the psychological implications of both physical and social aspects of residential experience. Thus we are led to formulations which deal with the functions and meanings of the residential area in the lives of working-class people.

THE NATURE OF THE LOSS IN RELOCATION: THE SPATIAL FACTOR

Any severe loss may represent a disruption in one's relationship to the past, to the present, and to the future. Losses generally bring about fragmentation of routines, of relationships, and of expectations, and frequently imply an alteration in the world of physically available objects and spatially oriented action. It is a disruption in that sense of continuity which is ordinarily a taken-for-granted framework for functioning in a universe which has temporal, social, and spatial dimensions. From this point of view, the loss of an important place represents a change in a potentially significant component of the experience of continuity.

But why should the loss of a place, even a very important place, be so critical for the individual's sense of continuity; and why should grief at such loss be so widespread a phenomenon? In order to clarify this, it is necessary to consider the meaning which this area, the West End of Boston, had for the lives of its inhabitants. In an earlier paper we tried to assess this, and came to conclusions which corroberate, although they go further, the results from the few related studies.

> In studying the reasons for satisfaction that the majority of slum residents experience, two major components have emerged. On the one hand, the residential area is the region in which a vast and interlocking set of social networks is localized. And, on the other, the physical area has considerable meaning as an extension of home, in which various parts are delineated and structured on the basis of a sense of belonging. These two components provide the context in which the residential area may so easily be invested with considerable, multiply-determined meaning.... the greatest proportion of this working-class group...shows a fairly common experience and usage of the residential area ... dominated by a conception of the local area beyond the dwelling unit as an integral part of home. This view of an area as home and the significance of local people and local places are so profoundly at variance with typical middle-class orientations that it is difficult to appreciate the intensity of meaning, the basic sense of identity involved in living in the particular area.[2]

Nor is the intense investment of a residential area, both as an important physical space and as the locus for meaningful inter-personalties, limited to the West End.[3] What is common to a host of studies is the evidence for the integrity of the urban, working-class, slum community as a social and spatial unit. It is the sense of belonging someplace, in a particular place which is quite familiar and easily delineated, in a wide area in which one feels "at home." This is the core of meaning of the local area. And this applies for many people who have few close relationships within the area. Even familiar and expectable streets and houses, faces at the window and people walking by, personal greetings and impersonal sounds may serve to designate the concrete foci of a sense of belonging somewhere and may provide special kinds of interpersonal and social meaning to a region one defines as "home."

It would be impossible to understand the reactions both to dislocation and to relocation and, particularly, the depth and frequency of grief responses without taking account of work-class orientations to residential areas. One of our primary theses is that the strength of the grief reaction to the loss of the West End is largely a function of prior orientations to the area. Thus, we certainly expect to find that the greater a person's pre-relocation commitment to the area, the more likely he is to react with marked grief. This prediction is confirmed again and again by the data.*† For the women, among those who had said they liked living in the West End *very much* during the pre-relocation interviews, 73 per cent evidence a severe post-relocation grief reaction; among those who had less extreme but positive feelings about living in the West End, 53 per cent show a similar order of grief; and among those who were ambivalent or negative about the West End, only 34 per cent show a severe grief reaction. Or, considering a

*The analysis involves a comparison of information from interviews administered *before* relocation with a depth of grief index derived from follow-up interviews approximately two years *after* relocation. The pre-relocation interviews were administered to a randomly selected sample of 473 women from households in this area at the time the land was taken by the city. The post-relocation interviews were completed with 92 per cent of the women who had given pre-relocation interviews and with 87 per cent of the men from those households in which there was a husband in the household. Primary emphasis will be given to the results with the women since we do not have as full a range of pre-relocation information for the men. However, since a split schedule was used for the post-relocation interviews, the depth of grief index is available for only 259 women.

†Dr. Jason Aronson was largely responsible for developing the series of questions on grief. The opening question of the series was: Many people have told us that just after they moved they felt sad or depressed. Did you feel this way? This was followed by three specific questions on which the index was based: (1) Would you describe how you felt? (2) How long did these feelings last? (3) How did you feel when you saw or heard that the building you had lived in was torn down? Each person was given a score from 1 to 4 on the basis of the coded responses to these questions and the scores were summated. For purposes of analysis, we divided the final scores into three groups: minimal grief, moderate grief, and severe or marked grief. The phrasing of these questions appears to dispose the respondent to give a "grief" response. In fact, however, there is a tendency to reject the idea of "sadness" among many people who show other evidence of a grief response. In cross-tabulating the "grief" scores with a series of questions in which there is no suggestion of sadness, unhappiness, or dissatisfaction, it is clear that the grief index is the more severe criterion. Those who are classified in the severe grief category almost invariably show severe grief reactions by any of the other criteria; but many who are categorized as "minimal grief" on the index fall into the extremes of unhappiness or dissatisfaction on the other items.

more specific feature of our formulation, the pre-relocation view of the West End as "home" shows an even stronger relationship to the depth of post-relocation grief. Among those women who said they had no real home, only 20 per cent give evidence of severe grief; among those who claimed some other area as their real home, 34 per cent fall into the severe grief category; but among the women for whom the *West End* was the real home, 68 per cent report severe grief reactions. Although the data for the men are less complete, the results are substantially similar. It is also quite understandable that the length of West End residence should bear a strong relationship to the loss reaction, although is it less powerful than some of the other findings and almost certainly it is not the critical component.

More directly relevant to our emphasis on the importance of places, it is quite striking that the greater the area of the West End which was known, the more likely there is to be a severe grief response. Among the women who said they knew only their own block during the pre-relocation interview, only 13 per cent report marked grief; at the other extreme, among those who knew most of the West End, 64 per cent have a marked grief reaction. This relationship is maintained when a wide range of interrelated variables is held constant. Only in one instance, when there is a generally negative orientation to the West End, does more extensive knowledge of the area lead to a somewhat smaller proportion of severe grief responses. Thus, the wider an individual's familiarity with the local area, the greater his commitment to the locality. This wider familiarity evidently signifies a greater sense of the wholeness and integrity of the entire West End and, we would suggest, a more expanded sense of being "at home" throughout the entire local region. It is striking, too, that while familiarity with, use of, and comfort in the spatial regions of the residential area are closely related to extensiveness of personal contact, the spatial patterns have independent significance and represent an additional basis for a feeling of commitment to that larger, local region which is "home."

THE SENSE OF SPATIAL IDENTITY

In stressing the importance of places and access to local facilities, we wish only to redress the almost total neglect of spatial dimensions in dealing with human behavior. We certainly do not mean thereby to give too little emphasis to the fundamental importance of interpersonal relationships and social organization in defining the meaning of the area. Nor do we wish to underestimate the significance of cultural orientations and social organization in defining the character and importance of spatial dimensions. However, the crisis of loss of a residential area brings to the fore the importance of the local spatial region and alerts us to the greater generality of spatial conceptions as determinants of behavior. In fact, we might say that a *sense of spatial identity* is fundamental to human functioning. It represents a phenomenal or ideational integration of important experiences concerning environmental arrangements and contacts in relation to the individual's conception of his own body in space.* It is based on spatial memories, spatial imagery, the spatial framework of current activity, and the implicit spatial components of ideals and aspirations.

It appears to us also that these feelings of being at home and of belonging are, in the working class, integrally tied to a *specific* place. We would not expect similar effects or, at least, effects of similar proportion in a middle-class area. Generally speaking, an integrated sense of spatial identity in the middle class is not as contingent on the external stability of place or as dependent on the localization of social patterns, interpersonal relationships, and daily routines. In these data, in fact, there is a marked relationship between class status and depth of grief; the higher the status, by any of several indices, the smaller the proportions of severe grief. It is primarily in the working class, and largely because of the importance of external stability, that dislocation from a familiar residential area has so great an effect on fragmenting the sense of spatial identity.

External stability is also extremely important in interpersonal patterns within the working class. And dislocation and relocation involve a fragmentation of the external bases for interpersonal relationships and group networks. Thus, relocation undermines the established interpersonal relationships and group ties of the people involved and, in effect, destroys the sense of group identity of a great many individuals. "Group identity," a concept originally formulated by Erik Erikson, refers to the individual's sense of belonging, of being a part of larger human and social entities. It may include belonging to organizations or interpersonal networks with which a person is directly involved; and it may refer to "membership" in social groups with whom an individual has little overt contact, whether it be a family, a social class, an ethnic collectivity, a profession, or a group of people sharing a common ideology. What is common to these various patterns of group identity is that they represent an integrated sense of shared human qualities, of some sense of communality with other people which is essential for meaningful social functioning. Since, most notably in the working class, effective relationships with others are dependent upon a continuing sense of common group identity, the

*Erik Erikson . . . includes spatial components in discussing the sense of ego identity and his work has influenced the discussion of spatial variables. In distinguishing the sense of spatial identity from the sense of ego identity, I am suggesting that variations in spatial identity do not correspond exactly to variations in ego identity. By separating these concepts, it becomes possible to study their interrelationships empirically.

experience of loss and disruption of these affiliations is intense and frequently irrevocable. On the grounds, therefore, of both spatial and interpersonal orientations and commitments, dislocation from the residential area represents a particularly marked disruption in the sense of continuity for the majority of this group.

THE NATURE OF THE LOSS IN RELOCATION: SOCIAL AND PERSONAL FACTORS

Previously we said that by emphasizing the spatial dimension of the orientation to the West End, we did not mean to diminish the importance of social patterns in the experience of the local area and their effects on post-relocation loss reactions. Nor do we wish to neglect personality factors involved in the widespread grief reactions. It is quite clear that pre-relocation social relationships and intra-psychic dispositions *do* affect the depth of grief in response to leaving the West End. The strongest of these patterns is based on the association between depth of grief and pre-relocation feelings about neighbors. Among those women who had very positive feelings about their neighbors, 76 per cent show severe grief reactions; among those who were positive but less extreme, 56 per cent show severe grief; and among those who were relatively negative, 38 per cent have marked grief responses. Similarly, among the women whose five closest friends lived in the West End, 67 per cent show marked grief; among those whose friends were mostly in the West End or equally distributed inside and outside the area, 55 per cent have severe grief reactions; and among those whose friends were mostly or all outside, 44 per cent show severe grief.

The fact that these differences, although great, are not as consistently powerful as the differences relating to spatial use patterns does not necessarily imply the *greater* importance of spatial factors. If we hold the effect of spatial variables constant and examine the relationship between depth of grief and the interpersonal variables, it becomes apparent that the effect of interpersonal contacts on depth of grief is consistent regardless of differences in spatial orientation; and, likewise, the effect of spatial orientations on depth of grief is consistent regardless of differences in interpersonal relationships. Thus, each set of factors contributes independently to the depth of grief in spite of some degree of internal relationship. In short, we suggest that *either* spatial identity or group identity may be a critical focus of loss of continuity and thereby lead to severe grief; but if *both* bases for the sense of continuity are localized *within the residential area* the disruption of continuity is greater, and the proportions of marked grief correspondingly higher.

It is noteworthy that, apart from local interpersonal and social relationships and local spatial orientations and use (and variables which are closely related to these), there are few other social or personal factors in the pre-relocation situation which are related to depth of grief. These negative findings are of particular importance in emphasizing that not all the variables which influence the grief reaction to dislocation are of equal importance. It should be added that a predisposition to depression markedly accentuates the depth of grief in response to the loss of one's residential area. But it is also clear that prior depressive orientations do not account for the entire relationship. The effects of the general depressive orientation and of the social, interpersonal, and spatial relationships within the West End are essentially additive; both sets of factors contribute markedly to the final result. Thus, among the women with a severe depressive orientation, an extremely large proportion (81 per cent) of those who regarded the West End as their real home show marked grief. But among the women without a depressive orientation, only a moderate proportion (58 per cent) of those who similarly viewed the West End as home show severe grief. On the other hand, when the West End is not seen as the person's real home, an increasing severity of general depressive orientation does *not* lead to an increased proprtion of severe grief reactions.

THE NATURE OF THE LOSS IN RELOCATION: CASE ANALYSES

The dependence of the sense of continuity on external resources in the working class, particularly on the availability and local presence of familiar places which have the character of "home," and of familiar people whose patterns of behavior and response are relatively predictable, does not account for all of the reaction of grief to dislocation. In addition to these factors, which may be accentuated by depressive predispositions, it is quite evident that the realities of *post*-relocation experience are bound to affect the perpetuation, quality, and depth of grief. And, in fact, our data show that there is a strong association between positive or negative experiences in the post-relocation situation and the proportions who show severe grief. But this issue is complicated by two factors: (1) the extent to which potentially meaningful post-relocation circumstances can be a satisfying experience is *affected* by the degree and tenaciousness of previous commitments to the West End, and (2) the post-relocation "reality" is, in part, *selected* by the people who move and thus is a function of many personality factors, including the ability to anticipate needs, demands, and environmental opportunities.

In trying to understand the effects of pre-relocation orientations and post-relocation experiences of grief, we must bear in mind that the grief reactions we have described and analyzed are based on responses given approximately two years after relocation. Most people manage to achieve some adaptation to their experiences of loss and grief, and learn to deal with new situations and new experiences on their own terms. A wide variety of adaptive methods can be employed to salvage fragments of the sense of continuity, or to try to re-establish it on new grounds. Nonetheless, it is the tenaciousness of the imagery and affect of grief, despite these efforts at dealing with the altered reality, which is so strikingly similar to mourning for a lost person.

In coping with the sense of loss, some families tried to remain physically close to the area they knew, even though most of their close interpersonal relationships remain disrupted; and by this method, they appear often to have modified their feelings of grief. Other families try to move among relatives and maintain a sense of continuity through some degree of constancy in the external bases for their group identity. Yet others respond to the loss of place and people by accentuating the importance of those role relationships which remain. Thus, a number of women report increased closeness to their husbands, which they often explicitly relate to the decrease in the availability of other social relationships for both partners and which, in turn, modifies the severity of grief. In order to clarify some of the complexities of pre-relocation orientations and of post-relocation adjustments most concretely, a review of several cases may prove to be instructive.

It is evident that a very strong positive pre-relocation orientation to the West End is relatively infrequently associated with a complete absence of grief; and that, likewise, a negative pre-relocation orientation to the area is infrequently associated with a strong grief response. The two types which are numerically dominant are, in terms of rational expectations, consistent: those with strong positive feelings about the West End and severe grief; and those with negative feelings about the West End and minimal or moderate grief. The two "deviant" types, by the same token, are both numerically smaller and inconsistent: those with strong positive pre-relocation orientations and little grief; and those with negative pre-relocation orientations and severe grief. A closer examination of these "deviant" cases with strong pre-relocation commitment to the West End and minimal post-relocation grief often reveals either important reservations in their prior involvement with the West End or, more frequently, the denial or rejection of feelings of grief rather than their total absence. And the association of minimal pre-relocation commitment to the West End with a severe grief response often proves on closer examination to be a function of a deep involvement in the West End which is modified by markedly ambivalent statements; or, more generally, the grief reaction itself is quite modest and tenuous or is even a pseudo-grief which masks the primary of dissatisfaction with the current area.

GRIEF PATTERNS: CASE EXAMPLES

In turning to case analysis, we shall concentrate on the specific factors which operate in families of all four types, those representing the two dominant and those representing the two deviant patterns.

1. The Figella family exemplifies the association of strong positive pre-relocation attachments to the West End and a severe grief reaction. This is the most frequent of all the patterns and, although the Figella family is only one "type" among those who show this pattern, they are prototypical of a familiar West End constellation.

Both Mr. and Mrs. Figella are second-generation Americans who were born and brought up in the West End. In her pre-relocation interview, Mrs. Figella described her feelings about living in the West End unambiguously: "It's a wonderful place, the people are friendly." She "loves everything about it" and anticipates missing her relatives above all. She is satisfied with her dwelling: "It's comfortable, clean and warm." And the marriage appears to be deeply satisfying for both husband and wife. They share many household activities and have a warm family life with their three children.

Both Mr. and Mrs. Figella feel that their lives have changed a great deal since relocation. They are clearly referring, however, to the pattern and conditions of their relationships with other people. Their home life has changed little except that Mr. Figella is home more. He continues to work at the same job as a manual laborer with a modest but sufficient income. While they have many economic insecurities, the relocation has not produced any serious financial difficulty for them.

In relocating, the Figella family bought a house. Both husband and wife are quite satisfied with the physical arrangements but, all in all, they are dissatisfied with the move. When asked what she dislikes about her present dwelling, Mrs. Figella replied simply and pathetically: "It's in Arlington and I want to be in the West End." Both Mr. and Mrs. Figella are outgoing, friendly people with a very wide circle of social contacts. Although they still see their relatives often, they both feel isolated from them and they regret the loss of their friends. As Mr. Figella puts it: "I come home from work and that's it. I just plant myself in the house."

The Figella family is, in many respects, typical of a well-adjusted working-class family. They have relatively few ambitions for themselves or for their children. They continue in close contact with many people; but they no longer have the same extensiveness of mutual cooperation in household activities, they cannot "drop in" as casually as before, they do not have the sense of being surrounded by a familiar area and familiar people. Thus, while their objective situation is not dramatically altered, the changes do involve important elements of stability and continuity in their lives. They manifest the importance of externally available resources for an integral sense of spatial and group identity. However, they have always maintained a very close marital relationship, and their family provides a substantial basis for a sense of continuity. They can evidently cope with difficulties on the strength of their many internal and external resources. Nonetheless, they have suffered from the move, and find it extremely difficult to reorganize their lives completely in adapting to a new geographical situation and new patterns of social affiliation. Their grief for a lost home seems to be one form of maintaining continuity on the basis of memories. While it prevents a more wholehearted adjustment to their altered lives, such adjustments would imply forsaking the remaining fragments of a continuity which was central to their conceptions of themselves and of the world.

2. There are many similarities between the Figella family and the Giuliano family. But Mrs. Giuliano shows relatively little pre-relocation commitment to the West End and little post-relocation grief. Mr. Giuliano was somewhat more deeply involved in the West End and, although satisfied with the change, feels that relocation was "like having the rug pulled out from under you." Mr. and Mrs. Giuliano are also second-generation Americans, of similar background to the Figellas'. But Mrs. Giuliano only moved to the West End at her marriage. Mrs. Giuliano had many objections to the area: "For me it is too congested. I never did care for it . . . too many barrooms, on every corner, too many families in one building. . . . The sidewalks are too narrow and the kids can't play outside." But she does expect to miss the stores and many favorite places. Her housing ambitions go beyond West End standards and she wants more space inside and outside. She had no blood relatives in the West End but was close to her husband's family and had friends nearby.

Mr. Giuliano was born in the West End and he had many relatives in the area. He has a relatively high status manual job but only a modest income. His wife does not complain about this although she is only moderately satisfied with the marriage. In part she objected to the fact that they went out so little and that he spent too much time on the corner with his friends. His social networks in the West End were more extensive and involved than were Mrs. Giuliano's. And he missed the West End more than she did after the relocation. But even Mr. Giuliano says that, all in all, he is satisfied with the change.

Mrs. Giuliano feels the change is "wonderful." She missed her friends but got over it. And a few of Mr. Giuliano's hanging group live close by so they can continue to hang together. Both are satisfied with the house they bought although Mrs. Giuliano's ambitions have now gone beyond this. The post-relocation situation has led to an improved marital relationship: Mr. Giuliano is home more and they go out more together.

Mr. and Mrs. Giuliano exemplify a pattern which seems most likely to be associated with a beneficial experience from relocation. Unlike Mr. and Mrs. Figella, who completely accept their working-class status and are embedded in the social and cultural patterns of the working class, Mr. and Mrs. Guiliano show many evidences of social mobility. Mr. Giuliano's present job is, properly speaking, outside the working-class category because of its relatively high status and he himself does not "work with his hands." And Mrs. Giuliano's housing ambitions, preferences in social relationships, orientation to the class structure, and attitudes toward a variety of matters from shopping to child rearing are indications of a readiness to achieve middle-class status. Mr. Giuliano is prepared for and Mrs. Giuliano clearly desires "discontinuity" with some of the central bases for their former identity. Their present situation is, in fact, a transitional one which allows them to reintegrate their lives at a new and higher status level without too precipitate a change. And their marital relationship seems sufficiently meaningful to provide a significant core of continuity in the process of change in their patterns of social and cultural experience. The lack of grief in this case is quite understandable and appropriate to the patterns of social orientation and expectation.*

. . .

CONCLUSIONS

Grieving for a lost home is evidently a widespread and serious social phenomenon following in the wake of urban dislocation. It is likely to increase social and psychological "pathology" in a limited number of instances; and it is also likely to create new opportunities for some, and to increase the rate of social mobility for others. For the greatest number, dislocation is unlikely to have either effect but does lead to intense personal suffering despite moderately successful adaptation to the total situation of relocation. Under these circumstances, it becomes most critical that we face the realities of the effects of relocation on working-class residents of slums and, on the basis of knowledge and understanding, that we learn to deal more effectively with the problems engendered.

In evaluating these data on the effect of pre-relocation experiences on post-relocation reactions of grief, we have arrived at a number of conclusions:

1. The affective reaction to the loss of the West End can be quite precisely described as a grief response showing most of the characteristics of grief and mourning for a lost person.
2. One of the important components of the grief reaction is the fragmentation of the sense of spatial identity. This is manifest not only in the pre-relocation experience of the spatial area as an

*[Editor's note: The "deviant" examples have here been omitted.]

expanded "home," but in the varying degrees of grief following relocation, arising from variations in the pre-relocation orientation to and use of local spatial regions.

3. Another component, of equal importance, is the dependence of the sense of group identity on stable social networks. Dislocation necessarily led to the fragmentation of this group identity which was based, to such a large extent, on the external availability and overt contact with familiar groups of people.

4. Associated with these "cognitive" components, described as the sense of spatial identity and the sense of group identity, are strong affective qualities. We have not tried to delineate them but they appear to fall into the realm of a feeling of security in and commitment to the external spatial and group patterns which are the tangible, visible aspects of these identity components. However, a predisposition to depressive reactions also markedly affects the depth of grief reaction.

5. Theoretically, we can speak of spatial and group identity as critical foci of the sense of continuity. This sense of continuity is not *necessarily* contingent on the external stability of place, people, and security or support. But for the working class these concrete, external resources and the experience of stability, availability, and familiarity which they provide are essential for a meaningful sense of continuity. Thus, dislocation and the loss of the residential area represent a fragmentation of some of the essential components of the sense of continuity in the working class.

It is in the light of these observations and conclusions that we must consider problems of social planning which are associated with the changes induced by physical planning for relocation. Urban planning cannot be limited to "bricks and mortar." While these data tell us little about the importance of housing or the aspects of housing which are important, they indicate that considerations of a non-housing nature are critical. There is evidence, for example, that the frequency of the grief response is not affected by such housing factors as increase or decrease in apartment size or home ownership. But physical factors may be of great importance when related to the subjective significance of different spatial and physical arrangements, or to their capacity for gratifying different socio-cultural groups. For the present, we can only stress the importance of local areas as *spatial and social* arrangements which are central to the lives of working-class people. And, in view of the enormous importance of such local areas, we are led to consider the convergence of familiar people and familiar places as a focal consideration in formulating planning decisions.

We can learn to deal with these problems only through research, through exploratory and imaginative service programs and through a more careful consideration of the place of residential stability in salvaging the precarious thread of continuity. The outcomes of crises are always manifold and, just as there is an increase in strain and difficulty, so also there is an increase in opportunities for adapting at a more satisfying level of functioning. The judicious use of minimal resources of counseling and assistance may permit many working-class people to reorganize and integrate a meaningful sense of spatial and group identity under the challenge of social change. Only a relatively small group of those whose functioning has always been marginal and who cannot cope with the added strain of adjusting to wholly new problems are likely to require major forms of intervention.

In general, our results would imply the necessity for providing increased opportunities for maintaining a sense of continuity for those people, mainly from the working class, whose residential areas are being renewed. This may involve several factors: (1) diminishing the amount of drastic redevelopment and the consequent mass demolition of property and mass dislocation from homes; (2) providing more frequently for people to move within their former residential areas during and after the renewal; and (3) when dislocation and relocation are unavoidable, planning the relocation possibilities in order to provide new areas which can be assimilated to old objectives. A closer examination of slum areas may even provide some concrete information regarding specific physical variables, the physical and spatial arrangements typical of slum areas and slum housing, which offer considerable gratification to the residents. These may often be translated into effective modern architectural and areal design. And, in conjunction with planning decisions which take more careful account of the human consequences of urban physical change, it is possible to utilize social, psychological, and psychiatric services. The use of highly skilled resources, including opportunities for the education of professional and even lay personnel in largely unfamiliar problems and methods, can minimize some of the more destructive and widespread effects of relocation; and, for some families, can offer constructive experiences in dealing with new adaptational possibilities. The problem is large. But only by assuring the integrity of some of the external bases for the sense of continuity in the working class, and by maximizing the opportunities for meaningful adaptation, can we accomplish planned urban change without serious hazard to human welfare.

NOTES

1. Abraham, K., "Notes on the Psycho-analytical Investigation and Treatment of Manic-Depressive Insanity and Allied Conditions" (1911), and "A Short Study of the Development of the Libido, Viewed in the Light of Mental Disorders" (1924), in *Selected Papers of Karl Abraham*, Vol. I, New York: Basic Books, 1953; Bibring,

E., "The Mechanisms of Depression," in *Affective Disorders*, P. Greenacre, ed., New York: International Univ. Press, 1953; Bowlby, J., "Processes of Mourning," *Int. J. Psychoanal*, 42: 317—340, 1961; Freud, S., "Mourning and Melancholia" (1917), in *Collected Papers*, Vol. III, New York: Basic Books, 1959; Hoggart, R., *The Uses of Literacy: Changing Patterns in English Mass Culture*, New York: Oxford Univ. Press, 1957; Klein, M., "Mourning and Its Relations to Manic-Depressive States," *Int. J. Psychoanal.*, 21:125—153, 1940; Lindemann, E., "Symptomatology and Management of Acute Grief," *Am. J. Psychiat.*, 101:141—148, 1944; Marris, P., *Widows and Their Families*, London: Routledge and Kegan Paul, 1958; Rochlin, G., "The Dread of Abandonment," in *The Psychoanalytic Study of the Child*, Vol. XVI, New York: International Univ. Press, 1961; Volkart, E. H., with S. T. Michael, "Bereavement and Mental Health," in *Explorations in Social Psychiatry*, A. H. Leighton, J. A. Clausen, and R. N. Wilson, eds., New York: Basic Books, 1957.

2. Fried, M., and Gleicher, P., "Some Sources of Residential Satisfaction in an Urban Slum," *J. Amer. Inst. Planners*, 27 : 305—315, 1961.

3. Gans, H., *The Urban Villagers*, New York: The Free Press of Glencoe, 1962; Gans, H., "The Human Implications of Current Redevelopment and Relocation Planning," *J. Amer. Inst. Planners*, 25 : 15—25, 1959; Hoggart, R., *op. cit.*; Hole, V., "Social Effects of Planned Rehousing," *Town Planning Rev.*, 30/ 161—173; 1959; Marris, P., *Family and Social Change in an African City*, Evanston, Ill.: Northwestern Univ. Press, 1962; Mogey, J. M., *Family and Neighbourhood*, New York: Oxford Univ. Press, 1956; Seeley, J., "The Slum: Its Nature, Use, and Users," *J. Amer. Inst. Planners*, 25 : 7—14, 1959; Vereker, C., and Mays, J. B., *Urban Redevelopment and Social Change*, New York: Lounz, 1960; Young, M., and Willmott, P., *Family and Kinship in East London*, Glencoe, Ill.: The Free Press, 1957.

CHAPTER 3   SUGGESTIONS FOR FURTHER READING

Feagin, Joe R. *Subordinating the Poor* (Englewood Cliffs, N.J.: Prentice-Hall, 1975). This book provides an overview of American attitudes, both elite and rank-and-file attitudes, toward poverty, antipoverty programs, the traditional American welfare systems, and new federal antipoverty strategies such as guaranteed-annual-income programs.

Haveman, Robert (ed.). *A Decade of Federal Antipoverty Programs* (New York: Academic Press, 1977). This is probably the best one-volume review and critical evaluation of the problems, failures, and successes of the widely-heralded War-on-Poverty programs. A number of experienced scholars review the overall impact of these liberal reform programs, including health-care, educational, legal-service, community-organization, and anti-discrimination programs.

Piven, Frances Fox, and **Richard A. Cloward.** *Regulating the Poor* (New York: Random House, 1972). One of the most important recent books by social scientists on poverty and welfare, this volume defends a controversial thesis: that welfare and relief programs are expanded by capitalist elites in times of economic and political crisis, and intentionally contracted in times of economic and political stability.

4

Black Americans in Urban Ghettos

The emergence and growth of large cities have been social developments of great interest to students of human societies for centuries. Why this should be the case is not difficult to comprehend.

> Almost all social changes of any significance move people from place to place. Almost all movements of people from place to place call for changes, temporary or permanent, in their relations to other people. We do not need to know any more than that to understand why migration fascinates students of social organization.[1]

Looking at the effects of white and nonwhite migrants on cities, and of cities on migrants, has seemed to many to be the best way to understand what cities are all about.

A thoroughgoing conceptualization of the process of urban migration would encompass more than the migrating units (individuals or families) and the receiving cities, the aspects of population movement that have received the greatest attention. Of great importance are the points of origin and the larger social structure within which migration occurs.[2] Research on points of origin, for example, can lead to new perspectives on the ongoing urban trek. While analysts have often emphasized the movement from country to city, other types of migration have also been of significance, including not only moves from city to country but also moves from one urban place to another. Thus, many readers may be surprised to learn that for the last few decades the typical migrant to a large American city has not come from a rural area but from another *urban* setting. Moreover, in recent years Americans have continued to freely exchange one place of residence for another; for example, between March 1969 and March 1970 no less than 13.3 million persons moved from one county to another, most from one urban place to another.[3]

In the following article Charles Tilly examines common misconceptions about the character and process of migration to American cities. A number of the arguments made apply to whites and blacks alike, but the central concern is with the migration of black Americans. Historically, the great migration of black Americans to the cities began just after the turn of this century, precipitated both by the economic "pull" of industrialization at points of destination in the North and by the "push" of a declining agricultural situation and of an increasingly racist system in Southern sending areas. For the first few decades of the twentieth century the cityward migration primarily involved rural Southerners moving to the urban North. But surprisingly, in the last few decades the majority of black migrants to most large cities, North and South, have come from other urban places. "One of the great American dramas — the mass movement of Negroes from the villages and open country of the South to the metropolises of both North and South — is ending a fifty-year run."[4] Moreover, by the mid-1970's some census tabulations showed more black Americans moving out of the North, to the South, than moving out of the South to the North.

Provocative, too, is Tilly's critique of conventional wisdom about the "who" and "why" of urban migration. While many city officials seem determined to propagate the myth of the typical nonwhite migrant as a drifter or problem case seeking to misuse the city's public services or to create disorder in the central city, Tilly shows these misconceptions to be wrong-headed on several counts. In the first place, research has shown that public services play a minor role in shaping the flow of migrants to particular cities; most who move to a particular city do so primarily for employment reasons. Researchers have also discovered that migrants to the cities come from the most vigorous elements at points of origin. Urban migrants rank higher in education and occupation than other persons (of their own racial group) at the point of origin, and those in the city of destination as well. Ironically, if the desires of officials who would like to reduce black migration to their areas — and spur blacks already there to leave — were to be implemented, the result would be to depress the average levels of educational and occupational qualification among the city's black residents.

One might well argue that black migrants have been widely utilized as a major explanation for critical urban problems; black migrants have been blamed for a variety of urban ills running from crime and juvenile delinquency to welfare problems, family disorganization, and urban rioting. However, Tilly, buttressing his contentions with data, argues that there is little evidence to show that migrant families are more unstable than those who do not migrate. As for the issues of crime and delinquency, what data there are point to the conclusion that natives are more likely to become juvenile delinquents and to have higher rates of imprisonment than are black newcomers. Likewise, Tilly notes that analysis of black rioters has shown the majority to be native-born or long-term residents rather than recent arrivals. The critical factors determining major urban problems seem to be associated with what happens to people within the urban setting, rather than with the wrenching effects of migration per se.

The concluding policy-oriented section is a welcome addition to the migration discussion. There Tilly suggests that cities should provide new aid and opportunities for migrants, perhaps by breaking down barriers in the areas of housing or employment, perhaps by extending public services immediately, perhaps by establishing well-run urban reception services. Migration in itself does not seem to be the current problem; rather, the unwillingness of white residents in cities to integrate nonwhites into urban life is one of the most serious dilemmas facing contemporary American cities, North and South.

The second selection in this chapter explores the racial segregation faced both by those blacks (and other nonwhites) who have migrated to cities and by their descendants. Looking in detail at statistical data from the 1970 census, Karl Taeuber raises questions about certain traditional pictures of blacks in cities. As of 1970 black Americans were a majority in the central cities of only three of the nation's 243 metropolitan areas; in his estimation eight more of these 243 cities will have black majorities by 1980. Taeuber suggests that it is naive for anyone to think in terms of blacks "taking over" most central cities. Black urbanization, already at a high point, cannot continue at its former pace. Taeuber is even more critical of those optimists about residential desegregation who accent the point that 5 percent of those who live outside central cities (that is, in what they term "suburbia") are now black. In the South much of the black population in suburbia is still in highly segregated areas, and in the North the relatively small numerical increases in the black population outside central cities seem to be concentrated in older suburban areas in essentially "the same kind of blacks-replacing-whites in segregated neighborhoods that occurs in central cities." Looking at the determinants of housing segregation, Taeuber suggests that *intentional discrimination* continues to be very important, particularly in well-institutionalized (if increasingly subtle) public housing and private real estate operations. Segregation in housing patterns persists, North and South, in central cities and in suburbs. In conclusion, Taeuber underscores the critical point that segregated housing is closely linked to segregation in other sectors, including schooling and employment.

In their thought-provoking analysis of American racial patterns, Stokely Carmichael and Charles Hamilton defined "racism" as the "predication of decisions and policies on considerations of race for the purpose of *subordinating* a racial group and maintaining control over that group."[5] Arguing that such racism has long characterized white actions toward black Americans, they described two types of racism: individual and institutional. Individual racism encompasses overt actions by white individuals to injure persons or destroy property, for example, the bombing of a black church; institutional racism is less overt, less dramatic, and more difficult to attribute to specific individuals. Institutional racism resulting in great racial inequalities is constantly manifested in the ordinary operation of the organizations and institutions in the society and stems from the actions of established and "respectable" persons. The focus is on the institutionalizing of discriminatory *behavior*. Although a number of analysts of American society have used terms such as "institutional racism" and "internal colonialism," and although much social science research has been devoted to examining prejudice and stereotyping among whites, few studies have examined the critical aspects of institutional racism in any detail or depth. One that does, William K. Tabb's *The Political Economy of the Black Ghetto*, provides the third selection in this chapter. In the preface to his book Tabb states:

> The purpose of this work is to describe the economic factors which help explain the origins of the black ghetto, and the mechanisms through which exploitation and deprivation are perpetuated; and to explore strategies for ending them.
>
> In the emotional discussion of race it is too easily forgotten that the same economic laws operate in this area as elsewhere. The systematic racism so often described cannot be effectively fought by merely denouncing bigotry and calling for more legislation: the important enemies are not the crude bigots, and there are already too many laws which are not being enforced. Racism is perpetuated by elements of oppression within an economic and political system which must be understood *as a system.*[6]

What are the basic structural features of the ghetto marketplace? Viewing the ghetto's economic system as an indicator of internal colonialism, Tabb describes a number of important structural features of the ghetto marketplace: bait advertising, switch sales, misrepresentative sales contracts, specialized sales and credit techniques, and profiteering in slum housing. Yet the exploitation of the ghetto consumer is not simply the result of the actions of a few disreputable business people. Laws and courts tend to favor business people over the nonwhite consumer, even when the consumer has been victimized. Banks and other reputable lending organizations buy up ghetto purchase contracts often without questioning how they were obtained, thus playing an important role in keeping black urbanites encapsulated in areas of poor-quality housing.

Following on his analysis of these and other important aspects of the economic situation of the ghetto, Tabb explores several strategies for remedying the existing situation — helping individual black business people, placing plants owned by white-controlled corporations in black ghettos, and creating community-controlled development corporations. He provides an intriguing analysis of the first two alternatives in terms of the structural situation in ghetto economies and raises serious questions about "black capitalism." Policy issues quickly come to the forefront in this discussion, and the community-controlled development corporation is explored as a possible way around the individualistic focus of black capitalism schemes.

NOTES

1. Charles Tilly, *Migration to an American City* (Newark, Del.: Division of Urban Affairs and School of Agriculture, University of Delaware, 1965), p. 1.
2. Ibid.
3. U.S. Bureau of the Census, "Mobility of the Population of the United States: March 1969 to March 1970," *Current Population Reports*, Series P-20, no. 210 (Washington, D.C.: U.S. Government Printing Office, 1970), pp. 1—2.
4. Charles Tilly, "Race and Migration to the American City," in *The Metropolitan Enigma*, James Q. Wilson, ed. (Cambridge, Mass.: Harvard University Press, 1968), p. 136.
5. Stokely Carmichael and Charles V. Hamilton, *Black Power* (New York: Vintage, 1967), p. 3.
6. William K. Tabb, *The Political Economy of the Black Ghetto* (New York: Norton, 1970), p. vii.

From
The Metropolitan Enigma:

Race and Migration to the American City

Charles Tilly

Not long ago, the movement of Negroes from rural to urban areas in the United States reached a crucial marker: a higher proportion of Negroes than of whites is now living in cities, especially big cities. For a long time, a majority of the nation's Negro population has lived outside the rural South. Most other "nonwhite" groups in the United States have spent most of their time in big cities; American Indians are the major exception. Anyone who keeps echoing the old idea of nonwhite migration to cities as simply an invasion of bewildered country folk is now, at best, behind the times.

Not that migration, or even migration from rural areas, has stopped. Americans are still very much on the move, and the countryside is still sending millions of people to the city each decade. But with increasing exchanges of inhabitants among cities and a shrinking share of the total population in rural areas, *the majority of migrants to most American cities, whatever their color, are now coming from other urban areas.*

One of the great American dramas — the mass movement of Negroes from the villages and open country of the South to the metropolises of both North and South — is ending a fifty-year run. It has left a mark; the very title of Claude Brown's *Manchild in the*

*I am grateful to S. D. Clark, Roger Davidson, William Michelson, Morton Rubin, Louise Tilly, Ian Weinberg, and James Q. Wilson for advice and criticism, not all of which I had the wit or knowledge to act on.

Promised Land recalls the hopeful exodus to the North. A thousand theories about the peculiarities of Negro life in the United States rest on beliefs about the wrenching effects of that migration.

Migration could plausibly explain such serious matters as the pattern of racial segregation in large cities, the bad housing and inferior services in urban areas inhabited by racial minorities, the violent outbursts of the nation's ghettos during the last few summers, and the white flight from the central cities of major northern metropolitan areas. Plausibly, but not certainly. This analysis will review some of the plausible relationships between migration and the living conditions of Negroes in cities, consider which of those relationships are solidly established, and offer some thoughts on what might be done to change them.

HOW MANY MIGRANTS, WHERE, AND WHEN?

Although they have probably moved around locally more often, America's racial minorities have generally done less long-distance migrating than have whites. We know surprisingly little about the volume and direction of their migration before the last few censuses. As a rough-and-ready approximation, we might say that in an average recent year five million of the twenty-odd million nonwhite Americans moved from one dwelling to another. Of them, some four million stayed in the same county, and the remaining million divided more or less equally between people moving elsewhere in the same state and people moving from one state to another.[1] Even more so than in the case of whites, the long-distance migrants were only a small minority of all the nonwhite movers.

Where did the interstate migrants go? If you took a map of the United States and drew a broad straight line from Tallahassee to Boston, another heavy line from New Orleans to Chicago, and a spindly one from Houston to Los Angeles, then sketched branching lines leading to the cities along the way — thicker for the bigger cities and the ones farther south — the three trees on your map would represent quite well the main established paths of nonwhite migration. The 1960 Census showed the importance of those paths.[2] In most states outside the South, about half the nonwhite population consisted of persons born in other states. Migration, that is, has added enormously to the nonwhite populations of northern and western states.

The states of origin and destination are most commonly on the same tree. For example, the South Atlantic states (from Delaware down to Florida and Georgia) were by far the most frequent places of birth reported for nonwhite persons; such northern states as New York, New Jersey, and Pennsylvania drew very heavily on them for their nonwhite migrants. But the state contributing the most to Illinois' population was outside the South Atlantic area. It was Mississippi, with Tennessee, Alabama, and Arkansas next but far behind. The chief feeder to California was Texas, followed by Louisiana. The "migration trees" are still very much alive.

But their shapes are changing. A growing number of Negro migrants are moving from one northern or western metropolitan area to another, and the number going directly from the rural South to big cities of the North and West has shrunk. Although during the late 1950's most of the nonwhite migrants to big southern cities like Atlanta and Memphis were still coming from small towns and the country, the majority of nonwhite migrants to big northern metropolitan centers like Detroit and Philadelphia were coming from *other* metropolitan areas. In the previous forty years so many Negroes had made the move from farm to village, village to town, and town to city that in 1960 the Negro population still contained much more than its share of people who at some time in their lives had made a major change in the *kind* of community they lived in. Nevertheless, only a fifth of the 1960 nonwhite population of American metropolitan areas (as compared with a tenth of the white population) consisted of persons born on farms. And the people then on the move were more urban than that.

Even in Wilmington, Delaware — a city of 100,000 located in a largely southern state with many Negroes in rural communities — well over half the nonwhite migrants by 1960 were coming to the city from other metropolitan centers.[3] In fact, by that time, once occupational differences were taken into account, there was little difference in urban experience between white and nonwhite migrants to Wilmington. Many Negroes were coming from Philadelphia, or Baltimore, or Detroit. The branches of the migration trees are crossing increasingly, and are growing to be more substantial than the trunks that used to support them.

THE IMPACT OF BIG CITIES

Most urban Americans have noticed at least one part of this complex process: the swelling of the nonwhite population of the central selection of major metropolitan areas. They have noticed the changes in New York's Bedford-Stuyvesant, Chicago's West Side, Cleveland's Hough, Boston's Roxbury. In all these cities and many more, the white population has dwindled since 1940 or so, as the net effect of many moves into central cities and many more moves out of them. At the same time, Negroes in cities have more than reproduced themselves and migration has added mightily to their numbers. One result has been the familiar but still impressive rise in the proportion of

Negroes in central cities. Over the decade 1950—1960 the percentage nonwhite in Washington went from 35 to 55, in New York from 10 to 15, in Cleveland from 16 to 29, in Boston from 5 to 10, in Chicago from 14 to 24; in all these cities the nonwhite population was over nine-tenths Negro. If we play the risky game of projecting these increases in a straight line, for the year 1980 we arrive at the following percentages nonwhite:

- Washington   95
- Cleveland   55
- Chicago   44
- New York   25
- Boston   20

As predictions, these numbers are worthless. As signs of what has been going on, they are very telling.

The less obvious part of this process was the bleaching of the suburbs through the addition of huge numbers of whites and almost no Negroes. Some of the bleaching occurred because of the flight of whites from the problems and people of the central city, some of it because jobs and housing attracted new white migrants directly to the suburbs rather than to central cities, more of it because, in the normal process of moving around and out toward the sites of new housing, low incomes and organized discrimination barred Negroes from taking part. A second result, then, has been the emergence of increasingly black central cities surrounded by increasingly white suburbs. This is the situation that gave one of the last decade's most intelligent essays on big cities the title *The Metropolitan Area as a Racial Problem.*[4]

At least the flight of the whites left some small benefits for Negroes. Though the piling up of families in the constricted central city housing market of the 1940's had actually increased crowding and decreased the average quality of dwellings available to Negroes in many cities, the loosening of the 1950's and 1960's gave them more choice, more room, and better quality. Many whites moved out of housing in good condition, public action like highway construction or urban renewal flattened many of the worst dwellings, a smaller number of new dwellings open to Negroes went up, and some landlords, faced with less of a seller's market than before, renovated their properties.[5]

Of course, these changes meant that Negroes ended up paying much higher rents; the regularity with which urban renewal programs subtract low-rent housing from the stock and replace it with fewer units of high-priced housing is only one example. These changes also look much less impressive when compared with the even greater gains in space, choice, and housing quality whites made throughout

American metropolitan areas. The multiple shifts of population and housing stock, taken all together, left big-city Negroes with an absolute improvement and a relative loss.

These streams of migration, local moves, and housing changes depend on each other so intricately that it is hard to say what difference migration in itself makes. In a strict sense, migration — in the form of net movements of Negroes into big cities and net movements of whites away from central cities and from areas of expanding Negro population — accounts directly for the pattern of segregation. Furthermore, the tendency of those migrants who come to the city through contacts with friends or kinsmen to settle first with them or near them, as well as the tendency of other Negro families to seek protection and familiar surroundings near the ghetto, add a measure of self-segregation to the city. Yet these tendencies toward a voluntary clustering of the Negro population are surely far less important than the extraordinarily limited range of dwellings open to the newcomer; besides the deliberate discrimination of owners and agents, the range is limited by the insufficient information concerning the market which new arrivals have at their disposal, their low incomes, and the problem of travelling to work in those central city enterprises which employ Negroes in any number.

These factors affect not only the location but the *quality* of housing available to racial minorities. A highly segregated market gives the minority group less room to compare or bargain, and in that sense any regional and local moves that raise the level of racial concentration also aggravate the housing situation. Still, it is not so simple. Despite the common-sense presumption that in a restricted market there would be more for everyone if fewer new people came to town, and despite the near certainty that the piling up of new arrivals during the 1940's worsened the housing of Negroes, it looks as though over the long run the vitality of new construction in a metropolitan area — which depends on the area's general prosperity and is therefore related to its attractiveness to new migrants — matters a great deal more than the number of Negro newcomers.[6] Where plenty of new suburban housing is going up, vacancies appear in the older sections of the central city, and Negroes are in a better competitive position. Under these conditions, to be sure, the whites are usually improving their housing at an even faster rate, so the gap between the races is remaining or increasing. The "trickling down" of used housing to Negro families does improve their lot; it falls far short of equalizing their opportunity.

WHO MIGRATES? WHY?

We often encounter the argument that if a town improves its living conditions and public services too energetically, it will simply see its resources consumed by a rush of new, poor, dependent migrants — drifters, welfare chiselers, and problem families. There are two things wrong with this idea. First, living conditions and public services play only a small part in determining the number of migrants to any particular city. Second, migrants to cities are drawn especially from favored and vigorous elements of the general population.

When interviewers ask American migrants why they have moved, the migrants give answers relating to jobs far more than any other answers; the largest number usually report a specific job brought them to the city, but another sizable number say they came looking for work.[7] This is about as true for Negroes as it is for whites. However, since workers in relatively unskilled occupations more often migrate without having a job already nailed down, and since Negroes include a higher proportion of workers in relatively unskilled occupations, Negroes who migrate are more often looking for work than migrating whites.

Our information on why migrants choose one destination rather than another is less abundant.[8] For people who have received specific offers of jobs, the climate, amenities, and services of a given city normally enter in a secondary way into their evaluation of the offer. For people retiring or in bad health they often determine the choice. But for people moving without a guarantee of a job the presence of friends and relatives matters a great deal more than such things as the housing supply or the availability of public assistance. If these conditions do make some marginal difference in the volume of a city's migration, most likely it is through the encouragement or discouragement friends and relatives already there give to potential migrants, rather than through a general spreading of the word among the would-be freeloaders.

If we move away from what people *say* about their own motives for moving and toward the *objective conditions* differentiating cities receiving many migrants from cities receiving few, we find jobs looming even more important than before. In the United States, the net migration to an area corresponds very closely to its income level and its production of new jobs as compared with other potential destinations for migrants. An exhaustive analysis of net migration from 1870 to 1950 conducted by the demographers and economists of the University of Pennsylvania shows that during this period Negroes as a group, even though they had less to hope for, responded more sharply to changes and regional variations in economic opportunity than did whites.[9] We have no good reason to think the situation has changed. Though booming cities often have both good public services and numerous migrants, there is no sign that public services themselves affect the volume of migration, and there is every sign that new employment does.

Anyway, who comes?[10] The "Grapes of Wrath" picture of migrants as the dispossessed has such a grip on American imaginations that one of the most popular explanations of the big-city riots of 1964, 1965, and 1966 has been the arrival of unhappy wanderers from the South. In reality, cityward migrants tend to be *above* the average in education and occupational skill at their points of origin. They come heavily concentrated in the most energetic age groups — the late teens and early twenties. *And they even tend to rank higher in education and occupation than the population already in the city.* (Of course, those who leave any particular city also average high in occupation and education, so the net effect of migration in and out is often to depress the level of skill in a city's population.)

People moving off farms are a little different. They are not consistently better off than the people they leave behind: both the least and the most educated predominating in the younger ages, the least educated in the older ones. They tend to be even younger than other migrants, and they are on the whole below the standard levels of education and occupational skill for the city's population. But migrants from farms are only a small part of all people coming to any particular city, and so their arrival does not significantly depress the population's level of qualifications.

We already know that nonwhite migrants to cities have more often come from farms and from regions with generally low educational standards than have white migrants. We also know that nonwhite persons, whether migrants or not, generally get less education and hold poorer jobs than white persons. No one should be surprised to learn that the average nonwhite migrant comes to the city with less education and occupational skill than either the white migrant or the bulk of the urban population. *But compared to the nonwhite population already in the city,* the average nonwhite migrant has a distinct *advantage* in age, occupation, and education.

These complicated comparisons hold an ironic implication for those city fathers who wish they could speed the departure of Negroes from their towns and keep new Negro migrants from coming in. Such a strategy would be a very good way to depress the average level of qualification of the city's Negro population. It would probably increase the proportion, if not the absolute number, of the Negro population heavily dependent on public services. The way to insure a young and skilled Negro population would be to attract new migrants and make sure that the mobile people already in the city were too satisfied to depart. Of course, stimulating job opportunities and providing a decent education for Negroes already in the city would complement such a policy.

One part of this prescription is already in effect without much help from the city fathers. More and more of the recent Negro migrants to big cities are people with relatively good job skills and educational backgrounds moving in from other metropolitan areas. If these new migrants have not attracted as much attention as the displaced croppers from depressed farming areas of the South, maybe it is because they do not fit everyday prejudices so well.

DOES MIGRATION DISORGANIZE?

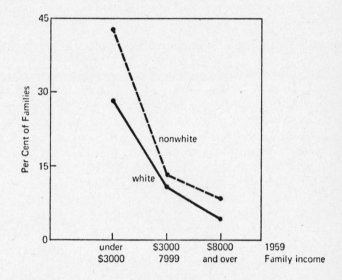

Percent of families headed by women, by income class: U.S. central cities, 1960

If we come to realize that most Negro migrants are neither drifters nor dregs, we may have to abandon other commonplace prejudices concerning the disorganizing effects of migration. No doubt it is true — as a long line of acute observers from W. E. B. DuBois to Gilbert Osofsky have noted — that migration from the South to an urban North in which Negro women had a niche (if not a very pleasant one), while Negro men often had no place at all, wrenched and reshaped the family lives of Negroes.[11] No doubt this wrenching even affected the later generations born in the city. Although the difference in family stability between whites and Negroes of the same income or occupations is less than many people think, Negro households do break up and regroup more often than do white ones. Rates of divorce and separation are generally higher for Negroes.[12] The greater frequency of divorce and separation in turn helps make families headed by women more common among Negroes. The figure above shows, for 1960, the proportion of female-headed families in various income and color groups, within central cities.[13] This comparison suggests (but certainly does not prove) that income is the big factor and racial difference in family life a somewhat smaller one. A finer comparison by income, indeed, would show less difference between the racial categories, since within each of these broad income classes the non-whites are concentrated toward the bottom. If so, Negroes still come out disadvantaged because their incomes are on the whole much lower and less reliable than those of whites. Though the majority of Negro families are unbroken, a substantially higher proportion of Negro children than of white children grow up without a father continuously at hand, and suffer both economically and psychologically from the absence of that father.

All this amounts to saying that the situation in the city, rather than the fact of moving, shook Negro family life in the time of the great northward migration. The distinction may seem academic: the impact of any move on the individual always includes the differences in living conditions between the origin and the destination. Yet it matters a great deal. For in the one case we might conclude that as migration slowed down and the immediate shock of moving faded, the troubles of Negro families would disappear. In the other case, we could hardly expect much improvement until the opportunities open to Negro men and women in the big city changed.

Oddly enough, there is no solid evidence indicating that migrant families are more unstable than immobile ones — or, for that matter, that the opposite is true. In principle, this should not be hard to find out; in practice, reliable measures and adequate data are painfully difficult to assemble. In the case of Wilmington, Delaware, Table 1

TABLE 1

Household types of whites and nonwhites migrating to Wilmington between 1955 and 1960

	PERCENT OF ALL HOUSEHOLDS CONSISTING OF					
	AN INDIVIDUAL LIVING ALONE		A MARRIED COUPLE WITH OR WITHOUT DEPENDENTS		A HEAD WITH NO SPOUSE PRESENT, PLUS OTHERS	
Moves made from 1955 to 1960	*White*	*Non-white*	*White*	*Non-white*	*White*	*Non-white*
Stayed in same house	20	28	62	47	18	25
Moved within the city of Wilmington	24	20	61	52	15	28
Moved into the city from the suburbs	23	18	62	56	15	26
Moved in from another metropolitan area	30	14	64	61	6	25
Moved in from a non-metropolitan area	36	7	54	91	10	2
Total	22	22	61	51	17	27

SOURCE: Unpublished tabulation of the 1960 Census of Population.

summarizes the relationship between color and mobility on the one hand and household composition on the other, as of 1960.

The white and nonwhite populations had about the same proportions of people living alone. But the relationship with mobility was quite different: among the whites, the bigger the move, the higher the proportion of solitary individuals; among the nonwhites, the bigger the move the smaller the proportion of solitary individuals. This does not mean there were more *unmarried* migrants among the whites, but that single nonwhite migrants were much more likely to lodge with friends or relatives instead of taking rented rooms. In fact, both single and married Negro migrants to Wilmington often come alone, and stay for at least a short time with friends or relatives. After finding jobs and getting used to the city, the married men ordinarily secure separate lodgings and then send for their families. The single men often continue to lodge with their friends or relatives for quite some time. The common picture of recent migrants as footloose, solitary individuals applies to the whites of Wilmington much more accurately than to the nonwhites.

The rest of the table contains an even more interesting message. Here we find the proportions of households headed by intact married couples contrasted with the proportions we might call "broken." The general comparison follows the national pattern: the whites have significantly more intact families. The comparisons in terms of mobility, however, look quite different for the two groups. The various categories of whites do not differ very much, except that the migrants from nonmetropolitan areas (which means essentially small towns and open country) include fewer married couples than the rest. Among the nonwhites, the bigger the move, the higher the proportion of married couples. The range goes from less than half for people staying in the same house between 1955 and 1960, up to more than nine-tenths for people moving in from nonmetropolitan areas. The statistics directly contradict everyday ideas on the subject.

Among both whites and nonwhites, the long-distance migrants include *fewer* broken families (compare the last two columns of the table). There are two significant differences between the white and nonwhite patterns. The white migrants from other metropolitan areas do not look much different from the local population. The comparison between white and nonwhite migrants from non-metropolitan areas goes the other way, with almost no broken families among the nonwhites coming from the countryside. If migration is disrupting family life in Wilmington, it must be doing so over a longer time span than the five years our table covers. Whatever the explanation of the greater instability of nonwhite households, it can hardly be the disruptive effects of migration.

While the great differences in size and in sources of migrants between the two cities produce some interesting variations in the

TABLE 2

Percentage of whites and nonwhites migrating to New York City between 1955 and 1960
(according to household composition)

| | PERCENT OF ALL HOUSEHOLDS CONSISTING OF | | | | | |
| | AN INDIVIDUAL LIVING ALONE | | A MARRIED COUPLE WITH OR WITHOUT DEPENDENTS | | A HEAD WITH NO SPOUSE PRESENT, PLUS OTHERS | |
Moves made from 1955 to 1960	White	Non-white	White	Non-white	White	Non-white
Stayed in same house	21	27	65	49	14	24
Moved within the central city	19	24	71	54	9	22
Moved into the city from the suburbs	28	23	63	64	9	12
Moved in from another metropolitan area	44	34	50	49	6	18
Moved in from a non-metropolitan area	38	23	50	63	12	14
Total	21	26	66	51	12	23

SOURCE: U.S. Census of Population, 1960, Subject Report PC(2)–2C, Mobility for Metropolitan Areas, calculated from table 4.

pattern, both Wilmington and New York display the same general tendencies. Table 2 is a parallel tabulation for New York City. A higher proportion of New York's recent migrants are living alone, and a few more of the migrants from nonmetropolitan areas are in broken families. Yet the main conclusion holds: if anything, the recent migrants are less likely than the rest to have broken families, and this is especially true within the nonwhite population.

When it comes to the related matter of emotional adjustment, it now looks as though major mental disorders are more common among long-distance migrants than in the general population (although even that fact could not in itself establish that mobility *causes* mental disorder), but comparisons for other types of personal disorganization remain inconclusive.[14]

As for the crime and delinquency so regularly attributed to the newcomers, what evidence there is points the other way: it takes some time in the city for the migrant to catch up with the old residents. A long series of studies first stimulated by arguments offered for the restriction of immigration after World War I showed lower rates of criminal activity for immigrants than for the native population. In a careful recent study of about 900 Negro boys from a high-delinquency section of Philadelphia, Leonard Savitz found the boys born and brought up in the city to have delinquency rates about 50 percent *higher* that the migrants from elsewhere, even after making allowance for the greater number of years the natives had been around to be caught. As Savitz summed up: "There was no confirmation of internal migration as a disorganizing process in modern life. The migrants not only tended to be lower than the native in the frequency and serious-ness of delinquencies, but also were less likely to come from broken homes, have illegitimate siblings or engage in considerable intracity mobility."[15] Most of the studies seeming to show otherwise, it turns out, establish that crime, delinquency, illegitimacy, and family instability concentrate in *areas* of high mobility, but fail to show that the mobile *persons* in those areas create disorder.

A detailed analysis of commitments to Pennsylvania prisons by Judith Kinman and Everett Lee brought out an even more interesting conclusion than that of Savitz.[16] As was already well established, they found the rates of imprisonment to be much higher for Negroes than for whites. Like Savitz, they also found that among Negroes the rates were higher for natives than for migrants. But among whites, it was the other way around: the migrants went to prison more often. Further-more, the really big differences showed up among migrants from the South, with the whites, compared with the natives and the whites from other regions, having exceptionally *high* rates of commitment, and the Negroes (likewise compared to the natives and the Negroes from other regions) having exceptionally *low* rates. So the most convenient explanation for the greater frequency with which Negroes are convicted of crimes — the disorientation of the new arrivals from the South — appears to be wrong on every count. Perhaps one part of the correct explanation is that the white criminal has an easier time escaping detection, conviction, and imprisonment than the Negro criminal. Perhaps another is that the Negro migrant from the South is more often drawn temporarily into a protective web of kinsmen and fellow migrants, whereas the white Southerner is more often cast into miserable circumstances on his own. Whatever the ultimate explana-tion, it must have more to do with what happens to migrants *after* they are in the city than with the shock of moving itself.

THE ASSIMILATION OF THE NEWCOMER

Sociologists and politicians alike have often tried to analyze what has been happening to racial minorities as a process of assimilation "into the mainstream of American life." They have relied on analogies with the fairly regular ways in which Italians or Poles went from isolation, deprivation, and cultural distinctness toward the normal rewards and involvements of American life.

The basic argument stands out in both the title and the text of Irving Kristol's stimulating *New York Times Magazine* article: "The Negro Today Is Like the Immigrant Yesterday."[17] The article rightly reminds us how much of the ugly language and uglier fact of current accounts of Negro urban life applied to the Irish of our cities only a few generations ago and holds out assurances that this crisis, too, will pass away. A number of historians of American immigration and assimilation, like Oscar Handlin, have urged the same thesis.[18]

The idea is attractive because of its simplicity and its optimism. Even if they didn't come from overseas, many Negroes have recently made the big move from region to region and from country to city. Over the last century Negroes and Orientals have won access to significantly better jobs, incomes, and education. These changes make the assimilationist idea plausible. The argument also makes it easier for the descendants of nineteenth- or twentieth-century immigrants to reply to Negro demands with: "We made it on our own . . . Why can't you?"

The idea of an inevitable movement toward assimilation faces some difficult facts, however. The ancestors of most of America's Negro population were here well before most of the Europeans on whose assimilation the scheme is based. Some forms of racial discrimination and segregation (the World War II roundup of Japanese, the rising residential segregation of big cities in the 1940's, the earlier elaboration of Jim Crow legislation are examples) have worsened several times in the memory of living men. And Negroes (if not Orientals or American Indians) have publicly expressed a greater sense of alienation from the rewards and involvement of American life in recent years than before.

In some broad ways, to be sure, assimilation has been moving on. Over the last few decades Negroes have been gaining better jobs, more education, higher incomes, sounder housing, fuller medical care, even greater life expectancy. But so have whites. In all these respects, the gap between whites and Negroes has closed little (if at all) over the last twenty years. Negro unemployment rates remain consistently higher, especially in bad times. Broken families remain common, illegitimacy rates rise, the need of Negro households for public assistance persists. The essence of assimilation is not just material improvement in absolute terms, but a closing of the gap between a group of newcomers and the rest of the nation. For a process often billed as steady and irreversible, the assimilation of Negroes does not seem to be working right.

At the beginning of their discussion of the position of Negroes in New York City, Nathan Glazer and Daniel Patrick Moynihan seem to accept the standard argument: "The Negro population is still in large part new to the city. In 1960 half of the entire nonwhite population of the city above the age of 20 had come from the South. These Americans of two centuries are as much immigrant as any European immigrant group, for the shift from the South to New York is as radical a change for the Negro as that faced by earlier immigrants."[19] Then the qualifications begin. As their analysis unfolds, Glazer and Moynihan slowly come to the conclusion that the conditions for getting ahead have changed too much, that the Negro family has suffered too much damage, that the internal cohesion of the Negro population is too low, for anyone to expect an updated repetition of the classic American success story. Now, this is not exactly the argument of civil rights leaders or of radical critics of American society, but it differs greatly from the more optimistic assimilationist account of what is going on.

At first glance, these disagreements may look like tedious professorial wrangling over definitions and historical analogies. In fact, they set the terms of one of the great questions for research and action in urban life over the next decade. Has there been a standard process of assimilation into an American mainstream via the big city, one that is still working today for Negroes and other racial minorities? Or have the mechanisms broken down, has the economic situation changed too much, has the system of exclusion become too efficient, are the groups now seeking inclusion too different in character? Or is the notion of assimilation into the mainstream itself based on mis-understanding of how American life works?

If the standard process of assimilation is still working, then designers of American public policy could reasonably seek ways to speed up an established pattern of change. If the process is not working, then they would have to envisage changes in the very structure of American society. For once, a problem with extensive theoretical implications and a question of great significance for public policy come together. Although I cannot guarantee that the social scientists, the policy makers, or the critics will come up with satisfactory answers, I am sure that they will all soon be pouring an extraordinary effort into the analysis of assimilation.

That prediction is all the safer because when forced to account for racial protests or ghetto riots, Americans so readily turn to migration and its aftermath as the explanations. The Governor's Commission on the Los Angeles Riots (the McCone Commission), after pointing out the hardships suffered by Negroes everywhere in the United States, had to ask, "Why Los Angeles?" Here is what they said:

> Yet the riot did happen here, and there are special circumstances here which explain in part why it did. Perhaps the people of Los Angeles should have seen trouble gathering under the surface calm. In the last quarter century, the Negro population here has exploded. While the County's population has trebled, the Negro population has increased almost tenfold, from 75,000 in 1940 to 650,000 in 1965. Much of the increase came through migration from Southern States and many arrived with an anticipation that this dynamic city would somehow spell the end of life's endless problems. To those who have come with high hopes and

great expectations and see the success of others so close at hand, failure brings a special measure of frustration and disillusionment. Moreover, the fundamental problems, which are the same here as in the cities which were racked by the 1964 riots, are intensified by what may well be the least adequate network of public transportation in any major city in America.[20]

Migration bears the blame.

That migration is to blame seems at first glance to be confirmed by the special census of South Los Angeles conducted after the Watts riots. From 1960 to 1965, unemployment stayed almost constant (in the face of dramatic increases in employment elsewhere), incomes had dropped, housing had deteriorated, and broken families had become more common.[21] When unveiling the census report, Andrew Brimmer, Assistant Secretary of Commerce for Economic Affairs, interpreted it to mean that "the most successful families had moved to more desirable neighborhoods and had been replaced by lower income groups moving in from other parts of the state and nation."[22] The new findings seemed to corroborate the Commission's explanation of the riots.

But the facts are more complicated. If migration is such a powerful factor, we should find that cities receiving many underprivileged migrants are more violent than the rest, we should expect violence in those sections of cities where populations are swelling with new migrants, and we should discover that recent migrants are peculiarly prone to violence. What is the evidence?

The efforts of sociologists to get at the origins of collective violence have not revealed any reliable tendency for high-migration cities to produce more interracial mayhem or more frequent ghetto explosions than the rest. An analysis of 76 urban riots during the years 1913—1963 done by Stanley Lieberson and Arnold Silverman of the University of Wisconsin identified some revealing tendencies for riots to break out in cities where Negroes were underrepresented in the police force or in the city council, but detected no difference attributable to migration.[23] In any case, the Watts of just before the 1965 riots was actually a *declining* community in population as well as in standard of living, not a staging area for new arrivals. And the Los Angeles County Probation Department found:

1. Over half the juveniles picked up for participation in the riots were California born.
2. More than three-quarters had lived in the county at least five years.
3. Only one in twenty had been there less than a year.
4. The proportions of natives and long-term residents were even higher among those juveniles whose cases the courts considered worth prosecuting.[24]

The findings sound something like the studies of crime and delinquency we reviewed earlier. It apparently takes time to learn to riot. Again we discover that the way assimilation to the city works is more important than how much stress and strain moving around creates.

MIGRATION AS A PROBLEM FOR PUBLIC POLICY

The most acute problems we have encountered in this survey of race and migration are not really problems created by migration at all. Some are difficulties faced by members of racial minorities wherever they are in America, difficulties that migration simply transplants and concentrates in cities. Job discrimination is one important example. In these cases, a change in the conditions of migration might affect which communities had to take the largest direct responsibility for meeting the problem, but it would not make much difference in the gravity of the problem as a whole.

Other problems are forms of discrimination more prominent in cities than elsewhere and therefore aggravated by the movement to the cities of more of the people they hurt. Big-city residential segregation is like that. In these cases, a slowdown of migration might ease the problem, but it certainly would not eliminate it.

As for problems directly produced by migration, my main message has been that they have been seriously misunderstood and exaggerated. Migrants as a group do not notably disturb public order, their arrival does not lower the quality of the city's population, they place no extraordinary demands on public services, and they do not arrive exceptionally burdened with personal problems. These things happen to them later. The difficulties faced by inhabitants of ghettos and by cities containing them are not to any large degree products merely of migration.

Yet in two ways the migrant *does* present a challenge to public policy. First, moving over long distances often imposes hardships and confusion on families at the same time as it cuts them off from the agencies that might be able to help them; instead of recognizing the special problems of people on the move, American public services tend to discriminate against them. Second, the newcomer — already by definition an innovator, having an advantage in age, education, and skill, bound to the old ways of his new city by fewer commitments and routines — is in an extraordinarily good position to take advantage of programs breaking down racial barriers, if only they are open to him. The challenge is to make maximum use of the migrant's talents, give him the greatest possible access to the rewards the city has to offer, make sure he can get past the personal crises almost all big moves involve without breaking down, and assure that he has attractive alternatives to the social and geographic isolation of the ghetto.

Open-housing arrangements directed to the newcomers would make sense. Some of the recent migrants might be too dependent on friends and relatives already in the city to consider living far from them. But we have seen that the more detached and highly skilled migrants from other big cities are increasing in number. They might well be more interested in integrated housing than the long-time ghetto residents who are the prime concern of most current open-housing programs. Since the creation of new jobs so regularly stimulates migration, why not encourage or require expanding firms to assure the availability of unsegregated housing?

Because migrants normally face their grimmest moments shortly after arrival, the usual residence requirements for public services have an unpleasant illogic to them. So long as cities think of themselves as involved in a curious sort of market in which generous public services infallibly attract more of the dispossessed, it is not hard to understand the occasional temptation to erect high walls and long waiting periods. But in fact, as we have seen, the quality of public services does not seem to make much difference to the flow of migrants, and the migrants who do come place no exceptional demand on services. In any case, equalizing the assistance available to newcomers in one city or another (possibly through federal programs concentrated in the first year of residence) would eliminate the competition among cities to keep migrants away. It would also mean the responsibility of paying for such assistance would be equally shared. Facilities like public housing are mostly paid for with funds coming from outside the city anyway. They ought to be available to those new arrivals who need them.

There are other services that need to be specially designed for migrants. Since the Welcome Wagon rarely calls in the ghetto, and social agencies do not usually make contact with a family until its serious troubles have begun, something as simple as a reception service could be very effective. Many migrants do not know where they can get medical attention, job information, help in finding housing, or legal assistance; they can only get unreliable, fragmentary information from their friends and neighbors. They are at a point where established routines and obligations are less likely to keep them from taking opportunities — for jobs, for housing, for training — outside the cramped circle of minority group life.

A well-run urban reception service would produce an important extra benefit: a good pool of information about current migration and migrants. For a country that has done so famously in the collection and storage of other kinds of data, the United States has pitifully little reliable information on migration. The Census does provide sound, voluminous data on long-term trends and new movements of population. Some scholars have learned to squeeze sources like city directories long and ingeniously enough to produce finer detail on who migrates and fuller descriptions of short-run fluctuations. Their procedures are still no substitute for the rich, accurate, up-to-date quantitative picture of migration to be gained from an intelligent combination of data already in the records of utilities installations, real-estate transactions, truck movements, new employment, school enrollments, and voting registrations, or for the full qualitative picture to be gained from the household interviews a reception service might conduct. At present the feedback of information on migrants to and from American cities is far too slow and fragmentary to permit effective action in meeting the pains they face or the problems they pose.

CONCLUSION

Migration, as such, is not a major public problem. But it points up grave problems. In the long run, the assimilation of racial minorities into the social life and opportunities of the city is the fundamental problem of American civil rights. Negroes, Orientals, and members of other racial minorities are increasingly concentrating in the great metropolitan centers. That is where the new opportunities and the possibilities of massive change are opening up. How cities meet the needs and aspirations of their nonwhite citizens will determine how America as a whole meets those needs and aspirations. If Negro separatism of any kind works effectively, it will have to work in the city. That is why the simple question, *"Is* the Negro today like the immigrant yesterday?"* matters so much, and is so likely to obsess scholars and policy makers over the next decade.

NOTES

1. For an excellent review of national and regional data concerning American internal migration, see Henry S. Shryock, Jr., *Population Mobility within the United States* (Chicago: Community and Family Study Center, University of Chicago, 1964).

2. See especially *U.S. Census of Population: 1960. Subject Reports: State of Birth*, Final Report PC(2)—2A, and *Lifetime and Recent Migration*, Final Report PC(2)—2D.

3. Charles Tilly, *Migration to an American City* (Newark, Delaware: Division of Urban Affairs and School of Agriculture, University of Delaware, 1965).

4. Morton Grodzins, *The Metropolitan Area as a Racial Problem* (Pittsburgh: University of Pittsburgh Press, 1959).

5. Karl E. Taeuber and Alma F. Taeuber, *Negroes in Cities* (Chicago: Aldine, 1965); Bernard Frieden, *The Future of Old Neighborhoods* (Cambridge: M.I.T. Press, 1964); Charles Tilly, Wagner D. Jackson, and Barry Kay, *Race and Residence in Wilmington, Delaware* (New York: Bureau of Publications, Teachers College, 1965).

6. See especially Taeuber and Taeuber, *Negroes in Cities*, chap. 7.

7. Ralph H. Turner, "Migration to a Medium-Sized American City," *Journal of Social Psychology*, 80 (1949), 229—249; Shryock, *Population Mobility*, chap. 12.

8. See Leonard Blumberg and Robert Bell, "Urban Migration and Kinship Ties," *Social Problems*, 6 (1959), 328—333; John S. MacDonald and Leatrice MacDonald, "Chain Migration, Ethnic Neighborhood Formation, and Social Networks," *Millbank Memorial Fund Quarterly*, 42 (1964), 82—97; Morton Rubin, "Migration Patterns of Negroes from a Rural Northeastern Mississippi Community," *Social Forces*, 39 (1960), 59—66; Harry Schwarzweller, *Family Ties, Migration, and Transitional Adjustment of Young Men from Eastern Kentucky* (Lexington: University of Kentucky Agricultural Experiment Station, 1964).

9. Hope T. Eldridge and Dorothy Swaine Thomas, *Demographic Analyses and Inter-relations* (Philadelphia: American Philosophical Society, 1964), vol. III of *Population Redistribution and Economic Growth, United States, 1870—1950*. Memoirs of the American Philosophical Society, no. 61.

10. In addition to Shryock, Taeuber and Taeuber, Rubin, Schwarzweller, and Eldridge and Thomas, cited above, see C. Harold Brown and Roy C. Buck, *Factors Associated with the Migrant Status of Young Adult Males from Rural Pennsylvania* (University Park: Pennsylvania State University Agricultural Experiment Station, 1961); Ronald Freedman, "Cityward Migration, Urban Ecology and Social Theory," in Ernest W. Burgess and Donald J. Bogue, eds., *Contribution to Urban Sociology* (Chicago: University of Chicago Press, 1964); C. Horace Hamilton, "Educational Selection of the Net Migration from the South," *Social Forces*, 38 (1959), 33—42; Arnold M. Rose, "Distance of Migration and Socio-economic Status of Migrants," *American Sociological Review*, 23 (1958), 420—423.

11. W. E. B. DuBois, *The Philadelphia Negro* (Philadelphia: University of Pennsylvania, 1899); Gilbert Osofsky, *Harlem: The Making of a Ghetto* (New York: Harper and Row, 1966).

12. See, for example, *Divorce Statistics Analysis* (Washington: U.S. Department of Health, Education and Welfare, Public Health Service, 1965; National Center for Health Statistics, Series 21, No. 7).

13. Data from *The Negroes in the United States* (Washington: United States Department of Labor, Bureau of Labor Statistics, 1966; Bulletin No. 1511), table IVA-5.

14. H. B. M. Murphy, "Migration and the Major Mental Disorders: A Reappraisal," in Mildred Kantor, ed., *Mobility and Mental Health* (Springfield, Ill.: Charles C. Thomas, 1965), plus other articles in the same volume.

15. Leonard Savitz, *Delinquency and Migration* (Philadelphia: Commission on Human Relations, 1960), p. 16.

16. Judith L. Kinman and Everett S. Lee, "Migration and Crime," *International Migration Digest*, 3 (1966), 7—14.

17. *New York Times Magazine*, Sept. 11, 1966.

18. Oscar Handlin, *The Newcomers* (Cambridge: Harvard University Press, 1959). See also Marc Fried, "The Transitional Functions of Working-Class Communities," in Kantor, *Mobility and Mental Health*.

19. Nathan Glazer and Daniel Patrick Moynihan, *Beyond the Melting Pot* (Cambridge: M.I.T. Press, 1963), p. 26.

20. *Violence in the City — An End or a Beginning?* (Los Angeles: Governor's Commission on the Los Angeles Riots, 1965), pp. 3—4.

21. U.S. Bureau of the Census, *Special Census Survey of the South and East Los Angeles Area, November, 1965* (Series P-23, no. 17, 1966).

22. According to a report in the *New York Times*, March 9, 1966.

23. Stanley Lieberson and Arnold R. Silverman, "The Precipitants and Underlying Conditions of Race Riots," *American Sociological Review*, 30 (1965), 887—898.

24. *Riot Participant Study, Juvenile Offenders* (Los Angeles County Probation Department, 1965). According to a *New York Times* article of September 4, 1966, a similar study of adult offenders done by the state's Bureau of Criminal Identification and Investigation yielded the same conclusions. After I wrote this paper, in 1966, much more evidence pointing in the same direction came in. See especially Louis H. Masotti, ed., "Urban Violence and Disorder," *American Behavioral Scientist*, 2 (March—April 1968), entire issue.

Racial Segregation:
The Persisting Dilemma

Karl E. Taeuber

The National Advisory Commission on Civil Disorders, appointed by President Johnson in response to the ghetto riots of the mid-1960s, reported in early 1968 its basic conclusion: "Our nation is moving toward two societies, one black, one white — separate and unequal."[1] The image of "two societies" took root in people's minds in a way that the commission's recommendations for action never could. Translated into geographic terms, this image now dominates the nation's perception of central city and suburbs: a black core surrounded by a white noose.

For decades scholars and the public have used battlefield imagery to describe residential patterns of blacks and whites. Early in this century, as black populations grew in the cities, the so-called colored were said to be threatening and invading white neighborhoods. During my childhood in World War II, a "Block-buster" was a bomb of awesome destructive power; in college in the 1950s I learned that a "block-buster" was an unscrupulous character who dared to sell or rent to Negroes in white areas. In the years since the Kerner Commission report, the imagery has become that of defeat and panic, of white flight to the suburbs in fear of blackening central cities.

*This paper is one in a series, "Studies in Racial Segregation," supported by funds granted to the Institute for Research on Poverty at the University of Wisconsin by the Department of Health, Education, and Welfare pursuant to the provisions of the Economic Opportunity Act of 1964. Conclusions and interpretations are the sole responsibility of the author.

Reprinted from "Racial Segregation: the Persisting Dilemma" by Karl E. Taeuber in Vol. 422 of *The Annals* of The American Academy of Political and Social Science. ©1975, by the American Academy of Political and Social Science. All rights reserved.

This racial battlefield imagery of cities and suburbs is, like the other city-suburban imagery, a gross exaggeration that nevertheless blinds the national perception to reality. Racial conflict is a prominent aspect of the American metropolitan scene, but the two-society image is too narrow a perspective. A survey of certain census data on population distribution and migration can broaden the perspective and provide a glimpse of both the uniformities of racial residential patterns throughout the nation and of the diversities in scale and character of the problems posed by these patterns in individual metropolitan areas.

THE BLACKENING OF CENTRAL CITIES

What did the 1970 census reveal about the so-called blackening of central cities? In the 243 metropolitan areas, blacks composed a majority of the population in only three central cities. These three cities — Washington, Newark and Atlanta — are each severely underbounded with respect to the spread of urbanization around them. (Washington had 26 percent of the metropolitan area's population; Newark, 21 percent; and Atlanta, 36 percent.) In the total metropolitan population of these three places, blacks were outnumbered three or four to one.

In only 12 other metropolitan areas did blacks in 1970 compose between 40 and 50 percent of the central city population. Four of these 12 were Southern cities in which the black percentage either declined or increased only slightly during the 1960s: Birmingham, Alabama; Charleston, South Carolina; Pine Bluff, Arkansas; and Richmond, Virginia. The other eight cities experienced rapid increases in percentage of blacks during the 1960s, and most will probably have black majorities by the time of the 1980 census. These eight, in declining order of city size, are Detroit, Baltimore, St. Louis and New Orleans, among the nation's large cities, and Savannah, Wilmington, Augusta and Atlantic City among the medium-size cities.

A few central cities other than these eight may experience such rapid white out-movement and black increase during the 1970s that they, too, will have black majorities by 1980. But in 211 of the 243 central cities, whites outnumbered blacks more than two to one in 1970. Many of the 32 cities in which blacks composed more than one-third of the 1970 population were medium-size Southern cities from which blacks were fleeing as fast as whites in the 1960s. In other medium-size cities whites were moving in, not out, and at a faster rate than blacks.

About one of every eight persons in the United States is Negro (according to census classification). A minority group, outnumbered seven to one, cannot "take over" all of the nation's central cities. Indeed, more than half of the nation's black population already lives in central cities of metropolitan areas. Black urbanization in the future cannot continue at the former pace. There are not enough blacks left in the rural South to provide a continuing large flow into the cities.

Although 198 of the 243 metropolitan areas experienced an increase during the 1960s in the percentage of blacks in the central city, there is no typical metropolitan area. Black population in New York City increased by more than half a million. In Provo-Orem, Utah, the black central city population increased from 18 to 28 persons. There are prevailing patterns of racial population change, but the specific pattern in each metropolitan area takes on a unique size and shape.

BLACK SUBURBANIZATION

Variety is the prominent feature of patterns of black suburbaniza-tion among the nation's metropolitan areas. In 1970 there were 70 million whites living in the suburbs (census definition) and 3.4 million blacks. Blacks composed about five percent of all suburban residents; but this aggregate figure of five percent is a misleading indication of the general pattern. In most of the old South, blacks lived in towns and villages and throughout the countryside. As metro-politan areas grew, they incorporated within their domain the pre-existing pattern of racial enclaves. Despite the exclusion of blacks from most of the new suburban housing of the past 50 years, in many of the South's metropolitan areas blacks compose from 10 to 40 percent of the suburban population. In every Northern metropolitan area and in some Southern areas, blacks compose less than 10 percent of the suburban population and often only a miniscule proportion.

During the 1950s and 1960s more blacks moved out of many Southern metropolitan areas than moved in; this was true of suburbs as well as central cities. The huge flow of black population to Northern central cities drew heavily from Southern urban blacks as well as from blacks in the rural hinterlands. With rapid white suburbanization in these Southern metropolitan areas, the percentage that blacks composed of the suburban population often fell.

In the Northern metropolitan areas, racial patterns of suburbaniza-tion varied. In many areas with rapid suburbanization of whites, the number of blacks has shown a sharp percentage increase. Some observers have seen in these demographic figures the harbinger of a new era of extensive black suburbanization. Caution is warranted, however, whenever one looks at percentage change data from a small base population. Between 1960 and 1970 the white suburban population in the Boston metropolitan area increased only 11 percent, while the black suburban population increased 53 percent. Numerically, however, the white suburbanization greatly outweighed the black: the white suburban population increased by 200,000, from 1.9 million to 2.1 million; the black suburban increase was less than 8,000, from 15,000 to 22,000. The *rate* of black suburbanization was greater, to be sure, and the percentage that blacks composed of Boston's suburban population did increase — from less than one percent to just over one percent. If this is the harbinger of a new era of black suburbanization, it is obvious that the old era will be with us for a long time before being ushered out.

Another kind of evidence shows that the black suburbanization currently occurring in a number of large metropolitan areas, whatever its numerical scale, is following the essential dynamics of the old era rather than ushering in a new era of race relations. This evidence pertains to the location of black suburbanites and the character of their new communities. Consider Chicago, for example, where the quantity of black suburbanization has been rather large. In the two decades from 1950 to 1970, the black suburban population in the Chicago area increased by 85,000 persons (from a 1950 base of 44,000). Nearly two-thirds of this increase occurred in nine old industrial suburbs (such as Joliet, Waukegan and Chicago Heights), each of which was experiencing the same kind of blacks-replacing-whites in segregated neighborhoods that occurs in central cities. Another one-fourth of the black suburban increase occurred in five "black suburbs" (such as Robbins and East Chicago Heights), small communities or neighborhoods in which new housing developments had been marketed directly to black families. The Chicago suburban territory, aside from these 14 communities, was home to more than 3 million whites in 1970, but it made room for a black increase of fewer than 10,000 persons during the 20-year period.

ECONOMICS OR DISCRIMINATION?

The residential segregation of blacks from whites within central cities and the exclusion of blacks from suburbs are often assumed to be a reflection of the relatively poorer economic circumstances of blacks. In fact, although metropolitan areas have both wealthier and poorer neighborhoods, most residential neighborhoods throughout the metropolis have housing that rents or sells for a wide range of prices. Thus, the first premise of the poverty interpretation of racial residential patterns is only a half-truth. The residential distribution of persons among neighborhoods in the metropolis is only in small part a function of housing costs, family income or other economic factors.

The second premise of the poverty interpretation of housing segregation is that blacks are poorer than whites. This is again only a partial truth. If the entire distribution of families by income is considered, rather than just average incomes, a considerable overlap is seen among races. Many wealthy and middle income black families have greater economic resources than do millions of poor white families.

The conclusion from the two premises of the poverty interpretation of residential segregation is that the residential locations of blacks and whites differ because of economic differences. The reality, alas, is not so simple. Sociologists and economists have devised various statistical techniques for assessing the influence of economic factors on the differential residential location of black and white households, but they have not reached any consensus beyond agreement that other factors are important. I have contributed to the esoteric literature on this topic, but I am more impressed by the results of common sense and simple statistics. Common sense and open eyes reveal that rich blacks do not live interspersed with rich whites. Poor whites do not live interspersed with poor blacks. Racial residential segregation exists to far too high a degree in all American cities for economic factors to be the primary cause. Simple statistics offer surprising confirmation. In Chicago in 1960, the average rent paid by white tenants was $88 a month; the average rent paid by black tenants was $88 a month. Black renters were highly segregated from white renters despite their obvious ability to pay as much.

But suburbanization is different, is it not? Granted that patterns of housing segregation in the central city are not primarily economic in origin, is it not true that economic factors play a more important role in suburban locations? Consider data for 29 of the nation's largest metropolitan areas.[2] Among white families with incomes of $5,000 to $6,999 (not a very good income even by 1969 standards), the proportion who lived in the suburbs was greater in every case than the suburban proportion among black families with incomes of $15,000 to $24,900. Consider also a specific metropolis. In Detroit in 1970, more than half of the white families in each income level, from very poor to very rich, lived in the suburbs. Among blacks, only one-tenth of the families at each income level (including very rich) lived in the suburbs.

I have concluded from my own research and a review of the work of others that the prime cause of residential segregation by race has been discrimination, both public and private.[3] Racial discrimination was influential in developing the racially segregated pattern of American cities. In recent years, despite court rulings and legislation clearly outlawing virtually all types of racial discrimination in housing, past patterns persist, and every investigation uncovers evidence that old impediments to free choice of residence by blacks continue. I refer specifically to practices such as:

1. racially motivated site selection and tenant assignment policies in public housing;

2. racially motivated site selection, financing, sales, and rental policies of other types of government subsidized housing, such as Federal Housing Administration and Veterans Administration insurance programs;
3. racially motivated site selection, relocation policies and practices, and redevelopment policies in urban renewal programs;
4. zoning and annexation policies that foster racial segregation;
5. restrictive covenants attached to housing deeds;
6. policies of financial institutions that discourage prospective developers of racially integrated private housing;
7. policies of financial institutions that allocate mortgage funds and rehabilitation loans to blacks only if they live in predominantly black areas;
8. practices of the real estate industry such as (a) limiting the access of black brokers to realty associations and multiple listing services; (b) refusals by white realtors to cobroke on transactions that would foster racial integration; (c) blockbusting, panic selling, and racial steering; (d) racially identifying vacancies, either overtly or by nominally benign codes (advertising housing according to racially identifiable schools or other neighborhood identifiers); (e) refusing to show houses or apartments or refusing to encourage blacks to consider housing in white neighborhoods; (f) reprimanding or penalizing brokers and salesmen who act to facilitate racial integration; and
9. racially discriminatory practices by individual homeowners and landlords.

MASS MIGRATION TO METROPOLIS

A century ago the black population in the United States was predominantly a rural agricultural one because the South of which blacks were a part was itself a rural agricultural region. As the South slowly urbanized, blacks participated. Southern cities, together with their outlying suburbs, grew with a pattern of separate housing for blacks. A slow northward movement of black population that had been occurring in the first half-century after the emancipation of slaves accelerated during the 1910—20 decade. Continuing for the next half-century and a few years beyond, the flow of blacks to Northern cities was truly a mass migration. Between 1920 and 1930 in Georgia and between 1940 and 1950 in Mississippi, nearly half of the young black males reaching adulthood left their states. In 1920, 1930 and 1950, in Michigan, Illinois and New York, from one-third to more than one-half of the young adult blacks enumerated in the census had moved to those states within the preceding 10 years.

The mass migration northward drew blacks from all over the South, from cities as well as villages and tenant farms. The Northern destinations, by contrast, were few in number. Of all Northern blacks in 1970, two-thirds lived in seven metropolitan areas containing more than 300,000 blacks each (New York, Chicago, Philadephia, Detroit, St. Louis, Newark and Cleveland). In the West, two-thirds of the blacks lived in Los Angeles or San Francisco. In the South, only five metropolitan areas contained more than 300,000 blacks each, and the 16 containing more than 100,000 blacks included only one-third of the region's total black population.

END OF AN ERA?

Any mass migration carries within itself the seeds of its own destruction. As youth move from one region to another, they transfer future natural increase from the place of origin to the place of destination. This demographic fact of life ensures that new generations will be born and raised in the destination places and that the supply of future migrants from the place of origin will be depleted. In addition, any mass migration is cause and effect of massive social and economic transformations at origin and destination.

During the half-century of massive black migration, the character of the migration was continually changing. By the time national attention was focused on the so-called urban crisis following the Watts riots of 1965, Northern black populations were increasingly Northern-born and Northern-raised. Northern blacks who migrated from the South were increasingly from the urban South. For blacks, as for whites, long distance migration was a feature of a metropolitan industrial economy in which those persons with greater education and marketable skills moved for economic benefit and for a better life. The poor and poorly educated rural blacks who were still being displaced from agriculture were far more likely to move a few miles to a Southern town or city than to take off directly for a Northern metropolis.

The steady aggregation of Americans, white and black, into metropolitan areas is a mass migration that must come to an end sometime. This migration has ebbed and flowed with economic circumstances — as in the slowdown during the depression of the 1930s — but at least until 1970 it was a continuing feature of American demographic history. No one foresaw the sudden cessation of this steady population concentration, but cessation is what appears to have happened since 1970. From 1970 to 1974, metropolitan areas lost migrants to non-metropolitan territories. Analysts first thought that the results might simply reflect a spilling over of metropolitan expansion beyond the current boundaries of metropolitan areas. Further investigation revealed, however, that the population in counties adjacent to metropolitan areas was growing less rapidly than the population in non-metropolitan counties not adjacent to any metropolitan area.

The national shift away from an ever-greater piling up of population in metropolitan areas has been matched by an extraordinarily sharp decline in black metropolitan movement. During the early 1970s there was still a slow rate of net in-movement of blacks to metropolitan areas, but it hardly compared to the rapid pace of the 1950s and 1960s. It is the nation's largest metropolitan areas that have experienced the sharpest shift in total migration rates, and it is these areas that in the past were most attractive to black migrants. As the black population has become increasingly urban, and as young blacks have become increasingly well educated, the character of black migration has increasingly resembled that of white migration. During recent decades white migration to central cities declined and then reversed, first in the largest cities and more recently in many of the medium-size centers. Already in the 1960s, blacks displayed a net out-movement from some central cities, and it should not have surprised us so much that this trend would gain momentum in the 1970s.

PERSISTING SEGREGATION

Recent information on population redistribution of both whites and blacks during the 1970s has surprised demographers and other social scientists. The sharp changes in fundamental long term trends were not anticipated and have not yet been investigated. It is difficult to change long-accustomed perceptions, and many observers suspect (or hope) that the latest demographic shifts are a temporary response to the unusual economic circumstances of the early 1970s. Taking cognizance of the fact that no trend continues forever, I am much less skeptical of the new information. We may well be entering a new era in American population distribution.

The identification of eras is an analytical distinction imposed on a continuous reality. The trends of population concentration in metropolitan areas have not suddenly been obliterated; rather, the magnitude of the former has declined, and we do not yet know how the pace of suburbanization has been and will be affected. Thus it is extraordinarily difficult to assess the future of black suburbanization.

In the early decades of the twentieth century, as the so-called Great Migration of blacks to Northern cities accelerated, the black newcomers to the cities behaved much like other newcomers of those times. Negro migrants repeated the behavior of Italian and Polish migrants and other ethnic groups in settling initially in certain downtown areas of inexpensive housing accessible to public transportation. As numbers grew, ethnic colonies spread. With time, increasing numbers of the group became familiar with the ways of the city, with how to get along economically, and with other residential choices that might be more pleasant than crowded central neighborhoods. From the beginning of mass concentration of each successive European ethnic group in New York, Chicago, Detroit and other great cities, some members of the group were moving elsewhere in the city, sometimes establishing secondary colonies, sometimes settling into ethnically heterogeneous neighborhoods. Many of the children and grandchildren, natives of America and of the city, exercised even wider ranges of choice of residence. Statistical measures of the degree of segregation of each major European ethnic group document declining segregation as time passed.[4]

For blacks, however, residential patterns took a different twist. The mechanisms of racial discrimination identified above were deliberately devised and elaborated to control the dispersal of blacks and to produce a more "orderly" channeling of rapidly growing black populations. Statistical measures document increasing segregation of blacks.[5] The residential segregation between blacks and whites increased well beyond the levels characteristic of turn-of-the-century ethnic group segregation in Northern cities. Some Southern cities that grew to prominence after the Civil War also experienced their first large influx of black population during this period, and their residential patterns developed similarly to those in the North. In some older Southern cities, where a large black population was present ever since the days of slavery, a more dispersed racial residential pattern survived for many decades. But even in those cities, such as Charleston, South Carolina, with its traditional pattern of backyard and alley dwellings for blacks, the modern national style of separate residential areas eventually took over. Urban renewal in the 1950s largely completed the task of racially modernizing these cities.

During the 1950s in the North, and during the 1960s in both Northern and Southern cities, the intensity of residential segregation of blacks and whites diminished somewhat from its peak levels.[6] These declines were too small to reflect or presage a new liberalism in race relations. Rather they arose, I believe, from the large scale of the white out-movement from central cities and from the simultaneous rapid increase in the numbers of black families (native Americans all and many second or third generation urbanites) who did not like the ghettos and who pursued as best they could — within the confines of a discriminatory housing market — the standard American dream of a decent home and a decent neighborhood in which to raise one's children.

The slight diminution in the degree of racial residential segregation within the central cities occurred during a period of rapid increase in white suburban populations. The 1970 census was the first to provide data for individual city blocks throughout the urbanized area, and hence for 1970 it is possible to calculate area-wide segregation indexes of the same sort described above for central cities. Among 40 of 44 Northern metropolitan areas, the segregation index for the total urbanized area is greater than that for the central city alone. Among Southern metropolitan areas, with their historical pattern of suburban black enclaves, the area index is higher in 27 of 44 cases.

These statistical data document the severity of the two-society pattern of increasingly black central cities and white suburbs. Until there is a much more even distribution of blacks and whites among central cities and suburbs, segregation indexes for metropolitan areas cannot fall. The evidence presented above indicates that black suburbanization to date, while numerically greater than ever before, remains a minor pattern in black population redistribution. Suburbia shows no signs of quickly becoming for blacks, as for whites, the primary destination of migrants. The evidence further shows that the suburbanization to date has occurred with the same racially discriminatory channeling of black residents into selected localities that characterizes central cities.

The lowered birth rate in the United States and the lowered rate at which whites and blacks are moving into metropolitan areas should sharply reduce population pressure on urban and suburban housing. Older and less desirable housing seems increasingly likely to be abandoned, as happened in the 1950s and 1960s even with growing populations. Reduction of central city densities should occur, and a potential exists for greatly increased black suburbanization. With black populations growing more slowly, and with blacks interested in the full spectrum of metropolitan residential neighborhoods, there could be rapid residential desegregation without the population pressures that in the past led so often to immediate resegregation. This pattern could develop, but there is no evidence yet that it will. Racial segregation persists in suburban housing because racial discrimination persists in suburbia.

Whether these patterns change depends not only on whether we develop the will and devise the means to enforce existing nationwide laws against all types of housing discrimination; change in the racial patterns of housing also depends on what happens to segregation in schooling and employment. It has become somewhat fashionable to recognize these linkages only to use them as an excuse. Segregated schools are said to depend on segregated housing, which depends on black poverty, which depends on occupational discrimination, which depends on earlier discrimination in Southern schooling, which depends on ante-bellum social institutions. This kind of logic rests on a specious reading of social science evidence. There is indeed a certain "unity of the Negro problem," as Gunnar Myrdal noted more than 30 years ago, but that unity may be expressed in the present tense, not only as a historical residue of slavery:

> Behind the barrier of common discrimination, there is unity and close inter-relation between the Negro's political power; his civil rights; his employment opportunities; his standards of housing, nutrition and clothing; his health, manners, and law observance; his ideals and ideologies. The unity is largely the result of cumulative causation binding them all together in a system and tying them to white discrimination.[7]

NOTES

1. National Advisory Commission on Civil Disorders *Report* (New York: Bantam Books, 1968), p. 1.
2. Albert I. Hermalin and Reynolds Farley, "The Potential for Residential Integration in Cities and Suburbs: Implications for the Busing Controversy," *American Sociological Review* 38 (October 1973), pp. 595—610.
3. This paragraph is taken from Karl E. Taeuber, "Demographic Perspectives on Housing and School Segregation," *Wayne Law Review* 31 (March 1975), pp. 840—841.
4. Stanley Lieberson, *Ethnic Patterns in American Cities* (New York: Free Press of Glencoe, 1963).
5. Karl E. Taeuber and Alma F. Taeuber, *Negroes in Cities: Residential Segregation and Neighborhood Change* (Chicago: Aldine, 1965).
6. Annemette Sørensen, Karl E. Taeuber, and Leslie J. Hollingsworth, Jr., "Indexes of Racial Residential Segregation for 109 Cities in the United States, 1940 to 1970," *Sociological Focus* 8 (April 1975), pp. 125—142.
7. Gunnar Myrdal, *An American Dilemma; The Negro Problem and Modern Democracy* (New York: Harper & Brothers, 1944), p. 77.

From
The Political Economy of the Black Ghetto:

Black Power—Green Power

William K. Tabb

If the ghetto is viewed as an internal colony, it becomes easier to see why white political and corporate leaders are working so hard to convince ghetto dwellers that what they really want is "black capitalism." However, the idea of black capitalism runs counter to an important anti-capitalist strand in the black power ideology.[1]

Black power demands black control over black institutions. This can be achieved in two ways. Individual blacks may own the important resources of the ghetto, or the black community may, in common, own and run its economy. Increasingly blacks are choosing the second course. The "white power structure," on the other hand, prefers individual ownership by blacks, which of necessity will have to be in cooperation with outside white interests. The reason for this choice is apparent. Such an arrangement is amenable to neo-colonial rule, since it guarantees the indirect control of the ghetto economy through a local native class essentially dependent on larger white businesses. The aim is twofold: to win loyalty of an important group of potentially influential local leaders, and to channel protest into less threatening, and incidentally, less useful goals. In this light, increasing the number of ghetto blacks in ownership positions appears to be an important prerequisite for ending ghetto unrest.[2] If blacks are upset because they lack control over the institutions of the ghetto, because they are charged high prices for inferior merchandise, victimized by credit racketeers, and exploited by employers, then perhaps — some would argue — greater black ownership will help end these conditions (or at least lessen anti-white feelings because the

Reprinted from *The Political Economy of the Black Ghetto* by **William K. Tabb.** By permission of W. W. Norton & Company, Inc. Copyright ©1970 by W. W. Norton & Company, Inc., pp. 35—57.

local merchants would be black). If the ghetto lacks leadership and a stable middle class, then enlarging the number of black entrepreneurs may provide such leadership and foster stability. If the problem is lack of racial confidence, the success of black capitalists would build pride. If riots are caused by people who have tenuous allegiance to our system, ownership is the best way to build a commitment to working for change within the system. Increasing the ownership class, in short, is a way to add stability, increase local leadership, lessen the visibility of white domination of the ghetto economy, and funnel ghetto discontent into acceptable channels.

Interest in black capitalism also strikes a responsive chord in the corporate sector. Proposals for black capitalism involve minimal direct government intervention. They provide for subsidies to cooperating private firms. Even though black hostility toward white businesses is increasing, the "Negro market, a market expected to reach $52 billion in 1975,"[3] cannot be ignored by even the largest firms. Market penetration is possible through joint corporations partly owned or managed by blacks. Franchising local blacks to distribute products in the ghetto and setting up independently owned but captive suppliers may also be in the corporation's interest. Banks limited by law to city boundaries find that as the black population grows they need to make more loans to minority-group businessmen to maintain their profit position.[4] Labor shortages in a period of rapid growth have sent many firms out to recruit in the ghetto, spurred on by Manpower Development and Training Act (MDTA) funds and a desire to get on better with the increasingly large number of blacks living in the inner city where their plants are located. Thus pushed by the demands of the black community and pulled by societal and corporate interest, government, industry, and black organizations are moving to promote black capitalism.

The purpose of this chapter is to assess the likely success of such efforts and to evaluate the strength and the nature of resistance to black capitalism. Three variations on the theme will be considered: attempts to help individual black small businesses, white corporate involvement in the ghetto, and proposals for community development corporations. Finally, different patterns of ghetto development and their impact on the economic structure of the ghetto will be considered. But it is first necessary to describe the ghetto marketplace itself.

THE GHETTO MERCHANT AND THE CONSUMER

Some economists draw a contrast between how markets work in the ghetto and how they operate elsewhere. There are differences, to be sure, but they should not be allowed to obscure the essential fact that the market mechanism works in the ghetto pretty much in the way traditional theory would lead us to expect. Low-income people, lacking purchasing power and information concerning the quality of available merchandise, and restricted to shopping in ghetto markets, end up with inferior merchandise at higher prices. Seeking to maximize profit, the ghetto merchants adjust their sales practices to the nature of their customers, who are characterized as having low incomes and comparatively limited education.

Shady business practices are often reported in ghetto areas: use of bait advertising of goods which are "sold out" when the customer arrives; the switch sale, where the customer comes in to look at specials and is told that the special is not of good quality and what he really wants is some more expensive item; the refusal to return deposits; the misrepresentative sales contract; the used furniture sold as new; the coercive pressures on buyers; the attempts to collect non-existent debts. All these practices so frequently complained of have their roots in the powerlessness and the lack of educational and financial resources of the urban poor. Deliberation in buying durable goods, surveys find, is more highly correlated with education than with income.[5] Judging quality in consumer durables takes some skill, and understanding credit arrangements is not easy. With a low income, one naturally is on the lookout for a "good deal."

A specialized sales network has developed to deal with low-income people. The friendly smooth-talking dealer who makes the un-educated, poorly-dressed customer feel at home, gaining his confidence, offering generous credit terms impossible to obtain else-where — and all this right in his own neighborhood — is much easier to deal with than a hostile downtown department store salesman. However, the prices paid reflect this special service. A recent Federal Trade Commission (FTC) report concludes:

> The low-income market is a very expensive place to buy durable goods. On television sets (most of which are the popular 19-inch black and white portables), the general market retailer price is about $130. In the low-income market a customer can pay up to $250 for similar sets. Other comparisons include a dryer selling for $149.95 from a general market retailer and for $299.95 from a low-income market retailer; and a vacuum cleaner selling for $59.95 in the general market and $79.95 in the low-income market.[6]

The same FTC study found investment credit used more extensively by retailers selling in low-income neighborhoods than by retailers selling to consumers elsewhere.[7] Further, given the greater risks involved, much higher carrying charges are exacted in ghetto stores than on the general market.

Speaking of the reluctance of the poor to seek legal aid even when they have clearly been victimized, Mary Gardiner Jones, an FTC commissioner, says the problem is not only that the poor lack financial resources to get legal assistance:

> With the poor, this reluctance is aggravated by their unfortunately realistic fears of retaliation by the merchant or credit agency on whom they are so dependent, by their inabilities to express themselves in the language of the Establishment and by their sense of inferiority, hopelessness and general mistrust of any government authority, which they regard not as the protector of their rights, but as the body which puts them into jail, evicts them from their apartment or garnishes their salary.[8]

This sort of explanation is not sufficient. The legal system does favor the businessman over the ghetto resident. Garnishing of salaries for nonpayment of debt is relatively easy, even when the debts were contracted in ignorance and the contract obtained by fraud. The small print on installment contracts, unread by the buyer, allows for easy repossession. The city marshals, paid by the taxpayer to act as collection agents, earn a commission for their services. The entire legal system is set up to protect property and ensure contracts. Nor is the Better Business Bureau of much help to the low-income consumer. Not only has it no legal enforcement power, but it serves as a lightning rod, absorbing anger while protecting both the image and the profits of business.

> Its claims notwithstanding, the Better Business Bureau is little more than a businessman's protective association often syphoning off consumer complaints that would be better directed to other agencies. That it has less than the consumer's interest at heart is indicated by the fact that in many states it has lobbied against consumer representation in government on the false premise that the Bureau is already doing the job of protecting the customers.[9]

David Caplovitz, whose studies of consumer practices of low-income families brought the unscrupulous dealings of ghetto merchants to the attention of the general public, has suggested that he may have "unwittingly created the impression . . . that these problems exist only because of a small class of disreputable sellers."[10] Caplovitz points out that the sellers could not exist without the banks and finance companies which buy up dishonestly obtained contracts. The finance companies know what they are doing, as do the highly respected banks who lend to the finance companies.[11] The involvement of the financial community in the exploitation of the poor is similar here to the role it plays in perpetuating housing segregation.

Again, as in the case of the slum landlord, the typical ghetto merchant does not appear to be making high profits. The market, with a large number of buyers and sellers and ease of entry and exit, assures that only normal profits are earned in the long run. In addition, the major studies in this area all show that marketing goods to low-income consumers is costly. Insurance premiums are high, pilfering and robbery are major problems, and the use of salesmen who canvass on a house-to-house basis, make home demonstrations, and collect debts is expensive. Summarizing a study of durable goods merchants, the FTC reports: "Practically all of the substantially higher gross margins of the low-income market retailers were offset by higher expenses and did not result in markedly higher net profits as a percentage of sales."[12]

It seems doubtful that exchanging black merchants for white in ghetto stores would make much of a difference, given the realities of doing business in the ghetto. The discussion of black capitalism which follows must be seen in the light of these economic realities.

BLACK CAPITALISTS

The small size of the black business class has generally been explained in two ways. First, there are barriers to an individual's advancement in business because he is black. Second, the nature of segregation and the economic relations between the black ghetto and the white society preclude, for the most part, the possibility of successful black businesses. Stressing one of these approaches over the other has major policy consequences; if blacks have not been successful because of discrimination, then classic civil rights strategies of groups like the Urban League and the NAACP should be followed. If the ghetto is viewed as an internal colony requiring collective liberation, then other strategies are called for.

Many scholars have pointed out the conspicuous absence of blacks in managerial and proprietary positions.[13] It has been argued that this situation exists because blacks are arriving in the cities at a time when opportunities for the establishment of small businesses are on the decline.[14] This may well be true, but the black man's failure to achieve success as a businessman must certainly be attributed more centrally to racism. As Eugene Foley has written, "The culture has simultaneously unduly emphasized achievement in business as the primary symbol of success and has blindly developed or imposed an all-pervading racism that denied the Negro the necessary opportunities for achieving this success."[15]

The only area in which black businessmen were able to gain entry was within their own segregated communities. In this regard the closing off of the ghetto may have helped black businessmen as a group. But even in the ghetto other groups often have the most prosperous businesses. In many cities Jews are more heavily represented in retail businesses than other groups as a result of past European restrictions on Jews which forced a disproportionate number to become traders and merchants because other professions were closed to them. Of the immigrant groups to come to America the Jews were as a result the group whose members went heavily into trade. In many ghettos anti-white feeling against merchants has taken on strong anti-semitic tones. However, a study of New Orleans, where the black ghetto businesses are heavily owned by Italians, showed the presence of strong anti-Italian feeling. In all cases hatred is aimed at the group which economically dominates the ghetto.[16]

In getting started in business the European immigrants had three major advantages over the blacks. First, the immigrants usually had a sense of clannishness. Glazer and Moynihan point out that because of such group solidarity, funds were more readily available. "Those who had advanced themselves created little pools for ethnic businessmen and professionals to tap."[17] This has not been as true of blacks, until the present decade, when a sense of identity and group pride has developed among a sizable number of blacks. Second, there is the legacy of slavery. Blacks have not only the "badge of color but also the ingrained burden of generations of cultural and economic deprivation."[18]

> The plantation system offered the Negro no experience with money, no incentive to save, no conception of time or progress — none of the basic experience to prepare him for the urban money economy. Instead, it indoctrinated him to believe in his own inferiority, to be resigned, while it held him in a folk culture dominated by a spiritual, other-worldly, escapist outlook. . . .[19]

This is a limited view of the effects of slavery. It ignores the "calculated cruelty . . . designed to crush the spirit," the malice and the hatred which blacks endured under slavery. Nor does such a view speak to the continuing record.

"When slavery ended and large scale physical abuse was discontinued, it was supplanted by different but equally damaging abuse. The cruelty continued unabated in thoughts, feelings, intimidation and occasional lynching. Black people were consigned to a place outside the human family and the whip of the plantation was replaced by the boundaries of the ghetto."[20]

Whether one blames the dominance of folk culture or at a more fundamental level the limits slavery placed on black development, it may be concluded that blacks do lack "managerial skills and attitudes. Negroes as a race have been little exposed to business operations and lack technical experience and entrepreneurial values that are necessary for succeeding in business."[21]

In the 1920s and 1930s West Indian-born blacks coming to this country did very well as a group, going into business and proving quite successful. They had drive and determination to succeed, and did so in surprisingly large numbers. Sociologists have attributed their success to the Jamaican social structure, where in spite of British colonial administration rule, there was upward mobility for blacks. Coming to this country, West Indians had separate customs and accents and an identity distinct from the masses of black descendants of American slaves. The Jamaicans showed the same self-confidence and motivation as did other immigrant groups.[22] While this experience is not conclusive evidence, certainly enough has been written about the debilitating effect of the slavery experience that it must be counted high as a cause of the lack of black entrepreneurship. It is also of interest to note that the race pride and self-help ethic preached by the Black Muslims may well be responsible for their success in numerous ghetto-based business operations.

A third and last factor, also difficult to assess, is the importance of an economic base in some occupation or trade in which the group has a special advantage — a phenomenon not found among the black population.

> Thus the Chinese in America, a small group who never dreamed until World War II of getting jobs in the general American community, had an economic base in laundries and restaurants — a peculiar base, but one that gave economic security and the wherewithal to send children to college. It has been estimated that the income of Chinese from Chinese-owned business is, in proportion to their numbers, *forty-five* times as great as the income of Negroes from Negro-owned business.[23]

The lack of business tradition may in and of itself be a handicap of some significance. The businessman is an important customer for other businessmen, and Italian bakeries are more likely to hire Italian truckers, suppliers, and so on.[24] Such ties are both natural and important. This is why black groups use their buying power to force white-owned businesses to hire black sales personnel. Black ownership could lead to the informal formation of "black" forward and backward linkages in procurement and sales patterns.

Another disadvantage the black businessman has is that he is limited to the ghetto as a place of business. This means that his customers have lower incomes than those of businessmen located elsewhere; his insurance rates, if indeed he can get insurance at all, tend to be much higher than elsewhere;[25] his customers are worse credit risks; loss rates from theft are higher; and so on. Further, when the black businessman goes to get bank loans, all of these disadvantages are thrown back at him. A commercial loan is "based on the proven management ability of the borrower in a stable industry and a stable locality."[26] Black businesses are for the most part marginal, unstable, and very poor credit risks. They also tend to be almost exclusively in retail and service trades. If "there exists, among Negroes, a rather low image of the significance and possibilities of business endeavors,"[27] this feeling seems justified. The evidence available suggests a low rate of return for black entrepreneurs.

There are black businessmen who have grown quite wealthy and others who are modestly well-to-do who have built up sizable businesses in the black communities of Atlanta, Durham, Chicago, and New York, but they have done so by overcoming extensive obstacles. The argument here is twofold. First, black business is much smaller and less profitable than white business. Further, small business — white or black — will not do well and is not what the ghetto needs.

In a 1964 study of the Philadelphia black ghetto it was found that "[p]ersonal services were the most numerous, hairdressing and barbering comprising 24 percent and 11 percent, respectively, of the total number of Negroes in business. Luncheonettes and restaurants comprised 11.5 percent of the total. Many of the businesses would be sub-marginal if free family labor were not available. For example, median sales for a sample of Negro-owned beauty shops were $2,500, for Negro-owned luncheonettes, $6,800, and for barber shops, $4,400."[28] It seems safe to say that the 1970s will not be the decade of the small businessman. The number of black-owned businesses decreased by more than a fifth between 1950 and 1960, faster than the also declining rate for white-owned small businesses.[29] In spite of the relatively unimportant and declining role of small businesses in the economy, blacks are being encouraged to open such businesses.

Restraining potential violence seems to be the major reason for the push for black ownership. One reporter making the ghetto tour in the spring of 1969 found:

> Despite the ruins and other physical deterioration, black leaders say there is a new spirit of restraint, and perhaps a little more hope, among the people. "A community that sees itself coming into ownership of business and other property," said Thomas I. Atkins, Negro member of the Boston City Council, "is not anxious to destroy that which it will own."[30]

A great effort is therefore being made to give more blacks "a piece of the action."

HELPING INDIVIDUAL BLACK BUSINESSMEN

One of the major differences in the ways white middle-class communities and black ghettos are organized is in the nature of formal and informal communication and decision-making. In white communities one of the most important groups on school boards, in charity fund raising, and in other commercial undertakings is the business community. The lack of black businessmen in the ghetto deprives the community of the important contribution such groups make elsewhere. A second disadvantage in this regard is absentee ownership. As James Q. Wilson has pointed out, "Communal social controls tend to break down when persons with an interest in, and the competence for, maintaining a community no longer live in the area. ..."[31] Residential businessmen, it is believed, add stability to their community.

The desirability of fostering the growth of small businesses has been recognized and accepted by the federal government for a long time. The Small Business Administration (SBA) makes loans to aid struggling businessmen. The extent of such aid going to blacks before the middle 1960s was minimal. A study of the ten and a half years of operation of the Philadelphia office of the SBA showed that out of 432 loans made through the fall of 1964, only seven had been to black businessmen.[32] Attempting to remedy this situation, the SBA set up a program on an experimental basis in Philadelphia to reach the "very" small businessmen, especially Negro businessmen, who operate a large segment of the very small business sector. The program involved loans up to $6,000 for six years (hence the name "6 × 6" Pilot Loan and Management Program). The SBA also offered individual training and counseling. The program was judged successful in overcoming traditional barriers faced by black businessmen, and, to the surprise of some old-time SBA people, the delinquency rate was very low.[33]

In the late 1960s the SBA accelerated its search for qualified black borrowers, instituting special outreach programs, lowering equity requirements (which in 1968 could be less than 15 percent), guaranteeing up to 90 percent of bank loans, and developing counseling programs in cooperation with volunteer groups such as the Service Corps of Retired Executives (SCORE) and Minority Advisors for Minority Entrepreneurs (MAME).[34] In fiscal 1968 the SBA aided 2,300 minority-owned businesses with various services and promised to increase this number in years to come.[35] One thousand six hundred seventy-six minority loans were approved in fiscal 1968, about 13 percent of total SBA loans, and five percent of the total value of loans made.[36]

Unfortunately, the rapid increase in the number of loans made to minority businesses was dramatically matched with climbing loss and default rates. In fiscal 1966 the loss rate was 3.6 percent. The next year it was 8.9 percent, and in fiscal 1968 the loss rate was nearly 12 percent of loan disbursement.[37] It was hinted in the spring of 1969 that the climbing rate of losses on loans might lead to cutbacks in the SBA program.[38] Once the best prospects were helped, the economies of the more typical ghetto business had become evident. Merchants with limited capital and markets purchase on a small scale and so must charge higher prices, creating customer resentment.

One way to minimize the failure rate of new businesses is through franchising, which utilizes a "proven" product, service, and marketing technique. The franchisor usually provides location analysis, helps negotiate a lease, obtains a loan, initiates training for the personnel, helps design and equip the store, and offers economies of centralized purchasing and advertising.[39] Franchising is also a safe way for white firms to enter the ghetto market. Franchising and the SBA programs are subject to the same criticism: small retail businesses are on the decline, and certainly to rely on small business as a way to promote black advancement in competition with white capitalism "is little more than a hoax."[40] An equally important criticism of attempts to create a greater number of black businessmen is that the economics of the ghetto may itself force the black capitalist to shortchange his "brothers," selling inferior merchandise at high prices just as other ghetto merchants do. For these reasons two other strategies seem more relevant to the economic development of the ghetto — the involvement of big business in partnership with the local community and local development corporations owned and operated by neighborhood residents.

THE WHITE CORPORATION IN THE BLACK GHETTO

The latter part of the 1960s witnessed the growing awareness on the part of the business community that it should become more "involved" in urban problems. Writing as a mayor of a large city with a background in business, Alfonso Cervantes stated in the fall of 1967 in the *Harvard Business Review* that before Watts he believed "businessmen should commit themselves to making money, politicians to saving the cities, do-gooders to saving the disadvantaged, and preachers to saving souls. . . . Observing the riots of Watts (and now Newark, Detroit, and other Harlems throughout the country) has converted me to an updated social orthodoxy. As a public administrator I have discovered that the economic credos of a few years ago no longer suffice; I now believe the profit motive is compatible with social rehabilitation."[41]

In a similar vein a group of corporation executives at the close of a Columbia University School of Business meeting devoted to "The Negro Challenge to the Business Community" spoke not only of the moral responsibility of business to take action, but of its self-interest in doing so. The report said, in part:

> Business cannot tolerate such disturbances. Business could be brought to a virtual standstill in such an atmosphere, as indeed it has in many parts of the world . . . the political realities are such that restrictions, legislation, and the direction of business could bring an end to what we call free enterprise.[42]

While involvement would unquestionably be of benefit to corporations as a whole, unless there is a profitable return to individual firms they will not participate.[43] The problem for government is to insure profitability through subsidies and tax incentives without allowing unearned windfall gains. As the Nixon Administration found out when it tried to make good on campaign promises, this [is] a difficult balance to achieve.[44]

The pattern of support that has emerged in the late Johnson and early Nixon years is that an independent corporation with a name like "Opportunity Unlimited" or "Economic Resources Corporation" is set up with a predominantly black board of directors, funded by Economic Development Administration grants and loans, Labor Department training funds, and perhaps an Office of Economic Opportunity grant and Department of Housing and Urban Development assistance.[45] The key ingredient is an ongoing relation between the newly established corporation and a large established firm which supplies know-how and a long-term contract for the independent firm's output. Thus, in one well-publicized case a black group, FIGHT, in Rochester, New York, was assisted by Xerox in getting started. The extent of dependency in such a relationship has been described as follows:

> FIGHT's venture would have been a pipedream without the unstinting support of Xerox Corporation — from planning to production. Xerox helped to define FIGHT's product-line — metal stampings and electrical transformers. The office-copier giant will lend FIGHT two key management advisors, conduct technical training, and open the doors to bank financing. Even more important, Xerox has guaranteed to buy $1.2 million of the firm's output over a two year period.[46]

In discussing the role of Xerox in getting the Rochester firm started, another writer stated:

> Here lies one of the principal strengths of the program: a corporation often initiates a company, guarantees it a market, helps set up the business, furnishes the training, and helps iron out any start-up problems. Indeed, all the manufacturing enterprises have been established so far at the instigation of potential corporate customers.[47]

The encouragement of black entrepreneurship not only raises the income of blacks who manage the new businesses, but changes or reinforces their attitudes towards the proper methods of achieving social change. One counselor who evidently learned "a good deal from his experience" in helping a black man enter the business world, describes in the following terms the enlightened attitude of his pupil toward Negro development:

> As a leading Negro, Howard has not been fully able to accept the rebellious nature of the present civil rights movement. Certainly, he resents the forces that have limited the Negroes' development, but in many ways he rises above this. He sees himself not only as a Negro but as a member of the society of man. As the movement advances and Negroes become more educated, Howard's values may be accepted. As he says, "Education without civilization is a disaster." He expresses his indebtedness to society when he says, "Let me be recognized, let me contribute."[48]

"Howard" would be described by some militants as an Oreo (black on the outside, white on the inside) or simply as a Tom. The achievement of such black men only reinforces the idea that blacks must struggle as individuals to escape their poverty. What is needed is not the salvation of a few but the redemption of all. This, militants argue, can be done only if all ghetto dwellers cooperatively own the economic resources of the ghetto and use these resources for the common good.

THE COMMUNITY DEVELOPMENT CORPORATION

The contrast between those who favor aiding individual blacks or encouraging white corporations to become involved in the ghetto and those who want independent black development is not always very distinct. Current proposals being put forward in the Congress have in fact adopted the rhetoric of militancy and the trappings of the radicals' own analysis. For example, Senator Jacob Javits, addressing the U.S. Chamber of Commerce in late 1968, compared the ghetto to an emerging nation which rejects foreign domination of its economy. He suggested:

> American business has found that it must develop host country management and new forms of joint ownership in establishing plants in the fiercely national-istic less-developed countries, [and so too] this same kind of enlightened partner-ship will produce the best results in the slums of our own country.[49]

In 1968 Javits along with others (including conservative Senator John Tower) proposed a bill which would establish community self-determination corporations to aid the people of urban (and rural) communities in, among other goals, "achieving the ownership and control of the resources of their community, expanding opportunity, stability, and self-determination."[50] The proposed "Community Self-Determination Act" had the support of some militant Black Power groups such as the Congress on Racial Equality (CORE) because it promised self-respect and independence through ownership by blacks and community control of its own development. The bill set as an important aim the restoration to the residents of local communities of the power to participate directly and meaningfully in the making of public policy decisions on issues which affect their everyday lives. "Such programs should," the bill stated, "aim to free local communities from excessive interference and control by centralized governments in which they have little or no effective voice." While the proposal was not enacted into law, it gives some indication of the type of thinking being done by influential groups and individuals. It has also directed attention to the community development concept.

Most schemes for community development corporations (CDC's) propose (1) expanding economic and educational opportunities through the purchase and management of properties and businesses; (2) improving the health, safety, and living conditions through CDC-sponsored health centers, housing projects, and so on; (3) enhancing personal dignity and independence through the expansion of opportunities for meaningful decision-making and self-determination; and (4) at the discretion of the corporation, using its profits to pay a "community dividend" rather than a return to stock-holders.[51] The relation between CDC-sponsored businesses and privately owned ones is hard to delineate satisfactorily.

Some proposals suggest that the CDC should also be a development bank to make loans and grants to local businesses in order to encourage ownership. Others suggest CDC's should bond black contractors and act as a broker between ghetto residents and outside groups for government grants, franchising, and subcontracting. Such an organization would be something on the order of a central planning agency, making cost-benefit studies of business potential in different lines, keeping track of vacancies, and conducting inventories of locally available skills.[52] One study in Harlem has made "feasibility analyses," detailed cost-benefit "profiles," for different industries which might be developed in the ghetto. These involve a consideration of employment and income-generating potential as well as any externalities not reflected in private profit calculations.[53] After detailing the best development plan (developed by technical analysis, subject to community approval under some suitable organizational form), a development planning group would make two final measures. First, an estimate would be made of the *efficiency gaps* (the expected differences in unit operating costs between Harlem projects' activities and similar businesses already operating outside the ghetto). "These gaps will suggest the magnitude of the public subsidies necessary to complement private capital in the implementation of the plan."[54] Second, estimates would be made of needed infrastructural requirements which would "permit the Project businesses to function efficiently. This bill of requirements will then be presented to local government officials,"[55] or funded by a well-financed CDC. Under such a plan the CDC would provide social infrastructure and funds but eschew an ownership role.

Such a development bank and planning agency approach would encourage black entrepreneurship through low-cost loans and technical help. It downplays mechanisms for community control while stressing neighborhood involvement in an individual entrepreneurial role, rather than community cooperation.

The CDC schemes are expected to be financed either through stocks and bonds sold in the local community or through funding by federal agencies. Some suggest that in addition to the Neighborhood CDC's there should be a national Urban Development Corporation (UDC). The UDC, it is suggested, would not engage in development projects but could give financial and technical advice to the CDC's. The UDC would sponsor experiments and demonstration projects. A UDC could "be a source of knowledge, as well as assistance, generating new ideas for community ventures. It would develop, test, and disseminate knowledge of new means for organizing and implementing projects for creating housing, nurturing new businesses, training the unskilled, and so forth."[56] By selective distribution of resources, based on performance measures, the UDC could increase the scale of operations of the more "effective" CDC's.[57] In this view, the CDC would be limited for funding to what it could earn and what the UDC allocated to it as a "reward for social effectiveness." Profit in the usual sense would not be the measure of efficiency.

The power relations here are subject to much debate. The idea behind the CDC is to give an organizational tool for ghetto development. The extent of control by any group outside the ghetto would in all likelihood be fought by the local leadership. Rosenbloom argues that a UDC would be needed as a "surrogate" for the market, since many CDC undertakings (day care centers, a community newspaper, health services, and so on) might not be run as profit-making ventures but are important programs worthy of financing. Through financial rewards, the UDC would recognize enterprises which improve community conditions. The danger that such controls might lead to covert or overt "manipulation" and the charges of "same old paternalism" have been recognized, but it is also pointed out that there must be an overseeing of public funds through audits and some sort of supervision.

Conflicts might also arise between CDC and powerful local interests. CDC housing rehabilitation programs might not get very much cooperation from local slumowners; buyers' cooperative stores might find local merchants using their influence to fight them; the community-run schools might have trouble reaching agreements with the city-wide board of education, the teachers' union, and so on. On the other hand, the inclusion of (white) businessmen in advisory capacities to take advantage of local expertise might be rejected by the community. The demand by the mayor and city council that they be given veto power over projects or that all money should be channeled through them would also be resisted vigorously. If poverty program experiences are indicative, militant local CDC's would find their funds cut off as political pressures of the vested interests made their power felt. The Model Cities Program has been carefully channeled through the local governments, and the ghetto has usually lost the battle for community control. Some of the problems involved, from the city council point of view, are shown in the vigorous resistance to giving neighborhood boards real power under Model Cities legislation.[58] This occurs partly because mayors and councilors do not like to "play second fiddle" to locally elected boards. There is a feeling that special consideration is unfair and that all parts of the city should be treated equally, and the argument that "fairness" requires restitution for past misallocation are rarely accepted by residents of the wealthier white neighborhoods. The narrow-mindedness of most local white electorates indicates that clashes between local autonomy and federal priorities may prove to be one of the more important conflicts in intergovernmental relations in the coming years.[59] Distinguishing among proposals which will encourage local control by black communities while not allowing racist policies in white neighborhoods which democratically vote to be racist is a problem that can be overcome through the application of the U.S. Constitution. It is not as difficult a task as some suggest; in fact, the suggestion that local control strengthens white bigotry, while real enough, is often stressed by those who do not want to see black communities gain real power. The inner-city blacks are asking only for the same degree of autonomy as is already enjoyed by the suburban whites who do run their police, school boards, etc. Each small town in suburbia duplicates facilities, some of which might on economic grounds be run on an area-wide basis. They do so to retain local control, even at the expense of the added financial burden.

BLACK COOPERATION

Corporations have been criticized by some for not going far enough in terms of ghetto autonomy. Others suggest that such proposals, by going too far towards ghetto autonomy, encourage black separatism.

The limits of black capitalism have been well stated by James Sundquist:

> Federal credit and technical assistance should be extended, and discrimination against Negro enterprises in such matters as surety bonds and other forms of insurance should be dealt with — if necessary, through federal legislation. Much can be said for a federal program to support and assist ghetto-based

community development corporations that will have power to operate or finance commercial and industrial enterprises. But even with all these kinds of encouragement, to suggest that Negro entrepreneurship can produce much more than a token number of new jobs for the hard-core unemployed, at least for a long time to come, is pure romanticism. Ghetto anarchy is impossible. Even if the ghetto markets could be walled off, in effect, through appeals to Negroes to "buy black," the market is not big enough to support significant manufacturing, and the number of white employees who could be replaced by black workers in retail and service establishments is limited.[60]

For the ghetto to develop a strong "export" sector would take a great deal of expertise and capital. Both would have to be imported from outside, and for this to happen, long-standing flow patterns would have to be reversed. There are three ways this could happen.

First, private funds could be guaranteed against "expropriation" and special tax treatment given to assure profitability. The difficulty here would be that given foreign ownership, decisions would be made externally and profits could be repatriated.

Second are the proposals usually offered to help any under-developed nation badly in need of capital: better terms of trade and technical assistance. Foreign aid could be used to build up social over-head capital, to make investment in human capital, and to give loans to local entrepreneurs. The ghetto's one major export, unskilled labor, could be aided through a continuing national commitment to full employment. Technical assistance would include economic consultants, the establishment of research facilities to study potentially profitable lines of ghetto development, and a financial commitment to pursue such avenues.

Third, if the problem is viewed as one of underdevelopment, efforts could be made to retain profits and wages of ghetto-based enterprises by demanding that those who work in the area live there. Those who hold jobs as policemen, teachers, postal employees, clerks, or small businessmen would have a greater interest in "their" community if they lived in it. Cooperative forms of ownership would also lead to greater community control and to a greater retention of capital in the ghetto.

. . .

NOTES

1. See Raymond S. Franklin, "The Political Economy of Black Power," *Social Problems*, Winter 1969; and Robert Blauner, "Internal Colonialism and Ghetto Revolt," *Social Problems*, Spring 1969.

2. See, for example, Robert B. McKersie, "Vitalize Black Enterprise," *Harvard Business Review*, September—October 1968.

3. "The Soul Market in Black and White," *Sales Management: The Marketing Magazine*, June 1, 1969.

4. See *Christian Science Monitor*, July 9, 1968.

5. See Louise G. Richards, "Consumer Practices of the Poor," in *The Ghetto as Marketplace*, ed. Frank D. Sturdivant (New York: The Free Press, 1969), p. 51.

6. Federal Trade Commission, "Economic Report on Installment Credit and Retail Sales Practices of District of Columbia Retailers," in Sturdivant, *The Ghetto as Marketplace*, p. 101.

7. *Ibid.*, p. 77.

8. Mary Gardiner Jones, "Deception in the Marketplace of the Poor: The Role of the Federal Trade Commission," in Sturdivant, *The Ghetto as Marketplace*, p. 252.

9. David Caplovitz, *The Poor Pay More: Consumer Practices of Low Income Families* (New York: The Free Press, 1967), p. xxiii.

10. *Ibid.*, p. xvii.

11. *Ibid.*, p. xvi.

12. Federal Trade Commission, "Economic Report on Installment Credit," p. 104.

13. See, for example, Nathan Glazer and Daniel Patrick Moynihan, *Beyond the Melting Pot* (Cambridge, Mass.: The M.I.T. Press and Harvard University Press, 1963), pp. 31—32; and Daniel Patrick Moynihan, "Employment, Income, and the Ordeal of the Negro Family," in *The Negro American*, ed. Talcott Parsons and Kenneth B. Clark (Boston: Beacon Press, 1967), p. 143.

14. Glazer and Moynihan, *Beyond the Melting Pot*, p. 143.

15. Eugene P. Foley, "The Negro Businessman: In Search of a Tradition," in Parsons and Clark, *The Negro American*, p. 572.

16. St. Clair Drake and Horace R. Clayton, *Black Metropolis*, vol. II (second edition; New York: Harcourt, Brace and World, 1962), p. 432.

17. Glazer and Moynihan, *Beyond the Melting Pot*, p. 33.

18. Jeanne R. Lowe, *Cities in a Race with Time* (New York: Vintage, 1967), p. 283.

19. *Ibid.*, p. 283.

20. [William H.] Grier and [Price M.] Cobbs, *Black Rage* [(New York: Bantam, 1968)], p. 20.

21. McKersie, "Vitalize Black Enterprise," p. 90.

22. Glazer and Moynihan, *Beyond the Melting Pot*, p. 34.

23. *Ibid.*, p. 37.

24. *Ibid.*, p. 31.

25. See The President's National Advisory Panel on Insurance in Riot-Affected Areas, *Meeting the Insurance Crisis of Our Cities* (Washington, D.C.: Government Printing Office, 1968). Also, *Hearings before The President's National Advisory Panel on Insurance in Riot-Affected Areas, November 8 and 9, 1967* (Washington, D.C.: Government Printing Office, 1968).

26. Foley, "The Negro Businessman: In Search of a Tradition," p. 560.

27. See National Conference on Small Business, *Problems and Opportunities Confronting Negroes in the Field of Business*, ed. H. Naylor Fitzhugh (Washington, D.C.: Government Printing Office, 1962), p. 8.

28. Foley, "The Negro Businessman: In Search of a Tradition," p. 561. For more recent evidence see James Heilbrun, "Jobs in Harlem: A Statistical Analysis," *Regional Science Association Papers*, 1970.

29. Eugene P. Foley, "Negroes as Entrepreneurs," in *The American Negro Reference Book*, ed. John P. Davis (Englewood Cliffs, N.J.: Prentice-Hall, 1966), p. 294.

30. John Herbers, "Mood of the Cities: New Stakes for Blacks May Cool Things Off," *The New York Times*, April 27, 1969, Section 4, p. 8e. See also Jacob Javits, "Remarks to the 56th Annual Meeting of the U.S. Chamber of Commerce," in U.S. *Congressional Record*, 90th Cong., 2nd Sess., May 7, 1968, p. S5053.

31. James Q. Wilson, "The Urban Unease: Community vs. City," *The Public Interest*, Summer 1968, p. 34.

32. Foley, "The Negro Businessman: In Search of a Tradition," pp. 574–575.

33. *Ibid.*, p. 575.

34. Small Business Administration, *Fact Sheet: Project Own* (Washington, D.C.: Small Business Administration, n.d. [received April 1969]).

35. Allen T. Demaree, "Business Picks up the Urban Challenge," *Fortune*, April 1969, p. 176.

36. Small Business Administration, Office of Reports, *Management Information Summary* (Washington, D.C.: Small Business Administration, May 1969), p. 25.

37. *The New York Times*, April 21, 1969, p. 27.

38. *Ibid.*

39. See U.S. Department of Commerce, *Franchise Company Data for Equal Opportunity in Business* (Washington, D.C.: Government Printing Office, 1966), especially p. 4.

40. W. Arthur Lewis, "The Road to the Top Is through Higher Education — Not Black Studies," *The New York Times Magazine*, May 11, 1969.

41. Alfonso J. Cervantes, "To Prevent a Chain of Super Watts," *Harvard Business Review*, September—October 1967, pp. 55–56.

42. The Conference Group, "Reports of Corporate Action," in *The Negro Challenge to the Business Community*, ed. Eli Ginzberg (New York: McGraw-Hill, 1964), p. 87.

43. Robin Marris, "Business Economics and Society," in *Social Innovation in the City: New Enterprises for Community Development*, ed. Richard S. Rosenbloom and Robin Marris (Cambridge, Mass.: Harvard University Program on Technology and Science, 1969), p. 30.

44. *The New York Times*, May 11, 1969, p. 1.

45. *The New York Times*, February 27, 1969, p. 1.

46. *Christian Science Monitor*, July 26, 1968.

47. McKersie, "Vitalize Black Enterprise," p. 98.

48. *Ibid.*, p. 96.

49. Javits, "Remarks to the Fifty-sixth Annual Meeting of the U.S. Chamber of Commerce," p. 5053.

50. U.S. Congress, Senate, *Hearings on S. 3876*, 90th Cong., 2d Sess., July 24, 1968, p. S9284. [Editor's note: The author probably means p. S928.]

51. *Ibid.*, pp. S927–S929.

52. *Ibid.*, Section 110; Richard S. Rosenbloom, "Corporations for Urban Development," in Rosenbloom and Marris, *Social Innovation in the City*; and Frederick D. Sturdivant, "The Limits of Black Capitalism," *Harvard Business Review*, January—February 1969.

53. Bennett Harrison, "A Pilot Project in Economic Development Planning for American Urban Slums," *International Development Review*, March 1968, p. 26.

54. *Ibid.*, p. 27.

55. *Ibid.*, p. 28.

56. *Ibid.*, p. 29.

57. Rosenbloom, "Corporations for Urban Development."

58. *Ibid.*

59. See Mahlon Apgar IV, and S. Michael Dean, "Combining Action and Research: Two Cases," in Rosenbloom and Marris, *Social Innovation in the City*, especially pp. 194—196.

60. James L. Sundquist, "Jobs, Training, and Welfare for the Underclass," in *Agenda for the Nation*, ed. Kermit Gordon (Washington, D.C.: The Brookings Institution, 1968), p. 58.

CHAPTER 4   SUGGESTIONS FOR FURTHER READING

Brooks, Glenwood C., and **William E. Sedlacek**, *Racism in American Education: A Model for Change* (Chicago: Nelson-Hall, 1976). This volume explores the way in which racism, both attitudinal and institutional, operates in American education and traces out specific, and workable, strategies for eradicating racial discrimination in education.

Feagin, Joe R., and **Clairece B. Feagin**, *Discrimination American Style* (Englewood Cliffs, N.J.: Prentice-Hall, 1978). After laying out a basic typology of individual and institutionalized discrimination, these authors systematically explore the ways in which overt and covert race (and sex) discrimination work in a number of areas, including employment, housing, and education. A concluding chapter explores the drift in equal opportunity and affirmative-action remedies.

Moore, Joan W. *Mexican Americans* (second edition; Englewood Cliffs, N.J.: Prentice-Hall, 1976). I am including this volume in the bibliography to suggest that black Americans are not the only ones facing problems in urban ghettos. This author makes clear that Mexican Americans, now a highly urbanized minority, have faced, and still face, race-related segregation and discrimination in American cities.

5

The Urban Environment:
A Focus on Transportation

In this chapter we deal with a number of interrelated issues centered on the urban environment. The reprinted selection by Bradford Snell examines the impact of transportation and related industrial choices on the environmental scene in cities. Noting the dominance of automobile, truck, and bus production by the Big Three automobile companies, Snell shows how the drive for profit expansion by these companies eliminated or reduced transportation alternatives to the automobile. By the 1970s there were no producers of electric streetcars or trolleys left in the United States, and few (passenger) railcar builders; diesel bus production was on the decline as well. In some detail Snell demonstrates how a large multinational corporation, General Motors, expanded into rail and bus production in a way that led to the decline of other sectors of the American transportation system. General Motors' involvement in bus building and operations accelerated the decline in passenger service on the railroads and the decline in the use of low-pollution electric vehicles in city bus systems. General Motors was even convicted, in 1949, of criminal conspiracy "to replace electric transportation with gas- and diesel-powered buses and to monopolize the sale of buses and related products to local transportation companies throughout the country." This penetration led to the demise of realistic people-moving alternatives to cars and diesel buses. Dieselization also contributed to the decline of American railroads. Snell further demonstrates the way in which the considerable political power of the automobile industry triggered a great flow of funds into highway development.

The implications of Snell's analysis for the urban environment in which most Americans now live are manifold. The environmental crisis is the work of human beings. The dominant means of personal transportation has altered the very shape of American cities. Instead of compact cities, we typically have scattered ones, often, as in Los Angeles, so large that it takes as long as two hours to drive across the city and its suburbs. Getting from one place to another in a reasonable length of time becomes virtually impossible during the better part of weekdays. Streets, either radiating out from central cities (as in many older cities) or more randomly patterned, become the central arteries of trade and industry. To a significant extent, these streets shaped the layout of business and industry. New residential areas also spread out along main arteries, with those areas designed for more affluent urbanites located on the suburban fringe. For the suburbanite, commuting becomes a daily scourge; for most urbanites, poor or affluent, largescale commuting brings pollution. The ever increasing use of automobiles had brought widespread, serious, choking pollution to cities, which might otherwise have been spared the personal health and environmental damage problems that such pollution creates. The huge growth in the number and size of highways means the publicly sanctioned and sponsored destruction of houses, and even communities, in many urban areas. Accidents and deaths* became more numerous. These and numerous related problems can be traced back to a common origin: the profit-maximization decisions and associated political actions of a few automobile-centered corporations. The American city's form might well carry a GM-made label.

Because of the short length of this reader I have not reprinted here other selections that would probe further such issues as pollution, urban renewal, and housing. The reader interested in these matters should note the suggestions for further reading on urban renewal and housing at the end of this chapter.

---

*Up to the 1970's, an estimated 1.7 million Americans had died in motor vehicle accidents since 1900, while only one million Americans have died in *all* American wars since 1776. Annual figures now run as follows: 25 million accidents, 5 million injuries, 55 thousand deaths. For a lucid discussion of this and other critical environmental problems, see Charles H. Anderson, *The Sociology of Survival* (Homewood, Ill.: The Dorsey Press, 1976), especially chapters 1—2.

American Ground Transport

Bradford C. Snell

INTRODUCTION AND SUMMARY OF FINDINGS

This is a study of the social consequences of monopoly. It shows that excessive economic concentration can restructure society for corporate ends. As an illustration, it focuses on three powerful automobile companies which eliminated competition among themselves, secured control over rival bus and rail industries, and then maximized profits by substituting cars and trucks for trains, streetcars, subways, and buses. In short, it describes how General Motors, Ford, and Chrysler reshaped American ground transportation to serve corporate wants intead of social needs.

This is not a study of malevolent or rapacious executives. Rather, it maintains that as a result of their monopolistic structure the Big Three automakers have acted in a manner detrimental to the public interest. More specifically, it demonstrates that in the absence of vigorous competition, the automakers were naturally inclined to build oversized, high-profit cars which were energy-inefficient, unreliable, costly, unsafe, and destructive to the environment. It also demonstrates General Motors to be a sovereign economic state, whose common control of auto, truck, bus and locomotive production was a major factor in the displacement of rail and bus transportation by cars and trucks. It notes, moreover, that these displaced methods of travel were energy-conserving, dependable, economical, safe, and environmentally compatible. In sum, this study strongly suggests that a monopoly in ground vehicle production has led inexorably to a breakdown in this Nation's ground transportation.

*[Editor's note: Footnotes and diagrams in the original have been deleted here.]

Reprinted by permission of the author from **Bradford C. Snell**, *American Ground Transport*, a Committee Print of the Subcommittee on Antitrust and Monopoly of the Committee on the Judiciary, U.S. Senate, February 26, 1974.

We are witnessing today the collapse of a society based on the automobile. Unlike every other industrialized country, we have come to rely exclusively on large, gas-guzzling cars and trucks for the movement of passengers and freight. In the process, we have consumed much of the Nation's supply of oil, fouled our urban air with poisonous exhausts, and turned our cities into highways and parking lots. Now we are confronted with an energy crisis that threatens to paralyze motor vehicle travel and reduce us to a level of mobility common only to less advanced countries.

The roots of our transportation malaise are several. This study purports neither to define nor to resolve all of them. They include, for example, a government bias in favor of highways rather than rail transit, an industry failure to produce transport vehicles consistent with energy resources and environmental constraints, and a consumer dependence on private automobiles to the exclusion of public transport. This study will argue, however, that to a considerable extent these are but outgrowths of a more fundamental problem: the economic and political control by three powerful automobile firms of all forms of ground travel. ...

...

INTERINDUSTRY COMPETITION BETWEEN MOTOR VEHICLES AND TRANSPORT BY BUS AND RAIL

Evaluated in terms of ... structural criteria ... the manufacture of ground transportation equipment is one of this Nation's least competitive industrial activities. More specifically, interindustry diversification and asymmetry have seriously upset the naturally competitive relationships among industries in this vital sector of the economy.

Ground transport is dominated by a single, diversified firm to an extent possibly without parallel in the American economy. General Motors, the world's largest producer of cars and trucks, has also achieved monopoly control of buses and locomotives which compete with motor vehicles for passengers and freight. Its dominance of the bus and locomotive industries, moreover, would seem to constitute a classic monopoly. Although GM technically accounts for 75 percent of current city bus production, its only remaining competitor, the Flxible Co., relies on it for diesel propulsion systems, major engine components, technical assistance, and financing. In short, Flxible is more a distributor for GM than a viable competitor; virtually its sole function is the assembly of General Motors' bus parts for sale under the Flxible trade name. Likewise, in the production of intercity buses, its only remaining competitor, Motor Coach Industries, is wholly dependent upon GM for diesel propulsion systems and major mechanical components. In addition, General Motors accounts for 100 percent of all passenger and 80 percent of all freight locomotives manufactured in the United States. Such concentration in a single firm of control over three rival transportation equipment industries all but precludes the existence of competitive conduct and performance.

The distribution of economic power in this sector is remarkably asymmetrical. ... [E]conomic power is fundamentally a function of concentration and size. In terms of concentration, the ground transport sector is virtually controlled by the Big Three auto companies. General Motors, Ford, and Chrysler account for 97 percent of automobile and 84 percent of truck production; GM alone dominates the bus and rail locomotive industries. Accordingly, the automakers have the power to impose a tax, in the form of a price increase, on purchasers of new cars to underwrite political campaigns against bus and rail systems.

In terms of size, there is an enormous divergence between the competing automotive and nonautomotive industries. Moreover, General Motors' diversification program has left only a small portion of the bus and rail industries in the hands of independent producers. As measured by aggregate sales, employment, and financial resources, therefore, the independent bus and rail firms are no match for the automakers. The Big Three's aggregate sales of motor vehicles and parts amount to about $52 billion each year, or more than 25 times the combined sales of trains, buses, subway, and rapid transit cars by the four largest firms other than GM which produce bus and rail vehicles: Pullman and Budd (railway freight and passenger cars, subway and rapid transit cars); Rohr (buses and rapid transit cars); General Electric (commuter railcars and locomotives). The Big Three automakers employ nearly 1½ million workers, or more than three times as many as their four principal rivals: General Motors alone maintains plants in 19 different States. The Big Three also excel in their ability to finance lobbying and related political activities. GM, Ford, and Chrysler annually contribute more than an estimated $14 million to trade associations which lobby for the promotion of automotive transportation. By contrast, their four leading rivals contribute not more than $1 million, or less than one-tenth this amount, to rail transit lobbies. The magnitude of their sales, employment, and financial resources, therefore, affords the automakers overwhelming political influence.

It may be argued, moreover, that due to their conflicting interlocks with the motor vehicle manufacturers, these bus and rail firms would be reluctant to set their economic and political resources against them. Eighty percent of Budd's sales, for example, consist of automotive components purchased by the Big Three; Rohr, which also owns the

Flxible Co., is wholly dependent upon GM for major bus components; Pullman derives more income from manufacturing trailers for highway trucks than from selling freight cars to the railroads; and General Electric manufactures a vast range of automotive electrical equipment, including about 80 percent of all automotive lamps. In sum, the independent bus and rail equipment manufacturers are probably unable and possibly unwilling to oppose the Big Three automakers effectively in political struggles over transportation policy.

Lacking a competitive structure, the group of industries responsible for providing us with ground transportation equipment fail to behave competitively. Diversification by General Motors into bus and rail production may have contributed to the displacement of these alternatives by automobiles and trucks. In addition, the asymmetrical distribution of economic and political power may have enabled the automakers to divert Government funds from rail transit to highways.

The Big Three automakers' efforts to restrain nonautomotive forms of passenger and freight transport have been perfectly consistent with profit maximization. One trolley coach or bus can eliminate 35 automobiles; 1 streetcar, subway, or rapid transit vehicle can supplant 50 passenger cars; an interurban railway or railroad train can displace 1,000 cars or a fleet of 150 cargo-laden trucks. Given the Big Three automakers' shared monopoly control of motor vehicle production and GM's diversified control of nonautomotive transport, it was inevitable that cars and trucks would eventually displace every other competing form of ground transportation.

The demise of nonautomotive transport is a matter of historical record. By 1973 viable alternatives to cars and trucks had all but ceased to exist. No producers of electric streetcars, trolley coaches, or interurban electric trains remained; only two established railcar builders (Pullman and Rohr) were definitely planning to continue production; a single firm (General Electric) still manufactured a handful of electric locomotives; and General Motors accounted for virtually all of an ever-shrinking number of diesel buses and locomotives.

There were, of course, a number of factors involved in this decline. For example, the popularity of motor vehicles, due in large part to their initial flexibility, most certainly affected public demand for competing methods of travel. On the other hand, the demise of bus and rail forms of transport cannot, as some have suggested, be attributed to the public's desire to travel exclusively by automobile. Rather, much of the growth in autos as well as trucks may have proceeded from the decline of rail and bus systems. In short, as alternatives ceased to be viable, automobiles and trucks became indispensable.

The sections which immediately follow relate in considerable detail how General Motors' diversification into bus and rail production generated conflicts of interest which necessarily contributed to the displacement of alternatives to motor vehicle transportation. A subsequent section will consider how asymmetry in the ground transport sector led to the political restraint of urban rail transit.

Before considering the displacement of bus and rail transportation, however, a distinction between intent and effect should be carefully drawn. This study contends that certain adverse effects flow inevitably from concentrated multi-industry structures regardless of whether these effects were actually intended. Specifically, it argues that structural concentration of auto, truck, bus, and rail production in one firm necessarily resulted in the promotion of motor vehicles and the displacement of competing alternatives. Whether that firm's executives in the 1920's actually intended to construct a society wholly dependent on automobiles and trucks is unlikely and, in any case, irrelevant. That such a society developed in part as the result of General Motors' common control of competing ground transport industries is both relevant and demonstrable.

1. The Substitution of Bus for Rail Passenger Transportation

By the mid-1920's, the automobile market had become saturated. Those who desired to own automobiles had already purchased them; most new car sales had to be to old car owners. Largely as a result, General Motors diversified into alternative modes of transportation. It undertook the production of city and intercity motor buses. It also became involved in the operation of bus and rail passenger services. As a necessary consequence, it was confronted with fundamental conflicts of interest regarding which of these several competing methods of transport it might promote most profitably and effectively. Its natural economic incentives and prior business experience strongly favored the manufacture and sale of cars and trucks rather than bus, and particularly rail, vehicles. In the course of events, it became committed to the displacement of rail transportation by diesel buses and, ultimately, to their displacement by automobiles.

In 1925, General Motors entered bus production by acquiring Yellow Coach, which at that time was the Nation's largest manufacturer of city and intercity buses. One year later, it integrated forward into intercity bus operation by assisting in the formation of the Greyhound Corp., and soon became involved in that company's attempt to convert passenger rail operations to intercity bus service. Beginning in 1932, it undertook the direct operation and conversion of interurban electric railways and local electric streetcar and trolleybus systems to city bus operations. By the mid-1950's, it could lay claim to having played a prominent role in the complete replacement of electric street transportation with diesel buses. Due to their high cost of operation and slow speed on congested streets, however, these buses ultimately contributed to the collapse of several hundred public transit systems and to the diversion of hundreds of thousands of patrons to automobiles. In sum, the effect of General Motors' diversification program was threefold: substitution of buses for passenger trains, streetcars, and trolleybuses; monopolization of bus production; and diversion of riders to automobiles.

Immediately after acquiring Yellow Coach, General Motors integrated forward into intercity bus operation. In 1926, interests allied with GM organized and then combined with the Greyhound Corp. for the purpose of replacing rail passenger service with a GM-equipped and Greyhound-operated nationwide system of intercity bus transportation. By mutual arrangement, Greyhound agreed to purchase virtually all of its buses from GM, which agreed in turn to refrain from selling intercity buses to any of Greyhound's bus operating competitors. In 1928, Greyhound announced its intention of converting commuter rail operations to intercity bus service. By 1939, six major railroads had agreed under pressure from Greyhound to replace substantial portions of their commuter rail service with Greyhound bus systems: Pennsylvania RR. (Pennsylvania Greyhound Lines), New York Central RR. (Central Greyhound Lines), Southern Pacific RR. (Pacific Greyhound Lines), New York, New Haven & Hartford RR. (New England Greyhound Lines), Great Northern RR. (Northland Greyhound Lines), and St. Louis Southwestern Railway (Southwestern Greyhound Lines). By 1950, Greyhound carried roughly half as many intercity passengers as all the Nation's railroads combined.

During this period, General Motors played a prominent role in Greyhound management. In 1929, for example, it was responsible for the formation, direct operation, and financing of Atlantic Greyhound, which later became Greyhound's southeastern affiliate. Three years later, in 1932, when Greyhound was in serious financial trouble, it arranged for a million dollar cash loan. In addition, I. B. Babcock, the president of GM's bus division, served on Greyhound's board of directors until 1938, when he was replaced by his successor at GM, John A. Ritchie. Until 1948, GM was also the largest single shareholder in the Greyhound Corp. In short, through its interlocking interests in and promotion of Greyhound, General Motors acquired a not insignificant amount of influence over the shape of this Nation's intercity passenger transportation. As the largest manufacturer of buses, it inevitably pursued a policy which would divert intercity traffic from rails to the intercity buses which it produced and Greyhound operated. Although this policy was perfectly compatible with GM's legitimate interest in maximizing returns on its stockholders' investments, it was not necessarily in the best interest of the riding public. In effect, the public was substantially deprived of access to an alternative form of intercity travel which, regardless of its merits, was apparently curtailed as a result of corporate rather than public determination.

After its successful experience with intercity buses, General Motors diversified into city bus and rail operations. At first, its procedure consisted of directly acquiring and scrapping local electric transit systems in favor of GM buses. In this fashion, it created a market for its city buses. As GM General Counsel Henry Hogan would observe later, the corporation "decided that the only way this new market for (city) buses could be created was for it to finance the conversion from streetcars to buses in some small cities." On June 29, 1932, the GM-bus executive committee formally resolved that "to develop motorized transportation, our company should initiate a program of this nature and authorize the incorporation of a holding company with a capital of $300,000." Thus was formed United Cities Motor Transit (UCMT) as a subsidiary of GM's bus division. Its sole function was to acquire electric streetcar companies, convert them to GM motorbus operation, and then resell the properties to local concerns which agreed to purchase GM bus replacements. The electric streetcar lines of Kalamazoo and Saginaw, Mich., and Springfield, Ohio, were UCMT's first targets. "In each case," Hogan stated, GM "successfully motorized the city, turned the management over to other interests and liquidated its investment." The program ceased, however, in 1935 when GM was censured by the American Transit Association (ATA) for its self-serving role, as a bus manufacturer, in apparently attempting to motorize Portland's electric streetcar system.

As a result of the ATA censure, GM dissolved UCMT and embarked upon a nationwide plan to accomplish the same result indirectly. In 1936 it combined with the Omnibus Corp. in engineering the tremendous conversion of New York City's electric streetcar system to GM buses. At that time, as a result of stock and management interlocks, GM was able to exert substantial influence over Omnibus. John A. Ritchie, for example, served simultaneously as chairman of GM's bus division and president of Omnibus from 1926 until well after the motorization was completed. The massive conversion within a period of only 18 months of the New York system, then the world's largest streetcar network, has been recognized subsequently as the turning point in the electric railway industry.

Meanwhile, General Motors had organized another holding company to convert the remainder of the Nation's electric transportation systems to GM buses. In 1936, it caused its officers and employees, I. B. Babcock, E. J. Stone, E. P. Crenshaw, and several Greyhound executives to form National City Lines, Inc. (NCL). During the following 14 years General Motors, together with Standard Oil of California, Firestone Tire, and two other suppliers of bus-related products, contributed more than $9 million to this holding company for the purpose of converting electric transit systems in 16 States to GM bus operations. The method of operation was basically the same as that which GM employed successfully in its United Cities Motor Transit program: acquisition, motorization, resale. By having NCL resell the properties after conversion was completed, GM and its allied companies were assured that their capital was continually reinvested in the motorization of additional systems. There was, moreover, little possibility of reconversion. To preclude the return of electric vehicles to the dozens of cities it motorized, GM extracted from the local transit companies contracts which prohibited their purchase of "any new equipment using any fuel or means of propulsion other than gas."

The National City Lines campaign had a devastating impact on the quality of urban transportation and urban living in America. Nowhere was the ruin more apparent than in the Greater Los Angeles metropolitan area. Thirty-five years ago it was a beautiful region of lush palm trees, fragrant orange groves, and clean, ocean-enriched air. It was served then by the world's largest interurban electric railway system. The Pacific Electric system branched out from Los Angeles for a radius of more than 75 miles reaching north to San Fernando, east to San Bernardino, and south to Santa Ana. Its 3,000 quiet, pollution-free, electric trains annually transported 80 million people throughout the sprawling region's 56 separately incorporated cities. Contrary to popular belief, the Pacific Electric, not the automobile, was responsible for the area's geographical development. First constructed in 1911, it established traditions of suburban living long before the automobile had arrived.

In 1938, General Motors and Standard Oil of California organized Pacific City Lines (PCL) as an affiliate of NCL to motorize west coast electric railways. The following year PCL acquired, scrapped, and substituted bus lines for three northern California electric rail systems in Fresno, San Jose, and Stockton. In 1940 GM, Standard Oil, and Firestone "assumed the active management of Pacific (City Lines)" in order to supervise its California operations more directly. That year, PCL began to acquire and scrap portions of the $100 million Pacific Electric system including rail lines from Los Angeles to Glendale, Burbank, Pasadena, and San Bernardino. Subsequently, in December 1944, another NCL affiliate (American City Lines) was financed by GM and Standard Oil to motorize downtown Los Angeles. At the time, the Pacific Electric shared downtown Los Angeles trackage with a local electric streetcar company, the Los Angeles Railway. American City Lines purchased the local system, scrapped its electric transit cars, tore down its power transmission lines, ripped up the tracks, and placed GM diesel buses fueled by Standard Oil on Los Angeles' crowded streets. In sum, GM and its auto-industrial allies severed Los Angeles' regional rail links and then motorized its downtown heart.

Motorization drastically altered the quality of life in southern California. Today, Los Angeles is an ecological wasteland: The palm trees are dying from petrochemical smog; the orange groves have been paved over by 300 miles of freeways; the air is a septic tank into which 4 million cars, half of them built by General Motors, pump 13,000 tons of pollutants daily. With the destruction of the efficient Pacific Electric rail system, Los Angeles may have lost its best hope for rapid rail transit and a smog-free metropolitan area. "The Pacific Electric," wrote UCLA Professor Hilton, "could have comprised the nucleus of a highly efficient rapid transit system, which would have contributed greatly to lessening the tremendous traffic and smog problems that developed from population growth." The substitution of GM diesel buses, which were forced to compete with automobiles for space on congested freeways, apparently benefited GM, Standard Oil, and Firestone, considerably more than the riding public. Hilton added: "[T]he (Pacific Electric) system, with its extensive private right of way, was far superior to a system consisting solely of buses on the crowded streets." As early as 1963, the city already was seeking ways of raising $500 million to rebuild a rail system "to supersede its present inadequate network of bus lines." A decade later, the estimated cost of constructing a 116-mile rail system, less than one-sixth the size of the earlier Pacific Electric, had escalated to more than $6.6 billion.

By 1949, General Motors had been involved in the replacement of more than 100 electric transit systems with GM buses in 45 cities including New York, Philadelphia, Baltimore, St. Louis, Oakland, Salt Lake City, and Los Angeles. In April of that year, a Chicago Federal jury convicted GM of having criminally conspired with Standard Oil of California, Firestone Tire, and others to replace electric transportation with gas- or diesel-powered buses and to monopolize the sale of buses and related products to local transportation companies throughout the country. The court imposed a sanction of $5,000 on GM. In addition, the jury convicted H. C. Grossman, who was then treasurer of General Motors. Grossman had played a key role in the motorization campaigns and had served as a director of PCL when that company undertook the dismantlement of the $100 million Pacific Electric system. The court fined Grossman the magnanimous sum of $1.

Despite its criminal conviction, General Motors continued to acquire and dieselize electric transit properties through September of 1955. By then, approximately 88 percent of the nation's electric streetcar network had been eliminated. In 1936, when GM organized National City Lines, 40,000 streetcars were operating in the United States; at the end of 1955, only 5,000 remained. In December of that year, GM bus chief Roger M. Kyes correctly observed: "The motor coach has supplanted the interurban systems and has for all practical purposes eliminated the trolley (streetcar)."

The effect of General Motors' diversification into city transportation systems was substantially to curtail yet another alternative to motor vehicle transportation. Electric street railways and electric trolley-buses were eliminated without regard to their relative merit as a mode of transport. Their displacement by oil-powered buses maximized the earnings of GM stockholders; but it deprived the riding public of a competing method of travel. Moreover, there is some evidence that in terms of air pollution and energy consumption these electric systems were superior to diesel buses. In any event, GM and its oil and tire coconspirators used National City Lines as a device to force the sale of their products regardless of the public interest. As Professor Smerk, an authority on urban transportation, has written, "Street railways and trolley bus operations, even if better suited to traffic needs and the public interest, were doomed in favor of the vehicles and material produced by the conspirators."

General Motors' substitution of buses for city streetcar lines may also have contributed in an indirect manner to the abandonment of electric railway freight service. During the 1930's merchants relied extensively on interurban electric railways to deliver local goods and to interchange distant freight shipments with mainline railroads. The Pacific Electric, for example, was once the third largest freight railroad in California; it interchanged freight with the Southern Pacific, the Union Pacific, and the Santa Fe. In urban areas, these railways often ran on local streetcar trackage. The conversion of city streetcars to buses, therefore, deprived them of city trackage and hastened their replacement by motor trucks, many of which, incidentally, were produced by GM.

General Motors also stood to profit from its interests in highway freight transport. Until the early 1950's, it maintained sizable stock interests in two of the Nation's largest trucking firms, Associated Transport and Consolidated Freightways, which enjoyed the freight traffic diverted from the electric railways. By 1951, these two companies had established more than 100 freight terminals in 29 States coast-to-coast and, more than likely, had invested in a substantial number of GM diesel-powered trucks.

GM's diversification into bus and rail operations would appear not only to have had the effect of foreclosing transport alternatives regardless of their comparative advantages but also to have contributed at least in part to urban air pollution problems. There were in fact some early warnings that GM's replacement of electric-driven vehicles with diesel-powered buses and trucks was increasing air pollution. On January 26, 1954, for instance, E. P. Crenshaw, GM bus general sales manager, sent the following memorandum to F. J. Limback, another GM executive:

> There has developed in a number of cities "smog" conditions which [have] resulted in Anti-Air Pollution committees, who immediately take issue with bus and truck operations, and especially Diesel engine exhaust. In many cases, efforts are being made to stop further substitution of Diesel buses for electric-driven vehicles....

Three months later, in April 1954, the American Conference of Governmental Industrial Hygienists adopted a limit of five parts per million for human exposure to nitrogen oxides. Diesel buses, according to another report by two GM engineers, emitted "oxides of nitrogen concentrations over 200 times the recommended" exposure limit. Nevertheless, the dieselization program continued. Chenshaw reported to Limback in 1954:

> The elimination of street-cars and trolley-buses and their replacement by our large GM 51-passenger Diesel Hydraulic coaches continues steadily . . . in Denver, Omaha, Kansas City, San Francisco, Los Angeles, New Orleans, Honolulu, Baltimore, Milwaukee, Akron, Youngstown, Columbus, etc.

2. The Displacement of Bus Transit by Automobiles

Diversification into bus production and, subsequently, into bus and rail operation inevitably encouraged General Motors to supplant trains, streetcars and trolleybuses with first gasoline and then diesel buses. It also contributed to this firm's monopolization of city and intercity bus production. The effect of GM's mutually exclusive dealing arrangement with Greyhound, for example, was to foreclose all other bus manufacturers and bus operating concerns from a substantial segment of the intercity market. At least by 1952, both companies had achieved their respective monopolies: GM dominated intercity bus production and Greyhound dominated intercity bus operation. By 1973, GM's only competitor, Motor Coach Industries (established in 1962 by Greyhound as the result of a Government antitrust decree), was wholly dependent on it for major components; and Greyhound's only operating competitor, Trailways, had been forced to purchase its buses from overseas. In the process, a number of innovative bus builders and potential manufacturers, including General Dynamics' predecessor (Consolidated Vultee) and the Douglas Aircraft Co., had been driven from the industry.

Likewise, in the city bus market, GM's exclusive bus replacement contracts with National City Lines, American City Lines, Pacific City Lines, the Omnibus Corporation, Public Transport of New Jersey, and practically every other major bus operating company foreclosed competing city bus manufacturers from all but a handful of cities in the country and assured GM monopoly control of this market as well. Since 1925 more than 50 firms have withdrawn from city bus manufacturing including Ford, ACF-Brill, Marmon-Herrington, Mack Trucks, White Motor, International Harvester, Studebaker Twin Coach, Fifth Avenue Coach, Chrysler (Dodge), and Reo Motors. By 1973, only the Flxible Company, which had been established and controlled until 1958 by C. F. Kettering, a GM vice-president, remained as effectively a competitor-assembler of GM city buses. One other firm, AM General (American Motors), had announced its intention to assemble GM-powered city buses for delivery in late 1973. The ability of this firm, or for that matter Flxible and Motor Coach Industries, to survive beyond 1975, however, was seriously doubted by industry observers. That year a Government antitrust decree compelling GM to supply bus assemblers with diesel engines, transmissions, and other major components will expire.

Monopolization of bus production and the elimination of electric street transportation has brought an end to price and technological competition in these industries. In this regard, several cities led by New York have filed a lawsuit charging that General Motors sets higher-than-competitive prices for its diesel buses and receives millions of dollars annually in monopoly profits. The suit also alleges that GM may be disregarding technological innovations in propulsion, pollution control, and coach design, which would help attract patrons out of their automobiles.

In light of our dwindling petroleum supplies and mounting concerns about air pollution, the decline of technological competition in bus manufacturing is particularly unfortunate. ACF-Brill, Marmon-Herrington, Pullman-Standard, Twin Coach, and St. Louis Car once built electric buses and electric streetcars. Other firms manufactured steam-driven buses. According to a number of studies, these alternative forms of motive power would be preferable in terms of energy consumption, efficiency, pollution, noise, and durability to the diesel engine. Exclusion of these innovative firms, however, and GM's apparent disinterest in steam- or electric-powered vehicles (whose longer life, fewer parts, and easier repair would drastically reduce replacement sales), have precluded the availability of these technological alternatives today. Moreover, domination of domestic bus manufacturing by the world's largest industrial concern tends to deter entry by smaller, innovative firms. Lear Motors, for example, has developed quiet, low-pollution steam turbine buses; Mercedes-Benz, which sells buses in 160 countries, has produced low-pollution electric buses. Neither these nor any other firms, however, have been able to break into the GM-dominated American bus market. Furthermore, GM's conversion of much of this country's streetcar and interurban trackage to bus routes has precluded the survival of domestic streetcar builders and deterred entry by foreign railcar manufacturers. As a result, there remain few transit alternatives to GM diesel buses. None of the early White or Doble steam buses are still in operation. The last electric streetcars were built in 1953; only one electric bus (built in Canada) has been delivered since 1955. In 1973, only five American cities continued to operate electric buses, and eight ran a handful of ancient streetcars.

General Motors' gross revenues are 10 times greater if it sells cars rather than buses. In theory, therefore, GM has every economic incentive to discourage bus ridership. In fact, its bus dieselization program may have generated that effect. Engineering studies strongly suggest that conversion from electric transit to diesel buses results in higher operating costs, loss of patronage, and eventual bankruptcy. They demonstrate, for example, that diesel buses have 28 percent shorter economic lives, 40 percent higher operating costs, and 9 percent lower productivity than electric buses. They also conclude that the diesel's foul smoke, ear-splitting noise, and slow acceleration may discourage ridership. In short, by increasing the costs, reducing the revenues, and contributing to the collapse of hundreds of transit systems, GM's dieselization program may have had the long-term effect of selling GM cars.

Today, automobiles have completely replaced bus transportation in many areas of the country. Since 1952, the year GM achieved monopoly control of bus production, ridership has declined by 3 billion passengers and bus sales have fallen by about 60 percent. During that same period, GM automobile sales have risen from 1.7 million to more than 4.8 million units per year. By 1972, in a move which possibly signified the passing of bus transportation in this country, General Motors had begun converting its bus plants to motor home production.

3. The Displacement of Railroad Transportation by Automobiles and Trucks

As described in the preceding section, General Motors' diversification into bus transportation contributed to two developments: the displacement of passengers from rail to bus and eventually to automobile travel, and the shift in freight from rail to trucks. GM's integration into locomotive production was arguably an additional factor in the diversion of rail passenger to automobiles and rail freight to trucks. In 1930, it entered the locomotive industry by acquiring Winton Engine and Electro-Motive. At that time, Winton was the largest manufacturer of heavy diesel engines. Electro-Motive, a principal customer of Winton, was the leading firm in the application of diesel engines to railroad motive power. By combining these firms, GM became the Nation's largest manufacturer of train locomotives.

As the world's largest manufacturer of cars and trucks, General Motors was inherently ill suited to promote train transportation. Indeed, it had very economic incentive to repress this method of travel. A single GM-powered passenger train could displace as many as 1,000 GM cars; a GM-powered freight train could supplant a fleet of 150 GM trucks. From the standpoint of economics, moreover, GM's gross revenues were from 25 to 35 times larger if it sold cars and trucks rather than train locomotives.

In fact, General Motors' diversification into railroads probably weakened this industry's ability to compete with motor vehicles. More specifically, GM eliminated technological alternatives in train motive power which were arguably more efficient than the diesel combustion system it promoted. Its production of diesels rather than electric- or steam-driven locomotives, however, was entirely rational in terms of profit maximization. First, dieselization would vastly increase locomotive sales. A diesel locomotive, for example, lasted one-half as long, did one-third the work, and cost three times more than an electric locomotive. Second, as compared with railroad electrification, dieselization was substantially less of a threat to car and truck transportation. Diesel trains were sluggish, noisy, and generally less attractive to passengers than rapid, quiet, pollution-free electric trains. In addition, they were less powerful and therefore not as efficient in hauling freight. As the Nation's largest shipper of freight, GM was able to exert considerable influence over the locomotive purchasing policies of the Nation's railroads. It used this powerful form of leverage to sell its diesel locomotives. Before long, it had dieselized the entire American railroad industry, and simultaneously had obtained a monopoly in the production of locomotives. As a consequence, alternative forms of motive power, such as electricity which might have enabled the railroads to compete more effectively with cars and trucks, were disregarded.

General Motors dieselized the Nation's railroads by using its freight business to coerce them to purchase its diesel locomotives. In 1935, with barely 2.4 percent of industry sales, it embarked upon a dual plan to monopolize locomotive production and to dieselize the American railroad industry. At that time, electric locomotives outnumbered diesel units 7 to 1, and several firms were developing a steam turbine engine to replace the conventional steam locomotive. In November, GM ordered its traffic division to begin routing freight over railroads which agreed reciprocally to scrap their electric and steam equipment for GM diesels. For the next 35 years it used its formidable leverage as the largest commercial shipper to exclude locomotive competitors and to force the railroads to convert to all-diesel operation. By 1970, it had effectively dieselized the entire industry: steam units were virtually extinct; and diesels, 80 percent of which were manufactured by GM, outnumbered electric locomotives 100 to 1.

The dieselization of America's railroads did not require blatant acts of coercion. Rail executives were fully aware of GM's formidable freight leverage. As an interoffice legal memorandum drafted by GM's antitrust attorneys stated, "GM could, in all probability, have successfully capitalized upon the railroad's sensitivity to reciprocity by frequently reminding them of GM's considerable traffic, and could have done so without ever interfering substantially with the economical routing of traffic." Nevertheless, on occasion, GM may have resorted to blatant pressure.

In November 1948, for instance, Roy B. White, president of the Baltimore & Ohio Railroad, was apparently contacted by Alfred P. Sloan, Jr., chairman of General Motors, regarding GM's offer to locate one of its warehouses on B. & O.'s tracks in return for B. & O.'s agreement to convert to GM diesels. Later that month, White replied by letter to Sloan to the effect: "Here is your Christmas present . . . we will purchase 300 diesel locomotives . . . we now expect to receive a New Year's gift from you . . . locate your warehouse near our tracks." Likewise, in the fall of 1958 a General Motors official informed Gulf, Mobil & Ohio Railroad that certain GM traffic would not be routed over its lines because other railroads had purchased more GM diesel locomotives than Gulf.

Through its shrewd use of freight leverage, GM eliminated all but one of its competitors by 1970. Westinghouse, a pioneer in railway electrification, announced its departure from the industry in 1954. Baldwin-Lima-Hamilton, one of the Nation's oldest railroad builders, built its last locomotive in 1956. Fairbanks-Morse, which attempted to enter in 1944, was forced out by 1958. In 1969, American Locomotive, an aggressive manufacturer of gas turbine, electric, steam turbine as well as diesel locomotives, and the leading exporter of rail equipment, was purchased by one of GM's automotive parts suppliers (Studebaker-Worthington) and immediately withdrawn from locomotive production. By 1973, 99 percent of the locomotive fleet was dieselized and GM's only competitor, General Electric, accounted for less than 17 percent of total production.

The immediate effect of dieselization was suppression of an alternative system of train propulsion: namely, electrification. In 1935, when GM initiated its dieselization program, two of the country's major railroads had electrified their systems and several others contemplated similar action. The New York, New Haven & Hartford had constructed the world's first 11,000-volt, 25-cycle alternating current system along 500 miles of New England track. The Pennsylvania had inaugurated electric passenger and freight train operations between New York and Washington. By dieselizing these and other roads, GM may have curbed in its incipiency a trend toward electrification. By 1960, when virtually every other industrialized Nation in the world was electrifying [its] trains, America was locked-in to GM diesel locomotives.

The long-term effect of dieselization was impairment of the railroads' ability to compete effectively with cars and trucks. By vastly increasing operating, maintenance, and depreciation costs, dieselization contributed to the curtailment of maintenance and service, and eventual bankruptcy of many American railroads. This process was arguably apparent in General Motors' conversion of the New Haven system from electric to diesel power. In 1956, GM reportedly used its freight leverage to coerce the railroad into scrapping all of its electric passenger and freight locomotives in favor of GM diesel passenger units. The conversion was followed by loss of a substantial portion of the New Haven's passenger and freight traffic to cars and trucks. Dieselization may have been the responsible factor. The slower GM diesels were less attractive to New Haven passengers accustomed to rapid electric trains. They were also less powerful and, consequently, less suitable for moving freight than the electric locomotives they replaced. Within a short time the company began to experience serious operating deficits. These deficits coupled with the diesel's higher operating and depreciation costs compelled, in turn, cutbacks in maintenance and service, which generated another round of traffic diversion to cars and trucks.

A subsequent investigation by the Interstate Commerce Commission in 1960 confirmed that in fact dieselization had contributed to the New Haven's severe financial crisis and eventual bankruptcy. Observing that "without an intelligent locomotive policy, no efficient railroad operation can possibly be conducted," the ICC hearing officers stressed the significant economic advantages which the New Haven had derived from the durability, efficiency, and extraordinary power of electric locomotives. They noted that the life of an electric locomotive was about twice that of a diesel (30 years versus 15 years, respectively) and, being a less complicated, more efficient, and less delicate piece of machinery, was substantially cheaper to operate and maintain. In addition, they emphasized that a single electric locomotive could do the work of three diesels and that new electric locomotives cost only one-third as much as the diesel locomotives sold to the New Haven by General Motors. The examiners found, however, that despite the numerous advantages of electric operation as compared with diesel and contrary to the advice of its own independent engineering consultants, the New Haven had relied instead on General Motors' "ridiculous" representations as to the savings to be derived from dieselization.

According to the ICC officials, GM's claims of anticipated savings proved to be "a mirage." The New Haven's replacement of its electric locomotives with GM diesels generated higher operating, maintenance and depreciation expenses and substantial losses in passenger and freight revenues. During 50 years of electrified operation, it had never failed to show an operating profit. In 1955, the year before dieselization, it earned $5.7 million carrying 45 million passengers and 814 thousand carloads of freight. By 1959, seven years after GM dieselization began, it lost $9.2 million hauling 10 million fewer passengers and 130 thousand fewer carloads of freight. In 1961, it was declared bankrupt; by 1968, when it was acquired by the Penn Central, it had accumulated a capital deficit of nearly $300 million.

In 1961, the ICC upheld the hearing officers' recommended report on the bankrupt New Haven and censured General Motors for contributing to the railroad's financial ruin. Of the several factors it listed as responsible for the New Haven's downfall, it placed special emphasis on the elimination of electric locomotives. Although it refrained from suggesting that GM was guilty of fraudulent mis-representation, the Commission found the automakers' estimates of savings from conversion to diesels "erroneous," "inflated," and "manifestly absurd." Referring to the "great advances in railway electrification made in Europe and in the Soviet Union," it concluded with a recommendation that the trustees undertake a study of the economic feasibility of complete reelectrification of the New Haven's main line.

The New Haven was probably not the only casualty of GM's dieseli-zation program. All six of the major railroads serving the Northeast corridor are today bankrupt, and those in the rest of the country are earning an average of less than 2 percent on investment. Had these roads electrified, they might have fared better financially and might have been better able to compete effectively with motor vehicles. That technological option, however, was foreclosed to them as a result, in part, of GM's diversification into railroad locomotives.

Since GM began its dieselization campaign in 1935, the railroads have progressively lost traffic first to buses and then to cars and trucks, most of which are manufactured by GM. In 1939 they carried half a million passengers and accounted for 75 percent of all freight revenues; by 1972 they had lost 50 percent of their passengers to cars, and nearly 75 percent of all freight revenue to trucks. Whether this result was actually intended by GM is irrelevant. Nonetheless, it is difficult to believe that a firm fundamentally interested in marketing cars and trucks would develop an efficient high-speed train system that might diminish their sales.

The impact of dieselization on this Nation's railroads has been the subject of expert scrutiny. H. F. Brown, an international authority on railroad motive power, has concluded that dieselization "was the single most important factor responsible for the demise of America's railroads." Significantly, his studies of America's experience with GM diesels helped persuade Parliament to electrify rather than dieselize the British railway system.

4. The Political Restraint of Rail Transit

General Motors' diversification into streetcar, bus, and railroad transportation was very likely a significant factor in their eventual displacement by automobiles and trucks. A second structural feature, the asymmetrical distribution of economic power in the ground transport sector, may also have generated the political restraint of a third alternative to automobile transportation: rail rapid transit (subways).

As discussed [previously] small deconcentrated industries are less able to influence government policymaking as effectively as their concentrated rivals. This may explain, in part, the political disregard until quite recently of rail transit as an alternative in congested urban areas to automotive transportation. Due to its high concentration and gigantic sales volume, the auto industry has accumulated hundreds of millions of dollars in revenues from higher-than-competitively-priced motor vehicles. It has used some of these revenues to finance political activities which, in the absence of effective countervailing activities by competing ground transport industries, induced government bodies to promote their product (automobiles) over other alternatives, particularly rail rapid transit.

Every industry, of course, has the constitutionally protected right to petition Government bodies and to mobilize public opinion as a means of shaping Government policies to its own private corporate advantage. This study does not take exception with that privilege. It does, however, suggest that the presence of a relatively large and highly concentrated automotive industry in the important multi-industry ground transportation sector may have resulted in the distortion of political processes to the advantage of this industry and to the disadvantage of the riding public. The effect, in short, may have been to deprive the public of the opportunity of choosing among competing transportation alternatives. More specifically, an imbalanced distribution of political power in favor of the automakers may have encouraged the Government to allocate overwhelmingly disproportionate sums of money to highways rather than to rail systems.

Generally, the automakers' political activities have been twofold in nature: establishment of a powerful lobbying organization to promote the public financing of highways, and participation in competing associations which favored the construction of subways.

On June 28, 1932, Alfred P. Sloan, Jr., president of General Motors, organized the National Highway Users Conference to combine representatives of the Nation's auto, oil, and tire industries in a common front against competing transportation interests. Sloan became its permanent chairman and served in that capacity until 1948, when he was succeeded by the new chairman of GM, Albert Bradley, who continued as its chairman through 1956. Its announced objectives were dedication of highway taxes solely to highway purposes, and development of a continuing program of highway construction.

In a statement issued the following January, NHUC formally proclaimed its political commitment to automotive transportation: "Until now those interested in automotive transportation have fought their battles independently. Participating in the National Highway Users Conference are a large majority of the interested groups. The manufacturers of motorcars and accessories have joined with the users of their equipment in the common cause of defense." The "interested groups" included the Motor Vehicle Manufacturers Association (representing automobile and truck companies), the American Petroleum Institute (spokesman for the oil industry), the American Trucking Association (representing the trucking interests), the Rubber Manufacturers Association (comprising the tire companies), and the American Automobile Association (purporting to speak for the Nation's millions of motorists). Although it disclaimed any intention of lobbying on behalf of these highway interests, it proposed to serve as "an agency for the coordination of activities of interested groups" and to cooperate with "such State organizations as are set up along the same lines as the national body." Implicitly, therefore, its function was to influence Congress and the State legislatures where it claimed "the membership may be badly informed or where a considerable part of it may yield to the influence of selfish interests."

During the succeeding 40 years, the National Highway Users Conference has compiled an impressive record of accomplishments. Its effect, if not purpose, has been to direct public funds away from rail construction and into highway building. At the State level, its 2,800 lobbying groups have been instrumental in persuading 44 of the Nation's 50 legislatures to adopt and preserve measures which dedicated State and local gasoline tax revenues exclusively to highway construction. By promoting these highway "trust funds," it has discouraged governors and mayors from attempting to build anything other than highways for urban transportation. Subways and rail transit proposals have had to compete with hospitals, schools, and other governmental responsibilities for funding. By contrast, highways have been automatically financed from a self-perpetuating fund which was legally unavailable for any other purpose. Largely as a result, highways, not subways, have been built. From 1945 through 1970, States and localities spent more than $156 billion constructing hundreds of thousands of miles of roads. During that same period, only 16 miles of subway were constructed in the entire country.

Likewise, at the Federal level this organization has been very successful in promoting highways over rail transportation. For example, under the early and exceptionally capable leadership of GM's Sloan and Bradley, it became a principal architect of the world's largest roadbuilding effort, the 42,500-mile, $70-billion Interstate Highway System. During the years prior to passage in 1956 of the Interstate Highway Act, NHUC and allied highway groups had worked assiduously building support among Congressmen, Federal administrators, academicians, and engineers. They contributed to congressional campaigns, placed their members in important administrative posts, and granted millions of dollars to highway research.

At the time, few opposed the idea of building a system of interstate highways. Only one witness during more than two years of congressional hearings even raised the issue of what effect it might have on the Nation's railroads. In retrospect, a national highway program was unquestionably needed. Whether its tremendous scope and budgetary commitment, however, might preclude Federal financing of alternative rail transport systems was a point which should have been debated at that time. The uneven distribution of political resources between automakers and rail manufacturers may explain why this important question received virtually no political attention.

When Congress finally began hearings on the Interstate Highway Act in 1956, the outcome was a foregone conclusion. Only the manner of financing the program was at issue. In the end, the National Highway Users Conference managed to persuade Congress to adopt the same trust fund arrangement which it had successfully promoted earlier to the State legislatures. The impact of the Federal Highway Trust Fund on transportation spending was similar to that which occurred at the State level. While urban rail proposals were forced to compete for funds with dozens of Federal priorities including national defense, health, and social security, thousands of miles of highways were built automatically with gasoline tax revenues unavailable for any other purpose. From 1956 through 1970, the Federal Government spent approximately $70 billion for highways; and only $795 million, or 1 percent, for rail transit.

Today, the National Highway Users Conference, now known as Highway Users Federation for Safety and Mobility (HUFSAM), works effectively with highway-related groups such as the Motor Vehicle Manufacturers Association (MVMA) to promote the automakers' interest in more highways and less rail transit. With combined annual budgets of nearly $16 million, most of which comes from the Big Three auto companies, HUFSAM and MVMA fight State and Federal attempts to "divert" highway funds for rail transit purposes. In this regard they are aided by a score of allied highway interests which collectively spend an estimated $500 million a year lobbying to preserve highway trust funds. They are also active in financing research groups which invariably conclude that automobiles, trucks, and, if necessary, "bus transit" complete with underground diesel "busways" can satisfy every ground transportation need.

By comparison, the three leading transit lobby groups are financially weak and torn by the conflicting interests of their membership. The American Transit Association, the largest element of the transit lobby, operates on an annual budget of about $700,000 which must be apportioned between the conflicting political needs of its bus and rail transit manufacturing members. The Railway Institute spends an estimated $600,000 a year. The third and smallest element of the transit body, the Institute for Rapid Transit, operates on a meager budget of about $200,000 a year. In short, HUFSAM and

MVMA alone outspend the three principal transit organizations by more than 10 to 1. Furthermore, General Motors, whose personnel organized and continue to direct the highway lobby, has secured the power to influence the policies of two of these three transit groups. Due to its position as the Nation's largest producer of bus and rail vehicles, it is a major financial contributor to both the American Transit Association and the Railway Progress Institute. It is also an influential member of the Institute for Rapid Transit.

Without a powerful and unequivocal rail transit lobby, those interested in balanced transportation are no match for the organized highway interests. Legislators including Senators Kennedy, Muskie, and Weicker, citizen and municipal groups such as the Highway Action Coalition and the League of Cities, Mayors Alioto (San Francisco), White (Boston), Daley (Chicago), and numerous others have failed repeatedly to shift anything other than token amounts of State and Federal gas tax revenues from highways to rail transit. As an apparent consequence, national transportation policy principally reflects the legislative objective of the automakers: building more highways which sell more cars and trucks.

Publicly, the automakers proclaim their support for mass transit. They cultivate this seemingly paradoxical image for two reasons. First, a protransit posture at a time of petroleum shortages and environmental concerns is good for public relations. Second, and perhaps more importantly, they seek to control and direct the development of nonautomotive transport technology in a manner least threatening to their fundamental interest: selling cars. In this regard, Ford is developing "horizontal elevators" and PRT (personal rapid transit) vehicles capable of moving people short distances within strictly downtown areas. Ford's transit vehicles would compete, therefore, not with automobiles but with pedestrians. Likewise, General Motors is engaged in a continuing effort to divert Government funds from rapid rail transit, which seriously threatens the use of cars in metropolitan areas, to GM buses, which fail consistently to persuade people to abandon their autos. In place of regional electric rail systems, for instance, it promotes diesel-powered "bus trains" of as many as 1,400 units, each spaced 80 feet apart. Instead of urban electric rail, it advocates the use of dual-mode gas/electric vehicles which would be adapted from GM's minimotor homes. In sum, the automakers embrace transit in order to prevent it from competing effectively with their sales of automobiles.

General Motors' diversification into the bus and rail industries and the asymmetrical distribution of power between automakers and rail builders would appear to have contributed at least in part, therefore, to the decline of competing alternatives to motor vehicles. By 1973 five different forms of nonautomotive transportation had either disappeared or been seriously impaired: electric streetcars, trolley coaches, interurban electric railways, buses, and trains. In short, diversification and asymmetry in ground transport manufacturing may have retarded the development of mass transportation and, as a consequence, may have generated a reliance on motor vehicles incompatible with metropolitan needs.

5. Current Performance of the Ground Transportation Sector

Due to its anticompetitive structure and behavior, this country's ground transport sector can no longer perform satisfactorily. It has become seriously imbalanced in favor of the unlimited production of motor vehicles. Unlike every other industrialized country in the world, America has come to rely almost exclusively on cars and trucks for the land transportation of its people and goods. Cars are used for 90 percent of city and intercity travel; trucks are the only method of intracity freight delivery and account for 78 percent of all freight revenues. This substitution of more than 100 million petroleum-consuming cars and trucks for competing forms of alternatively powered ground transportation is a significant factor in this sector's unacceptable level of inefficient and nonprogressive performance.

Efficiency in terms of market performance may be defined as a comparison of actual prices or costs with those that would obtain in a competitively structured market. Currently, Americans pay $181 billion per year for motor vehicle transportation. In terms of high energy consumption, accident rates, contribution to pollution, and displacement of urban amenities, however, motor vehicle travel is possibly the most inefficient method of transportation devised by modern man.

More specifically, the diversion of traffic from energy-efficient electric rails to fuel-guzzling highway transport has resulted in an enormous consumption of energy. Rails can move passengers and freight for less than one-fifth the amount of energy required by cars and trucks. The displacement of rails by highways, therefore, has seriously depleted our scarce supplies of energy and has increased by several billion dollars a year the amount consumers must pay for ground transportation. It has been estimated, for example, that the diversion of passengers in urban areas from energy-efficient electric rail to gasoline automobiles results in their paying $18 billion a year more in energy costs alone. In addition, economists have found that the inefficient diversion of intercity freight from rail to trucks costs consumers $5 billion per year in higher prices for goods.

The substitution of highways for rails has also reduced efficiency by imposing higher indirect costs on the public in the form of accidents, pollution, and land consumption. Rail travel is 23 times as safe as travel by motor vehicles. The diversion to highways has cost the public an estimated $17 billion each year in economic damages attributable to motor vehicle accidents. This figure, however, cannot reflect the incalculable human costs of motor vehicle accidents: the violent deaths each year by car and truck of 55,000 Americans, more than all who died in the entire 12 years of our involvement in Vietnam, and the serious injuries to an additional 5 million of our citizens.

Likewise, the costs of urban air pollution have been greatly accentuated by the imbalance in favor of cars and trucks. Motor vehicles annually consume 42 billion gallons of petroleum within the densely populated 2 percent of the U.S. geographic area classified as urban. The consumption of this enormous quantity of fuel in urban areas produces in excess of 60 million tons of toxic pollutants, which in turn cost urban residents more than $4 billion in economic damages.

The presence of high concentrations of these motor vehicle pollutants, particularly oxides of nitrogen, in densely populated areas has also generated a crisis in urban public health. In Los Angeles alone, more than 500 persons die each year of ailments attributable to motor-vehicle-generated smog. The hazards of carbon monoxide and hydrocarbon emissions from automobiles have been widely acknowledged. Less well known are the potentially more serious effects of oxides of nitrogen produced primarily by diesel trucks and buses in high concentrations on congested city streets. When inhaled, these oxides combine with moisture in the lungs to form corrosive nitric acid which permanently damages lung tissues and accelerates death by slowly destroying the body's ability to resist heart and lung diseases. By contrast, if electric rail transportation were substituted in cities for motor vehicles, urban air pollution might be reduced substantially. Although the burning of fuels to generate this increased electrical energy would produce some pollution, it would pose a substantially less serious hazard to public health. Electric powerplants can often be located in areas remote from population centers. Moreover, the increased pollution by generating facilities would be offset by a reduction in pollution due to oil refinery operations. Furthermore, the abatement of air pollution at a relatively small number of stationary powerplants would represent a far easier task than attempting to install and monitor devices on 100 million transient motor vehicles.

The diversion of traffic from rail to highways has imposed a third cost on consumers — the consumption of vast amounts of taxable urban landscapes [:] from 60 to 65 percent of our cities' land area is devoted to highways, parking facilities, and other auto- and truck-related uses. In downtown Los Angeles, the figure approaches 85 percent. This has led to an erosion in the cities' tax base and, concomitantly, to a decline in their ability to finance the delivery of vital municipal services. Electric rail transportation, by comparison, requires less than one-thirteenth as much space as highways to move a comparable amount of passengers or goods, and in many cases can be located underground.

Progressiveness in terms of market performance is generally under-stood as a comparison of the number and importance of actual inno-vations with those which optimally could have been developed and introduced. The substitution of highways for rails has resulted in a decrease in mobility and has precluded important innovations in high-speed urban and intercity ground transportation. The decrease in mobility is most acute in urban areas. The average speed of rush hour traffic in cities dependent on motor vehicles, for example, is 12 miles per hour. Studies indicate that city traffic moved more quickly in 1890. Moreover, 20 percent of our urban population (the aged, youth, disabled, and poor) lack access to automobiles and, due to the non-existence of adequate public transportation, are effectively isolated from employment or educational opportunities and other urban amenities. Substitution of highways for rails has also retarded inno-vations in high-speed urban and intercity transport. Technologically advanced rail transit systems, which currently operate in the major cities of Europe and Japan, would relieve congestion and contribute to urban mobility. High-speed intercity rail systems, such as Japan's 150-mile-per-hour electric Tokaido Express, would help relieve mounting air traffic congestion and offer a practical alternative to slower and more tedious travel by car or truck. But the political pre-dilections of the automakers have become the guidelines for American transportation policy. In contrast to the advanced rail transport emphasis of Europe and Japan, this country has persisted in the expansion of highway transport. As a result, America has become a second-rate nation in transportation.

There are strong indications, moreover, that due to mounting con-cerns about air pollution and a worldwide shortage of petroleum, our motor-vehicle-dominated transportation system will perform even worse in the future. The Environmental Protection Agency has warned that by 1977 motor vehicle emissions in major urban areas may compel a cutback in automobile, truck, and diesel bus use of as much as 60 percent. In addition, the Department of the Interior has forecast that the current petroleum crisis might cripple transportation and cause "serious economic and social disruptions." More precisely, an excessive reliance in the past on fuel-guzzling motor vehicles for transport has contributed to a crisis in energy which now threatens to shut down industries, curb air and ground travel, and deprive our homes of heating oil for winter.

Despite these adverse trends, the automakers appear bent on further motorization. Henry Ford II, for instance, has noted that notwith-standing "the energy crisis, the environmental crisis, and the urban crisis" new car sales in the United States "have increased by more than a million during the past 2 model years." General Motors' chief operating executive has predicted that soon each American will own a "family of cars" for every conceivable travel activity including small cars for trips, recreational vehicles for leisure, and motor homes for mobile living. GM is also engaged in the displacement of what little remains of this Nation's rail systems. To that end, it is developing 750-horsepower diesel engines to haul multiple trailers at speeds of 70 miles per hour along the nearly completed Interstate Highway System. These "truck trains" are slated to replace rail freight service. As substitutes for regional subway systems, GM is also advocating 1,400-unit diesel "bus trains," which would operate on exclusive bus-ways outside cities and in bus tunnels under downtown areas. Both diesel truck trains and underground bus trains, however, would seem grossly incompatible with public concerns about petroleum shortages and suffocating air pollution.

The automakers' motorization program, moreover, is worldwide in scope. The superior bus and rail systems which flourish in the rest of the industrialized world interfere with the sale of cars and trucks by the Big Three's foreign subsidiaries. "The automobile industry put America on wheels," said GM Chairman Gerstenberg in September of 1972. "Today," he added, "expanding markets all around the world give us the historic opportunity to put the whole world on wheels."

RESTRUCTURING GROUND TRANSPORTATION: A FIRST APPROXIMATION

As demonstrated [previously] the anticompetitive structure of the automobile, truck, bus, and rail industries enabled General Motors, Ford, and Chrysler to suppress price, product, and technological com-petition in motor vehicle production and to restrain practical alter-natives to motor vehicle transportation. This section considers a first approximation at restructuring these industries. In brief, it proposes reorganization of the automobile and truck industries into their con-stituent elements and divestiture of General Motors' bus and loco-motive production facilities. The objectives are threefold: to restore competition and innovation to the motor vehicle industries; to promote a balanced and technologically advanced ground transportation system comprising low-pollution cars, trucks, and buses, as well as high-speed rail transport; and to secure the additional social advantages of energy conservation, expanded employment, and a more favorable balance of trade.*

---

*[Editor's note: The details of Snell's break-up proposals have been omitted. Interested students should secure the longer paper.]

CHAPTER 5   SUGGESTIONS FOR FURTHER READING

Hartman, Chester. *Yerba Buena: Land Grab and Community Resistance in San Francisco* (San Francisco: Glide Publications, 1974). To my knowledge this is the only in-depth, A-to-Z study of the impact of a government urban renewal program on the physical and social environment of a central business area. The critical questions of who was hurt and who profited from this attempt to remake the physical structure of the urban environment are carefully explored.

Lupo, Alan, Frank Colcord, and Edmund P. Fowler. *Rites of Way: The Politics of Transportation in Boston and the U.S. City* (Boston: Little, Brown, 1971). Here two political scientists and a journalist, with the aid of some photographers, explore the destruction of neighborhoods by the ever-present highway expansion process in several urban areas. Public protest against highway expansion is documented.

Wolman, Harold. *Politics of Federal Housing* (New York: Dodd, Mead, 1971). Wolman argues that a critical aspect of the urban environment is the federal government. He dissects numerous federal housing programs, from the FHA programs that bailed out the loan and construction industries in the 1930's, to public housing, to more recent housing subsidy programs for low-income families.

6

The Future
of Urban Society:
The Struggle for Power

In numerous social science books on the city, surprisingly, the future of America's urban places receives remarkably little attention, at least beyond concern with projected demographic growth and the short-range urban-planning process. Neither the possible shapes that the urban *economic* and *political* future might take nor the possibility and character of a long-range urban-planning process have undergone much systematic analysis.

In the excerpt from *Future Shock* presented in this concluding chapter, Alvin Toffler grapples with some of these extraordinarily important issues touching on the urban political process. The basic argument of *Future Shock* is that modern American society, unless its members learn to adapt quickly and adopt radical new planning procedures, is headed for a massive breakdown — the result of bombardment by a myriad of profound social changes. "Future shock" is the phrase used to "describe the shattering stress and disorientation that we induce in individuals by subjecting them to too much change in too short a time."[1] Yet individuals are not the only ones who seem unable to cope with too much change. Governments, too, often appear incapable not only of developing mechanisms and policies to deal with the problems created by societal change but also of clearly determining the long-range goals toward which the society should be directed.

Rejecting the procedures of technocratic planning, as well as the "hang loose" philosophy of some of the young among the New Left, Toffler argues for a new approach which he terms "social futurism" a strategy that he sees as more far-sighted, humanized, and democratic than most strategies of the past. One aspect of this social futurism would be the development and periodic review of social indicators, which could be used to determine what is actually happening over time in this society. An established system for regularly evaluating social and cultural indicators is deemed essential by Toffler to the technical equipment of a society before "it can successfully reach the next stage of eco-technological development." Indeed, this would be the first step in the direction of humanizing the entire urban-planning process.

In defending the need for long-term, future-oriented planning, Toffler presses hard against those whom he sees as basically conservative, those who argue that the future is unknowable and not predictable, those who see Americans as helpless in the face of rapid social and cultural change. Indeed, a limited amount of scientific effort directed at predicting the future has already begun. Dramatic expansion of these experimental efforts is advocated by Toffler, together with the development in a variety of existing organizations and institutions of what he calls "imaginetic centers" — "think tanks" where people with wide-ranging imaginations and probing minds can speculate freely about possible and probable developments in such areas as race relations, urban transportation, education, and pollution. In addition, these "imagineers" might explore possibilities and probabilities for the future of modern urban society as a whole, dissecting and laying out the various utopias that reflect different values and perspectives.

Social futurism as a strategy should not be limited to think tanks and the development of institutions to assess social indicators; social futurism has implications for the *political* arena as well. Answers to a number of basic questions about the future come up hard against government and economic arrangements currently grounded in a top leadership structure composed of a small number of (mostly older, white male) Americans. Critical questions arise about *who* will determine the values, possible futures, and goals to be pursued by a society. In most scenarios focusing on the near future, traditionally prominent elites have been seen — or have seen themselves — as controlling the planning process. Yet with regard to social futurism and long-range planning this will not suffice.

Toffler argues for a new, more democratic approach to the setting of societal goals and the shaping of the urban future. Elitist processes of goal determination are no longer efficient in rapidly changing super-industrial societies. Greatly increased democratic participation in information-gathering and decision-making is critical, not just for idealistic but for practical reasons. Popular democracy is more efficient, he argues, because it allows for greater feedback than other arrangements in rapidly changing, complex urban societies: "As the number of social components grows and change makes the whole system less stable, it becomes less and less possible to ignore the demands of political minorities — hippies, blacks, lower-middle-class Wallacites, school teachers, or the proverbial little old ladies in tennis shoes." Here we have a call for full-fledged *participatory democracy*.

The author of the second selection goes even farther than Toffler in the direction of democratic participation and control, extending this idea to the economic system as well as to politics and planning. David Mermelstein underscores the emphasis in the last decade on enforced austerity both in public policy and in planning for the economic (and social) problems of cities. This fiscally conservative strategy aims at reducing social welfare programs in crisis-plagued cities (e.g., New York) in order that taxes may be reduced, at increasing unemployment in order that wages of workers and union militancy can be reduced as well. Indeed, government budget-cutting and tax reduction are now accepted by conservatives and by many liberals. All this is done in the name of improving the current rate of monetary profit for business and industry. Privately-controlled profit is indeed the incentive corporate propagandists say it is, and urban workers are caught in the bind of cooperating in this new austerity or of destroying the (private) profit-maximizing incentive that generates the capital investment cycle. Mermelstein thinks the way out is the *democratic socialist* alternative. The goal is to transform our society "into something more genuinely democratic, more egalitarian and more humane." To do this several changes are recommended:

(1) property and the productive apparatus must be taken out of the hands of a small profit-oriented capitalist class;
(2) critical resources must be owned by all workers;
(3) decisions about the use of resources and profits must be made collectively and democratically;
(4) privileges and resources must be more equally distributed.

Mermelstein concludes by noting problems in implementing these changes. Yet he provides little analysis of how these human-needs changes might be achieved. Current and future generations of Americans may well have to work out that analysis on their own.

NOTES

1. Alvin Toffler, *Future Shock* (New York: Random House, 1970), p. 4.

From
Future Shock:

The Strategy of Social Futurism

Alvin Toffler

Can one live in a society that is out of control? That is the question posed for us by the concept of future shock. For that is the situation we find ourselves in. If it were technology alone that had broken loose, our problems would be serious enough. The deadly fact is, however, that many other social processes have also begun to run free, oscillating wildly, resisting our best efforts to guide them.

Urbanization, ethnic conflict, migration, population, crime — a thousand examples spring to mind of fields in which our efforts to shape change seem increasingly inept and futile. Some of these are strongly related to the breakaway of technology; others partially independent of it. The uneven, rocketing rates of change, the shifts and jerks in direction, compel us to ask whether the techno-societies, even comparatively small ones like Sweden and Belgium, have grown too complex, too fast to manage?

How can we prevent mass future shock, selectively adjusting the tempos of change, raising or lowering levels of stimulation, when governments — including those with the best intentions — seem unable even to point change in the right direction?

Thus a leading American urbanologist writes with unconcealed disgust: "At a cost of more than three billion dollars, the Urban Renewal Agency has succeeded in materially reducing the supply of low cost housing in American cities." Similar debacles could be cited in a dozen fields. Why do welfare programs today often cripple rather than help their clients? Why do college students, supposedly a pampered elite, riot and rebel? Why do expressways add to traffic congestion rather than reduce it? In short, why do so many well-intentioned liberal programs turn rancid so rapidly, producing side effects that cancel out their central effects? No wonder Raymond Fletcher, a frustrated Member of Parliament in Britain, recently complained: "Society's gone random!"

If random means a literal absence of pattern, he is, of course, overstating the case. But if random means that the outcomes of social policy have become erratic and hard to predict, he is right on target. Here, then, is the political meaning of future shock. For just as individual future shock results from an inability to keep pace with the rate of change, governments, too, suffer from a kind of collective future shock — a breakdown of their decisional processes.

With chilling clarity, Sir Geoffrey Vickers, the eminent British social scientist, has identified the issue: "The rate of change increases at an accelerating speed, without a corresponding acceleration in the rate at which further responses can be made; and this brings us nearer the threshold beyond which control is lost."

THE DEATH OF TECHNOCRACY

What we are witnessing is the beginning of the final breakup of industrialism and, with it, the collapse of technocratic planning. By technocratic planning, I do not mean only the centralized national planning that has, until recently, characterized the USSR, but also the less formal, more dispersed attempts at systematic change management that occur in all the high-technology nations, regardless of their political persuasion. Michael Harrington, the socialist critic, arguing that we have rejected planning, has termed ours the "accidental century." Yet, as Galbraith demonstrates, even within the context of a capitalist economy, the great corporations go to enormous lengths to rationalize production and distribution, to plan their future as best they can. Governments, too, are deep into the planning business. The Keynesian manipulation of post-war economies may be inadequate, but it is not a matter of accident. In France, Le Plan has become a regular feature of national life. In Sweden, Italy, Germany and Japan, governments actively intervene in the economic sector to protect certain industries, to capitalize others, and to accelerate growth. In the United States and Britain, even local governments come equipped with what are at least called planning departments.

Why, therefore, despite all these efforts, should the system be spinning out of control? The problem is not simply that we plan too little; we also plan too poorly. Part of the trouble can be traced to the very premises implicit in our planning.

First, technocratic planning, itself a product of industrialism, reflects the values of that fast-vanishing era. In both its capitalist and communist variants, industrialism was a system focused on the maximization of material welfare. Thus, for the technocrat, in Detroit as well as Kiev, economic advance is the primary aim; technology the primary tool. The fact that in one case the advance redounds to private advantage and in the other, theoretically, to the public good, does not alter the core assumptions common to both. Technocratic planning is *econocentric*.

Second, technocratic planning reflects the time-bias of industrialism. Struggling to free itself from the stifling past-orientation of previous societies, industrialism focused heavily on the present. This meant, in practice, that its planning dealt with futures near at hand. The idea of a five-year plan struck the world as insanely futuristic when it was first put forward by the Soviets in the 1920's. Even today, except in the most advanced organizations on both sides of the ideological curtain, one- or two-year forecasts are regarded as "log-range planning." A handful of corporations and government agencies, as we shall see, have begun to concern themselves with horizons ten, twenty, even fifty years in the future. The majority, however, remain blindly biased toward next Monday. Technocratic planning is *short-range*.

Third, reflecting the bureaucratic organization of industrialism, technocratic planning was premised on hierarchy. The world was divided into manager and worker, planner and plannee, with decisions made by one for the other. This system, adequate while change unfolds at an industrial tempo, breaks down as the pace reaches super-industrial speeds. The increasingly unstable environment demands more and more non-programmed decisions down below; the need for instant feedback blurs the distinction between line and staff; the hierarchy totters. Planners are too remote, too ignorant of local conditions, too slow in responding to change. As suspicion spreads that top-down controls are unworkable, plannees begin clamoring for the right to participate in the decision-making. Planners, however, resist. For like the bureaucratic system it mirrors, technocratic planning is essentially *undemocratic*.

The forces sweeping us toward super-industrialism can no longer be channeled by these bankrupt industrial-era methods. For a time they may continue to work in backward, slowly moving industries or communities. But their misapplication in advanced industries, in universities, in cities — wherever change is swift — cannot but intensify the instability, leading to wilder and wilder swings and lurches. Moreover, as the evidences of failure pile up, dangerous political, cultural and psychological currents are set loose.

One response to the loss of control, for example, is a revulsion against intelligence. Science first gave man a sense of mastery over his environment, and hence over the future. By making the future seem malleable, instead of immutable, it shattered the opiate religions that preached passivity and mysticism. Today, mounting evidence that society is out of control breeds disillusionment with science. In consequence, we witness a garish revival of mysticism. Suddenly astrology is the rage. Zen, yoga, seances, and witchcraft become popular pastimes. Cults form around the search for Dionysian experience, for non-verbal and supposedly non-linear communication. We are told it is more important to "feel" than to "think," as though there were a contradiction between the two. Existentialist oracles join Catholic mystics, Jungian psychoanalysts, and Hindu gurus in exalting the mystical and emotional against the scientific and rational.

This reversion to pre-scientific attitudes is accompanied, not surprisingly, by a tremendous wave of nostalgia in the society. Antique furniture, posters from a bygone era, games based on the remembrance of yesterday's trivia, the revival of Art Nouveau, the spread of Edwardian styles, the rediscovery of such faded pop-cult celebrities as Humphrey Bogart or W. C. Fields, all mirror a psychological lust for the simpler, less turbulent past. Powerful fad machines spring into action to capitalize on this hunger. The nostalgia business becomes a booming industry.

The failure of technocratic planning and the consequent sense of lost control also feeds the philosophy of "now-ness." Songs and advertisements hail the appearance of the "now generation," and learned psychiatrists, discoursing on the presumed dangers of repression, warn us not to defer our gratifications. Acting out and a search for immediate payoff are encouraged. "We're more oriented to the present," says a teen-age girl to a reporter after the mammoth Woodstock rock music festival. "It's like do what you want to do now.... If you stay anywhere very long you get into a planning thing.... So you just move on." Spontaneity, the personal equivalent of social planlessness, is elevated into a cardinal psychological virtue.

All this has its political analog in the emergence of a strange coalition of right wingers and New Leftists in support of what can only be termed a "hang loose" approach to the future. Thus we hear increasing calls for anti-planning or non-planning, sometimes euphemized as "organic growth." Among some radicals, this takes on an anarchist coloration. Not only is it regarded as unnecessary or unwise to make long-range plans for the future of the institution or society they wish to overturn, it is sometimes even regarded as poor taste to plan the next hour and a half of a meeting. Planlessness is glorified.

Arguing that planning imposes values on the future, the anti-planners overlook the fact than non-planning does so, too — often with far worse consequence. Angered by the narrow, econocentric character of technocratic planning, they condemn systems analysis, cost benefit accounting, and similar methods, ignoring the fact that, used differently, these very tools might be converted into powerful techniques for humanizing the future.

When critics charge that technocratic planning is anti-human, in the sense that it neglects social, cultural and psychological values in its headlong rush to maximize economic gain, they are usually right. When they charge that it is shortsighted and undemocratic, they are usually right. When they charge it is inept, they are usually right.

But when they plunge backward into irrationality, anti-scientific attitudes, a kind of sick nostalgia, and an exaltation of now-ness, they are not only wrong, but dangerous. Just as, in the main, their alternatives to industrialism call for a return to pre-industrial institutions, their alternative to technocracy is not post-, but pre-technocracy.

Nothing could be more dangerously maladaptive. Whatever the theoretical arguments may be, brute forces are loose in the world. Whether we wish to prevent future shock or control population, to check pollution or defuse the arms race, we cannot permit decisions of earth-jolting importance to be taken heedlessly, witlessly, planlessly. To hang loose is to commit collective suicide.

We need not a reversion to the irrationalisms of the past, not a passive acceptance of change, not despair or nihilism. We need, instead, a strong new strategy. For reasons that will become clear, I term this strategy "social futurism." I am convinced that, armed with this strategy, we can arrive at a new level of competence in the management of change. We can invent a form of planning more humane, more farsighted, and more democratic than any so far in use. In short, we can transcend technocracy.

THE HUMANIZATION OF THE PLANNER

Technocrats suffer from econo-think. Except during war and dire emergency, they start from the premise that even non-economic problems can be solved with economic remedies.

Social futurism challenges this root assumption of both Marxist and Keynesian managers. In its historical time and place, industrial society's single-minded pursuit of material progress served the human race well. As we hurtle toward super-industrialism, however, a new ethos emerges in which other goals begin to gain parity with, and even supplant, those of economic welfare. In personal terms, self-fulfillment, social responsibility, aesthetic achievement, hedonistic individualism, and an array of other goals vie with and often over-shadow the raw drive for material success. Affluence serves as a base from which men begin to strive for varied post-economic ends.

At the same time, in societies arrowing toward super-industrialism, economic variables — wages, balance of payments, productivity — grow increasingly sensitive to changes in the non-economic environment. Economic problems are plentiful, but a whole range of issues that are only secondarily economic break into prominence. Racism, the battle between the generations, crime, cultural autonomy, violence — all these have economic dimensions; yet none can be effectively treated by econocentric measures alone.

The move from manufacturing to service production, the psychologization of both goods and services, and ultimately the shift toward experiential production all tie the economic sector much more tightly to non-economic forces. Consumer preferences turn over in accordance with rapid life style changes, so that the coming and going of subcults is mirrored in economic turmoil. Super-industrial production requires workers skilled in symbol manipulation, so that what goes on in their heads becomes much more important than in the past, and much more dependent upon cultural factors.

There is even evidence that the financial system is becoming more responsive to social and psychological pressures. It is only in an affluent society on its way to super-industrialism that one witnesses the invention of new investment vehicles, such as mutual funds, that are consciously motivated or constrained by non-economic considerations. The Vanderbilt Mutual Fund and the Provident Fund refuse to invest in liquor or tobacco shares. The giant Mates Fund spurns the stock of any company engaged in munitions production, while the tiny Vantage 10/90 Fund invests part of its assets in industries working to alleviate food and population problems in developing nations. There are funds that invest only, or primarily, in racially integrated housing. The Ford Foundation and the Presbyterian Church both invest part of their sizeable portfolios in companies selected not for economic payout alone, but for their potential contribution to solving urban problems. Such developments, still small in number, accurately signal the direction of change.

In the meantime, major American corporations with fixed investments in urban centers, are being sucked, often despite themselves, into the roaring vortex of social change. Hundreds of companies are now involved in providing jobs for hard-core unemployed, in organizing literacy and job-training programs, and in scores of other unfamiliar activities. So important have these new involvements grown that the largest corporation in the world, the American Telephone and Telegraph Company, recently set up a Department of Environmental Affairs. A pioneering venture, this agency has been assigned a range of tasks that include worrying about air and water pollution, improving the aesthetic appearance of the company's trucks and equipment, and fostering experimental preschool learning programs in urban ghettos. None of this necessarily implies that big companies are growing altruistic; it merely underscores the increasing intimacy of the links between the economic sector and powerful cultural, psychological and social forces.

While these forces batter at our doors, however, most technocratic planners and managers behave as though nothing had happened.

They continue to act as though the economic sector were hermetically sealed off from social and psychocultural influences. Indeed, econocentric premises are buried so deeply and held so widely in both the capitalist and communist nations, that they distort the very information systems essential for the management of change.

For example, all modern nations maintain elaborate machinery for measuring economic performance. We know virtually day by day the directions of change with respect to productivity, prices, investment, and similar factors. Through a set of "economic indicators" we gauge the overall health of the economy, the speed at which it is changing, and the overall directions of change. Without these measures, our control of the economy would be far less effective.

By contrast, we have no such measures, no set of comparable "social indicators" to tell us whether the society, as distinct from the economy, is also healthy. We have no measures of the "quality of life." We have no systematic indices to tell us whether men are more or less alienated from one another; whether education is more effective; whether art, music and literature are flourishing; whether civility, generosity or kindness are increasing. "Gross National Product is our Holy Grail," writes Stewart Udall, former United States Secretary of the Interior, "... but we have no environmental index, no census statistics to measure whether the country is more livable from year to year."

On the surface, this would seem a purely technical matter — something for statisticians to debate. Yet it has the most serious political significance, for lacking such measures it becomes difficult to connect up national or local policies with appropriate long-term social goals. The absence of such indices perpetuates vulgar technocracy.

Little known to the public, a polite, but increasingly bitter battle over this issue has begun in Washington. Technocratic planners and economists see in the social indicators idea a threat to their entrenched position at the ear of the political policy maker. In contrast, the need for social indicators has been eloquently argued by such prominent social scientists as Bertram M. Gross of Wayne State University, Eleanor Sheldon and Wilbert Moore of the Russell Sage Foundation, Daniel Bell and Raymond Bauer of Harvard. We are witnessing, says Gross, a "widespread rebellion against what has been called the 'economic philistinism' of the United States government's present statistical establishment."

This revolt has attracted vigorous support from a small group of politicians and government officials who recognize our desperate need for a post-technocratic social intelligence system. These include Daniel P. Moynihan, a key White House adviser; Senators Walter Mondale of Minnesota and Fred Harris of Oklahoma; and several former Cabinet officers. In the near future, we can expect the same revolt to break out in other world capitals as well, once again drawing a line between technocrats and post-technocrats.

The danger of future shock, itself, however, points to the need for new social measures not yet even mentioned in the fast-burgeoning literature on social indicators. We urgently need, for example, techniques for measuring the level of transience in different communities, different population groups, and in individual experience. It is possible, in principle, to design a "transience index" that could disclose the rate at which we are making and breaking relationships with the things, places, people, organizations and informational structures that comprise our environment.

Such an index would reveal, among other things, the fantastic differences in the experiences of different groups in the society — the static and tedious quality of life for very large numbers of people, the frenetic turnover in the lives of others. Government policies that attempt to deal with both kinds of people in the same way are doomed to meet angry resistance from one or the other — or both.

Similarly, we need indices of novelty in the environment. How often do communities, organizations, or individuals have to cope with first-time situations? How many of the articles in the home of the average working-class family are actually "new" in function or appearance; how many are traditional? What level of novelty — in terms of things, people or any other significant dimension — is required for stimulation without overstimulation? How much more novelty can children absorb than their parents — if it is true that they can absorb more? In what way is aging related to lower novelty tolerances, and how do such differences correlate with the political and intergenerational conflict now tearing the techno-societies apart? By studying and measuring the invasion of newness, we can begin, perhaps to control the influx of change into our social structures and personal lives.

And what about choice and overchoice? Can we construct measures of the degree of significant choice in human lives? Can any government that pretends to be democratic not concern itself with such an issue? For all the rhetoric about freedom of choice, no government agency in the world can claim to have made any attempt to measure it. The assumption simply is that more income or affluence means more choice and that more choice, in turn, means freedom. Is it not time to examine these basic assumptions of our political systems? Post-technocratic planning must deal with precisely such issues, if we are to prevent future shock and build a humane super-industrial society.

A sensitive system of indicators geared to measuring the achievement of social and cultural goals, and integrated with economic indicators, is part of the technical equipment that any society needs before it can successfully reach the next stage of eco-technological development. It is an absolute precondition for post-technocratic planning and change management.

This humanization of planning, moreover, must be reflected in our political structures as well. To connect the super-industrial social

intelligence system with the decisional centers of society, we must insti-
tutionalize a concern for the quality of life. Thus Bertram Gross and
others in the social indicators movement have proposed the creation
of a Council of Social Advisers to the President. Such a Council, as
they see it, would be modeled after the already existing Council of
Economic Advisers and would perform parallel functions in the social
field. The new agency would monitor key social indicators precisely
the way the CEA keeps its eye on economic indices, and interpret
changes to the President. It would issue an annual report on the
quality of life, clearly spelling out our social progress (or lack of it) in
terms of specified goals. This report would thus supplement and
balance the annual economic report prepared by the CEA. By
providing reliable, useful data about our social condition, the Council
of Social Advisers would begin to influence planning generally,
making it more sensitive to social costs and benefits, less coldly
technocratic and econocentric.[1]

The establishment of such councils, not merely at the federal level
but at state and municipal levels as well, would not solve all our problems; it would not eliminate conflict; it would not guarantee that
social indicators are exploited properly. In brief, it would not
eliminate politics from political life. But it would lend recognition —
and political force — to the idea that the aims of progress reach beyond
economics. The designation of agencies to watch over the indicators of
change in the quality of life would carry us a long way toward that
humanization of the planner which is the essential first stage of the
strategy of social futurism.

TIME HORIZONS

Technocrats suffer from myopia. Their instinct is to think about
immediate returns, immediate consequences. They are premature
members of the now generation.

If a region needs electricity, they reach for a power plant. The fact
that such a plant might sharply alter labor patterns, that within a
decade it might throw men out of work, force large-scale retraining of
workers, and swell the social welfare costs of a nearby city — such considerations are too remote in time to concern them. The fact that the
plant could trigger devastating ecological consequences a generation
later simply does not register in their time frame.

In a world of accelerant change, next year is nearer to us than next
month was in a more leisurely era. This radically altered fact of life
must be internalized by decision-makers in industry, government and
elsewhere. Their time horizons must be extended.

To plan for a more distant future does not mean to tie oneself to
dogmatic programs. Plans can be tentative, fluid, subject to continual

revision. Yet flexibility need not mean shortsightedness. To transcend technocracy, our social time horizons must reach decades, even generations, into the future. This requires more than a lengthening of our formal plans. It means an infusion of the entire society, from top to bottom, with a new socially aware future-consciousness.

One of the healthiest phenomena of recent years has been the sudden proliferation of organizations devoted to the study of the future. This recent development is, in itself, a homeostatic response of the society to the speed-up of change. Within a few years we have seen the creation of future-oriented think tanks like the Institute for the Future; the formation of academic study groups like the Commission on the Year 2000 and the Harvard Program on Technology and Society; the appearance of futurist journals in England, France, Italy, Germany and the United States; the spread of university courses in forecasting and related subjects; the convocation of international futurist meetings in Oslo, Berlin and Kyoto; the coalescence of groups like Futuribles, Europe 2000, Mankind 2000, the World Future Society.

Futurist centers are to be found in West Berlin, in Prague, in London, in Moscow, Rome and Washington, in Caracas, even in the remote jungles of Brazil at Belém and Belo Horizonte. Unlike conventional technocratic planners whose horizons usually extend no further than a few years into tomorrow, these groups concern themselves with change fifteen, twenty-five, even fify years in the future.

Every society faces not merely a succession of *probable* futures, but an array of *possible* futures, and a conflict over *preferable* futures. The management of change is the effort to convert certain possibles into probables, in pursuit of agreed-on preferables. Determining the probable calls for a science of futurism. Delineating the possible calls for an art of futurism. Defining the preferable calls for a politics of futurism.

The worldwide futurist movement today does not yet differentiate clearly among these functions. Its heavy emphasis is on the assessment of probabilities. Thus in many of these centers, economists, sociologists, mathematicians, biologists, physicists, operations researchers and others invent and apply methods for forecasting future probabilities. At what date could aquaculture feed half the world's population? What are the odds that electric cars will supplant gas-driven automobiles in the next fifteen years? How likely is a Sino-Soviet détente by 1980? What changes are most probable in leisure patterns, urban government, race relations?

Stressing the interconnectedness of disparate events and trends, scientific futurists are also devoting increasing attention to the social consequences of technology. The Institute for the Future is, among other things, investigating the probable social and cultural effects of advanced communications technology. The group at Harvard is concerned with social problems likely to arise from bio-medical advances. Futurists in Brazil examine the probable outcomes of various economic development policies.

The rationale for studying probable futures is compelling. It is impossible for an individual to live through a single working day without making thousands of assumptions about the probable future. The commuter who calls to say, "I'll be home at six" bases his prediction on assumptions about the probability that the train will run on time. When mother sends Johnny to school, she tacitly assumes the school will be there when he arrives. Just as a pilot cannot steer a ship without projecting its course, we cannot steer our personal lives without continually making such assumptions, consciously or otherwise.

Societies, too, construct an architecture of premises about tomorrow. Decision-makers in industry, government, politics, and other sectors of society could not function without them. In periods of turbulent change, however, these socially-shaped images of the probable future become less accurate. The breakdown of control in society today is directly linked to our inadequate images of probable futures.

Of course, no one can "know" the future in any absolute sense. We can only systematize and deepen our assumptions and attempt to assign probabilities to them. Even this is difficult. Attempts to forecast the future inevitably alter it. Similarly, once a forecast is disseminated, the act of dissemination (as distinct from investigation) also produces a perturbation. Forecasts tend to become self-fulfilling or self-defeating. As the time horizon is extended into the more distant future, we are forced to rely on informed hunch and guesswork. Moreover, certain unique events — assassinations, for example — are, for all intents and purposes, unpredictable at present (although we can forecast classes of such events).

Despite all this, it is time to erase, once and for all, the popular myth that the future is "unknowable." The difficulties ought to chasten and challenge, not paralyze. William F. Ogburn, one of the world's great students of social change, once wrote: "We should admit into our thinking the idea of approximations, that is, that there are varying degrees of accuracy and inaccuracy of estimate." A rough idea of what lies ahead is better than none, he went on, and for many purposes extreme accuracy is wholly unnecessary.

We are not, therefore, as helpless in dealing with future probabilities as most people assume. The British social scientist Donald G. MacRae correctly asserts that "modern sociologists can in fact make a large number of comparatively short-term and limited predictions with a good deal of assurance." Apart from the standard methods of social science, however, we are experimenting with potentially powerful new tools for probing the future. These range from complex ways of extrapolating existing trends, to the construction of highly intricate models, games and simulations, the preparation of detailed speculative scenarios, the systematic study of history for relevant analogies, morphological research, relevance analysis, contextual mapping and the like. In a comprehensive investigation of technological forecasting, Dr. Erich Jantsch, formerly a consultant to the OECD and a research associate at MIT, has identified scores of distinct new techniques either in use or in the experimental stage.

The Institute for the Future in Middletown, Connecticut, a prototype of the futurist think tank, is a leader in the design of new forecasting tools. One of these is Delphi — a method largely developed by Dr. Olaf Helmer, the mathematician-philosopher who is one of the founders of the IFF. Delphi attempts to deal with very distant futures by making systematic use of the "intuitive" guesstimates of large numbers of experts. The work on Delphi has led to a further innovation which has special importance in the attempt to prevent future shock by regulating the pace of change. Pioneered by Theodore J. Gordon of the IFF, and called Cross Impact Matrix Analysis, it traces the effect of one innovation on another, making possible, for the first time, anticipatory analysis of complex chains of social, technological and other occurrences — and the rates at which they are likely to occur.

We are, in short, witnessing a perfectly extraordinary thrust toward more scientific appraisal of future probabilities, a ferment likely, in itself, to have a powerful impact on the future. It would be foolish to oversell the ability of science, as yet, to forecast complex events accurately. Yet the danger today is not that we will overestimate our ability; the real danger is that we will under-utilize it. For even when our still-primitive attempts at scientific forecasting turn out to be grossly in error, the very effort helps us identify key variables in change, it helps clarify goals, and it forces more careful evaluation of policy alternatives. In these ways, if no others, probing the future pays off in the present.

Anticipating *probable* futures, however, is only part of what needs doing if we are to shift the planner's time horizon and infuse the entire society with a greater sense of tomorrow. For we must also vastly widen our conception of possible futures. To the rigorous discipline of science, we must add the flaming imagination of art.

Today as never before we need a multiplicity of visions, dreams and prophecies — images of potential tomorrows. Before we can rationally decide which alternative pathways to choose, which cultural styles to pursue, we must first ascertain which are possible.

Conjecture, speculation and the visionary view thus become as coldly practical a necessity as feet-on-the-floor "realism" was in an earlier time.

This is why some of the world's biggest and most tough-minded corporations, once the living embodiment of presentism, today hire intuitive futurists, science fiction writers and visionaries as consultants. A gigantic European chemical company employs a futurist who combines a scientific background with training as a theologian. An American communications empire engages a future-minded social critic. A glass manufacturer searches for a science fiction writer to imagine the possible corporate forms of the future. Companies turn to these "blue-skyers" and "wild birds" not for scientific forecasts of probabilities, but for mindstretching speculation about possibilities.

Corporations must not remain the only agencies with access to such services. Local government, schools, voluntary associations and others also need to examine their potential futures imaginatively. One way to help them do so would be to establish in each community "imaginetic centers" devoted to technically assisted brainstorming. These would be places where people noted for creative imagination, rather than technical expertise, are brought together to examine present crises, to anticipate future crises, and to speculate freely, even playfully, about possible futures.

What, for example, are the possible futures of urban transportation? Traffic is a problem involving space. How might the city of tomorrow cope with the movement of men and objects through space? To speculate about this question, an imaginetic center might enlist artists, sculptors, dancers, furniture designers, parking lot attendants, and a variety of other people who, in one way or another, manipulate space imaginatively. Such people, assembled under the right circumstances, would inevitably come up with ideas of which the technocratic city planners, the highway engineers and transit authorities have never dreamed.

Musicians, people who live near airports, jack-hammer men and subway conductors might well imagine new ways to organize, mask or suppress noise. Groups of young people might be invited to ransack their minds for previously unexamined approaches to urban sanitation, crowding, ethnic conflict, care of the aged, or a thousand other present and future problems.

In any such effort, the overwhelming majority of ideas put forward will, of course, be absurd, funny or technically impossible. Yet the essence of creativity is a willingness to play the fool, to toy with the absurd, only later submitting the stream of ideas to harsh critical judgment. The application of the imagination to the future thus requires an environment in which it is safe to err, in which novel juxtapositions of ideas can be freely expressed before being critically sifted. We need sanctuaries for social imagination.

While all sorts of creative people ought to participate in conjecture about possible futures, they should have immediate access — in person or via telecommunications — to technical specialists, from acoustical engineers to zoologists, who could indicate when a suggestion is technically impossible (bearing in mind that even impossibility is often temporary).

Scientific expertise, however, might also play a generative, rather than merely a damping role in the imaginetic process. Skilled specialists can construct models to help imagineers examine all possible permutations of a given set of relationships. Such models are representations of real-life conditions. In the words of Christoph Bertram of the Institute for Strategic Studies in London, their purpose is "not so much to predict the future, but, by examining alternative futures, to show the choices open."

An appropriate model, for example, could help a group of imagineers visualize the impact on a city if its educational expenditures were to fluctuate — how this would affect, let us say, the transport system, the theaters, the occupational structure and health of the community. Conversely, it could show how changes in these other factors might affect education.

The rushing stream of wild, unorthodox, eccentric or merely colorful ideas generated in these sanctuaries of social imagination must, after they have been expressed, be subjected to merciless screening. Only a tiny fraction of them will survive this filtering process. These few, however, could be of the utmost importance in calling attention to new possibilities that might otherwise escape notice. As we move from poverty toward affluence, politics changes from what mathematicians call a zero sum game into a non-zero sum game. In the first, if one player wins another must lose. In the second all players can win. Finding non-zero sum solutions to our social problems requires all the imagination we can muster. A system for generating imaginative policy ideas could help us take maximum advantage of the non-zero opportunities ahead.

While imaginetic centers concentrate on partial images of tomorrow, defining possible futures for a single industry, an organization, a city or its subsystems, however, we also need sweeping visionary ideas about the society as a whole. Multiplying our images of possible futures is important; but these images need to be organized crystallized into structured form. In the past, utopian literature did this for us. It played a practical, crucial role in ordering men's dreams about alternative futures. Today we suffer for lack of utopian ideas around which to organize competing images of possible futures.

Most traditional utopias picture simple and static societies — i.e., societies that have nothing in common with super-industrialism. B. F. Skinner's *Walden Two*, the model for several existing experimental communes, depicts a pre-industrial way of life — small, close to the earth, built on farming and handcraft. Even those two brilliant anti-utopias, *Brave New World* and *1984*, now seem over-simple. Both describe societies based on high technology and low complexity: the machines are sophisticated but the social and cultural relationships are fixed and deliberately simplified.

Today we need powerful new utopian and anti-utopian concepts that look forward to super-industrialism, rather than backward to simpler societies. These concepts, however, can no longer be produced in the old way. First, no book, by itself, is adequate to describe a super-industrial future in emotionally compelling terms. Each conception of a super-industrial utopia or anti-utopia needs to be embodied in many forms — films, plays, novels and works of art — rather than a single work of fiction. Second, it may now be too difficult for any individual writer, no matter how gifted, to describe a convincingly complex future. We need, therefore, a revolution in the production of utopias: collaborative utopianism. We need to construct "utopia factories."

One way might be to assemble a small group of top social scientists — an economist, a sociologist, an anthropologist, and so on — asking them to work together, even live together, long enough to hammer out among themselves a set of well-defined values on which they believe a truly super-industrial utopian society might be based.

Each member of the team might then attempt to describe in nonfiction form a sector of an imagined society built on these values. What would its family structure be like? Its economy, laws, religion, sexual practices, youth culture, music, art, its sense of time, its degree of differentiation, its psychological problems? By working together and ironing out inconsistencies, where possible, a comprehensive and adequately complex picture might be drawn of a seamless, temporary form of super-industrialism.

At this point, with the completion of detailed analysis, the project would move to the fiction stage. Novelists, film-makers, science fiction writers and others, working closely with psychologists, could prepare creative works about the lives of individual characters in the imagined society.

Meanwhile, other groups could be at work on counter-utopias. While Utopia A might stress materialist, success-oriented values, Utopia B might base itself on sensual, hedonistic values, C on the primacy of aesthetic values, D on individualism, E on collectivism, and so forth. Ultimately, a stream of books, plays, films and television programs would flow from this collaboration between art, social science and futurism, thereby educating large numbers of people about the costs and benefits of the various proposed utopias.

Finally, if social imagination is in short supply, we are even more lacking in people willing to subject utopian ideas to systematic test. More and more young people, in their dissatisfaction with industrialism, are experimenting with their own lives, forming utopian communities, trying new social arrangements, from group marriage to living-learning communes. Today, as in the past, the weight of established society comes down hard on the visionary who attempts to practice, as well as merely preach. Rather than ostracizing utopians, we should take advantage of their willingness to experiment, encouraging them with money and tolerance, if not respect.

Most of today's "intentional communities" or utopian colonies, however, reveal a powerful preference for the past. These may be of value to the individuals in them, but the society as a whole would be better served by utopian experiments based on super- rather than pre-industrial forms. Instead of a communal farm, why not a computer software company whose program writers live and work communally? Why not an education technology company whose members pool their money and merge their families? Instead of raising radishes or crafting sandals, why not an oceanographic research installation organized along utopian lines? Why not a group medical practice that takes advantage of the latest medical technology but whose members accept modest pay and pool their profits to run a completely new-style medical school? Why not recruit living groups to try out the proposals of the utopia factories?

In short, we can use utopianism as a tool rather than an escape, if we base our experiments on the technology and society of tomorrow rather than that of the past. And once done, why not the most rigorous, scientific analysis of the results? The findings could be priceless, were they to save us from mistakes or lead us toward more workable organizational forms for industry, education, family life or politics.

Such imaginative explorations of possible futures would deepen and enrich our scientific study of probable futures. They would lay a basis for the radical forward extension of the society's time horizon. They would help us apply social imagination to the future of futurism itself.

Indeed, with these as a background, we must consciously begin to multiply the scientific future-sensing organs of society. Scientific futurist institutes must be spotted like nodes in a loose network throughout the entire governmental structure in the techno-societies, so that in every department, local or national, some staff devotes itself systematically to scanning the probable long-term future in its assigned field. Futurists should be attached to every political party, university, corporation, professional association, trade union and student organization.

We need to train thousands of young people in the perspectives and techniques of scientific futurism, inviting them to share in the exciting venture of mapping probable futures. We also need national agencies to provide technical assistance to local communities in creating their own futurist groups. And we need a similar center, perhaps jointly funded by American and European foundations, to help incipient futurist centers in Asia, Africa, and Latin America.

We are in a race between rising levels of uncertainty produced by the acceleration of change, and the need for reasonably accurate images of what at any instant is the most probable future. The generation of reliable images of the most probable future thus becomes a matter of the highest national, indeed, international urgency.

As the globe is itself dotted with future-sensors, we might consider creating a great international institute, a world futures data bank. Such an institute, staffed with top caliber men and women from all the sciences and social sciences, would take as its purpose the collection and systematic integration of predictive reports generated by scholars and imaginative thinkers in all the intellectual disciplines all over the world.

Of course, those working in such an institute would know that they could never create a single, static diagram of the future. Instead, the product of their effort would be a constantly changing geography of the future, a continually re-created overarching image based on the best predictive work available. The men and women engaged in this work would know that nothing is certain; they would know that they must work with inadequate data; they would appreciate the difficulties inherent in exploring the uncharted territories of tomorrow. But man already knows more about the future than he has ever tried to formulate and integrate in any systematic and scientific way. Attempts to bring this knowledge together would constitute one of the crowning intellectual efforts in history — and one of the most worthwhile.

Only when decision-makers are armed with better forecasts of future events, when by successive approximation we increase the accuracy of forecast, will our attempts to manage change improve perceptibly. For reasonably accurate assumptions about the future are a precondition for understanding the potential consequences of our own actions. And without such understanding, the management of change is impossible.

If the humanization of the planner is the first stage in the strategy of social futurism, therefore, the forward extension of our time horizon is the second. To transcend technocracy, we need not only to reach beyond our economic philistinism, but to open our minds to more distant futures, both probable and possible.

ANTICIPATORY DEMOCRACY

In the end, however, social futurism must cut even deeper. For technocrats suffer from more than econo-think and myopia; they suffer, too, from the virus of elitism. To capture control of change, we shall, therefore, require a final, even more radical breakaway from technocratic tradition: we shall need a revolution in the very way we formulate our social goals.

Rising novelty renders irrelevant the traditional goals of our chief institutions — state, church, corporation, army and university. Acceleration produces a faster turnover of goals, a greater transience of purpose. Diversity or fragmentation leads to a relentless multiplication of goals. Caught in this churning, goal-cluttered environment, we stagger, future shocked, from crisis to crisis, pursuing a welter of conflicting and self-cancelling purposes.

Nowhere is this more starkly evident than in our pathetic attempts to govern our cities. New Yorkers, within a short span, have suffered a nightmarish succession of near disasters: a water shortage, a subway strike, racial violence in the schools, a student insurrection at Columbia University, a garbage strike, a housing shortage, a fuel oil strike, a breakdown of telephone service, a teacher walkout, a power blackout, to name just a few. In its City Hall, as in a thousand city halls all over the high-technology nations, technocrats dash, fire-bucket in fist, from one conflagration to another, without the least semblance of a coherent plan or policy for the urban future.

This is not to say no one is planning. On the contrary, in this seething social brew, technocratic plans, subplans and counter-plans pour forth. They call for new highways, new roads, new power plants, new schools. They promise better hospitals, housing, mental health centers, welfare programs. But the plans cancel, contradict and reinforce one another by accident. Few are logically related to one another, and none to any overall image of the preferred city of the future. No vision — utopian or otherwise — energizes our efforts. No rationally integrated goals bring order to the chaos. And at the national and international levels, the absence of coherent policy is equally marked and doubly dangerous.

It is not simply that we do not know which goals to pursue, as a city or as a nation. The trouble lies deeper. For accelerating change has made obsolete the methods by which we arrive at social goals. The technocrats do not yet understand this, and, reacting to the goals crisis in knee-jerk fashion, they reach for the tried and true methods of the past.

Thus, intermittently, a change-dazed government will try to define its goals publicly. Instinctively, it establishes a commission. In 1960 President Eisenhower pressed into service, among others, a general, a judge, a couple of industrialists, a few college presidents, and a labor leader to "develop a broad outline of coordinated national policies and programs" and to "set up a series of goals in various areas of national activity." In due course, a red-white-and-blue paperback appeared with the commission's report, *Goals for Americans*. Neither the commission nor its goals had the slightest impact on the public or on policy. The juggernaut of change continued to roll through America untouched, as it were, by managerial intelligence.

A far more significant effort to tidy up governmental priorities was initiated by President Johnson, with his attempt to apply PPBS (Planning-Programming-Budgeting-System) throughout the federal establishment. PPBS is a method for tying programs much more closely and rationally to organizational goals. Thus, for example, by applying it, the Department of Health, Education and Welfare can assess the costs and benefits of alternative programs to accomplish specified goals. But who specifies these larger, more important goals? The introduction of PPBS and the systems approach is a major governmental achievement. It is of paramount importance in managing large organizational efforts. But it leaves entirely untouched the profoundly political question of how the overall goals of a government or a society are to be chosen in the first place.

President Nixon, still snarled in the goals crisis, tried a third tack. "It is time," he declared, "we addressed ourselves, consciously and systematically, to the question of what kind of a nation we want to be ..." He thereupon put his finger on the quintessential question. But once more the method chosen for answering it proved to be inadequate. "I have today ordered the establishment, within the White House, of a National Goals Research Staff," the President announced. "This will be a small, highly technical staff, made up of experts in the collection ... and processing of data relating to social needs, and in the projection of social trends."

Such a staff, located within shouting distance of the Presidency, could be extremely useful in compiling goal proposals, in reconciling (at least on paper) conflicts between agencies, in suggesting new priorities. Staffed with excellent social scientists and futurists, it could earn its keep if it did nothing but force high officials to question their primary goals.

Yet even this step, like the two before it, bears the unmistakable imprint of the technocratic mentality. For it, too, evades the politically charged core of the issue. How are preferable futures to be defined? And by whom? Who is to set goals for the future?

Behind all such efforts runs the notion that national (and, by extension, local) goals for the future of society ought to be formulated at the top. This technocratic premise perfectly mirrors the old bureaucratic forms of organization in which line and staff were separated, in which rigid, undemocratic hierarchies distinguished leader from led, manager from managed, planner from plannee.

Yet the real, as distinct from the glibly verbalized, goals of any society on the path to super-industrialism are already too complex, too transient and too dependent for their achievement upon the willing participation of the governed, to be perceived and defined so easily. We cannot hope to harness the runaway forces of change by assembling a kaffee klatsch of elders to set goals for us or by turning the task over to a "highly technical staff." A revolutionary new approach to goal-setting is needed.

Nor is this approach likely to come from those who play-act at revolution. One radical group, seeing all problems as a manifestation of the "maximization of profits," displays, in all innocence, an econo-centricism as narrow as that of the technocrats. Another hopes to plunge us willy-nilly back into the pre-industrial past. Still another sees revolution exclusively in subjective and psychological terms. None of these groups is capable of advancing us toward post-technocratic forms of change management.

By calling attention to the growing ineptitudes of the technocrats and by explicitly challenging not merely the means, but the very goals of industrial society, today's young radicals do us all a great service. But they no more know how to cope with the goals crisis than the technocrats they scorn. Exactly like Messrs. Eisenhower, Johnson and Nixon, they have been noticeably unable to present any positive image of a future worth fighting for.

Thus Todd Gitlin, a young American radical and former president of the Students for a Democratic Society, notes that while "an orientation toward the future has been the hallmark of every revolutionary — and, for that matter, liberal — movement of the last century and a half," the New Left suffers from "a disbelief in the future." After citing all the ostensible reasons why it has so far not put forward a coherent vision of the future, he succinctly confesses: "We find ourselves incapable of formulating the future."

Other New Left theorists fuzz over the problem, urging their followers to incorporate the future in the present by, in effect, living the life styles of tomorrow today. So far, this has led to a pathetic charade — "free societies," cooperatives, pre-industrial communes, few of which have anything to do with the future, and most of which reveal, instead, only a passionate penchant for the past.

The irony is compounded when we consider that some (though hardly all) of today's young radicals also share with the technocrats a streak of virulent elitism. While decrying bureaucracy and demanding "participatory democracy" they, themselves, frequently attempt to manipulate the very groups of workers, blacks or students on whose behalf they demand participation.

The working masses in the high-technology societies are totally indifferent to calls for a political revolution aimed at exchanging one form of property ownership for another. For most people, the rise in affluence has meant a better, not a worse, existence, and they look upon their much despised "suburban middle class lives" as fulfillment rather than deprivation.

Faced with this stubborn reality, undemocratic elements in the New

Left leap to the Marcusian conclusion that the masses are too bourgeoisified, too corrupted and addled by Madison Avenue to know what is good for them. And so, a revolutionary elite must establish a more humane and democratic future even if it means stuffing it down the throats of those who are too stupid to know their own interests. In short, the goals of society have to be set by an elite. Technocrat and anti-technocrat often turn out to be elitist brothers under the skin.

Yet systems of goal formulation based on elitist premises are simply no longer "efficient." In the struggle to capture control of the forces of change, they are increasingly counter-productive. For under super-industrialism, democracy becomes not a political luxury, but a primal necessity.

Democratic political forms arose in the West not because a few geniuses willed them into being or because man showed an "unquenchable instinct for freedom." They arose because the historical pressure toward social differentiation and toward faster paced systems demanded sensitive social feedback. In complex, differentiated societies, vast amounts of information must flow at even faster speeds between the formal organizations and subcultures that make up the whole, and between the layers and substructures within these.

Political democracy, by incorporating larger and larger numbers in social decision-making, facilitates feedback. And it is precisely this feedback that is essential to control. To assume control over accelerant change, we shall need still more advanced — and more democratic — feedback mechanisms.

The technocrat, however, still thinking in top-down terms, frequently makes plans without arranging for adequate and instantaneous feedback from the field, so that he seldom knows how well his plans are working. When he does arrange for feedback, what he usually asks for and gets is heavily economic, inadequately social, psychological or cultural. Worse yet, he makes these plans without sufficiently taking into account the fast-changing needs and wishes of those whose participation is needed to make them a success. He assumes the right to set social goals by himself or he accepts them blindly from some higher authority.

He fails to recognize that the faster pace of change demands — and creates — a new kind of information system in society: a loop, rather than a ladder. Information must pulse through this loop at accelerating speeds, with the output of one group becoming the input for many others, so that no group, however politically potent it may seem, can independently set goals for the whole.

As the number of social components multiplies, and change jolts and destabilizes the entire system, the power of subgroups to wreak havoc on the whole is tremendously amplified. There is, in the words of W. Ross Ashby, a brilliant cyberneticist, a mathematically provable law to the effect that "when a whole sytem is composed of a number of subsystems, the one that tends to dominate is the one that is *least* stable."

Another way of stating this is that, as the number of social components grows and change makes the whole system less stable, it becomes less and less possible to ignore the demands of political minorities — hippies, blacks, lower-middle-class Wallacites, school teachers, or the proverbial little old ladies in tennis shoes. In a slower-moving, industrial context, America could turn its back on the need of its black minority; in the new, fast-paced cybernetic society, this minority can, by sabotage, strike, or a thousand other means, disrupt the entire system. As interdependency grows, smaller and smaller groups within society achieve greater and greater power for critical disruption. Moreover, as the rate of change speeds up, the length of time in which they can be ignored shrinks to near nothingness. Hence: "Freedom now!"

This suggests that the best way to deal with angry or recalcitrant minorities is to open the system further, bringing them into it as full partners, permitting them to participate in social goal-setting, rather than attempting to ostracize or isolate them. A Red China locked out of the United Nations and the larger international community is far more likely to destabilize the world than one laced into the system. Young people forced into prolonged adolescence and deprived of the right to partake in social decision-making will grow more and more unstable until they threaten the overall system. In short, in politics, in industry, in education, goals set without the participation of those affected will be increasingly hard to execute. The continuation of top-down technocratic goal-setting procedures will lead to greater and greater social instability, less and less control over the forces of change; an ever greater danger of cataclysmic, man-destroying upheaval.

To master change, we shall therefore need both a clarification of important long-range social goals *and* a democratization of the way in which we arrive at them. And this means nothing less than the next political revolution in the techno-societies — a breathtaking affirmation of popular democracy.

The time has come for a democratic reassessment of the directions of change, a reassessment made not by the politicians or the sociologists or the clergy or the elitist revolutionaries, not by technicians or college presidents, but by the people themselves. We need, quite literally, to "go to the people" with a question that is almost never asked of them: "What kind of a world do you want ten, twenty, or thirty years from now?" We need to initiate, in short, a continuing plebiscite on the future.

The moment is right for the formation in each of the high-technology nations of a movement for total self-review, a public self-examination aimed at broadening and defining in social, as well as merely economic, terms, the goals of "progress." On the edge of a new millennium, on the brink of a new stage of human development, we are racing blindly into the future. But where do we want to go?

What would happen if we actually tried to answer this question?

Imagine the historic drama, the power and evolutionary impact, if each of the high-technology nations literally set aside the next five years as a period of intense national self-appraisal; if at the end of five years it were to come forward with its own tentative agenda for the future, a program embracing not merely economic targets but, equally important, broad sets of social goals — if each nation, in effect, stated to the world what it wished to accomplish for its people and mankind in general during the remaining quarter century of the millennium.

Let us convene in each nation, in each city, in each neighborhood, democratic constituent assemblies charged with social stock-taking, charged with defining and assigning priorities to specific social goals for the remainder of the century.

Such "social future assemblies" might represent not merely geographical localities, but social units — industry, labor, the churches, the intellectual community, the arts, women, ethnic and religious groups, students — with organized representation for the unorganized as well. There are no sure-fire techniques for guaranteeing equal representation for all, or for eliciting the wishes of the poor, the inarticulate or the isolated. Yet once we recognize the need to include them, we shall find the ways. Indeed, the problem of participating in the definition of the future is not merely a problem of the poor, the inarticulate and the isolated. Highly paid executives, wealthy professionals, extremely articulate intellectuals and students — all at one time or another feel cut off from the power to influence the directions and pace of change. Wiring them into the system, making them a part of the guidance machinery of the society, is the most critical political task of the coming generation. Imagine the effect if at one level or another a place were provided where all those who will live in the future might voice their wishes about it. Imagine, in short, a massive, global exercise in anticipatory democracy.

Social future assemblies need not — and, given the rate of transience — cannot be anchored, permanent institutions. Instead, they might take the form of ad hoc groupings, perhaps called into being at regular intervals with different representatives participating each time. Today citizens are expected to serve on juries when needed. They give a few days or a few weeks of their time for this service, recognizing that the jury system is one of the guarantees of democracy, that, even though service may be inconvenient, someone must do the job. Social future assemblies could be organized along similar lines, with a constant stream of new participants brought together for short periods to serve as society's "consultants on the future."

Such grass roots organisms for expressing the will of large numbers of hitherto unconsulted people could become, in effect, the town halls of the future, in which millions help shape their own distant destinies.

To some, this appeal for a form of neo-populism will no doubt seem naive. Yet nothing is more naive than the notion that we can continue politically to run the society the way we do at present. To some, it will appear impractical. Yet nothing is more impractical than the attempt to impose a humane future from above. What was naive under industrialism may be realistic under super-industrialism; what was practical may be absurd.

The encouraging fact is that we now have the potential for achieving tremendous breakthroughs in democratic decision-making if we make imaginative use of the new technologies, both "hard" and "soft," that bear on the problem. Thus, advanced telecommunications mean that participants in a social future assembly need not literally meet in a single room, but might simply be hooked into a communications net that straddles the globe. A meeting of scientists to discuss research goals for the future, or goals for environmental quality, could draw participants from many countries at once. An assembly of steel-workers, unionists and executives, convened to discuss goals for automation and for the improvement of work itself, could link up participants from many mills, offices and warehouses, no matter how scattered or remote.

A meeting of the cultural community in New York or Paris — artists and gallery-goers, writers and readers, dramatists and audiences — to discuss appropriate long-range goals for the cultural development of the city could be shown, through the use of video recordings and other techniques, actual samples of the kinds of artistic production under discussion, architectural designs for new facilities, samples of new artistic media made available by technological advance, etc. What kind of cultural life should a great city of the future enjoy? What resources would be needed to realize a given set of goals?

All social future assemblies, in order to answer such questions, could and should be backed with technical staff to provide data on the social and economic costs of various goals, and to show the costs and benefits of proposed trade-offs, so that participants would be in a position to make reasonably informed choices, as it were, among alternative futures. In this way, each assembly might arrive, in the end, not merely in vaguely expressed, disjointed hopes, but at coherent statements of priorities for tomorrow — posed in terms that could be compared with the goal statements of other groups.

Nor need these social future assemblies be glorified "talkfests." We are fast developing games and simulation exercises whose chief beauty is that they help players clarify their own values. At the University of Illinois, in Project Plato, Charles Osgood is experimenting with computers and teaching machines that would involve large sectors of the public in planning imaginary, preferable futures through gaming.

At Cornell University, José Villegas, a professor in the Department of Design and Environmental Analysis, has begun constructing with the aid of black and white students a variety of "ghetto games" which reveal to the players the consequences of various proposed courses of action and thus help them clarify goals. *Ghetto 1984* showed what would happen if the recommendations made by the Kerner riot commission — the U.S. National Advisory Commission on Civil Disorder — were actually to be adopted. It showed how the sequence in which these recommendations were enacted would affect their ultimate impact on the ghetto. It helped players, both black and white, to identify their shared goals as well as their unresolved conflicts. In games like *Peru 2000* and *Squatter City 2000*, players design communities for the future.

In *Lower East Side*, a game Villegas hopes actually to play in the Manhattan community that bears that name, players would not be students, but real-life residents of the community — poverty workers, middle-class whites, Puerto Rican small businessmen or youth, unemployed blacks, police, landlords and city officials.

In the spring of 1969, 50,000 high school students in Boston, in Philadelphia and in Syracuse, New York, participated in a televised game involving a simulated war in the Congo in 1975. While televised teams simulated the cabinets of Russia, Red China, and the United States, and struggled with the problems of diplomacy and policy planning, students and teachers watched, discussed, and offered advice via telephone to the central players.

Similar games, involving not tens, but hundreds of thousands, even millions of people, could be devised to help us formulate goals for the future. While televised players act out the role of high government officials attempting to deal with a crisis — an ecological disaster, for example — meetings of trade unions, women's clubs, church groups, student organizations and other constituencies might be held at which large numbers could view the program, reach collective judgments about the choices to be made, and forward those judgments to the primary players. Special switchboards and computers could pick up the advice or tabulate the yes-no votes and pass them on to the "decision-makers." Vast numbers of people could also participate from their own homes, thus opening the process to unorganized, otherwise non-participating millions. By imaginatively constructing such games, it becomes not only possible but practical to elicit futural goals from previously unconsulted masses.

Such techniques, still primitive today, will become fantastically more sophisticated in the years immediately ahead, providing us with a systematic way to collect and reconcile conflicting images of the preferable future, even from people unskilled in academic debate or parliamentary procedure.

It would be pollyanna-like to expect such town halls of the future to be tidy or harmonious affairs, or that they would be organized in the same way everywhere. In some places, social future assemblies might be called into being by community organizations, planning councils or government agencies. Elsewhere, they might be sponsored by trade unions, youth groups, or individual, future-oriented political leaders. In other places, churches, foundations or voluntary organizations might initiate the call. And in still other places, they might arise not from a formal convention call, but as a spontaneous response to crisis.

It would similarly be a mistake to think of the goals drawn up by these assemblies as constituting permanent, Platonic ideals, floating somewhere in a metaphysical never-never land. Rather, they must be seen as temporary direction-indicators, broad objectives good for a limited time only, and intended as advisory to the elected political representatives of the community or nation.

Nevertheless, such future-oriented, future-forming events could have enormous political impact. Indeed, they could turn out to be the salvation of the entire system of representative politics — a system now in dire crisis.

The mass of voters today are so far removed from contact with their elected representatives, the issues dealt with are so technical, that even well-educated middle-class citizens feel hopelessly excluded from the goal-setting process. Because of the generalized acceleration of life, so much happens so fast between elections, that the politician grows increasingly less accountable to "the folks back home." What's more, these folks back home keep changing. In theory, the voter unhappy with the performance of his representative can vote against him the next time around. In practice, millions find even this impossible. Mass mobility removes them from the district, sometimes disenfranchising them altogether. Newcomers flood into the district. More and more, the politician finds himself addressing new faces. He may never be called to account for his performance — or for promises made to the last set of constituents.

Still more damaging to democracy is the time-bias of politics. The politician's time horizon usually extends no further than the next election. Congresses, diets, parliaments, city councils — legislative bodies in general — lack the time, the resources, or the organizational forms needed to think seriously about the long-term future. As for the citizen, the last thing he is ever consulted about is the larger, more distant goals of his community, state or nation.

The voter may be polled about specific issues, never about the general shape of the preferable future. Indeed, nowhere in politics is there an institution through which an ordinary man can express his ideas about what the distant future ought to look, feel or taste like. He is never asked to think about this, and on the rare occasions when he does there is no organized way for him to feed his ideas into the arena of politics. Cut off from the future, he becomes a political eunuch.

We are, for these and other reasons, rushing toward a fateful breakdown of the entire system of political representation. If legislatures are to survive at all, they will need new links with their constituencies, new ties with tomorrow. Social future assemblies could provide the means for reconnecting the legislator with his mass base, the present with the future.

Conducted at frequent and regular intervals, such assemblies could provide a more sensitive measure of popular will than any now available to us. The very act of calling such assemblies would attract into the flow of political life millions who now ignore it. By confronting men and women with the future, by asking them to think deeply about their own private destinies as well as our accelerating public trajectories, it would pose profound ethical issues.

. . .

NOTE

1. Proponents differ as to whether the Council of Social Advisers ought to be organizationally independent or become a part of a larger Council of Economic *and* Social Advisers. All sides agree, however, on the need for integrating economic and social intelligence. [Editor's note: This is an asterisked footnote at the bottom of p. 405 in the original.]

Austerity, Planning and the Socialist Alternative

David Mermelstein

Few Americans pay sufficient attention to the business press. For those who do, *Business Week* sounded an ominous warning in November 1974:

> Finally, and most distressing of all, it is not at all certain how graciously Americans, or any other people for that matter, will accept what is plainly today's (and history's) economic reality: that there is no such thing as perpetual plenty and no party that does not eventually end.

Not everyone, of course, had attended the gala affair. Poor people at home and abroad were generally excluded. Millions of others had their lives devastated by a faraway war in Vietnam which did much to create the party in the first place. However, most Americans, both black and white, *did* prosper during the sixties and had expectations that good times would never end.

Sadly they did. The "depression" of 1974—1975 was steep enough to challenge the euphemistic nomenclature fashionable in the postwar epoch. In spite of an economic recovery that at present writing is more than a year old, unemployment at 7½ percent still exceeds past recessionary highs. National averages by definition understate the hardships of particular localities and groups in the population.

The level and pervasiveness of current unemployment flow from an emerging corporate strategy of forced austerity. Its roots lie in the crisis of profitability.[1] By potentially reducing property taxes (or at least not permitting the increases of the past), by making loanable

Source: **David Mermelstein,** "Austerity, Planning and the Socialist Alternative" in *The Fiscal Crisis of American Cities,* David Mermelstein and Roger E. Alcaly Eds. (New York: Random House, 1976). Reprinted by permission of David Mermelstein.

funds more readily available to private enterprise and by dampening wage rates and labor militancy through unemployment, it is hoped that cutbacks will eventually aid in restoring the health of the economy, in particular its rate of profit. In short, in the peculiar world of capitalism, bad news is good news; cutbacks are necessary for recovery, while a slow-paced upturn is welcomed as a brake on inflation and an indicator of a prolonged expansion.

As necessity is the mother of invention, the "need" for austerity creates an appropriate ideology. For example, at the very moment pollutant controls are being removed in the name of economic recovery, ecological principles themselves are being harnessed (in distorted fashion) to justify lower standards of living. Among politicians, Zen Master Brown of California is only the most flamboyant of the purveyors of this new ideology of "declining expectations."[2] Carter rose to prominence as one untainted by a spend-thrift Washington connection. Budget cutting is currently the mood of the nation, whether engaged in by true believers Ford and Reagan or reluctantly accepted by pragmatists Carey and Beame.

The question arises, Why do people accept this ideology of sacrifice? In good part the answer lies in the simple fact that they are in no position to do otherwise. Given a capitalist economy, there is truth to corporate slogans that "What's good for General Motors is good for the country" or Mobil Corporation ads proclaiming that jobs and "progress" (or at least rising levels of production — the two are not synonymous) are dependent on corporate health. The latter, in turn, requires substantial profits. Whether one views them as justifiable returns to risk or a rake-off which the wealthy impose for providing us with jobs, profits are the prime financial source for new investment. In short, profits *are* the incentives corporate propagandists say they are. Without the prospect that investment will turn a healthy profit, the wheels of industry will, as they say, grind to a halt, and to some extent in 1974—1975, did. Their livelihoods and well-being thus dependent on the health and viability of the corporate system, workers are ideological captives of the capitalist class. It is hardly surprising, then, that many tend to see events in accordance with capitalist nostrums which emphasize the essential benevolence of the institutions of private property and the profit system. They dismiss its defects as exceptions. To challenge those institutions, to see them as essentially malevolent and the source of our problems is to destroy the comforting set of values most people live by. Such understanding is difficult to develop. The result is that most Americans have no conception of economic disorder resulting from a myriad of forces in which the role of the private corporation is decisive.

In effect, workers are in a double bind. If they fight for increased wages and full employment, they undermine corporate profitability and run the risk of pushing the nation into a depression. To do other-wise — cooperate with capital — is to cooperate in wage cuts and layoffs. Held over such a barrel, it is no wonder that workers are demoralized and divided. Separated on other levels as well, by skill, occupation, race, region, sex, ethnicity, and so on, workers have learned they must look out for themselves. They forsake joint endeavors because, by and large, historical experience teaches them that to do otherwise is personally costly. Not expecting to win, few want to be suckers.

PLANNING FOR PROFITS

There is, to be sure, one powerful alternative to this double bind. Workers can opt out of the system altogether. A remote prospect, perhaps, but there *is* precedent for a radical response to hard times. The Great Depression, for example, unleashed forces that overcame repression in defense of an open shop and a previous generation's reluctance to bargain collectively. The hardships of the late nineteenth century gave birth to Debs and the considerable socialist movement of that era. There is no immutable law of capitalist development that requires workers to remain forever divided any more than there is a law of class cohesion.

The dialectics of history are not unappreciated by far-seeing defenders of capitalist class interest. They know that too brutal a dose of austerity risks a counterattack by those whose backs are forced against the wall. Thus it is no surprise that an alternate strategy has emerged for revitalizing profits and achieving capitalist prosperity. It calls for *increased* economic planning and an *enlarged* role for the state rather than the diminished one contemplated by the budget cutters.

Congressional expression of this viewpoint is incorporated in the Humphrey-Hawkins bill promoting full employment and the Humphrey-Javits bill on behalf of balanced growth and economic planning. Although Democrats presumably are preponderant, the New Planners include luminaries from both parties: Thomas B. Watson of IBM, Henry Ford II, perhaps Arthur F. Burns, who has been advocating some form of wage-price controls, and Felix Rohatyn. The latter is chairman of New York's Municipal Assistance Corporation, a director of such corporate titans as ITT and partner in the influential investment banking house, Lazard Frères. He has explicitly called for state planning and the creation of a new Reconstruction Finance Corporation which would serve as an "instrument of both rescue and stimulus."[3]

These men and others want to extend the system of capitalist planning beyond the Keynesian regulatory framework, which is general in nature, to *individual* controls on prices, wages and resource allocation. They hope to create new federal agencies, like Rohatyn's RFC, to mobilize huge agglomerations of capital for needed private investment that otherwise might not be made, especially in the development of new sources of energy.

This movement for overt corporate-government planning appears to be in conflict with the dominant ideology of free enterprise promoted by the budget cutters. In reality, this ideology has veiled a vast system of government subsidy and waste designed to promote profits and prosperity. In this fashion, corporations can have their cake and eat it too: a government thoroughly oiled and geared to their needs, yet a populace concerned with government restrictions on business and with handouts squandered on the undeserving poor. The following captures what is at issue:

> When the state is used surreptitiously to socialize the costs of businesses which appropriate the benefits for themselves, it proves that the benefits from state actions are invisible relative to the burdens of its costs. When the prime resources of the nation are used for private purposes, the leftovers available to the state cannot serve as demonstrations of the state's potential. In this way, the business system has killed two birds with one stone: it achieves its guaranteed survival through the needed and enlarged state and then can appear as an underdog and champion of efficiency in the ideological attack on the wastes and bureaucratic inefficiencies that are visible and allegedly inherent in under-financed and over-used state activities. . . . When the economy falters, it can be blamed on the errors of government policies; when the economy succeeds, it is due to the dynamic qualities of the private sector.[4]

Nonetheless, such past ideological obfuscations may not be possible in a regime of planning. From the capitalist point of view, planning like austerity carries grave risks (not least of which is the politicalization of income distribution through a system of imposed wage schedules). More important, capitalists are also placed in a double bind: if controls work badly, all of the problems of unemployment, inflation and profitlessness continue apace. But if they work well, the working class may begin to reassess its bias against socialism so carefully cultivated all these years by the culture of capitalism.

THE SOCIALIST ALTERNATIVE

Many . . . suggest that a meaningful and progressive solution to America's urban and economic problems cannot be achieved within a capitalist framework. Those who reject the corporate solutions of austerity or capitalist planning generally believe that ultimately America's ills require a socialist transformation. Similarly, in response to a question about solutions to the most recent crisis of capitalism, Joan Robinson told of a traveler who stops by the side of the road to ask the way to Oklahoma. "I don't know the way to Oklahoma," the guide replies, "but I sure wouldn't start from here."

Since the notion of socialism tends to be bandied about and loosely used, some elaboration is needed.

Socialists are of the belief that like the economic systems which preceded it, capitalism, too, is a transitory phenomenon which sooner or later will be forced to give way to more rational forms. As Marx wrote more than a hundred years ago,

> The growing incompatibility between the productive development of society and its hitherto existing relations of production expresses itself in bitter contradictions, crises, spasms. The violent destruction of capital not by relations external to it, but rather as a condition of its self-preservation, is the most striking form in which advice is given to be gone and to give room to a higher state of social production.[5]

Ideologues like Ayn Rand would have us believe that the contemporary capitalist system is a mixed economy, part capitalist and part socialist, that somehow we have departed from "true" capitalism, which is some kind of perfect political state, like the notion of God transferred to politics. True capitalism is a hypothetical laissez-faire construct, one which never has existed in reality and never will. Eternal, and "existing" only in the mind, this approach is totally ahistorical.

It ignores first of all the brutal origins of capitalism. As Marx put it, "If money . . . comes into the world with a congenital blood-stain on one cheek, capital comes dripping from head to foot, from every pore with blood and dirt." It also ignores the entire history of its development, one in which the capitalist class itself increasingly made use of state power to increase its profits and ensure its survival. If it is silly to believe that Richard Nixon — a reactionary Republican of long standing, with close ties to big business — became a socialist on August 15, 1971, when he promulgated a wage-price freeze to solve the problems of capitalism, it is absolutely ludicrous to call state planning under Nelson Rockefeller "socialism." We'll know that socialism has arrived when we see Nelson enter a cab and sit down behind the wheel!

Social complexity being what it is, it is hardly surprising that no single definition of socialism can command the allegiance of all who advocate it.[6] Socialists have in mind the transformation of existing capitalist society into something more genuinely democratic, more egalitarian and more humane. At the very least, this implies that society's property and technological-productive apparatus cannot be owned, controlled and developed by the few (the capitalist class) in the interests of their own private profit. These resources must be owned by all and democratically controlled to create a sane and healthful pattern of existence, compatible with real human needs, and with the environment as well. Moreover, decisions made at the workplace and in government must be democratic not just in name, but in the fundamental sense that everyone to the extent humanly possible participates as an equal. At the same time, the right of minorities to freely dissent from majority rule must be cultivated and safeguarded.

Socialism, then, is not only an economic mode of production and distribution but a social-cultural system in which social, political and economic privilege has been eradicated (or at least the direction of movement is continuously toward this ideal). The socialist goal is that everyone should live up to potential or at least not be denied the opportunity to do so because of an inegalitarian system of power and stratification.

No one seriously denies the enormous obstacles standing in the way of achieving such a goal. One immediate problem is the strength of capitalist ideology already alluded to, especially its ability to create divisions within the working classes (all those who labor for wages). Behind this lies the immense repressive apparatus the capitalist class can bring to bear against those who seek fundamental social change. Given this context of political struggle, socialists have usually hesitated to present blueprints of how socialism will work, believing that any future revolutionary condition will be considerably different from what now exists.

The idea that socialism can only be introduced after "the revolution" is not without challenge. On the other hand, many question whether it is possible to introduce socialism piecemeal: perhaps "socialized" medicine here, public housing there; perhaps the nationalization of energy here and of transportation there. Such efforts may result in more massive and oppressive state bureaucracies. Workers may make gains, but in ways that reinforce the capitalist ideology (co-optation). The piecemeal approach to socialism is therefore viewed skeptically since it fails to destroy a state apparatus dedicated to maintaining capitalist forms, capitalist privilege and a capitalist class structure. Nevertheless, some socialists (the Communist party of Italy, at least implicitly) believe that this state apparatus can be effectively neutralized by a strong working-class movement during a period of transition. If so, socialist modes of thought and socialist structures can take root and be partially introduced within the context of electoral politics. The danger here is that capital will go on strike, so to speak, sabotage such efforts and cause such a socialist party to discredit itself by moving too quickly (or not moving at all).

Regardless of the route taken to *achieve* socialism, certain key and unresolved issues present themselves. For example, how centralized or decentralized shall decision making in the economic sphere be? Some insist that decisions be made locally in small units. Decentralized decision making is considered preferable, since it reduces the number of intermediaries between the people and their leaders. Yet a New

England town-meeting style of socialism is probably not feasible in a modern industrial nation of more than 200 million people. For example, a local decision to produce more steel may adversely affect the river life of another area. This suggests that some kind of democratically elected national economic council with the power to veto projects of subunits is needed. Centralization may also be needed on the morrow of the revolution to counter patterns of sexual and racial discrimination in those spheres where capitalist ideology still holds sway.

Another question is that of incentives. Since it is not likely that centuries of capitalist conditioning can be erased overnight, it is unrealistic to expect that people will initially work out of a sense of socialist commitment. On the other hand, there is no justification for wage differentials of the magnitude we are accustomed to in capitalist America. In the end, the line between moral and material incentives will undoubtedly be pragmatically drawn. Related to this is the role played by small-scale capital, such as the family farm, neighborhood grocery or small manufacturer. Small businesses — even those motivated by self-interest and greed — may be necessary for the flexibility they provide, not to speak of the fact that they are repositories of distributive and productive know-how. This may be tolerable as long as the socially controlled large-scale productive forces are used to narrow sharply differentials in income. To the extent that creativity, equality and democratic participation [are] socially encouraged both on the job and off, individuals may less feel the need to own their own business. Also, to the extent that investment is directed more toward social and communal consumption — for example, parks, recreation facilities, dining areas — there is less need for individuals to have the extra income that private enterprise offers.

This discussion also poses the question of what role the market should play in contrast to that of a central plan. Complex industrial economies are not easily planned in the absence of a market for goods and labor — even with computers and such economic techniques as input-output and linear programming — without creating serious problems relating to inefficiency, bureaucracy and coercion. (A case in point: the Soviet economy.) On the other hand, the capitalist market gives rise to the inefficiency and coercion of advertising, sales pressure, monopoly, imperialism and an economy misdirected away from human needs. In the long period of readjustment, there may be a realistic place for the market mechanism as long as it exists within a socialist framework, one in which investment is controlled by the people at large, and the fruits of progress are largely directed to those most needy.

Socialists are also committed to democratizing the workplace. Here, too, a compromise must be fashioned between the interests of society as a whole and the rights of workers to make decisions affecting their lives. Workers' control must inevitably be a part of a national plan — a plan, moreover, having the flexibility to tolerate strikes or errors of judgment by workers themselves. Within such a framework, concrete decisions on wages, working conditions, pensions, etc., must be made. Another problem: years of capitalist oppression do not prepare workers to be confident, independent participants in new forms of industrial democracy. For this reason, workers' control is not a panacea. Problems that arise from the spiritually destructive form of society we now have are from a socialist point of view essentially *transitional* problems, likely to diminish as the new socialist ethic emerges.

In the last analysis, these remarks on how socialism works, or can work, rest upon a faith that humankind need not live in the kind of societies which have to now dominated existence, that once people get fed up with the malfunctions and disasters of capitalist modes they have the intelligence and capacity to create a better social order. In this sense, *socialism represents a qualitative step forward, not utopia.* By the same token, economic issues are not fundamental barriers. They are more in the nature of technical problems, surmountable by a people energized enough to want to create something better for themselves and posterity.

For those who reject socialism because of its negative features where it already exists (or in countries describing themselves as socialist), I would counter with an old, yet valid argument: these experiments in socialism have taken place in backward countries where the need was to build a modern industrial economy on an underdeveloped, agricultural base. These were countries lacking traditions of democracy and civil liberties; moreover, they were surrounded by hostile and aggressive capitalist powers.

The United States is hardly economically backward — many would call it *over*developed. We are also a people who cherish our civil liberties and democratic processes, however much we have permitted them to erode. Should America become socialist, no hostile capitalist power of any consequence is apt to threaten our existence.

American socialism, then, when and if it arrives, will necessarily be qualitatively different from what now exists. Its specific features are of course unknown at present, but it will obviously reflect our level of development. Socialism, though, is no more around the corner than Hoover's prosperity. The question is whether or not the economic crisis will be used to reorganize capitalist society along increasingly regimented lines, or alternatively, whether the crisis can be used to build a popular, socialist movement which will in the short run protect the living standard of working people and in the long run prepare the way for the eventual reorganization of our society along more humane lines.

NOTES

1. . . . Some students of capitalism believe we are in the early stages of a reorganization of the world capitalist order under the aegis of the multinational corporation, following which a new prosperity may emerge. Others hold that capitalist development leads to permanent stagnation. Another view is that we are "simply" in a cyclical downturn, albeit one of serious proportions. These are not necessarily mutually exclusive approaches. Whatever proves to be the case about the long-run workings of capitalism, the point here is that the present epoch is one of hard times and economic austerity.
2. The phrase is from Felix Kramer, "The Revolution of Declining Expectations," unpublished manuscript.
3. See Rohatyn's article in the *New York Times* (December 1, 1974), reprinted in David Mermelstein, ed., *The Economic Crisis Reader* (New York: Vintage Books, 1975).
4. Mark Rosenblum and Raymond Franklin, "New York: A Case of Ideological Bankruptcy," unpublished manuscript.
5. Karl Marx, *Grundrisse* (Baltimore: Penguin Books, 1973), pp. 749—750.
6. The following material was developed in collaboration with my colleague Louis Menashe.

CHAPTER 6   SUGGESTIONS FOR FURTHER READING

Altshuler, Alan A. *Community Control* (Indianapolis, Indiana: Bobbs-Merrill, 1970). Altshuler sees the implementation of large-scale community control as the practical solution for the numerous urban problems growing out of the impotence of non-white minorities encapsulated in the ghettos of central cities.

Downs, Anthony. *Urban Problems and Prospects* (second edition; Chicago: Rand McNally, 1976). This collection of articles, by one of the most provocative urban analysts of our time, is full of practical suggestions for dealing with present and future urban problems. For example, alternative forms of future urban growth and their consequences are explored in the first article.

Mermelstein, David, and **Roger E. Alcaly** (eds.). *The Fiscal Crisis of American Cities* (New York: Random House, 1976). This useful collection of critical and radical essays probes a wide range of urban fiscal-crisis issues, with a particular focus on the past, present, and future fiscal crises of New York City. Numerous liberal, conservative, and socialist strategies for avoiding future urban fiscal calamities are considered.